THE
UNITED NATIONS,
IRAN, AND
IRAQ

CAMERON R. HUME

THE UNITED NATIONS, IRAN, AND IRAQ

How Peacemaking Changed

*An Institute for
the Study of Diplomacy Book*

INDIANA UNIVERSITY PRESS · BLOOMINGTON · INDIANAPOLIS

Prepared with the encouragement and support of the Institute for
the Study of Diplomacy, Georgetown University, and the Center for
International Affairs, Harvard University. The views expressed
represent those of the author and not necessarily those of the
U.S. Department of State or the Institute for the Study of
Diplomacy.

The paper used in this publication meets the minimum requirements of American
National Standard for Information Sciences—Permanence of Paper for Printed
Library Materials, ANSI Z39.48-1984.

♾ ™

Manufactured in the United States of America

Library of Congress Cataloging-in-Publication Data
Hume, Cameron R., date
    The United Nations, Iran, and Iraq : how peacemaking changed /
Cameron R. Hume.
        p.   cm.
    "An Institute for the Study of Diplomacy book."
    Includes bibliographical references and index.
    ISBN 0-253-32874-8
    1. United Nations—Iraq.   2. United Nations—Iran.   3. United
Nations. Security Council—History.   I. Title.
JX1977.2.I7H85   1994
341.5'2—dc20   93-26951

2 3 4 5   99 98 97 96 95

In memory of my father,
who taught me the value of getting things right

CONTENTS

PREFACE

This book examines the most significant development in diplomacy during the past decade: how the Security Council became in the late 1980s the central authority for peacemaking, as intended in the UN Charter. Before 1985 the council had not played this role with any consistency; since then it has had success, even if reviews remain mixed. As crises in ex-Yugoslavia and Somalia show, there are still unanswered questions, such as whether the international community has a duty to interfere when a state massively violates the rights of its citizens, or how to authorize the legitimate use of force. By examining the past this book aims to contribute to the search for answers to such questions.

This examination has a story. The Security Council is the focal point, with three themes always within the field of vision: the progression from using the gentler provisions of the council's authority, as stated in the UN Charter, to using its more muscular provisions; the change in Security Council diplomacy over a period of forty-five years as it dealt with a series of conflicts involving Iran and Iraq; and the growing bond between diplomacy as practiced in the Security Council and the bilateral policies of the major powers.

This story is told in terms accessible to any interested reader. Students and practitioners of diplomacy will find it contains information not available elsewhere.

In August 1986 I joined the U.S. delegation to the United Nations as a regional affairs expert responsible for the Middle East. I was arriving from Beirut, where I had been political counselor for U.S. ambassador Reginald Bartholomew. The three major items in my new portfolio were Lebanon, the Arab-Israeli conflict, and the Iran-Iraq war. Was there any possibility that in the next few years the United Nations might play a role in ameliorating at least one of these crises?

The prospects did not seem good. U.S. diplomats had been trying to get the United Nations, particularly the Security Council, to play a more realistic and constructive role, but the United States was frequently isolated on questions relating to the Middle East. It appeared to me then that outsiders had already been too involved in Lebanon, and there was little prospect for a constructive initiative through the United Nations. Any diplomat should maintain a sense of humility when contemplating the possibility of resolving the Arab-Israeli conflict. Perhaps because I knew less about the Iran-Iraq war, I wondered why the major powers could not agree on a plan to contain the risks to which it was exposing other states.

The United Nations had little support in the United States. It was expensive for the U.S. taxpayer, unable to solve any international crises, and used by Third World radicals as a soapbox for attacking American values and policies.

I was privileged to be a firsthand witness, indeed at times a participant, as the Security Council changed from a forum for set-piece, acrimonious public diplomacy into a meeting place for governments to work together to settle regional disputes. The engines of change were not centered in the Security Council, but the new sense of collaboration there helped those engines to run more smoothly.

Skepticism and optimism are professional infirmities of diplomats, with skepticism dominating their judgments but with optimism often driving their actions. When the permanent members began to consult together in January 1987, few thought anything could be accomplished, and doubts about the intentions of the participating governments only gradually diminished. Even as late as September 1990 the majority of diplomats at the United Nations shared Saddam Hussein's assessment that the Security Council would not authorize the use of force against Iraq. Only hindsight makes clear a process of change.

Diplomacy, an art rather than a science, is best learned in a master's atelier. It was my good fortune to join the U.S. delegation when it was led by Ambassador Vernon Walters and by Ambassador Herbert S. Okun, the deputy permanent representative. Robert M. Immerman, the political minister, and Robert B. Rosenstock, the legal counselor, were demanding and creative colleagues. I was equally fortunate later to serve with Ambassador Thomas R. Pickering and political minister Robert T. Grey.

Diplomacy engenders discussion. My understanding of events depended often on discussion with other colleagues. While at times ambassadors of other countries, such as Britain's Sir Crispin Tickell, seemed to point the way in understanding the latent possibilities in any situation, at other times working-level colleagues had the most acute insights. Among those who never failed to deepen one's understanding I must mention Wang Xuerian (China), Sergei Smirnov (Soviet Union), David Blatherwick (United Kingdom), Ahmed Abul Gheit (Egypt), and Giandomenico Picco in the secretary-general's office.

In September 1989, after three years on the U.S. delegation, I was sent by the State Department to be a Fellow at Harvard's Center for International Affairs. It was a good opportunity to complete a paper for the International Peace Academy on negotiations and peacekeeping and to put the intense experience of the past few years behind me. With encouragement from Leslie Brown, the director of the Fellow's Program, and Professor Saadia Touval, I agreed to present a seminar paper on the Security Council and the Iraq-Iraq war.

In preparing for the seminar I compared the public record with my private experiences, gradually finding patterns in the changes that had been taking place. It seemed natural to explore the possibility of publishing an article on the subject. Georgetown's Institute for the Study of Diplomacy considered the proposal. Flattered and flabbergasted when the institute later suggested I write a book rather than an article, I quickly agreed. The institute's director, Ambassador David Newsom, and director of publications, Margery Boichel Thompson, put my efforts on the right track and kept them there.

Harvard gave me needed encouragement and advice. In addition to support from Leslie Brown, Professor Joseph Nye reviewed an initial outline and expressed confidence in the project. Professor Jorge Dominguez gave me invaluable advice at the outset and later reviewed the manuscript. During my year at Harvard I had the chance to work with Professor Roger Fisher and other members of the Harvard Negotiation Project, including the rare opportunity to help teach a training course organized by the Negotiation Project and the Soviet Diplomatic Academy for diplomats from twenty countries. I discussed this project at the Ford Foundation with Sir Brian Urquhart and Dr. Enid Shoettle.

Ambassador Pickering arranged for me to rejoin the U.S. delegation as a senior adviser for six months starting in July 1990. Little did I anticipate that events would extend the rate of change in Security Council practices, reaching the point of authorizing military action against Iraq.

It is too early to prepare a definitive analysis of the vast diplomatic changes of the last decade, but it is not too late to record, from the perspective of a participant and observer, the process that transformed Security Council diplomacy. Perhaps just in time, peacemaking changed.

Any useful insights this story contains are undoubtedly the distillation of discussions with others; any errors are the author's alone. The views contained in this book are the author's and do not necessarily represent those of the U.S. Department of State or the Institute for the Study of Diplomacy.

PART ONE

In the Postwar World

IN THE FALL OF 1990 the Security Council operated much as the founders of the United Nations must have hoped. Having determined that Iraq's invasion was a threat to international peace and security, the council adopted a graduated series of measures to counter Iraq's aggression—starting with diplomatic persuasion, through sanctions, to military action. In so doing, the council followed the progression of steps laid down in chapter VII of the Charter of the United Nations. But, far from being the normal practice at the United Nations, this was the first time in the history of the organization that the measures prescribed in the charter had been taken step by step.

The only way to understand how this breakthrough came about is to examine the history of the Security Council in its dealings with Iran and Iraq from 1945 to 1990. Soon after the council first met in 1945, it became a place for divisive public arguments rather than for solving conflicts through collective action. Then, starting in 1985, changed Soviet policies and improved superpower relations made cooperation within the council possible. In 1987 the council's permanent members cooperated to seek an end to the Iran-Iraq war. By 1990 such cooperation was an established practice, making possible for the first time the use of the UN Charter's progression of steps for collective security.

Iran and Iraq have long competed to dominate the Persian Gulf. In the 1960s and 1970s Britain's withdrawal from the gulf led to decisions by Iran and Iraq to use force or the threat of force against their smaller, weaker neighbors. By 1980 the rival ambitions of Iran and Iraq led to full-scale war. History and geography provided a bottom line for identifying winner and loser: Would the boundary between the two be in the middle of the Shatt al-Arab, Iran's objective, or on its eastern bank, Iraq's objective?

When the war started in 1980, the permanent members were deeply divided. Earlier in the year the Soviet Union had blocked the U.S. demand for Security Council sanctions to pressure Iran to release U.S. hostages it was holding. The Iranian revolution and the Soviet invasion of Afghanistan produced popular images of the "Arc of Crisis" and, later, "the Evil Empire." With the permanent members unable to cooperate, they dumped the task of mediating between Iran and Iraq on the secretary-general. A flock of other mediators crowded the field. They all failed to stop the fighting or to alleviate its consequences.

From the start of the war in September 1980 until early 1986 the war went through three phases. From September 1980 until the end of that year Iraqi forces invaded Iran and remained on the offensive. From the beginning of 1981 until mid-1982, while Iraqi occupying forces adopted defensive tactics in Iran, Iranian forces recovered strength and launched a series of offensives that caused Iraqi forces to withdraw from Iranian territory. From mid-1982, despite several Iranian offensives, there was a stalemate in the ground war; Iraq began to use its superior air power to strike at Iranian logistical targets behind the front lines and to attack Iranian shipping.

The United States, the Soviet Union, France, Britain, and China had separate national interests and perspectives toward relations with Iran, Iraq, and the other states in the region. On some points their interests coincided. They wanted to prevent outright dominance of the region by either Iran or Iraq, to keep the Persian Gulf open for shipping, to stop the use of chemical weapons, and to maintain the integrity of the Geneva Convention on prisoners of war. Other interests drew these states into conflict. Could these five states reconcile, or at least minimize or marginalize, their differences in order to build a basis for joint action?

In 1985 the Security Council looked as if it would be forever ineffective as a mechanism for diplomacy. Efforts to end or limit the fighting had failed—the Security Council gave the war only sporadic attention, Iran and Iraq rejected all offers of mediation, and both insisted on unreconcilable terms. Other countries adjusted to this impasse and sought to protect themselves from the consequences of war.

1

A Structure for Diplomacy

The New Era

At 4:30, Tuesday afternoon, 25 September 1990, Soviet Foreign Minister Eduard Shevardnadze called the Security Council to order. For eight weeks the council had been acting as directorate for a "New Era" in international relations that was rising from the ashes of the Cold War. The response to Iraq's invasion of Kuwait had triggered the use of the powers that the UN Charter provides for "collective security"—instead of states acting unilaterally or in competing coalitions, they would act as a community to deter aggression.

Twelve other foreign ministers joined Shevardnadze around the Security Council's horseshoe-shaped table. Only twice before, in almost three thousand meetings over forty-five years, had the ministers of the permanent members—China, France, the Soviet Union, the United Kingdom, and the United States—attended a meeting together. Five years had passed since the last time, and in 1985 the agenda had been purely ceremonial.

Shevardnadze called on Secretary-General Javier Pérez de Cuéllar, who had asked to make a brief statement. He pointed out that since Iraq's invasion of Kuwait on 2 August the Security Council was shouldering, in a way that had been impossible in the past, the responsibilities placed on it by the charter. The power at the disposal of the council was the solidarity of nations opposed to transgression of the charter, really a power of principle. "What makes the Council's task particularly onerous—and, I am sure, ultimately fruitful," he commented, "is that principles must be consistently applied and the Council's actions must be based on equity and perceived to be so."[1]

Pérez de Cuéllar recalled that the Security Council had little experience with applying the charter's enforcement powers. This unprecedented test would be qualitatively different from war: a collective engagement, minimizing undeserved human suffering and supporting states particularly affected by carrying out sanctions, demanding not surrender but that the wrong be righted, and keeping alive diplomatic efforts to arrive at a peaceful solution. He emphasized that the "effort to secure the correction of one international wrong [did] not mean that we leave other wrongs unaddressed. The world situation generally, and in particular the situation in the Middle East as a whole, presents itself as a proving ground for probity in establishing the rule of law. If peace is to be made secure, justice must have the last word."[2]

The business before the council was British Prime Minister Margaret Thatcher's proposal, prepared by ambassadors of the permanent members, to set up an air embargo against Iraq. Yemen's minister of state for foreign affairs Abdel Aziz Al-Dali and Cuba's ambassador Ricardo Alarcón, both expected to vote against, asked to speak before the vote. Yemen's Al-Dali, after pledging his government's support for the creation of a new world order, warned the council to avoid the disaster that war would be for his region. Yemen wanted an active peace process. To restore the Security Council's credibility, he concluded, "concrete measures must be taken to deal with the complex and chronic issues in our region, foremost among which is the question of Palestine."[3]

Ambassador Alarcón, who for over twenty years had led Cuba's delegations to the United Nations, rejected the conduct of Iraq but opposed an air embargo that "would not bring us close to a settlement of the conflict, but rather close to a military outbreak."[4] He chided the council for not having taken consistent action on other problems, including Palestine, and dissented from the prevailing euphoria. He doubted that, with the ending of the Cold War, cooperation among the Security Council's permanent members would usher in a new, more peaceful age. Using an odd quotation for a Communist revolutionary, he quoted Ecclesiastes 3:8 that there was "a time to love, and a time to hate; a time of war, and a time of peace." When the vote was taken, Yemen's minister surprised Alarcón by voting in favor.

Then other speakers interpreted the text of the resolution and expressed hopes for a better world. "The passing of the cold war has meant many things," said U.S. Secretary of State James Baker, "but above all, it has meant a rebirth of hope. The horizons of democracy, of human rights, of national dignity and of economic progress have all been extended, and the result has been a rebirth of the United Nations as well. Suddenly, the vision of the Charter and the promise of international co-operation do seem within reach. In Central America, in Namibia, and perhaps, hopefully soon, in Cambodia and Afghanistan, this Organization makes signal contributions as a peacemaker. . . . If this Organization is to fulfil its mission, if peace is to prevail, then Iraq's leader simply must not be allowed to gain from his assault on decency and his assault on basic human values."[5] Baker said nothing about the Arab-Israeli conflict.

Other ministers, including those of Britain, China, France, and the Soviet, said the Arab-Israeli conflict had to be resolved. Foreign Minister Abu Hassan of Malaysia, a government that supports Islamic and Arab causes, accused the Security Council of having a dismal record regarding Palestine and the Israeli occupation of Palestine. Vetoes had paralyzed the council and the secretary-general even on the humanitarian issue of treatment of Palestinians. "It is as if Israel has protectors in the Council and different standards are applied with regard to Israel. This does not speak well of the Council and those that wrongly protect Israel."[6] If the experiment with collective security in turning around Iraq's invasion of Kuwait were successful, Abu Hassan suggested, should it not be tried elsewhere?

At last Shevardnadze spoke. In language little reminiscent of Soviet policy from the founding of the United Nations until the recent past, he said, "The United Nations has assumed the role intended for it when it was founded, the transformation of the Security Council into an effective mechanism for the maintenance of international peace and security. By acting consistently and without delay the Council has justified the mandate entrusted to it by the Charter."[7] He sided with speakers calling for collective action without delay to deal with other problems of the region, foremost among them the questions of Palestine and Lebanon.

Shevardnadze presided over a ceremony that had more notes of self-congratulation than of sobriety. Ministers had spoken of a new beginning in the council's reaction to Iraq's invasion of Kuwait, claiming that success here should be a model for use elsewhere, especially on the Arab-Israeli conflict (if only the United States agreed). The issue was deciding how and when to use sanctions or force to counter aggression. The powers and procedures for Security Council action had existed in the charter for the previous forty-five years. Now they were being used.

Purposes and Principles

The victors of World War II founded the United Nations to moderate conflict, "to save succeeding generations from the scourge of war." Conflict is inherent in relations among sovereign states, and statesmen have long sought to limit conflict and resolve disputes by peaceful means. States manage conflict using the entire range of foreign policy instruments at their disposal, usually unilateral rather than collective means. More powerful states can rely more on unilateral action, and those with powerful or numerous friends might seek security in alliances. To what extent can states, guided by principles of international law, organize as a community to manage conflict, to provide collective security against aggression, and to reduce the risk of war?

The United Nations was designed to provide a structure for collective efforts to manage conflict, even if the record shows that frequently states have used diplomacy at the United Nations to sharpen conflict.[8] As a guide to this structure, when diplomats plot tactics or negotiate, they consult a small blue booklet that contains the text of the UN Charter.

The charter announces that the UN's first purpose is: "To maintain international peace and security, and to that end: to take effective collective measures for the prevention and removal of threats to the peace, and for the suppression of acts of aggression or other breaches of the peace, and to bring about, by peaceful means, and in conformity with the principles of justice and international law, adjustment or settlement of international disputes or situations which might lead to a breach of the peace."

The charter's article 2 restates general principles of international law, the basic rules of the game for UN diplomacy. But when applied, these rules can have unintended consequences. One rule is the sovereign equality of states, a useful legal concept that with the tripling of the number of states in the postwar era became elevated to the less useful role of political dogma. The injunction against interference in the domestic jurisdiction of any state aims to limit conflicts among states, but it has long been used to block international action to secure respect for human rights. Other principles enjoin members "to settle their international disputes by peaceful means in such a manner that international peace and security, and justice, are not endangered" and to "refrain in their international relations from the threat or use of force" (article 2:3–4). Most often these principles favor stability over change; but, paradoxically, the bias for a cease-fire immediately after fighting breaks out, which postpones withdrawal of forces and restoration of the status quo ante, benefits the preemptive use of force. Ambassadors cite these principles to define the issues, sort out precedents, and rally other governments to their side.

Jeane Kirkpatrick, the U.S. permanent representative to the United Nations from 1981 to 1985, earned the reputation of one who saw clearly the hypocrisy with which diplomats could apply these principles. A few weeks before the meeting presided over by Shevardnadze, she described signs of change in an article entitled "Doublespeak Days Are Over at the U.N." Kirkpatrick wrote that the string of resolutions condemning Iraq's invasion of Kuwait showed that the United Nations no longer worked the way it used to. The consensus of the permanent members—Britain, China, France, the Soviet Union, and the United States—showed that the world was changing with the transformation of the Soviet government and Soviet policies in the world. Previously ideology would have provided a rationale to justify almost any action, and the Soviet Union, to protect its Iraqi ally, would have sided with "the Kuwaiti revolution." According to Kirkpatrick, "Now Soviet officials mean by aggression what we mean by aggression and what the U.N. Charter means by aggression. And they are against it."[9] If the age of doublespeak had passed, Kirkpatrick suggested, one could finally see how useful the United Nations could be.

The Security Council

The Security Council's function is to organize collective security. Here a state sends its representative to invoke the charter's principles as guides for resolving a dispute. The charter, by defining the council's authority and structure, determines the parameters of the diplomatic process.

The Security Council has fifteen members. The charter lists five states (the Republic of China, France, the Union of Soviet Socialist Republics, the United Kingdom of Great Britain and Northern Ireland, and the United States of America) as permanent members. The other ten members, coming from the UN's five regional groups, are elected for two-year terms. A resolution needs nine affirmative votes to be adopted; it can still be rejected if any permanent member casts a negative vote. Strictly procedural decisions, such as invitations to nonmembers to participate in a debate, are not subject to the veto power. Voting, like the council's debates, takes place in the Security Council chamber.

Ambassadors at the United Nations often seek national advantage through public rhetorical victories, but rarely have they achieved through the Security Council the substantive cooperation or collective engagement needed to implement its decisions. This tendency appeared at the outset of the council's work when in early 1946 the United States used the council as a public platform to press for Soviet withdrawal from Iran, thereby setting the Cold War pattern of superpower clashes in the council. This inability to make its decisions effective prevailed from the 1960s into the 1980s, when the new majority of states were asserting their own leadership in the council, often at the expense of either the United States or the Soviet Union.

In chapter VI, "Pacific Settlement of Disputes," the charter lays out a simple, sensible progression for diplomacy, first describing how to bring issues before the council (see text in the Documentary Annex). Before the Iraq-Kuwait crisis of 1990 almost all activity of the Security Council was based on the authority of this chapter. For action aimed at the peaceful settlement of disputes, the operative verb here is "recommend," not "decide" or "demand."

Article 33:1 points out that parties to a dispute likely to endanger international peace and security have an obligation to seek a peaceful solution "by negotiation, enquiry, mediation, conciliation, arbitration, judicial settlement, resort to regional agencies or arrangements, or other peaceful means of their own choice." The council can call on the parties to settle their dispute by these means (article 33:2). The council has the authority to initiate action by investigating a dispute or any situation that might give rise to one (article 34) in order to determine if there is a risk to international peace and security. Any member of the United Nations can bring any such dispute or situation to the attention of the council (article 35).

The council has the authority, once an issue is before it, to recommend procedures for settling the dispute (article 36). If the parties fail to settle their dispute by the diplomatic means listed in article 33, they should refer the dispute to the council, which can recommend procedures or terms of settlement if it first decides that continuation of the dispute will endanger international peace and security (article 37). Or, when all the parties to the dispute so request, the council can recommend terms of settlement (article 38).

The theory is to engage the parties in a process of reconciliation that would end the threat to the peace and move the dispute toward settlement. Perhaps the best-known example is the framework for a negotiated settlement of the Middle East crisis, laid out in Security Council resolutions 242 (1967) and 338 (1973). Together these resolutions provided the basis for Kissinger's shuttle diplomacy following the 1973 Arab-Israeli war, for President Carter's mediation leading to the Camp David agreement between Egypt and Israel, and for the Madrid Peace Conference and the unfinished search for a Middle East peace. Chapter VI encourages a diplomatic process of investigation, recommendation, and negotiation.

Chapter VII ("Action with Respect to Threats to the Peace, Breaches of the Peace, and Acts of Aggression") provides for sterner action. Before 1987 it was rarely used. Article 39 authorizes the council to determine whether there is "any threat to the peace, breach of the peace, or act of aggression," to make recommendations, and to "decide" on nonmilitary or military measures "to maintain or restore international peace and security." Article 40 authorizes the council to recommend provisional measures (such as a cease-fire or a peacekeeping operation) without any determination that there is a threat to the peace.

If the council makes an article 39 determination, it can take mandatory measures. Article 41, before 1990 used only in the cases of South Africa and Rhodesia, provides for sanctions not involving the use of force—"complete or partial interruption of economic relations and of rail, sea, air, postal, telegraphic, radio, and other means of communication, and the severance of diplomatic relations." If those measures are inadequate, the council "may take such action by air, sea, or land forces as may be necessary to maintain or restore international peace and security. Such action may include demonstrations, blockade, and other operations by air, sea, or land forces" (article 42). The reluctance to invoke article 42, even in the case of Iraq, is explainable in part by the failure to activate the arrangements in subsequent articles to organize a military force under the direction of the Security Council.[10]

Those arrangements for a UN force were agreed on in 1945. Members would make available, through special agreements to be negotiated on the initiative of the Security Council, armed forces and facilities (article 43). No such agreements have been negotiated. Air force contingents would be kept immediately available for "combined international enforcement action" (article 45). The Security Council, assisted by the Military Staff Committee (article 46), would make plans for using this force. The Military Staff Committee, consisting of the chiefs of staff of the permanent members or their representatives, who could invite representatives of other members to join them, would "be responsible for the strategic direction of any armed forces placed at the disposal of the Security Council" (article 47). In practice the Military Staff Committee has been a moribund operation, holding perfunctory biweekly meetings for almost fifty years.

The next four articles deal with the impact on member states of decisions taken under chapter VII. Article 48 states that these decisions are mandatory as determined by the Security Council. Article 49 explains that members should provide mutual assistance in carrying out these decisions. Article 50 allows members "confronted with special economic problems arising from the carrying out of those measures," such as the economic embargo against Iraq, to consult the Security Council regarding a solution of those problems. Article 51, invoked to justify unilateral measures of self-help, states that nothing in the charter "shall impair the inherent right of individual or collective self-defense if an armed attack occurs against a Member of the United Nations, until the Security Council has taken measures necessary to maintain international peace and security." Following the Iraqi invasion of Kuwait, the United States relied on article 51 and requests from Kuwait and Saudi Arabia to justify its military deployments to Saudi Arabia and increased naval activity in the Persian Gulf.

Until early 1987, when Pérez de Cuéllar first called on the permanent members to agree on how to end the Iran-Iraq war, it did not seem realistic to use the charter provisions for collective security. Starting on that occasion the permanent members, consulting together as a group, began to identify, define, and develop areas of convergence in their policies toward the Iran-Iraq war. Precedent is important in UN diplomacy, and soon the permanent members were cooperating to use the Security Council for collective management of other regional conflicts. From this effort came the UN's second beginning, the new era confidently proclaimed in the fall of 1990.

The Security Council Process

There is a collegial spirit among the Security Council's fifteen ambassadors. During an ambassador's month-long term as council president, he (or she) guides the council's work through behind-the-scenes consultations and public meetings, shaping the process of diplomacy and encouraging good working relations. The president's role is symbolized in the lunch each president hosts for his fourteen peers in honor of "our" secretary-general. This tradition started in November 1955, when the new president, Nasrollah Entezam of Iran, who like Secretary-General Dag Hammarskjöld was a bachelor, replaced an elaborate dinner that included spouses with a business luncheon, a format that eventually became an informal executive session of the council.[11] At the end of the meal the president toasts the secretary-general for his work on behalf of the council. In response the secretary-general reviews the challenges before the council, compliments the members for their efforts in favor of peace, and pledges his loyal cooperation. It is very polite and usually predictable.

The president manages the council's work. Serving on a rotating basis according to English alphabetical order, a president acts not in a national capacity but as the representative of all council members. He must be available to meet with all delegations, even those with whom his own government does not maintain relations, and he needs the council's authorization for any public statement made as president. At the beginning of each month most presidents consult separately with all council members. Such consultations help the president control the process of negotiation, resolving separately differences that a group consultation among fifteen members could aggravate. Presidents report the substance of their bilateral meetings during informal consultations of the whole. If all members agree with the text of a resolution, the president can act as its sponsor, as is standard procedure for renewal of peacekeeping operations. The president chairs both the formal meetings of the council and the informal consultations of the whole that prepare for the formal meetings. The presidency is exceptionally demanding during a crisis.

Before bringing an issue to the council an ambassador should decide what outcome to aim for. Usually only the parties to a dispute place it before the council. Minimum action is for an ambassador to send an open letter to the secretary-general, making a public record of his government's position. She or he can simply meet with the president, asking that members be informed, as is standard practice when parties agree to renew a peacekeeping mandate. When a party wants a formal, public meeting, the ambassador tells the president whether he seeks only a debate without further action, or a debate ending with a statement by the president on behalf of the council's members, or a debate plus a decision on a resolution. An ambassador who wants a council statement or resolution should give the president a draft text or at least a list of desired points for inclusion in one.

The ambassador meets with the president in an office adjoining the Security Council chamber. In this area a series of rooms are available for confidential discussions. In addition to the president's office, the secretary-general and the secretariat support staff have offices for use during council meetings. There are phone booths for calls back to missions or capitals. Photocopiers stand ready to reproduce negotiating texts.

Adjacent to this area, three other rooms reflect the natural organization of group consultations. The traffic flow from one room to the next shapes the process through which diplomats prepare for Security Council meetings.

Ambassadors enter this area through a corridor where journalists lie in wait to glean useful sound bites or indiscreet quotations. Next door is a larger room that the UN's guidebook identifies as the "quiet room." It is a lounge reserved for delegates. The press is prohibited. On afternoons when the council is not meeting, the only diplomats likely to be present are those resting after a heavy lunch. Before, during, and after informal consultations the din of diplomatic gossip competes with the background noise of a television monitor tuned to CNN. Diplomats rarely negotiate texts here, but they consult on tactics and positions for informal consultations. Interested delegations that are not members of the council gather here to stay in touch with the latest developments.

A small room off to one side of this lounge is used predominantly by members of the nonaligned caucus. The caucus tries to act as a bloc, and during the years of East-West confrontation, it carved out a large area for initiative. Given the distribution of seats in the council, the caucus normally has five to seven members, and because resolutions require nine affirmative votes for adoption, the nonaligned have an effective veto over council decisions. Members of the nonaligned caucus have sponsored most of the council's resolutions on the Arab-Israeli conflict and Southern Africa. They do their drafting work in this small room, at times joined by other nonaligned delegations directly interested. In informal consultations, but not in formal meetings, caucus members often speak through a spokesman for the month.

After the council expanded from eleven to fifteen members in 1965, the practice of informal, behind-the-scenes diplomacy grew in importance. The council's "informal consultations" take place in a larger room between the quiet room and the president's office. Only a few secretariat officials and member delegations can enter this area or attend the informal consultations. There is translation, but no official records are kept. Here the president and the secretary-general report confidentially on their meetings or on negotiations conducted elsewhere. Here members can authorize the president to speak privately with the parties, to issue a public statement, or to brief the press. To decrease surprise, the members prepare here the agenda and scenario for formal meetings.

Next door, in the council's formal chamber, members sit in English alphabetical order around a horseshoe-shaped table. The president is at the head of the table, with the secretary-general on his right and the under secretary-general for Security Council affairs (traditionally until 1991 a citizen of the Soviet Union) on his left. When a president completes his month in office, the fifteen delegations shift to the right one seat so that the head of the next delegation can preside.

Shortly after a meeting begins, the president invites representatives of the parties to sit at either side of the open end of the table. Other nonmembers, if they inscribe to speak, sit at the sides of the chamber; they sit at the end of the table only when speaking. Toward the back of the chamber each UN member has a reserved seat; behind is a public gallery. One flight up, the press and translators work in booths along the sides of the chamber. In the middle of the horseshoe précis writers work at a rectangular table. Unlike the area with restricted access where there is real give and take among diplomats, on this public stage ambassadors act out positions that have already been set, as they seek media coverage or try to insert a legal point in the official record. Debates tend to be numbing.

2

Setting Out

The First Case

On Thursday, 17 January 1946, representatives of eleven countries gathered at Church House, London, for the Security Council's first meeting. The brief agenda included selecting a presiding officer, adopting rules of procedure, and recommending to the General Assembly a candidate for secretary-general. Because Australia came first in alphabetical order, its minister of the navy, N. J. O. Makin, presided. Other delegates—including Edward R. Stettinius, Jr., of the United States, Andrei A. Gromyko of the Soviet Union, and Ernest Bevin of the United Kingdom—congratulated Makin and expressed, in Gromyko's words, "the hope that the Security Council will fulfil the great historic task which has been given to it by the Charter of the United Nations."[1] Within only ten days the refusal of the Soviet Union to withdraw its forces from northern Iran deflated these lofty sentiments.

On Saturday the nineteenth the head of the Iranian delegation sent to Gladwyn Jebb, the UN executive secretary, a letter that accused the Soviet Union of interference in the internal affairs of Iran and explained that Iran's efforts to negotiate with the Soviet Union had met with no success.[2] The Iranians raised the matter "so that the Council may investigate the situation and recommend appropriate terms of settlement." Jebb circulated the letter to council members.

Gromyko responded two days later. A letter from the Soviet delegation asked the council to consider the situation caused by the presence of British troops in Greece;[3] a letter from the Ukrainian delegation asked for examination of the situation caused by the presence of British troops in Indonesia.[4] Any solidarity that remained from the permanent members' wartime alliance did not survive the council's first item of business.

Wartime arrangements provided the background for the Iranian complaint. Under the terms of the Tripartite Treaty of Alliance of 1942, Britain, the Soviet Union, and the United States had stationed troops in Iran, primarily to arrange for the shipment of lend-lease goods from Persian Gulf ports across Iran to the Soviet Union. Iran was divided into a Soviet zone north of Tehran and a British zone to the south. After the end of fighting in Europe Britain began to withdraw its troops. The Soviet Union refused to do likewise, although the 1942 treaty required it to do so within six months of the end of fighting. Those six months would expire on 2 March.[5]

Soviet forces were impeding efforts of the Tehran government to reestablish control over Azerbaijan, the northwestern province bordering on Turkey and the Soviet Union. Soviet troops were concentrated in the provincial capital of Tabriz. Soviet officials armed the provincial militia and supported the separatist leader of the provincial government, Ja'afar Pishevari. Western diplomats in Tehran were gloomy about prospects for the departure of Soviet troops in the near term and for the reimposition of central government control over Azerbaijan.[6]

By the time the council met on 28 January to consider the Iranian letter, Iranian Prime Minister Ibrahim Hakimi had resigned and been replaced by Qavam Es-Sultane. What line would the Iranian government pursue in negotiations with the Soviet Union or in the Security Council? An initial procedural question to address was whether the council would formally inscribe Iran's complaint on its agenda. Iranian representative Seyed Hassan Taqizadeh described events and asked that Soviet authorities stop interfering in Iran's internal affairs, that Soviet forces not hinder the deployment of Iranian security forces, and that all Soviet troops and officials be withdrawn by 2 March. Ambassador Andrei Vyshinsky (a prosecutor during Stalin's purge trials in the 1930s) rebutted Iran's position. He claimed that negotiations were taking place between the two sides and denied that the Security Council had jurisdiction over the matter.[7] Council members wanted to avoid a decision on inscription.

On 30 January Taqizadeh and Vyshinsky expanded and rebutted points already made. Taqizadeh, without requesting any other specific action, wanted the matter kept before the council; Vyshinsky did not, stating, "If the position is that the Union of Soviet Socialist Republics, in its action, must be placed under some sort of special supervision by the Security Council, I reject it as incompatible with the position of the Union of Soviet Socialist Republics among the Powers of the world, as incompatible with its dignity as a member of the Security Council, and as incompatible with the dignity of the United Nations."[8]

For two hours the council wrestled with procedure to frame a decision that would keep the issue before the council but not inscribe it on the agenda. The members eventually adopted resolution 2 (1946), which requested the parties to inform the council of results of their negotiations and retained the right to request information on the progress of negotiations. The question was temporarily shelved.

By early March events in capitals were setting patterns for Cold War diplomacy. On 18 February Prime Minister Qavam left Tehran with Princess Ashraf, the Shah's sister, for negotiations in Moscow. On 22 February George F. Kennan, then U.S. chargé d'affaires in Moscow, sent to Washington his "long telegram" that analyzed Soviet foreign policy and provided the intellectual framework for the policy of containment. Although Kennan's telegram mentioned Iran only in passing, he warned that "where individual governments stand in the path of Soviet purposes, pressures will be brought for their removal."[9] On 4 March Washington received Kennan's report of a conversation in which Qavam had told him that the Iranian side had reached no understanding at all with the Russians and that Stalin had been "very rough."[10] The State Department sent back urgent instructions for Kennan to deliver a note to Foreign Minister Vyacheslav Molotov, warning in threatening but ambiguous language that the failure of Soviet troops to depart Iran by the 2 March deadline had created a situation with regard to which the United States "cannot remain indifferent."[11] On 5 March Winston Churchill delivered in Fulton, Missouri, his "iron curtain" speech calling on the Western democracies to maintain their military strength to deter Soviet aggression. Wire service photographs showed President Truman applauding.[12] Kennan's demarche and news of Churchill's speech were delivered in Moscow on the same day.

Because the United Nations had departed London but not yet established itself in New York, the Security Council could not meet. Meanwhile in Tehran the U.S. and British ambassadors supported Prime Minister Qavam's resolve to reopen the issue in the council; the Soviet chargé d'affaires threatened Qavam that this "would be regarded as an unfriendly and hostile act and would have unfortunate results for Iran."[13] From Moscow Kennan advised Washington that the Soviet Union had no intention of withdrawing its troops from Iran and suggested that, when the Security Council met in New York, the United States should press for an early solution.

On 18 March Hussein Ala, Iran's ambassador in Washington who would represent Iran at the United Nations, met with the new secretary-general, Trygve Lie, at Blair House. Ala gave Lie a letter asking that the dispute be put on the agenda for the next meeting of the Security Council, set for 25 March.[14] In his memoirs Lie reports that he counseled against such a step: "I believed then, as I believe now, that open disagreements openly arrived at are not necessarily preferable to processes of diplomacy of a more discreet and effective character."[15] Gromyko asked in a letter that the meeting be postponed until 10 April, and Stettinius wrote to ask that the Iranian request be put at the head of the agenda.[16]

Between 26 March and 22 May the council met eleven times on this question in temporary quarters set up in the gymnasium of Hunter College in the Bronx. The debate focused only on the narrow question of whether this item should be on the agenda at all. Two early decisions put the item on the agenda and rejected a Soviet motion to defer consideration until 10 April. It took three meetings for the council to vote on Gromyko's motion for deferral; when his motion was defeated with only the Soviet Union and the Ukraine voting in favor, Gromyko announced he would not participate further in the discussion and led the Soviet delegation out of the hall, setting a Soviet practice of withdrawal that continued until after the start of the Korean war. This disaccord over procedure confirmed that the permanent members' public arguments in the Security Council would replace the image of their wartime cooperation.

The new U.S. secretary of state, James F. Byrnes, thought that the public airing of this conflict had positive effects. He later wrote:

> That meeting of the Council was a splendid demonstration of the power of the United Nations to focus the world's attention upon a government's violation of its treaty pledges and the principles of the Charter. The Soviets could not stand the spotlight, and the Security Council did not have to act formally on the grievance between the two countries. Stalin shortly announced, not to the Security Council but to the representative of a news agency, that his government was withdrawing its troops.[17]

Quieter diplomacy was already under way in Tehran between Qavam and Soviet ambassador Ivan C. Sadchikov. Soviet troops were evacuating several provinces in northern Iran. On 4 April Qavam told the U.S. ambassador that agreement had been reached on unconditional Soviet withdrawal to be completed within five to six months. In return Qavam agreed to withdraw the Iranian complaint at the United Nations, to give the Tudeh Party three places in the Iranian government, to enter into talks with the Azerbaijani Democratic Party, and in principle to set up a joint Soviet-Iranian company to exploit Iran's oil resources in the north.[18] Nevertheless, the United States determined that this issue should stay before the council and obtained the adoption of resolution 3 (1946) deferring further action until 6 May. Gromyko responded with a letter describing that resolution as "incorrect and illegal" because the matter had been settled by bilateral negotiations.[19] After a Soviet demarche in Tehran, the Iranian ambassador on 15 April sent a letter to withdraw the original complaint.[20]

Could the council retain jurisdiction? Trygve Lie set an important precedent for the powers of the secretary-general by submitting an unsolicited opinion. He advised that the council no longer had a basis for jurisdiction. Gromyko applauded Lie's initiative; not so the Americans. The United States, wanting to keep pressure on the Soviets to complete their withdrawal, argued that the council should retain jurisdiction. The U.S. side prevailed throughout. On 8 May the council adopted resolution 5 (1946) deferring the issue until Iran could report the withdrawal of all Soviet forces and asking for a report by 20 May. On 21 May a letter from Prime Minister Qavam stated, "No trace whatever of USSR forces, equipment, or means of transport was found, and . . . according to trustworthy local people, who were questioned in all these places, USSR troops evacuated Azerbaijan on 6 May."[21] Despite the withdrawal of the Iranian complaint and now the affirmation that Soviet forces had departed Iran, the United States convinced other council members to keep the item on its agenda by a decision to "adjourn the discussion of the Iranian question until a date in the near future."[22]

There it remained for three decades, until October 1976, when the secretary-general, following the receipt of letters from Iran and the United Kingdom, removed it from the agenda with the council's consent.[23]

The Security Council's first case raised the question whether debates in the council would amplify or muffle conflicts between the United States and the Soviet Union. Secretary of State Byrnes thought that public pressure on the Soviet Union was needed to pave the way for a solution. Had the council been less assertive, the hopes for collective security would have been dashed in its first case. Soviet statesmen, striking the pose of a party wronged by the U.S. use of public pressure despite the wartime relationship, complained that the council had been used in an "anti-Soviet campaign." At a dinner on 28 April given by Byrnes for Foreign Minister Molotov, Molotov and Vyshinsky explained to their host the thesis that great power relations were more important than the strict observance of the charter and that the actions and policies of these powers were in effect outside the jurisdiction of the Security Council.[24]

Given other Soviet actions that soon followed in Europe and which were contrary to agreements reached among the Big Four, it is evident why U.S. officials thought they ought not to remain quiet about Soviet actions in northern Iran. In hindsight, however, the extent to which ministers joined these issues directly in public debate is striking. There was as yet no established process through which ambassadors consulted informally to search for compromises that public meetings might later solemnify.

As this incident showed, the United States had replaced Britain and the Soviet Union as the foremost outside power in Tehran. Within months, on 26 September, the State Department asked the Joint Chiefs of Staff for their views on U.S. strategic interests in Iran. After responding in general terms, the chiefs recommended that, to strengthen the capacity of the government in Tehran to maintain internal security, the United States should respond positively to reasonable Iranian requests for military supplies and technical assistance.[25] Over the next three decades this judgment grew in significance.

Iraqi Ambitions and British Withdrawal from Kuwait

On 19 June 1961 Edward Heath, then Lord Privy Seal, announced to the House of Commons the cancellation of the Treaty of 1899 in which Kuwait, following a Turkish attempt to occupy the sheikdom, agreed to British protection. Heath explained that the United Kingdom would now provide protection for Kuwait upon a specific request of its ruler and act as a temporary channel for the conduct of foreign affairs until Kuwait set up its own foreign service. The United Kingdom would support an application by Kuwait for UN membership.[26] Iraq had different plans for Kuwait.

On 25 June Iraqi Premier Abd al Karim Qasim, who had consolidated his rule over Iraq after the overthrow of the Hashemite monarchy in 1958, told a Baghdad press conference that Kuwait was an integral part of Iraq. Qasim, of mixed Sunni-Shiite origin, came from southeastern Iraq, and he depended on support from pan-Arabists and Communists. The Baath Party led the opposition, as was evident in Saddam Hussein's part in the 1959 attempted assassination of Qasim. Qasim's government pursued a foreign policy of nationalism and anticolonialism and a domestic policy that improved the position of urban workers, peasants, and the middle class.[27] The 1899 treaty, he claimed with inconsistency, was not only forged but also imposed and obtained by the payment of fifteen thousand rupees. He announced the extension of Iraq's borders to the south of Kuwait and the appointment of Kuwait's ruler as the governor of the province of Kuwait. He explained, "The era of sheikdoms is over."[28]

Any legal basis for Iraq's claim would have to be found in a connection between Kuwait and the Ottoman Empire and the extent to which Iraq succeeded to the rights of the Ottoman Empire. The Turks never occupied or conquered Kuwait. Although evidence suggests the Sheiks of the house of Al-Sabah accepted the Turkish title of Qaim Maqam until 1896,[29] during the First World War Kuwait took part in fighting against the Ottomans, a good indication that Turkey had then no control over the territory. After the war Iraq was declared a British mandate by the League of Nations and succeeded to the Turkish provinces of Mosul, Baghdad, and Basra. Kuwait was outside the mandate. On 21 July and 10 August 1932 letters between the prime minister of Iraq and the ruler of Kuwait reaffirmed the existing frontier, a definition of which was included in the exchange of letters. Whatever doubtful legal validity a Turkish claim may have had, an Iraqi claim surely had even less. Whether in 1961 or subsequently, the Iraqi claim was based not on sound legal arguments but on the perceived ideological, economic, or security needs of Iraq.

Tensions mounted. On 1 July Kuwait, although not a member of the United Nations, asked the Security Council to meet because of the threats by Iraq "to the territorial independence of Kuwait which is likely to endanger the maintenance of international peace and security."[30] The British ambassador supported Kuwait's request.[31] The next day Iraq's ambassador asked the council to meet on a complaint "arising out of the armed threat by the United Kingdom to the independent and security of Iraq."[32] "Kuwait is not and has never been an independent State," he explained in a second letter. "It has always been considered, historically and legally, a part of the Basra province of Iraq. There can be no question of an international dispute arising between Iraq and Kuwait since the latter is an integral part of the Iraqi Republic."[33] When the council met later that day, the Soviet representative supported the Iraqi view that the agenda should include the Iraqi complaint regarding the armed threat by the United Kingdom. The council put both items on the agenda.

By 3 July the United Kingdom, which in May had received 39 percent of its petroleum imports from Kuwait, had positioned four thousand to five thousand troops in Kuwait. Prime Minister Harold Macmillan told Parliament that his government's actions were in "closest cooperation with the United States."[34] Kuwait applied for UN membership.

The council met on 5 July. Iraqi ambassador Adnan Pachechi, affirming Iraq's peaceful intention, cited examples from history to prove that "there is not and never has been a country or a national entity called Kuwait, never in history."[35] The British ambassador and Kuwait's representative rebutted Pachechi's case. The Soviet representative, who refused to support Kuwait's request to participate in the debate, dismissed the claim that there was an Iraqi military threat against Kuwait and called on the council to condemn the British presence, which he described as an example of a colonial power trying to keep a people under its control by all possible means. The U.S. representative supported the sovereignty and independence of Kuwait and the British response to Kuwait's request for assistance.

On 7 July the Soviet Union, opposing the British presence while nurturing its growing relationship with Iraq, vetoed a British draft resolution calling for respect for Kuwait's indepence and asking all concerned to work for peace and tranquility in the area.[36] An Egyptian draft that did not mention Kuwait's independence but did call for the withdrawal of British forces failed because it received only three votes in favor (Ceylon, Egypt, and the Soviet Union).[37] After the voting the Soviet ambassador said that, as long as British troops remained, Kuwait would lack real independence. Kuwait's representative regretted that the council took no measures to counter the real threat that Kuwait still faced.

Kuwait's government understood the need for active diplomacy outside the United Nations. On 20 July 1961, after Iraq's representative had walked out of a meeting of the council of the League of Arab States, the league's council admitted Kuwait by unanimous vote as its eleventh member and authorized the establishment of Arab League security forces in Kuwait.[38] Three months later the Kuwaiti government sent a telegram to the president of the Security Council announcing the completion of the withdrawal of the British forces and their replacement by Arab League forces.[39] On 30 November the Soviet representative in the Security Council, explaining that the 1961 treaty with Britain still subjected Kuwait to foreign influence, again vetoed Kuwait's application for membership. The Kuwaiti cause fared better in Washington. After the United States accepted the credentials of Kuwait's first ambassador, Iraq recalled its ambassador from Washington on 2 June 1962 and ordered the departure of the American ambassador from Baghdad.[40]

In February 1963 a bloody coup, organized by Arab nationalist army officers and the Baath party, took power in Baghdad and executed Qasim.[41] The Council of Ministers of the new government announced that it wanted to ease tensions with Kuwait and took steps to relinquish the Iraqi claim to Kuwait.[42] Within weeks TASS announced in Moscow that the Soviet Union and Kuwait, following a proposal by Kuwait, would establish diplomatic relations.[43] A month later Kuwait revived its application for UN membership. When the council met on 7 May, the Iraqi representative declared his government's reservations regarding the application and reaffirmed Iraq's legitimate rights, stating Iraq would never allow anything to affect its historical ties with Kuwait and its people. With the Soviet Union voting in favor, the council approved Kuwait's application unanimously. The Security Council vote signaled the end of the crisis.

By this time, fifteen years after the Azerbaijan case, divisions among the permanent members still ran too deep for collaboration, and the council had not yet established the practice of informal consultations through which diplomats can explore areas of cooperation. As for Iraq, once Britain had decided to reduce its role as the dominant outside power in the region, the government in Baghdad made claims to historic justice, backed them up by the power of nationalism and military force, and dismissed the prima facie legal validity of Kuwait's case. Kuwait relearned how much its security depended on good relations with outside powers. Kuwait's establishment of relations with the Soviet Union, a move not followed by any other gulf Arab state for more than twenty years, consolidated the Soviet Union's rejection of Iraq's claim to Kuwait.

On 4 October 1963 a Kuwaiti delegation visited Baghdad, leading to Iraq's official recognition of the government of Kuwait and a large, interest-free loan from Kuwait to Iraq.[44] The agreed minutes of the meeting, registered in the United Nations Treaty Series, state, "The Republic of Iraq recognizes the independence and complete sovereignty of the State of Kuwait, in accordance with the definition of its boundaries contained in the letter, dated 21 July 1932, of the Prime Minister of Iraq and the reply to the said letter, dated 10 August 1932, of the Ruler of Kuwait."[45] Five years later, in 1968, the Kuwaiti and British governments exchanged notes to terminate in three years the agreement of 1961, and that agreement ended on 13 May 1971.[46] Within two years, on 20 March 1973, Iraqi troops occupied a Kuwaiti frontier post to back up demands that Kuwait cede to Iraq the islands of Bubiyan and Warbah to improve Iraq's access to the Persian Gulf from the new port of Um Qasr.[47] The Iraqi government, in dealing with its small, rich neighbor, operated on the conviction that, when Baghdad wanted a concession to support its ambition for a growing role in the region, then it had a right to the concession. Kuwait refused the demand.

Iranian Ambitions and British Withdrawal from the Gulf

Britain's 1968 announcement that within three years it would withdraw from its security role in the Persian Gulf triggered the independence of Britain's remaining protectorates in the area—Bahrain, Qatar, and the

ns known as the Trucial States that later formed the United
With British withdrawal the primary responsibility for this
Western alliance shifted to the United States. During these
d States was extricating itself from direct involvement in
id putting in doubt U.S. readiness to use its own forces in
Europe and northeast Asia, the United States would limit commitments
to use its forces in peripheral areas. But, as President Nixon explained in
the "Guam Doctrine," the United States was ready to expand other forms
of military cooperation, including sales of sophisticated equipment, so that
friendly states could provide for their own security.

This policy had important implications for the Persian Gulf. The United
States maintained a modest naval presence there. Iraq had again broken
diplomatic relations with the United States following the 1967 Arab-Israeli
war, and the Baath party government that took power in 1968 expanded
economic and military ties to the Soviet Union. The United States announced a "twin pillar" policy of support for Saudi Arabia and Iran, both
of which already had close economic and military ties to the United States.
Saudi Arabia would station most of its naval units on the Red Sea rather
than in the Persian Gulf, build an air force to defend the kingdom's extensive borders, and forge economic and security ties among the small Arab
states on the southern side of the gulf.

Iran was expected to be the sturdier of the two pillars, because of the
preponderant size of its population, its location on the southern border of
the Soviet Union, and the ambitions of the Shah. He set for Iran the task
of becoming the foremost naval power in the gulf, deploying the most
advanced warships and extending the range of Iran's security responsibilities to cover the international shipping lanes. He stated, "I believe that
the Persian Gulf must always be kept open under Iranian protection, for
the benefit, not only of my country, but of the other Gulf countries and
the world."[48] His determination to make Iran the dominant maritime power
in the gulf precipitated conflicts with Iraq, Bahrain, and then the Trucial
States.

On 19 April 1969 Iran's deputy minister for foreign affairs told the Iranian
senate that Iran no longer considered valid its 1937 treaty with Iraq regulat-
ing the rights of the two sides in the Shatt al-Arab, the waterway forming
part of the boundary between Iran and Iraq, primarily because Iraq had
unilaterally collected tolls and used them for purposes other than the joint
maintenance of river facilities.[49] In a discussion four days earlier the Iraqi
under secretary for foreign affairs had told the Iranian ambassador in Baghdad that Iranian ships would be required to lower their flags while navi-
gating the Shatt al-Arab and that Iran would have to withdraw naval
personnel on such vessels.[50] On 20 April Iraq reserved its right to take full
measures to preserve its territorial integrity, and Iran put its navy and air
force on alert. On 22 and 25 April Iran sent down the Shatt two freighters,

escorted by jets and naval gunboats, that refused to pay the tolls.[51] There were no armed clashes.

Starting on 29 April each side sent a letter to the Security Council president to complain about the other's action, to emphasize its own good faith, and to express a desire to settle the dispute by peaceful means. Neither side asked for Security Council action. The first significant incident to take place after Britain's announcement that it would withdraw then faded away.

The next incident came in 1970, when Iran raised its dormant claim to Bahrain. Bahrain, long a center for trade in the central Persian Gulf, is an archipelago with a territory of 226 square miles near Saudi Arabia. In 1970 its 200,000 inhabitants lived on three main islands joined by roads. Thirteen years earlier the Shah had announced to the Iranian parliament his intention to annex Bahrain and had two seats set aside for representatives from Bahrain.[52] In response to requests from Britain and Iran, the sectetary-general agreed to help find a process to resolve the conflict between the British plan to grant Bahrain independence and the Iranian claim.

The secretary-general turned to Ralph Bunche, his under secretary-general for special political affairs. Bunche joined the United Nations in 1945 and had been awarded the Nobel Peace Prize for mediating the 1949 armistice agreements between Israel and its Arab neighbors. Through twenty-five years of UN service Bunche had a reputation as a skillful, dedicated, and impartial mediator, discreet in public but frank in private. Already terminally ill, Bunche took on his last mediation.

As a result of Bunche's efforts, on 28 March 1970 the secretary-general told the Security Council that Iran and the United Kingdom had accepted a proposal that the secretary-general exercise his good offices.[53] Accordingly the director-general of the UN's headquarters in Geneva, as the secretary-general's personal representative, would visit the area to ascertain the wishes of the people of Bahrain. This mandate, couched in neutral language, gave the Shah a face-saving way to yield on the Iranian claim (which partisans of the Islamic Republic of Iran would echo a decade later).

The secretary-general's personal representative visited Bahrain from 30 March until 18 April. His report, submitted to the Security Council on 30 April, explained how the mission gathered information from individuals and organizations from a broad cross-section of Bahraini society. Almost all Bahrainis wanted an independent state, and the great majority wanted it to be an Arab state. They hoped "that the cloud of the Iranian claim would be removed once and for all." The report concluded: "The overwhelming majority of the people of Bahrain wish to gain recognition of their identity in a fully independent and sovereign State free to decide for itself its relations with other States."[54]

The parties moved quickly to have the Security Council validate this conclusion. On 11 May, after representatives of Iran and the United Kingdom spoke briefly, the council adopted resolution 278 (1970) to welcome the report's conclusion. The scenario of mediation and face-saving worked flawlessly. The British ambassador, Lord Caradon, commemorated the session in verse:

> Rejoice, again I say, rejoice,
> We spoke with a united voice.
> The play is over. Witness now the
> Actors come to make their bow.
> All the endeavors were not vain.
> The people made their wishes plain.
> Their independence they retain.
> So let us all repeat again
> Good luck, God speed, to Bahrain.[55]

On 12 August Bahrain's Sheik Isa bin Suleiman al Khalifa announced that the country would declare its independence on 15 August and that he would send envoys to Saudi Arabia, Iran, and Iraq to explain this decision.[56] On the fifteenth Bahrain and the United Kingdom signed a friendship treaty that terminated previous agreements between the two sides. The next year Bahrain became a UN member.

Iran's next move came in the fall of 1971, on the eve of Britain's final withdrawal from the Trucial States. This time Iran wanted not face-saving but three islands astride the shipping lanes where the Persian Gulf narrows into the Straits of Hormuz: Abu Musa, with 800 inhabitants and thirty square miles of territory thirty miles offshore, was part of the sheikdom of Sharjah; Greater Tunb (150 inhabitants) and Lesser Tunb (uninhabited), about forty-five miles off the coast, were parts of Ras al-Khaymah.

There was no mediation. For several months the Iranian government had asserted its sovereignty over the islands. On 29 November Iranian forces occupied the two Tunbs in a military action causing fatal casualties among both the Ras al-Khaymah police force and the attacking force. The next day, despite an agreement made by the two sides to permit Iran to post soldiers on Abu Musa while Sharjah maintained administrative services and sovereignty, Iranian forces landed on the island, killed four policemen who resisted, and deported the inhabitants.[57] The Shah presented the world with a fait accompli.

On 3 December Algeria, Iraq, Morocco, and the People's Democratic Republic of Yemen requested an urgent meeting of the council to consider the dangerous situation arising from the Iranian action.[58] Preoccupied by Rhodesia and a war between India and Pakistan, the council delayed. On 8 December, with no reference to this request, the council unanimously approved the application of the United Arab Emirates, the new states formed by the seven sheikdoms, for UN membership. Representing the new state was Adnan Pachechi, who ten years earlier had presented Baghdad's claim to Kuwait.[59]

On 9 December, after expressions of condolences for the death of Ralph Bunche, the council debated but took no further action. Iraq's ambassador accused Britain and the United States of supporting Iran as part of their policy of preparing Iran to be the policeman of the gulf. Others saw British connivance because the Iranian attack took place on the last day before Britain relinquished its obligation to defend the Emirates. The British explanation did nothing to dampen these suspicions: "There is a French expression 'le mieux est l'ennemi du bien.' The over-all outcome—and I repeat once again, it was what the Arab states concerned repeatedly urged upon us—though it falls short of the ideal, represents a positive achievement and a contribution to peace. The alternative could well have been disorder and lasting animosity."[60]

Iran vs. Iraq: The Shatt al-Arab until the Algiers Accord of 1975

The border between Iran and Iraq has been one of the fault lines of history. Although Arabic and Persian speakers mingle along the length of the border, the predominant language to the east is Persian and to the west Arabic. Iraq's civilization has centered in the valley of the Tigris and Euphrates rivers, where the water from these rivers has sustained irrigated agriculture in the low-lying land of central and southern Iraq. In the seventh century Arab armies fighting in the name of Islam defeated Persian forces, thereby establishing Arab predominance in southern Iraq. Baghdad is only 80 miles from the border with Iran, and Basra, Iraq's second city, only 30 miles from the border. The center of Iranian civilization is far away, on an elevated plateau, without navigable rivers and surrounded by mountains. Tehran is 380 miles from the border.

Since the Arab conquest Sunni Muslims, including Ottoman Turks from the sixteenth to the twentieth centuries, have ruled Iraq. But a majority of Iraqis are Shiite Muslims, especially in southern Iraq. Here the important Shiite shrines of Karbala and An-Najf mark the sites where Sunni forces defeated the party of Ali (the Prophet Mohammed's son-in-law) and killed Hussein (Ali's son) in the early struggle for leadership of the Muslim world. Shiite Muslims (the partisans of Ali), whose religious rites emphasize the memory of Ali's defeat and Hussein's martyrdom, have ruled Iran since the seventeenth century.

The Shatt al-Arab, the 155-mile-long waterway formed by the confluence of the Tigris and Euphrates, has always been vital to the people in Iraq and their only outlet to the sea. Then, at the start of this century, with the discovery of oil in southwestern Iran and the growth of industry in Khorramshahr and Abadan, the Shatt took on vital importance for Iran.

The 17 May 1739 Treaty of Zohab between Sultan Murad IV of Turkey and Shah Safi of Persia and the 4 September 1746 Treaty of Kurdan assigned territories to the Ottoman and Persian states, but they did not delineate a precise boundary.[61] The first Treaty of Erzurum of 28 May 1823 confirmed these arrangements. Throughout this time the Shatt appeared to be under Turkish control.

From 1843 to 1847 Turkey and Persia held another round of conferences in Erzurum, Turkey, attended by Britain and Russia as mediating powers. Persia had recently extended its direct control over Khorramshahr and Abadan, an area previously ruled by tribal leaders who occasionally had paid tribute to both Ottomans and Persians. Britain and Russia muted their often conflicting interests in the Ottoman and Persian states to establish a line defining the boundary.

The second Treaty of Erzurum of 31 May 1847 recognized Persian sovereignty over the land east of the southern Shatt, including the city, port and anchorage of Mohammara (Khorramshahr), the island of Khizr, and an anchorage at Abadan. Otherwise the Shatt remained under Turkish sovereignty, and its eastern bank was referred to as the boundary. Persian vessels would have the right to navigate freely in the area up to where the land border met the Shatt upriver from Khorramshahr. In 1850–1852 the parties, with help from the mediating powers, tried but failed to define a mutually acceptable land border. Between 1869 and 1876 a renewed attempt, based on a large-scale map of the border area presented by the British and Russian ambassadors to the Turkish foreign minister, failed. Throughout this time Turkish sovereignty over the Shatt, with the exception of the anchorages at Khorramshahr and Abadan, was unchallenged.

Another round of negotiations, mediated by Britain and Russia, produced the Boundary Protocol of 1913 and led to an effort to demarcate the land boundary. Some adjustments were made, but the main line along the Shatt remained on the eastern bank. Colonel C. H. D. Ryder, a British official, wrote, "The frontier along the Shatt al-Arab was the left or Persian bank, and the Commission only had to make a trip down to the mouth of the river to make 'une acte de présence' and mark the frontier line on a map."[62]

In the next thirty years major changes took place. In 1923 Reza Shah replaced the Qajar dynasty and later took over the Persian throne, bringing with him ambitions for a vigorous foreign policy. On 3 October 1932 Iraq, which had been severed from the Ottoman Empire at the end of World War I and governed by Britain as the Mandatory Power, became independent. Economic development, led by the petroleum industry, made the southwestern corner of Iran, once peripheral to the central government's concerns, an area of greatest importance. Iran's anchorage at Khorramshahr was adequate, but at Abadan ships visiting the major oil refinery and port used an anchorage in Iraqi waters. Iraq's Port Authority of Basra was exclusively responsible for dredging and marking the channel for navigation, but 80 percent of the shipping on the Shatt was bound for these two Iranian ports.[63] In 1937 Iraq agreed to move the boundary to the *thalweg*, or middle of the navigable stream, for a span of about eight kilometers in the area of Abadan.[64] The Shatt would be open to the commercial vessels of all nations and the warships of the contracting parties. Iraq asserted its full right to maintain the waterway.

Despite these arrangements tensions remained after the 1969 incidents when Iran refused to pay tolls to Iraq. On 12 February 1974 Iraq sent a letter to the Security Council president to complain of Iranian aggression against Iraq and to request an urgent meeting.[65] The letter cited several armed clashes, including one on 10 February that caused twenty-one Iraqi casualties and seventy Iranian casualties.

In 1974 conflict between Iran and Iraq had come to include three main controversies. First, Iraq's Kurdish population, concentrated in the mountainous area in the northeast of the country along the borders with Iran and Turkey, was in semirebellion against Baghdad. The Shah's government allowed Iraqi Kurds to get enough supplies to keep up low-intensity warfare against the Iraqi army.[66] Second, the central border area (from Khanaqin to Basra on the Iraqi side, a distance of approximately 130 miles) still gave rise to conflicting claims; the commission to mark the boundary according to the terms of the 1913 Constantinople protocol never finished its work, which in 1937 Iran and Iraq had agreed to accept as binding. The 1974 clashes occurred here. Third, there was the perennial question of sovereignty over the Shatt.

The council met three times between 15 and 28 February 1974. The ambassadors of Iraq and Iran spoke with that high sense of justice and flare for fulminations which characterized the rhetoric of the two sides during their eight-year war. Arab delegations supported Iraq, then one of the council's members; the other fourteen members did not appear to take sides. On 28 February the council president issued an appeal to the parties to refrain from military action and requested the secretary-general to appoint a special representative to investigate.[67] China immediately disassociated itself from this request because it did "not favor United Nations involvement in any form in a border dispute."[68]

Secretary-General Kurt Waldheim appointed Luis Weckmann-Muñoz of Mexico to conduct the investigation. Weckmann-Muñoz first met in New York with secretariat officials and the ambassadors of the two sides, after which he arrived in Baghdad on 3 April. During a briefing at the Foreign Ministry he received an Iraqi map of the disputed sector, which he then inspected on the ground and by helicopter. He made a tour of the Shatt from Basra to Abadan. From 10 to 17 April he was in Iran, where he made a similar inspection of the border with Iranian maps. Before returning to New York he went back twice to Baghdad and once to Tehran.

According to Weckmann-Muñoz,[69] the immediate cause of the border clashes was that the two sides used different maps that located the border in different places. He explained that neither side was aware that its map was at variance with the other's and that both wanted to resolve their disputes by peaceful means. Accepting this discrepancy at face value, his report concluded (1) that it was important to delimit and demarcate the border line; (2) that notwithstanding the legal dispute over the Shatt al-Arab, there was a willingness to seek practical arrangements to ensure safe and unhampered navigation on the river; and (3) that the cease-fire in force since 7 March should be strictly observed and concentrations of military units in the border area decreased.

In resolution 348 (1974) the council welcomed the report's conclusions that the parties were ready to de-escalate the conflict and willing to resume conversations to settle bilateral issues, and in vague terms the council invited the secretary-general to "lend whatever assistance might be requested by both countries." China repeated its disclaimer.[70]

By midsummer the situation was deteriorating, and by the end of the year both sides reported border incidents, including the shooting down of two Iraqi planes and the bombing of an Iranian village. The elegant discovery of Weckmann-Muñoz—that unbeknownst to each other the two sides had been relying on different maps—did not create the trust and goodwill Iran and Iraq would need to resolve matters amicably.

To convince Baghdad of his point of view, the Shah stepped up Iran's support for the Kurdish insurgency in northeastern Iraq. By 1975 this fighting became a major drain on Iraqi resources, crippling plans for economic development and ambitions for a more forceful foreign policy, especially within the Arab world. Algerian mediators suggested a straightforward basis for a deal that became the Algiers Protocol and Baghdad Treaty of 1975: Iran would cut off support to the Kurds, and Iraq would recognize the *thalweg* as the boundary in the Shatt. The two sides affirmed intentions to maintain amicable relations, to adjust rights, and to demarcate the border in other areas. The text of the agreement stipulated a package deal—violation of a single provision could invalidate the whole. It must have galled Saddam Hussein to yield on the boundary in the Shatt, a line so freighted with historical significance, so that his government could be relieved of an internal threat that the Shah had encouraged. In explaining the joint basis for the accord the Shah cited one main point—"We both want to keep third parties out."[71]

Leaders in Baghdad and Tehran were drawing lessons from these incidents that did not augur well for the future. Iraq's early threat against Kuwait had been turned back only by the deployment of a British force and then strong Arab League support for Kuwait; there were no longer any British forces in the area. The Shah's success over the islands in the southern gulf and over the boundary line in the Shatt showed how useful the threat or use of force could be. As for the charter's prohibition against the threat or use of force, Cold War antagonisms among the permanent members made it seem unlikely that the council would ever activate the charter's provisions for collective security, including sanctions and military action, to counter a threat to the peace in the Persian Gulf.

3

Over the Edge to War

Hostages

On 9 November 1979 U.S. Ambassador Donald F. McHenry sent a letter to the council president to report that U.S. diplomatic personnel in Iran were held hostage and to ask the council to consider what should be done to secure their release.[1] Iran's revolution unleashed popular resentment against the United States for having supported the Shah for thirty years, and President Carter's decision to permit the Shah to enter the United States for treatment at New York's Memorial Hospital triggered the takeover of the embassy. After urgent consultations the council president issued a statement that emphasized the principle of the inviolability of diplomatic personnel, urged release of the hostages "in the strongest terms," and called on the secretary-general to use his good offices to this end.[2]

The unfolding drama set patterns for more than a decade of diplomacy: confrontation between Iran and the United States; Iran's rejection of international legal norms and adamant insistence on its own conception of justice, sustained by self-inflicted isolation and scorn for the Security Council; and the failure of the United States, because of Soviet opposition, to convince the council to impose economic sanctions against Iran.

Secretary of State Cyrus R. Vance has described the two-track strategy decided upon by the United States in November 1979 and maintained throughout the crisis. The first track was to open all channels of communication with Iranian authorities. The second track, somewhat contradictory to the first, was "to build intense political, economic, and legal pressure on Iran through the United Nations and other international bodies, increase Iran's isolation from the world community, and bring home to its leaders in Tehran the costs to the revolution and to Iran of continuing to hold the hostages in violation of international law."[3]

On 13 November Abholhassan Bani-Sadr, then Iran's foreign minister, wrote to Secretary-General Waldheim that "the United States is again striving, and in connexion with a crisis it has itself caused, to create a war psychosis." After denouncing the ignorance of the American people and U.S. protection of the Shah, he demanded the U.S. government "recognize an examination of the guilt of the former Shah" and agree that property and funds of the Shah, his family, and members of his regime be returned from the United States to Iran.[4] Bani-Sadr requested a meeting of the council. The United States blocked a meeting, because it was trying to establish through Waldheim a separate channel for negotiations.

Vance, accompanied by Assistant Secretary of State Harold Saunders, went to New York on 14 November to meet with Waldheim at his Sutton Place residence. Vance presented a package for transmission to the Iranians. It had four points: (1) the immediate release and departure of the hostages, (2) an international commission to inquire into allegations of human rights violations in Iran under the Shah, (3) availability of U.S. courts to the government of Iran to seek the return of the Shah's assets, and (4) affirmation by both Iran and the United States that they would strictly observe international conventions prohibiting interference in the internal affairs of other states and defining the rights of diplomats.[5]

Bani-Sadr sent to New York two representatives carrying a different package: (1) establishment of an international commission and U.S. recognition of the Shah's guilt, (2) return of all property and funds of the Shah that might be located in the United States, (3) a U.S.-Iranian declaration of principles similar to that proposed by the United States, and (4) evacuation of the U.S. embassy by the Iranian students and permission for U.S. citizens and employees to depart Iran.[6] By 25 November agreement was reached on a text close to the U.S. version, and Vance and Bani-Sadr were expected to go to New York to conclude the matter.

Waldheim later complained that the U.S. refusal to hold a meeting of the council while private negotiations were proceeding "gave the Iranians a chance to portray the Council as a mere tool of the Americans."[7] On 25 November, using a rarely used power that article 99 of the charter grants to the secretary-general, Waldheim requested that the council meet.[8] Little happened. Two days later the council met for twenty minutes to allow Waldheim to appeal for restraint. The council president announced that, out of respect for the Shiite holy days of Tassua and Ashura, the council would not meet until Saturday, 1 December, when Bani-Sadr would attend.[9] But three days later Bani-Sadr was dismissed as foreign minister. His replacement, Sadegh Ghotbzadeh, announced there was "no room for negotiations at present" and refused to go to New York.[10]

Washington's position was hardening. President Carter wrote on 27 November that he wanted to get the Shah out of the United States and to press the Security Council to condemn Iran. Next, until the hostages were released, he wanted to call for a total embargo on all goods shipped to Iran and to follow up by having the Security Council adopt a chapter VII resolution making the embargo a legal obligation of all UN members. In the same note Carter listed as possible options mining Iranian ports, destroying Iranian domestic petroleum facilities, and restricting Iran's access to international credit and foreign commerce.[11]

Ambassador McHenry was the first speaker in the late-night meeting on Saturday, 1 December. He emphasized that international law required release of the hostages and appealed to Iran to act accordingly. "No country can breach the most fundamental rules of the community of nations and at the same time expect that community to be helpful in the problems which it perceives for itself. In the simplest terms, no country can break and ignore the law while seeking its benefits."[12] All nineteen subsequent speakers that night and on Monday and Tuesday, including Soviet Ambassador Oleg Troyanovsky, urged Iran to meet its international legal obligations by releasing the hostages.

After the debate the council adopted resolution 457 (1979), repeating the main points of the 9 November statement: Iran should release the hostages, both sides should exercise restraint, and the secretary-general should lend his good offices. White House staff assessed the outcome with optimism and thought the United States had achieved "the further isolation of Iran, establishment of a strong mandate for the Secretary-General's good offices, proof that the non-aligned states would not support Iran's action, and provision of an argument to those Iranians in favor of releasing the hostages to restore broad international support for the Iranian revolution."[13]

The United States now sought by every means to secure the hostages' release. Vance used his attendance at the regularly scheduled December NATO ministerial meeting in Brussels to rally allied support for the increasingly hard American position. Without enthusiasm the allies agreed to support U.S. efforts to get UN sanctions and apparently to impose such sanctions even if the Soviet Union vetoed UN action. As Gary Sick, the National Security Council staff member working on the issue, later wrote: "On the whole, the European reaction was consistent with President Carter's initial assessment; at each stage they reluctantly took only what they considered to be the minimum steps necessary to prevent the United States from moving to a military solution."[14] Diplomatic cooperation was the one option the allies could offer to the United States if they wanted to avoid the possibility of a unilateral U.S. military response.

Moving toward Sanctions

On 22 December Waldheim gave the council a brief report that ruled out an early end to the crisis. "We are here dealing with an unusual and highly exceptional situation."[15] Ambassador McHenry, arguing that the council must act to enforce its call on Iran to release the hostages, immediately asked the council president to convene a meeting for this purpose.[16] McHenry set about enlisting support for sanctions.

The Soviet Union's Christmas Eve invasion of Afghanistan, which evoked memories of the 1946 Azerbaijan crisis, sharpened tensions both between the United States and the Soviet Union and between Iran and the Soviet Union. It did nothing to lessen tensions between the United States and Iran.

McHenry proposed to a White House meeting on 28 December that the

United States follow a two-step strategy in the Security Council—first, to seek adoption of a resolution sending Waldheim to Tehran and laying an explicit basis for sanctions, and then, if he did not report progress within a week, to ask for sanctions.[17] Although this procedure followed the careful step-by-step design of the charter's chapter VII, it would require two votes. McHenry suggested that agreement on the first step would improve chances that the council would later adopt sanctions.

Vance went back to New York to sell this approach. Waldheim told Vance that Iran's Revolutionary Council seemed ready for mediation but Ayatollah Ruhollah Khomeini rejected it. Reflecting on the charter obligation of UN members to resolve disputes by peaceful means, Vance, according to the account by Harold Saunders in *American Hostages in Iran*, "replied quickly and sternly that the Security Council needed to be told authoritatively that Khomeini was rejecting mediation."[18] (Waldheim did not do this.) Council members resisted Vance on the text of a resolution; they did not want to spell out in detail the sanctions to be selected.

Vance presented his case to the council on Saturday evening, 29 December. If Iran held the hostages after unanimous calls for their release, he argued, the council was obliged to adopt sanctions to promote a peaceful solution. He proposed a resolution requesting that the secretary-general go to Tehran; if the hostages were not released at an early date, the council should then adopt sanctions.[19] In the debate allies provided strong support, Third World countries were less supportive, China was distinctly cautious, and the Soviet Union opposed sanctions outright. The New Year's Eve vote on resolution 461 (1979) was 11-0-4 (the four abstentions being Bangladesh, Czechoslovakia, Kuwait, and the Soviet Union). This tally on the first step showed that the U.S. push for sanctions was almost certainly doomed.

In anticipation of the vote Waldheim had departed for Tehran with a grudging invitation from Iran that allowed him to come if he wanted.[20] Before leaving he met with Vance, who reaffirmed that the United States was willing to proceed with its earlier four-point proposal, to which Vance added a fifth point that the United States, once the hostages were released, would work to resolve all issues with Iran in accordance with the UN Charter.[21] Waldheim, who wanted to divorce his visit from the threat of sanctions being developed in the Security Council, issued before leaving a statement that the Secretary-General was in this case taking a special responsibility upon himself.[22] In other words he wanted to be seen as acting within his powers as secretary-general rather than as an agent of the council. Who in Tehran was likely to appreciate or be persuaded by such finesse?

Khomeini had already said, "I do not trust this man."[23] As Waldheim later described his stay in Tehran, "There seemed to be an orchestrated campaign to portray the United Nations as a servitor of the Iranian royal family and an institution which chose to ignore the sufferings of the Iranian people."[24] On arrival he was met by demonstrators bearing placards showing his kissing Princess Ashraf's hand; the evening news showed Waldheim's arrival on one half of a split screen, faced on the other half by victims of SAVAK, the Shah's political police. His itinerary included a meeting with alleged victims of SAVAK ("Many in the crowd, including children, were crippled, blind, or missing arms and legs.")[25] and a visit to graves in Behest Zahara Cemetery of those who had died for the revolution ("We got away by the skin of our teeth.").[26] He was not permitted to meet with the American hostages, nor did he meet with Ayatollah Khomeini.

Waldheim met with Foreign Minister Sadegh Ghotbzadeh on 1 and 3 January, meetings described in his report to the Security Council. Waldheim urged the release of the hostages, arguing that this could lead to a hearing for Iran's grievances. Ghotbzadeh stonewalled, insisting that Iran's grievances be dealt with before the hostages were released. On the evening of 3 January Waldheim made his case to the Revolutionary Council, chaired by Ayatollah Mohammed Beheshti. The council backed up Ghotbzadeh. Putting the best possible face on the outcome, Waldheim's report concluded: "Despite the many difficulties I encountered during my visit to Tehran owing to the particular power structure in that country, I consider that the trip was useful and helped me to understand better the many facets of the existing crisis."[27]

On 7 January Waldheim went to Washington and met with President Carter for two hours. After relating the details of his reception in Tehran, Waldheim said sanctions would not move things forward and urged the President to hold back.[28] Carter decided to push for sanctions. If the Security Council would not adopt sanctions, it would prove its irrelevance.

During Waldheim's trip the council was in the throes of a debate on the Soviet invasion of Afghanistan. On 3 January fifty-two delegations, including China, Britain, and the United States, requested an urgent meeting of the council, which then met six times from the fifth to the ninth of January. The Chinese statement used particularly colorful language, charging "hegemonism" and "naked military aggression," to lambast the Soviet invasion.[29] Pakistan, Britain, the United States, and others denounced the Soviet aggression with equal firmness. Iran kept silent. Ambassador Troyanovsky used Gromyko's argument in 1946, that there was no justification for a meeting; he then cast a veto against a draft resolution (sponsored by nonaligned members of the council) that called for "the immediate and unconditional withdrawal of all foreign troops from Afghanistan."[30]

On Friday evening, two days after this rancorous debate, the council postponed action to give time for negotiations on a U.S. draft that called for the imposition of comprehensive economic sanctions against Iran "until such time as the hostages are released and have safely departed from Iran."[31]

On Sunday night the council met to vote. Ambassador McHenry, citing the council's responsibilities and Iran's intransigence, asked that sanctions be adopted "to demonstrate that Iran's continued defiance of international law will result in its increased isolation from the international community."[32] Ambassador Troyanovsky objected to Iran's violation of diplomatic immunity but warned that the Soviet Union opposed "any steps by the United States aimed at putting pressure on Iran."[33] A Soviet veto defeated the resolution. The Chinese ambassador, in explaining why China did not choose to participate in the vote, called a spade a spade: "The performance of the Soviet Union on the question now under consideration shows that it intends to take advantage of the crisis in United States-Iranian relations to disguise itself as the 'guardian' of Iran and a 'natural ally' of the Islamic countries, so as to make cheap political capital out of it. We will certainly see through the intrigues of the Soviet Union and not allow it to succeed in its plot to sow discord and to fish in muddied waters."[34]

It seemed Iran had escaped UN pressure to release the hostages. But did it? Warren Christopher, the deputy secretary of state who played a key role in the negotiations that led to the hostages' eventual release, did not think so. "We received particular cooperation from an institution that many Americans have grown to resent and regard as hostile to our interests—the United Nations," Christopher later wrote. "In October 1980, when the new Iranian prime minister, Mohammed Ali Rajai, came to the United Nations seeking an international condemnation of Iraq for its September invasion, he received instead a steady round of reprimands from the U.N. missions of scores of countries, which made clear their lack of sympathy for a country that remained in continuous and flagrant violation of diplomatic norms and international law. . . . Countries we have often thought to be our antagonists within the U.N. system helped mightily and perhaps decisively to let Iran know that, for its own sake, it should resolve the crisis."[35] Christopher concluded: "Ultimately, the release of the hostages came about in substantial part because Iran found itself completely isolated in the world community—not because other countries necessarily were friendly to the United States, but because they almost universally were offended at Iran's transgressions against international law."[36]

No doubt Baghdad and Tehran saw different lessons in this episode. In Baghdad Saddam Hussein must have noticed that the council, even when a permanent member's interests were at stake, did not adopt sanctions or even give the secretary-general a strong mandate. In Iran the leadership was so absorbed in the internal dynamics of the Islamic revolution that the isolation suffered seemed less a penalty than a confirmation that the revolution's fate depended not on outsiders but on what happened at home. Despite much huffing and puffing by council members over the violation of international legal norms and charter obligations, the mandatory provisions of chapter VII, including sanctions, had so far proved to be a dead letter. Both governments had grounds to conclude that the Security Council was unlikely ever to take decisive action.

The Secretary-General

When the Security Council fails to act, attention shifts to the secretary-general and his ability to help end a crisis.[37] Waldheim, like other secretaries-general, has been criticized for his caution. What role, however, can a secretary-general or any third party play?

A third party can facilitate negotiations between states but rarely has the powers of an arbitrator and never those of a judge. He can:

Convene negotiations. The third party can identify the parties to include, arrange for them to come to the table, and establish a constructive ambiance.[38]

Facilitate the negotiating process. The third party can help the parties to clarify their interests in nonthreatening terms and to perceive opportunities for joint gains. He can open up the exploration of preferred solutions and help the parties settle on a procession for deal-making, whether exchanging package offers, working issue by issue, agreeing first on a principle and then generating the details for implementation, or starting with a single text and examining amendments. And, he can provide a rationale for agreement.[39]

Manipulate the rules. Any process is managed by rules, explicit or unspoken. The third party can assume authority for these rules, perhaps by setting deadlines, encouraging the involvement of additional parties, or leaving the parties on their own.[40]

Legitimize the outcome. The third party can lead the two sides to see the merit of an outcome and to legitimize it for others. Such action can include demonstrating that the proposed solution, whatever its defects, is preferable to alternatives, making a public endorsement, or providing assistance for the process of implementation.

The secretary-general is a special third party. As symbol of the United Nations and trustee of its charter, he can invoke the legal obligation of member states to abide by the charter's principles and to perform other duties of UN membership. The charter describes the secretary-general's role in bare-bones terms. He is the chief administrative officer, he appoints the staff, he makes an annual report to the General Assembly on the work of the organization, and he "may bring to the attention of the Security Council any matter which in his opinion may threaten the maintenance of international peace and security" (article 99).

Within this institutional framework the secretary-general can request action by the Security Council or communicate with the parties, he can facilitate negotiation among council members and between the parties, and he can solidify support for an outcome, for example by arranging for a peacekeeping force. He can draft proposals and resolutions for member states to consider.[41] Neutral in the sense of acting independently of any government, he is expected to remain impartial between the parties.

The secretary-general is "appointed by the General Assembly upon the recommendation of the Security Council" (article 97). In effect the permanent members, by controlling who cannot be secretary-general, decide who can be. While in office the secretary-general needs to maintain their support.

At the height of the Cold War Dag Hammarskjöld tried to fill the vacuum

ιe failure of the permanent members to act together. He dis-
.dea that the United Nations should be primarily a "state con-
:hinery" to resolve conflicts, served by a secretariat repre-
specific interests of its member states. Instead he saw "the
⌐ɪ₆ᵤᵣ........ n primarily as a dynamic instrument of governments through
which they, jointly and for the same purpose, should seek such reconciliation but through which they should also try to develop forms of executive
action, undertaken on behalf of all members, and aiming at forestalling
conflicts and resolving them, once they have arisen, by appropriate diplomatic or political means."[42] He counted on the medium-sized and smaller
states, whose number was expanding due to decolonization, for support.
If the permanent members could not agree on how to resolve a dispute,
they should support independent action by the secretary-general.

Thus, when a General Assembly resolution condemned Chinese actions
but asked Hammarskjöld to mediate with the Chinese government for the
release of U.S. pilots, he put aside the resolution as the basis for his mission
and publicly explained that he was acting rather on the basis of authorities
vested in him by the charter (as Waldheim did before his trip to Tehran).

While careful to avoid conflict with the permanent members, Waldheim
sought support from Third World states, many recently independent, who
often held the initiative in the Security Council during his decade in office.
Waldheim cautioned in 1972 that even détente would not create a basis for
permanent member leadership of the Security Council. "Even if the Security Council were to acquire a new effectiveness through great Power détente, the idea of maintaining peace and security in the world through
a concert of great Powers, although these Powers obviously have great
responsibilities in matters of peace and security, would seem to belong to
the nineteenth rather than to the twentieth century . . . however effective
in the past [this system] obviously cannot be acceptable, in the long run,
to the peoples of the world."[43]

War

By 1980 the Baghdad and Tehran governments were marching to very
different drummers. In Baghdad Baath Party ideology committed the government to a secular program oriented toward the Arab world. The Iraqi
government emphasized Arab nationalism and organized the Baghdad
Summit of 1978, which "expelled" Egypt from the Arab ranks because of
the Camp David treaty. Since 1979 the Tehran government had become
explicitly Islamic and intensely nationalistic. The new government scorned
the rules of diplomacy designed to promote stability and impede the export
of revolution. Khomeini's description of Saddam Hussein revealed the
abyss between the two sides: "This deviated person is completely uninformed about Islam, and, among other things, is an Arab. God, the Most
High, said, the Arabs are very hard in infidelity and hypocrisy and more

inclined not to know the limits that God has sent down unto His Messenger."[44]

Personal animosity played its part. After being exiled by the Shah in 1965, Ayatollah Khomeini settled in An-Najf in southern Iraq. There he developed his distinctive theory of rule by an Islamic jurisconsult (*vilayat il faqih*). Despite differences over religion and politics, there was little friction between Khomeini and Iraqi authorities, but by 1978 Khomeini was creating problems for the Shah. In February 1978 Saddam Hussein, at the Shah's request, expelled Khomeini. When Khomeini's entourage arrived at the border with Kuwait, Kuwaiti officials refused him entry for lack of a visa. Somewhat ironically, the Ayatollah's eventual exile in Paris gave him freer rein for subversive activities against the Shah than he had enjoyed in An-Najf. Khomeini's expulsion provided grounds for his personal animosity against Saddam Hussein.

In the first eight months of 1980 a series of bomb attacks inside Iraq prompted Iraqi authorities to charge that an Iranian-sponsored group was responsible. After Deputy Prime Minister Tariq Aziz was almost killed during a public meeting at Baghdad's Al Mustansiriyah University on 1 April, Iraq expelled to Iran tens of thousands of residents reportedly of Iranian origin. Throughout the summer incidents occurred along the border. Saddoun Hammadi, Iraq's foreign minister, explained, "After the Shah, the new regime in Iran did not evacuate the occupied areas along the land frontier. It resumed its military support to the Kurdish rebellion, and it began large-scale interference in Iraq's internal affairs. When we resisted, Iran took military action against us along the border. The 1975 agreement fell to pieces and war conditions were created. The Shah disappeared, but the new regime in Iran did not change the basic goal of their traditional policy—namely to expand and to dominate the other side of the Arabian Gulf."[45]

In early September Iraq occupied by force ninety square miles of territory, which, Iraq explained, it was entitled to according to the 1975 Algiers agreement but which Iran had failed to turn over. On 17 September Iraqi President Saddam Hussein stated that the 1975 agreement was "null and void" because Iran had failed in its obligations under the agreement and the agreement stood or fell as a package. "From here on in the Shatt al-Arab is totally Iraqi and totally Arab."[46] Fighting between Iranian and Iraqi patrol boats on the Shatt was reported two days later. Whatever date one gives for the start of the war, it had surely begun by 20 September, when Iraqi forces in large numbers crossed into Iranian territory.

In announcing the abrogation of the 1975 Algiers Protocol Iraq argued that the 1975 agreement was a package deal that Iran had violated by failing to evacuate certain areas, by border violations, and by fomenting violent opposition to the government in Baghdad. But stronger arguments than these supported Iran's claim to sovereignty up to the *thalweg* of the Shatt. Article 5 of the treaty describes the boundaries as "inviolable, permanent, and final." Even when international law recognizes grounds for the unilateral termination of treaties, termination "does not affect any right, obligation, or legal situation of the parties created through the execution of the treaty prior to its termination."[47] In particular, boundary treaties establish where states exercise their sovereign rights, and once executed the permanent territorial rights vest in the new sovereign. Despite Iran's violations of other provisions of the 1975 treaty, the case that the boundary in the Shatt still ran along the *thalweg* was on solid legal grounds.[48] If Saddam Hussein wanted to shift the boundary back to the left bank, he would have to secure Iranian agreement to the revision, and the only means likely to accomplish this was force.

On 21 September Saddoun Hammadi wrote to the secretary-general that "the Iraqi government now finds itself obliged to exercise its legitimate right to self-defense on [sic] sovereignty and territorial integrity and to recover its territories by force." Iraq, he wrote, "has no intention whatsoever of waging war on Iran . . . beyond the limits of defending its sovereignty and legitimate rights. The Iraqi Government sincerely hopes that the Iranian Government will accept the new situation and will act in the light of reason and wisdom."[49] Waldheim immediately appealed to the parties to end the fighting and to settle their differences by peaceful means, and he offered his good offices to help them do so.[50]

On the twenty-third Waldheim asked the Security Council to meet "in consultation." Already by 1980 informal consultations of the whole had become more frequent than formal meetings, permitting members to discuss issues in confidence before debating them in public. This time the consultations only authorized the president to issue a statement welcoming and echoing what the secretary-general had already done.[51] This was an exceptionally limp response to the outbreak of a war certain to have major consequences.

An acknowledged master of diplomacy at the United Nations was on hand to present Iraq's case. Throughout the war Ambassador Ismat Kittani played a major role, both at the United Nations and in arranging the reopening of diplomatic relations between Iraq and the United States in 1984. He merits introduction.

A Kurd, Kittani was born in Amadiya, a town in rural northeastern Iraq. In 1948, during the first Arab-Israeli war, he won a government scholarship to study abroad, and at the age of seventeen decided to go to the United States rather than to Britain. An older brother then studying for a doctorate at the University of California suggested that he try a small college. Kittani chose Knox College in Illinois.[52] Thirty-eight years later he told the Security Council, in the course of a statement expressing more sorrow than anger at U.S. protection of Israel, how he had seen, when the ship in which he was traveling to New York docked in Haifa, the destruction in Haifa's Arab quarter caused by Jewish forces. Throughout his career Kittani adeptly mixed personal and political elements.

After graduation he joined Iraq's foreign service and was in Cairo when Britain, France, and Israel attacked Egypt in 1956. In the 1960s he served seven years with the Iraqi mission to the United Nations, the last three as ambassador, before joining the UN secretariat. When George Bush was the U.S. permanent representative to the United Nations, Kittani was the assistant secretary-general coordinating the work of the specialized agencies. When his staff prepared Kittani's files for the day's meetings, one file always contained a photocopy of the *New York Times* crossword.

Kittani returned to Baghdad in 1978 to be the Foreign Ministry's undersecretary in charge of relations with international organizations. Iraq was then making its bid to lead the nonaligned movement. According to a scenario orchestrated by Kittani, at the 1979 nonaligned summit in Havana Saddam Hussein expanded his diplomatic contacts, particularly with Africans, and used offers of economic assistance to bolster Iraq's position in Third World capitals. The conference named Baghdad the site for the 1982 summit and thus Iraq as the head of the movement for the next three years. Because Saddam opposed a U.S. naval presence in the gulf and was disenchanted with Iraq's relationship with Moscow,[53] he wanted to gain greater Third World support for his foreign policy. He had chosen the right man for the job.

Kittani's personal stature with his colleagues made the difference during his 1981 campaign to be elected president of the General Assembly. Also running were the representatives of Bangladesh and Singapore. Aware that the war had dimmed Iraq's luster, Kittani campaigned for office on a personal basis, calling on all those ties built up over the years. He outpolled his opponents on the first ballot, but the runoff vote resulted in a tie. When, according to established procedure, the presiding officer then drew the winner's name out of the ballot box, Kittani won. Israel's delegate, Yehuda Z. Blum, condemned the result as "a measure of the regrettable decline of the United Nations's status."[54]

On 26 September, three days after its initial statement on the outbreak of the war, the council was preparing to meet again, this time at the prompting of Waldheim and the request of Mexico and Norway. The previous day, after a meeting with Foreign Ministry Gromyko, Secretary of State Edmund S. Muskie announced that the United States and the Soviet Union intended to pursue a policy of neutrality in the war.[55] At the United Nations, members of the Organization of the Islamic Conference (OIC) consulted on ways to end the fighting, and on Friday the twenty-sixth their foreign ministers decided on a "good-will" mission (not a formal mandate for good offices or mediation) that would be headed up by Pakistan's president Zia ul-Haq.

The council's half-hour evening meeting on the twenty-sixth accomplished nothing. The Mexican ambassador, in a brief statement, struck two notes that would be heard in changed circumstances later—he stressed the role of the nonpermanent members of the council and stated that the

deliberations of the council "should culminate, where appropriate, in decisions of a binding nature—not just in declarations or recommendations."[56]
Kittani simply quoted his foreign minister on Iraq's limited and reasonable
objectives and asked the council to defer substantive discussions until his
foreign minister could attend in person. The next morning the *New York
Times* reported that Kittani's request was part of a move to block the immediate passage of a resolution calling for a cease-fire.[57] If so, it worked. Sir
Brian Urquhart, Ralph Bunche's successor as under secretary-general, later
observed, "It was impossible to avoid the conclusion that the members of
the Security Council, under strong Iraqi pressure, were sitting on their
hands hoping that the Iraqi victory would be quick and total."[58]

In the next forty-eight hours Iraq pressed attacks along a broad front,
near the cities of Dezful, Khorramshahr, and Abadan. On 27 September
Zia ul-Haq arrived in Tehran to be told by Prime Minister Mohammed Ali
Rajai that Iran would not accept mediation.[59] On the twenty-eighth Saddam Hussein announced he would welcome a cease-fire and direct talks
(while indicating Iraq's territorial claims had to be satisfied).[60] Now Iraq
was ready for the council to meet.

After a two-hour delay, the meeting came to order at 5:15 P.M., Sunday
the twenty-eighth. Members by unanimity adopted resolution 479 (1980)
to ask for a cease-fire but not a withdrawal of forces. Gary Sick later criticized the resolution for its "lackadaisical approach," because it referred to
the war merely as a "situation," not even as a "dispute," when surely there
was already a breach of the peace.[61] There was no debate, but members
did explain their votes afterward.

Then Kittani spoke. After chiding the council because it did not wait
until his minister arrived in New York to address the council, he pointed
out that everyone in the room already knew that Iran had rejected a cease-
fire. He quoted Saddam Hussein: "Iraq is ready to stop the fighting immediately, if the other side responds to this sincere call."[62] Perceptions count
in diplomacy, and Iraq was already co-opting members of the Security
Council into seeing things its way.

For the next two weeks Waldheim worked on what appeared to be a
manageable problem: getting the parties to allow foreign vessels caught in
the Shatt to depart. To avoid arguments over sovereignty of the waterway,
Waldheim proposed that these ships fly a UN flag. Iran agreed; Iraq insisted that the ships fly the Iraqi flag while on an Iraqi river. The ships
were trapped. Meanwhile Zia ul-Haq announced that his mission to Iran
and Iraq had failed.[63] From Tehran President Bani-Sadr told the secretary-
general that Iran would not accept a cease-fire as long as Iraqi troops were
on Iranian soil.[64]

The council met five more times during October on the war. On 15
October Iraqi foreign minister Saddoun Hammadi made an hour-long law-
yer-like presentation to explain how Iran had brought on the war by fomenting civil strife in Iraq, failing to respect the terms of the 1975 Algiers

agreement, and then violating Iraqi territory. He claimed that Iranian breaches of the Algiers agreement invalidated the entire accord, including the shift in the boundary to the middle of the Shatt. Finally, he justified Iraq's decision to take "direct preventive strikes against military targets in Iran" by quoting from the correspondence in the *Caroline Case*, in which Secretary of State Daniel Webster called on Great Britain to justify its cross-border raid from Canada into upstate New York in 1837 to capture one steamship by showing a "necessity of self-defense, instant, overwhelming, leaving no choice of means and no moment for deliberation."[65] Hammadi thought Iraq's invasion met this test.

Iranian prime minister Rajai spoke two days later. Rajai was a school-teacher on his first trip outside of Iran. It is difficult to believe that the Iranian delegation could have expected his statement, although often moving and persuasive, to convince his audience inside the council that the war was somehow caused by the "fight of the super-Powers against the Islamic revolution." Or worse, was Rajai really so inexperienced that he did expect to convince this audience? Rajai's statement was Iran's last in the council on the war for eight years. "We wish to declare that a fair end to this war can be found only if the aggressor is vanquished and punished. That is our final position. . . . The decision of the Council, whatever it may be, will not change anything for us. For our people, with the help of God, will fight Saddam and his oppressive regime with their own hands. Our people will win."[66]

Rajai met separately with other delegations and the secretary-general. Waldheim tried to convince him that, as long as Iran held the American hostages, it would get little support. In his memoirs Waldheim recalled that Rajai "could not understand why the Iranians, so evidently the victims of aggression, did not get a more sympathetic reception."[67]

For three more meetings delegations read into the record pious hopes for a cease-fire. On 5 November the council president issued a brief statement welcoming the secretary-general's intent to send a representative to the region.[68] The war would rage on, but the council would not consider it again until July 1982. Without any framework of support from the council, the initiative had been returned to the secretary-general and his newly appointed representative, former Swedish prime minister Olof Palme.

4

Five Years of War

To June 1982: Olof Palme's Mediation

Before Olof Palme lay the daunting task of mediating a raging conflict. The opening phase of the war, Iraq's offensive into Iran, was ending; the second phase, in which the Iranians regrouped and then eventually drove the Iraqi invaders out of Iran, would last a few months longer than Palme's mediation. The Security Council had issued only a feeble call for a cease-fire, Iran and Iraq hardened their positions through public statements, and Waldheim could not play an active part because of the unhappy experience of his trip to Tehran earlier in the year. The council president described Palme's mission as merely "facilitating authoritative contacts with and between the governments concerned in order to clear the way for peace negotiations within the near future."[1] Palme modestly said his mission would be to gather information rather than to conduct negotiations.[2] It seemed a reasonable way to start.

Beginning in November 1980 Palme conducted five rounds of talks with the parties, the last in March 1982. According to his closest collaborator, Ambassador Jan Eliasson of Sweden, Palme followed two main approaches—at times aiming for a comprehensive settlement that included both a cease-fire and withdrawal of forces plus talks on disputed issues, and at other times seeking more modest agreements on arrangements to reduce the level of fighting or lessen its impact.[3] Palme sought commitments from the parties vis-à-vis the secretary-general rather than directly to each other. "It may be crazy to send a pragmatic Scandinavian with no knowledge on this mission," Palme said of his own involvement, "but I have no prejudgments and I like [both parties]."[4]

Palme entered a field already crowded with mediators. On 28 September 1980, soon after the opening of the Iraqi offensive, Saddam Hussein announced that Iraq would accept a cease-fire if Iran recognized Iraq's legal rights (meaning sovereignty over the Shatt) and agreed to hold direct talks. Iraq, always insisting on the condition of sovereignty over the Shatt, agreed on 5 October to the proposal by Pakistan's President Zia ul-Haq, representing the Islamic Conference, for a unilateral three-day cease-fire and for merchant ships to be allowed to leave the Shatt al-Arab (if flying the Iraqi flag). On 16 October Iraq accepted a proposal by Habib Chatti, secretary-general of the Islamic Conference, for negotiations (if Iran recognized Iraq's claims to sovereignty over the Shatt). Iran throughout demanded the unconditional withdrawal of Iraqi forces before any cease-fire or negotiation and the condemnation of Iraq as the aggressor. In addition to Zia ul-Haq and Habib Chatti for the Islamic Conference, there were the PLO (both sides had rejected its 4 October four-point plan proposing a supervised withdrawal of Iraqi forces) and a nonaligned peace mission led by Cuban foreign minister Isidóro Malmierca and including Yugoslavia, India, Zambia, Pakistan, and the PLO.

When Palme arrived in Tehran on 20 November, Iraqi forces were reaching the full extent of their success. President Bani-Sadr announced, "As long as Iraqi armed forces are present in Iran, we cannot consider any peace proposal."[5] Prime Minister Rajai said Iran wanted the overthrow of Saddam Hussein and reportedly told Palme that his effort was a "waste of time."[6] After talks in Baghdad Palme returned to New York to report to Waldheim and announced an agreement in principle to free the sixty-three commercial vessels trapped in the Shatt by the fighting. If both sides could keep a commitment not to hinder the operation for ten days, there might be better prospects for arranging a comprehensive cease-fire. Palme noted two problems to be worked out: (1) Iran would have to allow Iraq to clear the shipping channel, and (2) Iraq insisted that the ships sail under a Red Cross flag (emphasizing the humanitarian aspects of the operations) rather than under a UN flag (on the theory that a UN flag might diminish Iraq's claim to sovereignty). His effort failed on 29 December when the International Committee of the Red Cross (ICRC), aware that most of the crews were already evacuated from vessels caught in the Shatt, announced in Geneva that its flag could not be used because "the urgent humanitarian need for protection has ceased to exist."[7]

In January 1981 Palme held a second round of talks. Public statements by both sides showed a hardening of attitudes. In Baghdad Palme's interlocutors said they were willing to engage in discussions of the issues,[8] but they repeated that peace talks and withdrawal of forces would be possible only when Iran recognized Iraqi sovereignty over the Shatt.[9] In Tehran the government spoke with multiple voices, and access to the ultimate authority, Khomeini, was difficult. Palme talked with Bani-Sadr, who despite his past as a shrill ideologue was now pragmatic in talks with Palme. Bani-Sadr announced that no solution could be accepted as long as Iraqi forces were in Iranian territory.[10] Speaker of Parliament Hojatolislam Ali Akhbar Rafsanjani was accessible and easy to engage in a dialogue. Rajai ignored questions put to him and insisted that before any negotiation Saddam Hussein had to be removed, Iraq condemned as the aggressor, and reparations paid.[11] After this round Palme claimed that, although both sides insisted on hard positions, he as mediator still saw possibilities for a solution that would safeguard the interests of both.[12]

In February Palme went back for a third trip, this time to focus on the fundamental issues at stake. Iran was now conducting counteroffensives against Iraqi forces. While willing to discuss principles that might later be applied in negotiations, Bani-Sadr and other Iranians insisted on no negotiations until Iraqi forces had left Iranian territory. Palme later told the press that time was "not yet ripe" for a negotiated settlement.[13]

None of the other mediators then active achieved anything. Between 28 February and 5 March 1981 an enlarged committee of the Islamic Conference (OIC), including the presidents of Bangladesh, Pakistan, Gambia, and Guinea, as well as representatives from Senegal, Turkey, the PLO, and the OIC secretariat, visited both capitals. Iran demanded unconditional withdrawal of Iraqi troops from its territory and a tribunal to condemn Iraq and assess damages; Iraq wanted a cease-fire and settlement by negotiations of outstanding issues before a withdrawal of forces.[14] The Islamic Conference plan called for: (1) a cease-fire as of 13 March, (2) a withdrawal of forces to begin on 20 March and to be completed within four weeks, (3) supervision of the cease-fire by the Islamic Conference, (4) sovereignty over the Shatt to be decided by the Islamic Conference, (5) negotiations on other matters, (6) mutual promises of noninterference in internal affairs, and (7) the Islamic Conference to oversee and observe implementation of these arrangements.[15] Iran rejected the proposal on 6 March. Iraq rejected it on 11 March, because it did not properly consider Iraq's claim to the Shatt. At the end of April Iran told an OIC delegation headed by Habib Chatti that the withdrawal of forces and payment of reparations had to be unconditional. The OIC tried again in May with a visit by President Zia ul-Rahman of Bangladesh (in March 1982 President Sékou Touré of Guinea came back on the same mission). No progress was registered. In June Iran refused an invitation for both sides to meet with the OIC mediation committee in Jeddah.

Palme returned to the area in June 1981. Iraq, already sensing the pressure generated by the regrouping of the Iranian military, offered one cease-fire for the holy month of Ramadan and another in November for the Shiite holy period of Muharram. Iran rejected both offers. Palme presented both sides the outlines of a comprehensive plan, but because the Iranian parliament was busy with impeachment proceedings against Bani-Sadr, Palme did not get much of a hearing.

Nonaligned mediators, who had visited both capitals in April, returned in August. Rajai told them that they were wasting their time. The Iranian counteroffensive began to make progress. After failing to retake territory elsewhere, at the end of September, one year after Iraq's invasion, Operation Thamin al-A'imma broke the Iraqi siege of Abadan, Iran's vital oil port on the Shatt. In early December Operation Jerusalem Way retook Bostan near the border in the central sector, putting pressure on Iraqi forces further east in Susangerd.

After Pérez de Cuéllar replaced Waldheim as secretary-general on 1 January 1982, Palme undertook his fifth and final round of talks on 24–28 February. A month earlier Iraq had rejected a Syrian offer to mediate. Because Iran's position was that withdrawal must be unconditional, Tehran rejected Palme's proposal that Iraq withdraw its forces and that borders be negotiated thereafter.[16] On 1 March in Stockholm Palme told reporters he had "exhausted all possibilities to mediate in the war between Iran and Iraq."[17]

Military setbacks soon caused Saddam to adjust Iraq's diplomacy but not to retreat from his demand for Iraqi sovereignty over the Shatt. On 9 March Ayatollah Khomeini stated, "Peace with the criminal is a crime against Islam." Within two weeks Iran launched an eleven-day offensive (Operation Undeniable Victory) that pushed back Iraqi forces in the Dezful-Shush area, one hundred kilometers north of Susangerd. On 12 April Saddam announced that Iraqi troops would withdraw from Iran if Iran would guarantee Iraq's borders and end the fighting. Iran refused. On 24 April Iran liberated Khorramshahr and by 25 May had reoccupied most of Khuzistan (Operation Jerusalem). In May Algerian foreign minister Mohammed Benyahia, who was working to revive the role Algeria played as mediator for the 1975 agreement and end the war on the same terms, died when his plane was shot down en route from Baghdad to Tehran (Algerian investigators reportedly established Iraq was responsible).[18] On 9 June Iraq repeated its willingness to withdraw and announced a unilateral cease-fire to begin on 10 June. Iran rejected the offer and demanded the removal of Saddam Hussein and the payment by Iraq of $150 billion in war reparations. On 20 June Iraq announced it would withdraw from all Iranian territory within ten days.

So far the Security Council, through almost two years of war, had done next to nothing. Iraq, even if in retreat more eager for a cease-fire and willing to withdraw, still demanded recognition of its sovereignty over the Shatt. Iran refused to negotiate while Iraqi forces were on Iranian soil and then added demands to condemn Iraq for aggression, to oust Saddam Hussein, and to receive war reparations. Even after Iraq withdrew from Iran, Iran continued offensive operations, passing what Gary Sick has described as a crucial threshold for launching a process of diplomacy that might have spared both sides another six years of war:

> If Iran had chosen to sue for peace in mid-1982, it would have been in a good position to influence the terms of a settlement. At that time, Iran was widely perceived as having snatched victory from the jaws of defeat, and its military forces were regarded as perhaps the most potent in the region. By pursuing peace, Iran could have gone far toward restoring its image with both the

tates and the international community, and it could have established
itself as a power broker in the region. Instead, Iran once again chose
, revolutionary fervor overcome a realistic appraisal of its own long-
terests.[19]

July 1982–March 1984: Iran Invades Iraq

After Iraq withdrew from Iran, the Security Council paid renewed attention
to the war, now in its third phase: a murderous stalemate on the ground
but expansion of air attacks on logistical targets behind the fronts and on
shipping. On 12 July 1982 the council adopted resolution 514 (1982) to call
for a cease-fire and the immediate withdrawal of all forces to recognized
international boundaries (something the council had not done while Iraqi
forces were inside Iran). The resolution authorized the dispatch of a UN
team to observe a cease-fire, urged the parties to continue mediation efforts
through the secretary-general, and asked other states to refrain from action
that might prolong the conflict. Surely the council's action was taken to
forestall a renewed Iranian offensive.

In less than twenty-four hours Iran launched Operation Ramadan, a
series of five large-scale offensive operations in the direction of Basra. In
preparation for the expected Iranian invasion, Iraq was doubling the size
of its army to some twenty divisions (475,000 troops) and erecting an extensive defensive system of fortified positions, earth walls, and water obstacles. The invading force, consisting of 100,000 troops, half from the regular
army and half Pasdaran (Revolutionary Guard) and Basij (youth brigade)
forces, drove five to ten miles into Iraqi territory. There were reports that
Iraq used nonlethal tear gas to turn back the Iranians. Two days into the
fighting the council issued a statement through its president expressing
concern that fighting continued.

Iraq committed its ground forces to a static defense but expanded the
range of the fighting by using its superior air force against Iranian
countervalue targets, including petroleum installations and logistic centers. After the July offensives Iraqi planes attacked the Kharg Island oil
complex, and on 12 August Iraq declared a northern gulf exclusion zone
to warn away international shipping from what had become a war zone.
Algeria renewed its offer of mediation, which on 26 July Iranian prime
minister Hussein Moussavi welcomed—as long as all of Iran's terms were
met. (When Algeria's new foreign minister visited Tehran in January and
May 1983, he registered no progress.)

Between 1 and 10 October 1982 (Operation Muslim Ibn Aqil) and between 1 and 11 November 1982 (Operation Muharram) Iraqi forces repulsed Iranian offensives in the directions of Baghdad and Al-Amarah, a
town on the road between Baghdad and Basra. On 4 October, just three
days after Iran launched Operation Muslim Ibn Aqil, the Security Council
adopted resolution 522 (1982), which only repeated the main points of

resolution 514 and welcomed the willingness of one of the parties (Iraq) to adhere to a cease-fire. After the offensives Iraqi planes attacked the Iranian cities of Dezful and Abadan, as well as oil tankers on their way to Iranian ports.

Ignoring the council's two recent resolutions, Iran did not change its war aims. On 23 October, during the lull between the two Iranian offensives, the Islamic Conference peace mission, now led by Senegal's foreign minister, visited Tehran. President Ali Khamenei said on 8 November that Iranian forces intended to "proceed toward Baghdad whenever they deem it necessary," and he demanded $150 billion in reparations from Iraq.

To make Khamenei's threat a reality, Iranian forces launched five ground offensives in 1983. In the central sector the offensives aimed at Al-Amarah (Operation Before Dawn from 6 to 16 February), in the area north of Bostan (Operation Dawn from 10 to 17 April), and in the Mehran area (Operation Dawn III from 30 July to 9 August). These were frontal infantry assaults, without proper armor, artillery, or air support; Iraq repulsed them with artillery and air power plus some armored counterattacks. In the north, Iranian offensives toward Kirkuk (Operation Dawn II from 22 to 30 July) and in the area of Penjwin (Operation Dawn IV from 20 October to 21 November) led to Iranian occupation of Iraqi territory but did not break the Iraqi defensive line.

Iraq responded on the military and diplomatic levels. On 2 March 1983 Iraqi planes attacked an Iranian offshore oil facility, causing a massive oil spill that covered a twelve-thousand-square-mile area in the gulf. Iraq used its air superiority to strike behind the front lines against logistical staging areas in Iran, attacks that Iran charged were against purely civilian targets. On 20 July Tariq Aziz announced Iraq would escalate attacks on oil installations in Iran. Iraqi officials justified this escalation of the war by pointing out that at the outset of fighting Iraq had lost the ability to export petroleum except via pipelines through Turkey and Saudi Arabia, while Iran, which refused a cease-fire, could ship from its Persian Gulf ports. During this period Iranian oil production was often twice that of Iraq, and not until the second half of 1986 did Iraqi production surpass that of Iran.[20]

In 1983 Saddam Hussein published a series of "open letters" addressed to the people of Iran. On 15 February and 14 March he offered assurances of Iraq's goodwill and willingness to end the war. On 16 April he offered to meet with Ayatollah Khomeini in Baghdad in order to end the war. On 7 June he called for a cease-fire during the month of Ramadan; another letter followed a week later. Iran rejected them all. On 1 October there was another unanswered Iraqi offer, this time by Tariq Aziz, who invited the General Assembly to establish an arbitration commission to decide who was responsible for the war. "Iraq is prepared to accept the results of such arbitration."[21]

International efforts aimed at peace were well-intentioned but ineffective. In May 1983 the International Committee of the Red Cross investigated the condition of prisoners of war and concluded that there had been "grave and repeated breaches of international humanitarian law" by both sides.[22] After a UN team visited Iranian and Iraqi war zones, the secretary-general reported to the council heavy destruction of civilian areas in Iran and light damage to Iraq's civilian areas.[23] Foreign ministers of Kuwait and the United Arab Emirates went to Tehran and Baghdad in May to present a Gulf Cooperation Council mediation plan. In August Japan's foreign minister Shintaru Abe urged Iran and Iraq to settle the conflict, and as first steps he suggested an end to attacks on civilian targets, no use of chemical weapons, respect for free navigation (including no further attacks on Kharg Island), and reopening of Iraqi ports.[24] These efforts were valid expressions of international concern, but they made no headway with the parties.

The Security Council did no better. Without any willingness to consider even a determination that the war constituted a threat to international peace and security, there was no possibility of using the authorities of the charter's chapter VII. The council reacted to Iran's February 1983 offensive in a presidential statement, merely expressing grave concern that its previous calls for a cease-fire had not been implemented. On 31 October, in the midst of a controversy over a sale of Super Etendard planes by France to Iraq, it adopted resolution 540 (1983), which requested the secretary-general to mediate, condemned violation of international humanitarian law, especially the Geneva Conventions of 1948, affirmed the right of free navigation and commerce in the gulf, and called for a cease-fire. The secretary-general renewed contract with the parties, but no positive results followed.

The dismal, inconclusive slaughter on the battlefields and ineffective diplomacy continued through 1984. In early February Iraq tried to forestall Iran's planned offensive by announcing eleven Iranian cities it would attack and giving the civilian population a week to evacuate; Iran threatened reprisals. When Iran launched a probing attack on 7 February, Iraqi air attacks began. Iranian reprisals against Iraqi cities set the pattern for what would be called the "war of the cities." From 15 to 24 February Iran launched Operations Dawn V and Dawn VI along a one-hundred-mile front in the central sector; once again the aim was to cut the Baghdad-Basra highway near Al-Amarah. Iran's one real success came in Operation Khaybar (from 24 February to 19 March), during which it captured the Majnoon Island oil field forty miles north of Basra. On both sides up to 500,000 troops were engaged in the fighting, with Iran's regular army playing only a minor role in support of Pasdaran and Basij forces. In retaliation for the capture of Majnoon Island, on 27 February Iraq announced a blockade of Iran's Kharg Island oil terminal.

The renewed fighting produced more violations of international humanitarian law. On 5 March the United States accused Iraq of using chemical weapons, a charge confirmed by the ICRC, and the secretary-general announced the dispatch of a UN mission to investigate. Based on the secretary-general's report, on 30 March the council president issued a statement condemning the use of chemical weapons and all violations of international humanitarian law.

April 1984 to April 1985: Tanker War, Stalemate, and a Plan

By the time the war was in its fourth year, despite its inexorably horrible cost in human life, the consequences to the international community were still contained. Oil still flowed, and neither side had upset the balance of power in the region. Under the caption "If not peace, then this will do," the *Economist* wrote in the summer of 1984: "If there cannot be a negotiated peace, then a grumbling stalemate will do quite well instead."[25]

In fact, during 1984 both sides stepped up attacks on tankers (thirty-seven by Iraq and seventeen by Iran). Iraq had already proclaimed a blockade of Iranian oil facilities on Kharg Island, and its attacks on ships sailing to and from Kharg increased to a rate of four per month. On 27 March Iraq announced it had used the Super Etendard fighters acquired from France for the first time. The Iranian response was cautious. Although Parliament Speaker Rafsanjani had previously warned, "If Iran's oil shipping were halted, then no country in the world would be able to use Persian Gulf oil," Iran did not close the Straits of Hormuz nor conduct a reprisal attack until 13 May, and that was against a Kuwaiti tanker.

Immediately following that attack, members of the Gulf Cooperation Council (GCC)—Bahrain, Kuwait, Oman, Qatar, Saudi Arabia, and the United Arab Emirates—activated the League of Arab States and then the Security Council. On 20 May the Arab League adopted a resolution accusing Iran of aggression against Saudi and Kuwaiti oil tankers. Less than two weeks later the Security Council adopted resolution 552 (1984), which demanded an end to all attacks on shipping to and from nonbelligerent states, condemned the recent attacks on shipping, and called on all states to respect both the right of free navigation in international waters and the territorial integrity of nonbelligerents. War seemed to threaten the secure supply of petroleum from the gulf to the rest of the world. This resolution was a sign that the international community, which had taken only half measures to urge the parties to end the fighting, might draw a line to prevent the war from spreading either to international shipping of nonbelligerents or to the territory of the oil-rich countries of the GCC.

In June 1984 there were two centers of renewed diplomatic activity. In New York the secretary-general appealed for Iran and Iraq to end deliberate attacks on civilian population centers, and on 10 June both sides accepted the appeal, with Iraq adding the condition that there be no military concentrations in civilian areas. On 15 June the Security Council accepted the secretary-general's plan to send inspection teams to verify compliance. At the London Economic Summit there was concern that the United States might opt for unilateral military action to protect shipping in the gulf, to which President Reagan responded that a U.S. intervention would not occur without an invitation from the gulf states and prior consultations with allies. The Tanker War would only gradually weaken Iran's economy, but Reagan had already made explicit conditions for a U.S. military intervention.

The fighting season that resumed in October 1984 culminated in an initiative by Secretary-General Pérez de Cuéllar six months later. The fighting began on 18 October, when Iran launched the week-long Operation Dawn VII on a twelve-mile front in the Mehran area, using mostly Pasdaran and basij troops. The offensive netted only a few square miles. Two months later, on 21 December, Iranian foreign minister Ali Akbar Velayati repeated to a conference of Islamic foreign ministers that Iran would oppose an end to the war as long as Saddam Hussein stayed in power. In January 1985 Iraq conducted an offensive along the central front in the Qasr-e-Shirin area, its first since 1980. It failed.

On 11 March Iran launched Operation Badr, with 100,000 troops, toward the Baghdad-Basra highway near the town of Qurena. Although eventually repulsed, the Iranians briefly cut the highway. Iraq responded, as it had the previous year, with aerial attacks against Iranian cities, including Tehran, Tabriz, Isfahan, and Bushehr. The "war of the cities" went on intensively for ten days before tapering off and ending three months later.

During March 1985 there was a reawakening of diplomacy. The council president issued two statements, the first urging a moratorium on attacks on civilian targets and a second expressing concern over the resumed fighting and calling for a peaceful solution. On 16 March, after the end of Iran's Operation Badr and before Iraq renewed the war of the cities, Iraq's foreign minister Tariq Aziz called for a UN force to oversee a cease-fire and a withdrawal of all forces to international borders. Trying to catch the moment, on 20 March the prime minister of India announced the dispatch of envoys to Iran and Iraq to discuss ending the war. The discussions must have been brief, for on 21 March Ayatollah Khomeini declared on TV that the war would continue until the world accepted Iran's right to punish the aggressor.

Now, without prompting or apparent backing from the Security Council, Pérez de Cuéllar launched an initiative based on his inherent, independent authority as secretary-general. On 26 March he met separately in New York with representatives of Iran and Iraq. He gave each a set of proposals, known as "the eight-point plan," and said he would like to visit both capitals to discuss the plan during a trip to the region that he would take in the next two weeks.[26] The invitation to visit Baghdad came quickly, but ten days passed before Tehran gave assurances permitting discussion of a "full-scale cessation of hostilities."[27]

On 28 March he told the Security Council members in informal consultations of his approach to the parties. His eight points were:

1. Aiming at an end to hostilities, drawing up with the parties a compre-

hensive schedule, with fixed dates, for implementing the specific measures that were to follow.

2. An end to the war of the cities.
3. An end to threats against civil aviation.
4. Confidential assurances that both sides would abide by the terms of the 1925 Geneva Protocol regarding chemical weapons.
5. An end to attacks against civilian shipping.
6. Arrangements to spare port facilities from attack so that they could be rebuilt and resume normal activities.
7. Affirmation of readiness to cooperate with the ICRC regarding the Third Geneva Convention of 1949 and arrangements for the release and repatriation of prisoners.
8. Each party to cooperate in good faith with the secretary-general and to continue discussions on additional measures to take to normalize the situation.

Pérez de Cuéllar explained that Iraq wanted the provisional measures in the plan tied to an end to hostilities, with the first step being a commitment to an immediate cease-fire. Iraq also wanted a complete exchange of prisoners of war and the withdrawal of troops to the international borders. Iran, while accepting the plan in principle, rejected any linkage between the eight points and a cease-fire.

The secretary-general told council members, "I want to reaffirm that my main goal is, as it ought to be, finding a way to end the tragic conflict and also to bring to an end the inadmissible practices that it has given rise to." These included attacks against civilian areas, use of chemical weapons, attacks against nonbelligerent shipping, and threats against civilian aviation.

Pérez de Cuéllar, accompanied by a few aides, visited Tehran on 7 April and Baghdad the next day. The parties were sharply divided. Tariq Aziz complained publicly that Iran insisted on limiting the talks to the question of stopping attacks on civilian targets.[28] When back in New York, Pérez de Cuéllar told council members Iran would stop the war only if it received reparations and if Iraq were condemned as the aggressor.[29] The positions of the parties were unchanged.

By the end of 1985 and the beginning of another fighting season, there were no signs that the situation was about to improve. Iraq still had on the table an offer for a cease-fire and demands that Iran withdraw its forces from Iraq and recognize Iraq's claim to full sovereignty over the Shatt. Although Iran's military advances cleared away one precondition for negotiations by expelling Iraqi forces from Iran, Iran had since added demands for reparations of $150 billion, for the ouster of Saddam Hussein, for the world community to condemn Iraq's aggression, and for recognition of Iran's right to punish Iraq. The Security Council had as yet neither considered whether the war was a threat to international peace and security nor tried to exert real pressure on the parties by indicating circumstances in which it would take action under chapter VII, such as adopting sanctions to stop the fighting. No wonder all the mediation efforts—by Olof Palme, by the Islamic Conference peace committee, by Algeria, by India, by the nonaligned, by Japan, by Syria, by Kuwait and the United Arab Emirates, and by the secretary-general—had failed.

The tolerance of other states for the inevitable negative consequences of the war was now being tested. The war had expanded to include attacks on Persian Gulf shipping, with a threat to the interests of gulf Arab states and of petroleum-importing nations. The integrity of the standards of international law regarding chemical weapons, treatment of prisoners of war, and freedom of navigation had been put at risk.

The United Nations at Forty

Six months after taking over as secretary-general in 1982, Pérez de Cuéllar posed the question of what role the United Nations was playing. His answer was disturbing. "We are perilously close to a new international anarchy."[30] His analysis pointed out ways that diplomacy at the United Nations should change.

Under the general charge that the Security Council's performance had "strayed far from the Charter in recent years," he listed several complaints:

1. Governments that believe they can win an international objective by force are ready to do so, and domestic opinion often applauds this course.
2. The Security Council is often unable to take decisive action to resolve conflicts, and its resolutions are defied or ignored by those strong enough to do so.
3. The council seems powerless to ensure that its decisions are respected, even when they are taken unanimously; this failing eviscerates the process for peaceful settlement of disputes prescribed by the charter.
4. It now seems impossible in a divided world community to have recourse to the stronger measures provided for in chapter VII of the charter.[31]

He asked for changes. In order to carry out its responsibilities for peace and security, the Security Council should set its own agenda and no longer defer to the judgment of the parties to determine its agenda or actions. Although the process of informal consultations can be invaluable, it must not be either a substitute for action or an excuse for inaction. Whatever the state of relations between the permanent members outside of the United Nations, they have a duty not to let their bilateral difficulties prevent effective action by the Security Council. Members had acted as if the adoption of a resolution absolved them of further responsibility; to the contrary it should be a springboard to motivate policies of governments outside of the United Nations. When the secretary-general is given responsibility to follow up on the implementation of a resolution, member states must continue to concert their diplomatic actions in support of his efforts. Members should exert collective influence to overcome the lack of respect for UN decisions by those to whom they are addressed.[32]

After Pérez de Cuéllar's analysis, others criticized the state of affairs at the United Nations. The Security Council had been changed "from a body which focussed on problem-solving, whose negotiation involved the principal parties to a problem, to a body before which certain melodramas are played out," U.S. ambassador Jeane Kirkpatrick said the following year. "It's not paralysis. There is a lot of activity. It's a sound and light show in which a country is identified as villain and victim."[33] Kirkpatrick criticized the frequent failing to include parties to a conflict (Israel and South Africa, in particular) directly in negotiations because they were never elected members of the Security Council. Public displays were all that was left.

In 1983 President Belisario Betancur Cuartas of Colombia, drawing a rare standing ovation from the General Assembly, put most of the blame on the great powers and the consequences of their conflicts.

> Since [the founding of the UN] 38 years have passed and, despite our constituent Charter, the world is moving farther away from [the] idea [of preserving peace]. An objective review of its actions of insanity reminds us that since that time there have been in succession 150 armed conflicts, waged in the name of the most senseless causes, each one reflecting an apparent yet absurd polarization. But the victims have come from the low-lying lands of the weak, not from the centres of arrogant power, and the blood has flowed in remote provinces, and not in the fortresses where the interests truly engaged in the conflict are to be found.[34]

In the middle of his paean to Third World statesmanship, Betancur asked, "By what means are we to bring the two great world Powers, each with a centripetal nucleus for friendly nations, to reopen the dialogue, to give more thought to mankind than to their own sometimes warped interests?"

Sir Anthony Parsons, then British ambassador, must have been frequently engaged by his colleagues in corridor conversations on the state of the organization. He later wrote an assessment with a sympathetic understanding for the UN's weaknesses. He judged that the United Nations was not an instrument for providing collective security; it was an instrument of persuasion only. "The UN is *not*, and should not try to be, a forum for the *solution* of disputes. If I have learned anything from my experience, it is that problems can ultimately be resolved peacefully only through direct negotiations between the parties themselves. It is no use expecting outside bodies, including the UN, to draw up detailed blueprints and to impose them on recalcitrant parties to a dispute. It simply does not work." Parsons identified three ways that action through the United Nations could persuade the parties—*public diplomacy,* especially the setting of guidelines by the Security Council, *private diplomacy* by the secretary-general, and providing an *escape route* (such as that offered to the Shah in order to liquidate Iranian claims to Bahrain).[35] He made no reference to the enforcement powers granted in the charter's chapter VII.

For its fortieth anniversary in 1985 the United Nations held an elaborate celebration. That year a record-setting number of heads of state or government spoke in the General Assembly, and the Security Council met at the ministerial level to commemorate the event. Ministers gave speeches that were soon forgotten and took no action to reform the Security Council, despite universal awareness of its failings. The lack of reform lent credibility to the view, prevalent in the United States, that the situation was beyond redemption.

"There are moments," commented Sir Brian Urquhart, "when I feel that only an invasion from outer space will re-introduce into the Security Council that unanimity and spirit which the founders of the Charter were talking about."[36]

The Economist argued that after forty years the United Nations needed an overhaul. "Some people would like to see it scrapped; the snag, however, is that there is no new and better model available to replace it. How about trying to make the machinery we have work better? . . . Modest reforms . . . would not, of course, transform the United Nations into the ideal international mechanism that features in some people's dreams. They could, however, bring it into closer correspondence with the reality of our world. They should have some appeal for those whose irritation with the UN's present performance leads them to talk of scrapping it, as well as for those who complain that its words and deeds command no respect nowadays. So forward, please, with the oilcan and the duster."[37]

5

The Permanent Members

In the Security Council

Britain, China, France, the Soviet Union, and the United States, as permanent members of the Security Council, have a special influence over Security Council diplomacy. Perhaps more important than their power to veto any substantive decision by the council is the strong influence they derive from the continuity of their presence, year after year, integrating the consequences of their membership on the council into the fabric of their foreign policy and relations with other states, including parties to a conflict. Beijing, London, Moscow, Paris, and Washington all follow the same diplomatic procedure, employed much less rigorously by most other capitals, of closely instructing their delegations, reinforcing the connection between government policy and actions taken in New York. As much as laymen criticize modern ambassadors for having to refer questions home for instructions, diplomats prefer assurance that an agreement represents the position of a government, not just that of an ambassador. Beyond what happens in New York, these five states, more frequently than most, see their national interests at stake in regional conflicts. They have both the ability and the desire to influence the diplomatic process.

During the 1980s these states adjusted their policies to the changed situation in the Persian Gulf area following the upheaval caused by the revolution in Iran. To recapitulate the situation at the start of the decade, since the Second World War the United States had taken over from Britain the role of opposing the southward push of Soviet power. The United States had played this role through its security relationships with Turkey and Iran, a modest naval presence in the gulf, and close economic and security ties to Iran and Saudi Arabia. During the 1960s and 1970s the Soviet Union built up a privileged relationship with Iraq. The 1973 Arab-Israeli war and the ensuing Arab oil embargo delivered one blow to the pattern of U.S. influence; in 1979 the Iranian revolution delivered another, even if revolutionary Iran wanted nothing to do with the Soviet Union. In 1980 the Soviet invasion of Afghanistan raised the threat of a permanent shift in the geopolitical map of the region. In the 1980s it was a changed

ıment, and there was much uncertainty how the permanent mem-
ould view their interests and shape their policies.[1]

th growing interests in the region and a more hostile and competitive
relationship, the superpowers' role will be more direct," one analyst predicted in 1980.

> This is especially clear from the Western perspective where acute dependence
> and Soviet proximity to the region are even more stark in the aftermath of
> Iran's upheaval. Past structures have broken down, and without regional states
> as buffers, the prospect for direct East-West confrontation arising from local
> instabilities has increased. Unlike the preceding era, the pressures on the
> superpowers in assuming a greater role in conflict management have intensi-
> fied. Their interests are greater and no obvious substitute exists. The issue in
> this case is not whether but how the superpowers can usefully play this role
> and what role exists for regional structures.[2]

The West was more vulnerable to upheaval in the area, and the Soviet
Union more interested in limiting foreign naval activity in the gulf, but
they shared an interest in the free transit of shipping and in avoiding the
risk that a regional conflict might lead to a general war. "If détente were
to be revived and given substance, the Persian Gulf, where interests overlap, could serve as an important test-case for restraint and for negotiations."[3]

If the permanent members were to cooperate in engaging the UN machinery, they would have to be convinced that doing so in the case at hand
would serve their national interests.[4] In other words, there was no need
that they agree in abstract on how to use the Security Council—what was
needed was an ad hoc agreement on how to proceed in a specific case.[5]
How did the policies of the permanent members toward the war develop
between its outbreak in 1980 and the end of the period of stalemate at the
beginning of 1986?

United States

At the start of the Iran-Iraq war the media described a Soviet strategy
aimed at the gulf from positions in Afghanistan, Ethiopia, and South
Yemen, which accompanying maps depicted as bastions of the Soviet
threat. The United States did not seem to be in any position to respond.
Since British military withdrawal, the United States had grown dependent
on its relations with Iran for the defense of a critical region that contains
approximately two-thirds of the world's proven reserves of petroleum. In
May 1972, several months after the dismemberment of Pakistan and one
month after Iraq and the Soviet Union had signed a defense agreement,
the Nixon administration decided to allow the Shah to buy any conventional arms he wished. Then the oil price rise of 1973 gave the Shah the
financial resources to change radically the consequences of this decision.

The other pillar of U.S. policy, Saudi Arabia, had limited military capabilities and reservations about political cooperation with the United States; it participated in the 1973 oil embargo against the United States because of U.S. support for Israel in the 1973 Arab-Israeli war, and it opposed the Camp David treaty. As for Iraq, it led the opposition to Camp David and U.S. policy in the region.

After the Iranian revolution ended the "twin pillar" policy, President Carter announced a new doctrine in his State of the Union message on 23 January 1980: "Any attempt by any outside force to gain control of the Persian Gulf region will be regarded as an assault on the vital interests of the United States of America, and such an assault will be repelled by any means necessary, including military force." The United States began to assemble a force identified for use in the Persian Gulf area. In January 1983 the Reagan Administration established the Central Command (CENT-COM), with earmarked forces totaling 230,000 military personnel. CENT-COM's mission was to assure access to Persian Gulf oil and prevent the Soviet Union from acquiring control of the area.[6]

At the start of the Iran-Iraq war the United States, beset by the hostage crisis with Iran, lacking diplomatic relations with Iraq, and opposing the Soviet invasion of Afghanistan, had limited policy options. It pledged neutrality in the war and called on others, especially the Soviet Union, not to interfere. President Carter hoped the conflict would be solved "peacefully and promptly with the aid of international institutions."[7] Carter and Secretary of State Edmund Muskie spoke out to support the unity and territorial integrity of Iran. Because, as the State Department said, "we are not neutral in meeting the legitimate defense needs of our friends,"[8] the United States sent four AWACS, with U.S. crews, to Saudi Arabia. It proposed to Britain, France, Japan, Italy, and the Federal Republic of Germany the establishment of a joint naval force to protect the flow of petroleum through the gulf, but the allies opted not to join in, after Iraq spoke out against the idea.[9] The subsequent release by Iran of the embassy hostages on 20 January 1981 caused no significant shift in U.S. policy.

Oddly, it was Israel's attack on Iraq's Osirak nuclear facility on 7 June 1981 that led to a diplomatic breakthrough between the United States and Iraq. Jeane Kirkpatrick, then U.S. ambassador to the United Nations, and her Middle East adviser, April Glaspie (later the U.S. ambassador in Baghdad), negotiated over a Security Council resolution until Iraq grudgingly accepted the text. Resolution 487 (1981) "strongly condemns the military attack by Israel in clear violation of the Charter of the United Nations and the norms of international conduct." Kirkpatrick explained that U.S. support was based solely on the conviction that Israel had failed to exhaust peaceful means to resolve the dispute.[10] Iraq complained that without the U.S. support for Israel the text would have better reflected world public opinion.[11] The first step had been taken in the thawing of U.S.-Iraqi relations.

After Iraqi forces withdrew from Iran in mid-1982, the United States became more friendly toward Iraq. The State Department removed Iraq from its list of countries supporting international terrorism. Although the United States remained "strictly neutral," concern was rising in Washington that the fall of Saddam Hussein would accelerate the spread of Islamic fundamentalism. Operation Staunch, the U.S. campaign to convince other states not to permit arms sales to Iran, began. "I think the Iranians pose a major threat without any question to the nations of the Middle East," said Secretary of Defense Caspar Weinberger. "They are a country run by a bunch of madmen."[12] For its part, Iraq wanted to improve relations with the United States, now its sixth largest trading partner, and Baghdad for the first time invited twenty U.S. companies to participate in the Baghdad Trade Fair.[13] By 1983 trade had climbed to $1 billion a year, supported by $435 million in U.S. agricultural credits.[14]

Iran gave a push to the U.S. tilt toward Iraq. After France decided in September 1983 to sell Super Etendard planes to Iraq, Iran threatened to close the gulf if Iranian shipping were halted; Washington warned Iran that the United States would keep the gulf open. On 23 October 1983 Iranian allies in Lebanon blew up the U.S. Marine barracks, killing 241 Marines. Then, on 12 December a truck bomb attack, most probably committed by a pro-Iranian group, blew up part of the U.S. embassy in Kuwait. A week later Donald Rumsfeld, the president's special representative for the Middle East, visited Baghdad, where he was the first senior-level U.S. visitor in sixteen years. His visit led to the decision to extend approximately $2 billion in commodity credits for the sale of U.S. farm products to Iraq. The State Department announced, "If there was a feeling on the part of Iraq that we should exchange ambassadors, the U.S. would be ready to do that."[15] On 23 January 1984 the State Department declared Iran to be a supporter of international terrorism and tightened controls on Iranian purchases of U.S. goods.

During 1984 the United States and Iraq moved to reestablish diplomatic relations. Nizar Hamdoon, who became the first Iraqi ambassador to Washington in seventeen years, described the conditions for opening relations as "1. Greater American understanding of Iraq's important role in the region. 2. A lessening of the regional threat to its sovereignty and security (to avoid any misinterpretation of its action). 3. An avoidance of the perception that Iraq's decision was an alignment with the American camp in terms of the global East-West conflict."[16] On 26 November, during a visit by Iraq's deputy prime minister Tariq Aziz to Washington that included a meeting with President Reagan, the two sides announced that relations were reestablished.[17] In 1984 the United States began to share intelligence with Iraq.[18]

According to congressional testimony by Assistant Secretary of State Richard Murphy in June 1984, "A victory by either side is neither militarily achievable nor strategically desirable."[19] Actions by the parties influenced

how this perspective was translated into policy. Iraq
relations with the United States. Iran, whose Lebanese
U.S. embassy in East Beirut in 1984 and began to take A
in West Beirut, emphasized its antagonism toward the Un
bers of the National Security Council staff, perhaps disc
events, sowed seeds for the initiative that became the Iran

Since 1980 the anchor of U.S. policy toward the regi⸻ ⸻ ⸺een its
economic and military ties to Saudi Arabia and the other GCC members—
Bahrain, Kuwait, Oman, Qatar, and the United Arab Emirates. The United
States had a privileged position in Riyadh as both an economic and a
military partner, despite congressional opposition to arms sales, French
inroads in the arms market, and competition for commercial sales. In February 1985 the Reagan administration prepared an arms sale package designed to give Saudi Arabia superior air combat and attack capability and
to demonstrate U.S. support for Saudi Arabia. The key to the package,
which included over $3.6 billion in immediate sales, was upgrading the
capabilities of Saudi Arabia's existing sixty F-15 C and D models. The package fell apart when the administration failed to counter anticipated congressional opposition with a coordinated effort led by the White House.[20]
Britain would now get its chance to enter the Saudi arms market.

Soviet Union

Two goals of Soviet policy—nurturing its relationship with Iraq and building new ties to Iran—were in conflict. In the 1970s Iraq was the only state
in the region without a close tie to any Western state. From 1970 to 1976
Iraq's share of Soviet trade with the Third World grew from 2.2 percent to
10.9 percent; Iraq's growing oil income and good repayment record solidified the relationship.[21] The number of Soviet and Eastern bloc economic
technicians working in Iraq doubled during the years 1977 to 1979,[22] and
by 1978 Iraq was the Soviet Union's most important Arab trade partner.
The Soviet Union and Warsaw Pact allies sold Iraq most of its arms.

Then, starting in the mid 1970s Iraq began to expand contacts with the
West, diversify its sources of high-technology arms, and supply its air force
with French aircraft. In 1978 Baghdad suppressed the Iraqi Communist
party and restricted the number of Soviet military advisers. As growing
oil revenues made hard currency available for trade with the West, the
percentage of Iraqi trade with the Soviet Union fell. By 1980 Iraqi-Soviet
relations were no longer flourishing.

Iranian-Soviet relations have always been complicated. Iran had a long
border with the Soviet Union; imperial Russia had seized large parts of
the Persian Empire in the nineteenth century; and the Muslim population
of these territories watched events in Iran with interest. The fall of the
Shah and the hostage crisis eliminated U.S. influence in Tehran, suggesting
an opening for Soviet policy. At the start of the war with Iraq the Soviet

on's minimum aims were to achieve working relations with Iran that
were as good as possible, at least up to the level enjoyed with the Shah,
and to promote strained relations between the United States and Iran to
prevent an American "comeback" in Iran. If possible, the Soviet Union
wanted improved relations, a regime friendly to the Soviet Union with
neutralist foreign policy, strained relations between Iran and the West,
and coordination (or at least consultation) on foreign policy.[23] The Soviet
invasion of Afghanistan blighted prospects for this policy.

The Soviet Union had minimal contacts and commerce with Arab gulf
states and diplomatic relations only with Kuwait. The Soviet Union wanted
to erode the privileged military and political position of the United States
with these states and to play for openings with Iran and Iraq to broker a
settlement of the war. The growth of the Soviet fleet in the Indian Ocean
was another sign of the times. Dennis Ross, who later directed the secretary of state's policy planning staff, wrote, "It would remind local states
that the Soviet Union (and not just the United States) was an arbiter of
local disputes, and that the USSR played an important role in local security
arrangements."[24]

The war revealed contradictions in the Soviet position. When Iraqi troops
crossed the border, Tariq Aziz was in Moscow to explain the Iraqi move
and seek more arms. The Soviets did not oblige. On 26 September 1980
Secretary of State Muskie and Foreign Minister Gromyko met in New York
and reaffirmed neutrality in the war. Expressing his concern that the
United States would turn the war to its advantage, General Secretary Leo-
nid Brezhnev warned an Indian delegation in Moscow that the United
States would use the war to recoup its old position and turn Iran into a
"military base and police outpost of imperialism." Neither Iran nor Iraq
had anything to gain from the war, Brezhnev explained, and "it is only
the third side, to which the interests of the people are alien, which stands
to gain."[25]

On 8 October in Moscow Brezhnev and Syrian president Hafez al-Assad
signed the USSR-Syrian Friendship treaty. At the state dinner for President
Assad Brezhnev said: "We are not going to intervene in the conflict between Iran and Iraq. We stand for its earliest political settlement by the
efforts of the two sides. And we resolutely say to others: Hands off these
events."[26] In Baghdad the treaty must have been seen as an anti-Iraqi move,
because Syria and Iraq had broken off relations in August of the same year
and Syria was close to Iran.

In Tehran Soviet policy initiatives were not well received. On 5 October
Radio Tehran reported that, because Iran was not ready to exchange its
independence for Soviet aid, it rejected an offer of arms transfers conveyed
by the Soviet ambassador. This report, in addition to showing a lack of
Iranian interest in closer relations with the Soviet Union, must have sapped
Iraqi confidence in its Treaty of Friendship with the Soviet Union and cast

doubt on Soviet claims of neutrality.[27] In November Tariq Aziz went back to Moscow to ask for arms, again without success.

During a state visit to New Delhi on 10 December, Brezhnev, seeking to escape the contradictions of Soviet relations with Iran and Iraq and the international opposition to the Soviet invasion of Afghanistan, issued a five-point doctrine addressed to the Western powers, China, and Japan. He called on them:

- Not to set up foreign military bases in the Persian Gulf area and on adjacent islands, [and] not to deploy nuclear or any other weapons of mass destruction there.
- Not to use or threaten to use force against the countries of the Persian Gulf area and not to interfere in their internal affairs.
- To respect the status of nonalignment chosen by the states of the Persian Gulf area, not to draw them into military groupings with nuclear powers.
- To respect the sovereign rights of the states of that area to their natural resources.
- Not to raise any obstacles or pose threats to normal trade exchanges and the use of sea lanes linking the states of the area with other countries.[28]

This initiative had scant appeal, especially for the Arab gulf states.

Soviet relations with Iraq and Iran stagnated. Iraq and the Soviet Union signed a technical aid agreement in April 1981, but the Soviet Union still restricted Iraqi access to Soviet arms. In November 1981 Saddam Hussein said Iraq's Treaty of Friendship and Cooperation with the Soviet Union had not worked during the war, suggesting that Soviet neutrality looked to Saddam like a tilt toward Iran. If there was a tilt, it did not earn favors in Tehran. By March 1982 Iran had further restricted relations with the Soviet Union, cut Soviet diplomatic, commercial, and cultural establishments in Iran, stepped up support for the Afghan resistance, appealed to Muslims in the Soviet Union, and restricted the Moscow-leaning Tudeh party.[29]

By the summer of 1982, when Iraq withdrew its forces across the border, Iran had not moved closer to the Soviet Union. Iraq, it now appeared, might turn further to the West for arms, commercial transactions, and diplomatic support. The Israeli Defense Force, using American and Israeli weapons, had just roundly defeated Syrian forces using Soviet weapons; it was no time for the Soviets to restrict arms transfers to Iraq and risk another failure of Soviet arms. In December 1982 Saddam Hussein announced resumption of Soviet arms sales, as per prepaid contracts signed before the war. Transfers would include MiG-25 jet fighters, T-72 tanks, and SAM-8 missiles. There were now between one thousand and twelve hundred Soviet technicians and advisers in Iraq.[30] In early 1983 a visit to Moscow by Deputy Prime Ministers Taha Yahsin Ramadan and Tariq Aziz, joined by Chief of Staff Abd al-Jabbar Shansal, led to more equipment and more Soviet experts.

Meanwhile, Soviet relations with Iran were suffering a severe setback. On 22 October 1982 the British Home Office announced that a Soviet diplomat who had served at the embassy in Tehran had defected and received permission to remain in the United Kingdom. Vladimir Kuzichkan, officially a vice consul, was reportedly a KGB officer.[31] Kuzichkan gave information on KGB operations in Iran to British authorities, who, to build up Britain's ties to Iran and curb Soviet influence there, shared it with Iran. On 7 February 1983 Iranian authorities, as part of a widespread crackdown, arrested the head of the Tudeh party on charges of spying for the Soviet Union. In May Iran expelled eighteen Soviet diplomats and banned the Tudeh party. Noureddin Kianouri, secretary-general of the Tudeh, stated on Iranian TV that "our violations consisted of the delivery of top secret military and political documents to our bosses at the Soviet embassy."[32] Demonstrations in Tehran subjected the Soviet Union to vilification on a par with that used for the United States, and Iran kept up support to the Afghan resistance fighting the Red Army.

The resumption of Soviet arms sales to Iraq did help to improve relations with Baghdad. In 1984 and 1985 Tariq Aziz made several trips to Moscow, usually shadowed within a week by an Iranian official. In December 1985 Saddam Hussein visited Moscow; this was his first visit to a non-Arab state since the start of the war. However, disagreements remained, as shown by the official characterization of the meeting as "businesslike, frank, and friendly."[33]

This time Tehran, because Iran and the Soviet Union shared an interest in maintaining a "balanced" Soviet position, agreed to a visit by First Deputy Foreign Minister Georgi Korniyenko. In February 1986 he was in Tehran for a three-day visit that he characterized as "useful, pleasant, and constructive."[34] Although no major deals were concluded, it was announced that Aeroflot would resume flights to Tehran and that a dormant joint economic commission would be reactivated. Baghdad's suspicious rulers must have noticed that within days Iran launched an offensive across the Shatt that resulted in the capture of the Fao peninsula, the narrow strip of land between the Shatt and the Kuwaiti border. Soviet and Iranian officials met again in August and December, with indications that Iran had contracted to resume exports of natural gas to the Soviet Union, up to three billion cubic feet annually by 1990.[35]

Whatever opportunities the war presented for Soviet diplomacy, in its first five years the Soviet Union had limited success exploiting them. Arms were flowing to Iraq, but Baghdad, remembering how the Soviets cut off arms at the start of the war and worried about Soviet flirtation with Iran, had limited confidence in its Soviet connection. Soviet relations with Iran were improving, but from a very low starting point. Relations with the GCC states were a plus—in 1984 Kuwait announced a deal to purchase $327 million in Soviet weapons (following a U.S. refusal to sell Stinger missiles), and Oman and the United Arab Emirates agreed to establish relations with the Soviet Union. The greatest liability for Soviet policy toward the region—one that crippled its diplomacy—was the Soviet occupation of Afghanistan. Moscow had not become the arbiter of conflicts in the region, and it saw the position of the United States getting stronger.[36]

France

Before the war France had built up a special relationship with Iraq, the one major oil exporter in the area where French firms did not confront privileged positions already held by U.S. and British firms. France, the only Western arms supplier to offer any competition to the Soviet Union, had extensive contracts to sell arms to Iraq. A 1977 contract provided for the sale of 36 Mirage F-1 fighter planes; another in 1979 added 24 more. Other Iraqi orders included 100 heavy tanks, 50 light tanks, 40 transport helicopters, and 20 light helicopters. By 1980 France was receiving 18 percent of its petroleum imports from Iraq, and French firms had contracts for major development projects, including the Osirak nuclear reactor.

Throughout the war France based its policy on three points. First, there should not be a victorious or a defeated party; after the Iraqi withdrawal from Iran, this led to a decided tilt in Iraq's favor. Second, France would maintain its existing contracts; as it happened, the contracts were mostly with Iraq. Third, France would stay within the majority trend in the Security Council.[37]

This policy produced a deterioration of Franco-Iranian relations in 1981. In February, when four planes were to be turned over to Iraq, France reaffirmed that it would perform these contracts: "The government has made it clear that its obligation under the agreement will be carried out."[38] An Iranian embassy spokesman in Paris retorted, "The Iranian people will never forget this act by the French government." Within a week Khomeini canceled pending contracts worth billions of French francs, including those for power plants and a metro for Tehran.[39] Franco-Iranian relations deteriorated further in July when President Bani-Sadr, fleeing his impeachment trial at home, arrived in Paris with a request for political asylum. He was accompanied by Massoud Rajavi, leader of the People's Mujahidin Group. Although Khomeini himself had benefited from France's traditional hospitality for political exiles, the Iranian government wanted Bani-Sadr back. On 5 August France refused Iran's request for extradition and asked French citizens in Iran to depart quickly. The Quasi D'Orsay recalled the French ambassador and reduced the embassy staff from sixty to three.[40]

In February 1983 the press reported that another twenty-nine of the already ordered Mirage F-1s would be delivered to Iraq in 1983 and that Iraq had requested five planes specifically equipped to carry the Exocet antiship missile.[41] On 24 June *Le Monde* indicated that France had agreed to "lend" to Iraq five Super Etendards equipped with the Exocets. At the time France was negotiating for Iraq to repay some of its $2.26 billion debt by shipping oil. Other Western states expressed concern to the French government that transfer of Super Etendards with Exocets could only increase the risk of attacks against oil tankers, but by September France confirmed its intention to go through with the sale. Heightening tensions, Baghdad announced that the Super Etendards, with retrained Iraqi pilots and the Exocets, were intended to sink ships: "We're not just taking the planes out to polish them."[42] France's justification for the transfer was more subtle: the planes would give Iraq a new military credibility and therefore give Iran an incentive to settle the war.[43]

In October, the month in which Iran's Lebanese Shiite allies blew up the French paratroopers' headquarters in Beirut as well as the U.S. Marine barracks, France worked in the Security Council for adoption of resolution 540 (1983) to affirm the right of free navigation in the gulf and to call for an end to hostilities in the gulf, including port facilities. According to one observer, the intent was to link Iraq's resumption of shipping through facilities in the northern gulf war zone to Iran's continued shipping outside of this zone.[44] The situation was tense—Iran warned that "the Persian Gulf's jugular is in our hands"[45] and suggested that, if its own shipping were halted, it might close the Straits of Hormuz. But Iran reacted elsewhere. Its official retaliation for the Super Etendard deal was to close the French commercial attaché's office and a French archeological institute in Tehran and to impose new sanctions against French banks.[46] There was little doubt of Iranian inspiration for the 12 December bomb blasts at the French and U.S. embassies in Kuwait that killed seven persons and injured sixty-six.

Terrorism and hostages plagued Franco-Iranian relations. In February 1986, after the Security Council adopted another resolution not favored by Iran and after France expelled four Iranians in connection with bombings in Paris, Iranian authorities detained five French nationals, including a third secretary at the French embassy in Tehran.[47] On 5 March Islamic Holy War, a group in Lebanon allied to Iran, announced that it had executed Michel Seurat, a French researcher, to protest French support for Iraq in the war.[48] Now a new French government, led by Prime Minister Jacques Chirac, decided to improve relations with Iran as a way to resolve France's hostage crisis. Chirac's government warned that if, after an improvement in relations, Iran failed to use its influence to secure the release of French hostages, French arms shipments to Iraq would be increased.[49] The warning repeated the logic used when Iraq received the Super Etendards in 1983: if Iran did not improve its performance regarding French interests, things would get worse for Iran.

France had interests at stake in relations with other gulf states, particularly because they were such significant customers for France's arms industry. France was, after the United States, the second largest source of arms for Saudi Arabia. By the autumn of 1980 Saudi Arabia had already bought twelve billion French francs' worth of equipment—450 Panhard APCs, 250 AMX-30 tanks, 150 AMX-10p infantry combat vehicles, Gazelle antitank helicopters, Crotale air defense missiles, and 155mm howitzers.[50] Between 1983 and 1987 France transferred to the Saudis equipment valued at $6.4 billion, including a $4 billion air defense system. For the same period this figure was $1.6 billion more than its sales to Iraq and only $.8 billion less than U.S. sales to Saudi Arabia.[51] With total sales between 1983 and 1987 of $12.33 billion to Iraq and the GCC states, France was the foremost source of Western arms to the region. In addition, a French military presence was constant: on 28 October 1980 France announced it would set up a special five-vessel minesweeping task force for possible use in the gulf;[52] France maintained a naval base in Djibouti; and throughout the war French naval vessels operated in the area.

French policy had some apparently contradictory elements. France wanted to influence U.S. policy as the surest way to influence security arrangements in the gulf, but it insisted on maintaining independent policies toward the area.[53] Put differently, France, even when exhibiting less unilateralism than characterized U.S. or Soviet policy, wanted to maintain the independence of its own decision whether or how to participate in security arrangements.

Britain

After Britain withdrew from the gulf in 1971, its interests were largely commercial and financial, as the growing presence of gulf Arabs in London's fashionable Knightsbridge section testified. "To put it bluntly," wrote Anthony Parsons, the last British ambassador to the Shah and Britain's representative to the United Nations at the start of the war,

> Britain in the 1980's sees the Gulf in terms of oil, finance, and commerce. This is not to say that Britain depends to an overriding extent on any or all of these elements for its prosperity and well-being. . . . Nevertheless Britain is conscious of the fact that the cumulative importance of the Gulf for the industrialized economies of the Western world as a whole, in particular those of certain Western European countries and Japan, is such that radical changes— for example, political chaos or the advent of hostile regimes—would, by extension, be seriously damaging to Britain.[54]

If Britain retained a privileged position in the area, it was not with Iran, Iraq, or Saudi Arabia, but with the five smaller Arab states Britain had once protected.

When war broke out, Britain had sanctions in force against Iran because it still held U.S. embassy hostages in Tehran. On 4 November 1980 Britain told other members of the European Community it had rejected twelve Iranian requests for weapons.[55] Nevertheless, Britain would consider any future request "based on its merits in light of the prevailing circumstances at the time."[56] Such requests seemed likely, because Iran had a large inventory of British tanks and armored cars, including 950 Chieftain tanks.[57] After U.S. hostages were released on 20 January 1981, Britain would eventually want better relations with Iran.

In January 1984 an article in the *Times* of London claimed, "Britain is quietly emerging as the prime architect and mover behind United Nations peace initiatives in the Gulf war." The article asserted that Sir John Thomson, Britain's new UN representative, had identified signs that Iran was ready to end its boycott of normal diplomatic practices. While aiming at an end to the war, Britain wanted to fill "the void that exists in Iran's relationship with the West" and balance France's relationship with Iraq. Thomson had "staunchly defended Iran" when the Security Council considered resolution 540 on freedom of navigation, for which Britain, however, voted. The article described the resolution as an "undisguised attempt by France to justify morally its delivery of the five Super Etendard aircraft and Exocet missiles to Iraq."[58]

In fact, just as Britain's UN ambassador was trying to balance France's relationship with Iraq, officials in London were working to conclude an arms sale to Iran. A 14 October 1984 Iranian document reported a deal with a commercial subsidiary of the British Ministry of Defense to resupply spare parts for tanks and armored vehicles and asked for transport from the United Kingdom to Iran in unmarked planes for fifteen planeloads of merchandise. Not until 27 September 1985 did British authorities confirm this transaction, which had been approved because it would not "prolong or exacerbate the conflict."[59] British arms sales to the belligerents from 1980 to 1987 were a relatively modest $350 million to Iraq and $210 million to Iran[60] (including new engines for the Chieftain tanks, Plessey air defense radars, and logistic support ships).[61] In London Iran located its Logistical Support Center in the Iranian National Oil Company building, where a staff of thirty civilians arranged worldwide purchases of arms.

But Britain never established good relations with Tehran. Ayatollah Khomeini's expression for Britain was "the aged wolf of imperialism."[62] After 1985 Britain faced, like the United States and France, the dilemma of hostages in Lebanon held by Shiite groups linked to Tehran. The foremost British hostage was Terry Waite, representative of the Archbishop of Canterbury, who was kidnapped on 23 January 1986. Diplomatic contretemps battered British-Iranian relations. In May 1986 Britain refused to accept as Iranian chargé d'affaires in London Mr. Hussein Malouk, a leader of the 1979 student takeover of the U.S. embassy; Iran then blocked the appointment of Hugh Arbuthnott as head of the British interests section in the Swedish embassy in Tehran.[63]

Britain wanted to expand relations with the five smaller GCC states and develop financial and commercial ties to Saudi Arabia. Some 6.5 percent of British exports were sold to the GCC countries, a total three and a half times more than Britain exports to the Soviet Union and Eastern Europe.[64]

Preparing for the possibility that the United States would drop out as the lead supplier to the Saudi air force, in January 1984 British defense minister Michael Heseltine met with Saudi defense minister Prince Sultan ibn Abdul Aziz in Riyadh to promote the virtues of the Tornado over the Mirage 2000.[65] In April 1985, shortly after political pressures on the White House and Congress had stopped the proposal for an arms sale including improvements for Saudi Arabia's 60 F-15 C/D planes, Prime Minister Margaret Thatcher visited King Fahd in Riyadh. In September the package was expanded to include 48 attack versions of the Tornado, 24 of the air defense versions of the Tornado, and 60 training aircraft (30 British Hawks and 30 Swiss Pilatus PC-9s). The final letter of acceptance, including provisions for partial payment in oil, was signed on 17 February 1986.[66]

For Britain, like France, policy toward the gulf was in part a function of relations with the United States. It wanted to promote its own political and economic ties with countries in the region, but Western Europe depended on U.S. military power to maintain access to vital oil supplies in the gulf. Britain, like other European countries, would therefore want to coordinate with the United States on foreign and defense policies toward the gulf.[67] The Western allies both wanted to prevent an outcome of the war that would give Khomeini the upper hand over the entire gulf area, or encourage the spread of Islamic fundamentalism and militarism, or provide opportunities to the Soviet Union. But British officials, like their continental colleagues, thought the United States often put too much emphasis on the military angle, especially regarding the Soviets, and should rely more on political diplomacy.[68]

China

China and Iran both bordered on the Soviet Union, with China and Iran separated by Afghanistan.

In August 1978 Chinese Communist party leader and Premier Hua Kuo-Feng visited Iran on the first trip ever by a Chinese Communist party chairman to a non-Communist country. The three stops on the trip, which took place several months after a Marxist coup in Afghanistan, demonstrated Chinese opposition to Soviet policies. After stops in Romania and Yugoslavia, on his arrival in Tehran Hua Kuo-Feng assailed big power "expansion, aggression, and domination."[69] A cultural agreement was signed, but no communiqué was issued. Diplomatic sources indicated the two sides reviewed the coup in Afghanistan as "the most unsettling element in the stability of the region."[70]

When the Iran-Iraq war began, China was sympathetic to Iran's security needs. Both governments firmly opposed the Soviet invasion of Afghanistan. In October 1980 China granted permission for overflights by Iranian planes en route to North Korea for military supplies.[71] China developed its position as an arms supplier to Iran. In March 1985 China and Iran negotiated an arms deal worth $1.6 billion, including J-6 fighters, T-59 tanks, heavy artillery, multiple rocket launchers, and surface-to-air missiles.[72] Iranian Parliament speaker Rafsanjani then visited China from 27 June to 1 July of that year. Between 1980 and 1987 cumulative Chinese deliveries had a value of $1.8 billion.[73]

China sold even more arms to Iraq, a total of $3.9 billion in the period 1980–1987. Arms sales became a major source of hard currency for China ($8.5 billion during these years), and during the eight years of the war Iran and Iraq accounted for two thirds of all sales.[74] Moreover, the Chinese army, which during the period of the war suffered from budget cutbacks, from 17.5 percent to 8.8 pecent of GNP,[75] had a strong incentive to sell abroad. Iraq wanted to expand sources of supply and to develop a Chinese stake in Iraq. By the end of the war twenty thousand Chinese workers were employed in Iraq in civilian projects.[76] As the war wound down the Chinese, like the British, looked for arms markets in Saudi Arabia.

There were no clashes between activists of the Islamic revolution and China. China had few commercial exports to the area and did not rely on petroleum imports. The key for China was that in the first five years of the war it made fully 78 percent of its arms sales here, supplying both sides. (Comparable figures for other permanent members were Britain 51 percent, France 68 percent, Soviet Union 33 percent, and United States 31 percent.)[77] China, with its interests not threatened, could be patient about ending the war.

PART TWO

The Turning Point

FOR THE SECURITY COUNCIL to use its chapter VII powers to confront a threat to the peace, the permanent members would have to agree to do so. The impediments were substantial: there was no precedent for such a move, the policies of member states toward the Iran-Iraq war would have to change, and the permanent members would need better relations among themselves, including a working relationship at the United Nations. At the end of 1986 it seemed unlikely that these conditions would ever be met.

But the seeds of radical change had in fact been planted and were growing. In early 1986 the fourth phase of the war began, bringing with it successful Iranian ground offensives into southern Iraq and extension of the scope of the war, through Iraqi air power, to Iranian urban areas and to shipping throughout the gulf. The Arab gulf states, previously opposed to the presence of outside military forces in the gulf, now wanted protection from the consequences of the war. The Iran-Contra scandal made the Reagan administration search for a more legitimate format for its policies. Gorbachev's accession to power in 1985 brought new flexibility in Soviet policy, suggesting that superpower relations might improve. And in 1986 the permanent members cooperated in the reelection of Pérez de Cuéllar.

In January 1987, days after Iraq checked a major Iranian offensive aimed toward Basra, the secretary-general challenged the permanent members to cooperate to end the war. In response, their ambassadors began to negotiate. They considered the possibility of determining the existence of a threat to the peace, thereby opening the way for using the powers authorized by chapter VII. The U.S. decision to reflag Kuwaiti tankers and to deploy a major naval force in the gulf raised the stakes, making diplomatic efforts to end the war more urgent. After several months, the process of consultation among the permanent members produced agreement on a mandatory chapter VII resolution to create a new basis for the secretary-general's mediation and a framework for follow-on action that could include economic sanctions.

On 20 July 1987, meeting at the level of foreign ministers, the Security Council adopted by unanimity resolution 598 (1987). According to Secretary of State Shultz, never before had the Soviet Union and the United States cooperated at the United Nations on a security issue of such importance and complexity. "A thaw in the cold war was clearly under way. Constructive action through the United Nations was now possible."*

Resolution 598 opened the way for renewed mediation by the secretary-general, now with the council's explicit mandate. The entry into the gulf of Western naval forces, particularly the U.S. Navy, to protect shipping changed the fighting to Iran's disadvantage. If the parties did not accept a cease-fire quickly, the permanent members were pledged among themselves to consider follow-on action.

The Soviet Union proposed forming a naval peacekeeping force; the United States, backed by Britain and France, argued for an arms embargo against Iran. Whether or not they agreed to adopt such measures, the permanent members were consolidating the practice of collaborating among themselves and preparing for any subsequent crisis in which they might decide to use the Security Council's enforcement powers.

---

*George P. Shultz, *Turmoil and Triumph: My Years as Secretary of State* (New York: Scribner's, 1993), p. 932.

6

Signs of Change

The Gulf Cooperation Council

From its opening shots in 1980, the Iran-Iraq war threatened Bahrain, Kuwait, Oman, Qatar, Saudi Arabia, and the United Arab Emirates. These states, all either small or sparsely populated, live in a dangerous neighborhood. Iran, with forty-five million inhabitants, controls the northern shore of the Persian Gulf. Iraq, with fifteen million inhabitants but only a twenty-mile shoreline, had shown a desire to extend its control down the southern shore. In Kuwait, Qatar, and the United Arab Emirates, more than half the total population were foreigners;[1] more than half of the citizen population of Bahrain and Qatar were Shias.[2] Several of these states had a long history of commercial relations with Iran, but Iran's revolutionary impulse made these governments uneasy. They wanted a quick end to the war, without a victor or vanquished.

During the January 1981 meeting of the Organization of the Islamic Conference in Taif, Saudi Arabia, these six states agreed to form the Gulf Cooperation Council (GCC). Reflecting fear of the threat posed by the Soviet invasion of Afghanistan and apprehension about the growing U.S. capacity to project military power to the area, they emphasized that "security and stability of the Gulf as well as the safety of its waterways are the absolute responsibility of the Gulf states without any foreign interference."[3] The GCC's charter, adopted on 25 May 1981, referred to cooperation and coordination in "various fields" but did not mention defense.[4] A declaration the next day reaffirmed the responsibility of states in the area for regional security and stability, rejected foreign interference, and stressed the need to keep away military fleets and foreign bases.[5] Six months later the next GCC declaration repeated the same themes.[6]

On 26 January 1982, after an abortive coup in Bahrain (allegedly by "saboteurs" trained by Iran), GCC defense ministers decided to allocate $30.6 billion for defense in 1982. They agreed in principle to a joint command structure and to link air and maritime defenses.[7] In November, after Iraq had withdrawn from Iran, the GCC's Supreme Council expressed concern over "the recent dangerous developments which were exemplified by Iran crossing the international border between it and Iraq, and by what these developments hold for the peace of the Arab nation, and by how they threaten its security and the violation of its sovereignty."[8] The ministers' views on security issues were changing, and their declaration dropped the reference to keeping out foreign forces. With Iran ascendant, U.S. military support, if kept "over the horizon," was no longer so offensive.

By the end of 1983 the problem of security for shipping in the gulf worried GCC governments. In May of that year the foreign ministers of Kuwait and the United Arab Emirates visited Tehran and Baghdad to discuss the war, along with how to limit damage from the giant oil spill caused by Iraq's attack on Iran's Nowruz oil field.[9] From 1981 to the end of 1983 Iraq had attacked forty-three targets in the tanker war; Iran had attacked none.[10] In October 1983, after Iraq acquired from France Super Etendard planes capable of attacking shipping in the southern part of the gulf, Iran threatened to attack shipping. Shortly after the Security Council adopted resolution 540 (1983), a GCC declaration noted with satisfaction Iraq's acceptance of that resolution, called on Iran not to threaten freedom of navigation in the gulf, and asked the permanent members of the Security Council "to shoulder their responsibilities in taking the necessary measures to implement the resolution."[11] Already the GCC states were exhorting the permanent members to protect them.

In April 1984 Iraq began using Super Etendards to attack Iranian shipping, and Iran retaliated with attacks on vessels bound for Kuwait and Saudi Arabia. Iraq hit two Saudi tankers in the vicinity of Iran's Kharg Island: the *Safina al-Arab* on 25 April and the *Al-Ahood* on 7 May. Iran hit the Kuwaiti vessel *Umm Casbah* on 13 May and the Saudi vessel *Yanbu* on 16 May. The GCC states asked for an urgent meeting of the Security Council "to consider Iranian aggressions on the freedom of navigation to and from the ports of our countries."[12] On 1 June the council adopted resolution 552 (1984) to call on all states to respect the right of free navigation and demand an end to attacks on commercial ships en route to Kuwait and Saudi Arabia. On 5 June Saudi Arabian F-15s, guided by a U.S.-supplied AWACS aircraft, shot down two Iranian F-4 Phantoms in Saudi airspace. Both Iran and Iraq were active in the tanker war in 1984, although it is uncertain which side hit more targets.[13]

The November 1984 GCC summit meekly noted Iraq's positive attitude toward UN resolutions and asked Iran to join in peace efforts.[14] By the next November the GCC states accepted that foreign forces might be needed to keep the sea lanes safe. Their summit declaration called on Iran to respect freedom of navigation in international waterways. It indicated that the GCC states were ready to "continue their endeavors with the parties concerned to end this destructive war in a manner that safeguards the legitimate rights and interests of the two sides in order to bring about the establishment of normal relations among the Gulf states."[15] This time it made no mention of keeping foreign military forces out of the gulf. Under the pressure of war attitudes were changing.

An Unusual Departure

On 9 February 1986, one week after Soviet Deputy Foreign Minister Korniyenko visited Tehran, Iran launched two offensives. The first was an attack across the Hawizah marshes north of Basra, which Iraqi forces repulsed. The second was a major amphibious offensive against Iraq's Fao peninsula, with successful night landings at six points along a forty-mile front. Within twenty-four hours Iranian forces controlled over three hundred square miles on the pensinula, and ten thousand Iraqi soldiers were taken prisoner. By 18 February Iraq deployed its superior air power, artillery, and armor units, and on 21 February the Iraqi presidential guard, normally held in reserve, sealed off the Iranian forces. Nevertheless, Iran had captured a significant piece of Iraqi territory and created a second front on the western bank of the Shatt—causing Iraq to shift up to fifty thousand troops to this sector, keeping them in static positions, and decreasing the effectiveness of Iraq's mobile reserves.

On 10 February, as soon as Iran launched its attacks, Ismat Kittani, again the Iraqi ambassador in New York, alerted the secretary-general to the dangers. At Kittani's instigation the Arab League Committee of Seven (Iraq, Jordan, Kuwait, Morocco, Saudi Arabia, Tunisia, and the Republic of Yemen), charged with coordinating diplomatic activity regarding the war, asked for an urgent meeting of the Security Council. There was a widespread feeling, as expressed on the sixteenth in a *New York Times* article by Flora Lewis, that although superpower cooperation was needed to end the war, it was still unrealistic to expect such cooperation. When the council president opened the debate on the eighteenth, Australia, Denmark, and France appealed to Iran to stop its boycott of the council and join the debate.

Kittani, working behind the scenes, prepared a paper containing points for a draft resolution and consulted members to see how far they would support Iraq in the debate and on the text of a resolution. Early on Kittani must have heard that some nonaligned delegations, to make the draft more favorable to Iran, might ask for changes to condemn the initiation of the conflict, to drop the call for withdrawal of forces, to call for a body to judge the question of aggression, or to include reparations as an element in a final settlement.

On 19 February Iraq informally circulated its draft. When the nonaligned caucus (Congo, Ghana, Madagascar, Trinidad and Tobago, and the United Arab Emirates) discussed the text, Ghana, Madagascar, and Trinidad and Tobago said the group should consider producing a draft naming Iraq as the aggressor.[16] The caucus then met with the other nonpermanent members (Australia, Bulgaria, Denmark, Thailand, and Venezuela), and together these ten delegations decided to prepare a draft that might lay a basis for Iranian cooperation with the council.

This "more balanced" draft was closer to the Iranian position, and by 21 February Kittani was negotiating for changes. On the afternoon and evening of the twenty-first these ten delegations met in the room used for informal council consultations, while diplomats from the permanent members congregated in the council chamber. Rather than sit in their seats scattered at the perimeter of the horseshoe table, they moved to the précis writers' table, chatting and waiting. Although the Iranian ambassador, Said Rajaie-Khorassani, had earlier urged the adoption of changes making the draft closer to Iran's position, he now passed word that Iran would not participate in the debate. His message threw the purpose of the nonaligned initiative into doubt.

During the evening the ambassador of Trinidad and Tobago, as representative of the ten delegations, presented a draft to the permanent members. This was a crucial point in the development of the diplomatic process, a tangible gesture that might engender a shift in working relationships, because the power of the nonaligned caucus inside the council derived in large measure from the lack of cooperation or even the antagonism between the Soviet Union and the United States. Diplomats representing the permanent members recognized that this approach to them as a group was a novelty. After each permanent member's delegation had reviewed the text independently, the French, Soviet, and U.S. delegations found that they shared objections to the draft because of several points that moved it closer to the Iranian position. Both Britain, whose ambassador Sir John Thompson may have instigated the nonaligned effort,[17] and China were more open to Iranian views. At the end of this first round each of these five delegations passed back its comments to the drafting group individually.

After more consultations among the ten delegations now working together, the ambassador of Trinidad and Tobago asked to meet with the permanent members as a group. Again the initiative came from the nonpermanent members. After consulting bilaterally among themselves and overcoming an initial objection by the British delegation, the permanent members regrouped at the précis writers' table to hammer out a joint counterproposal. They then presented this unified position to the ambassador of Trinidad and Tobago, who took it back to the consultation room.

Repeated contacts confirmed that the permanent members were now together in rejecting the new points intended to entice Iran. On 24 February the council adopted resolution 582 (1986). Its one new point was to deplore the initial acts that caused the war, at most a veiled concession to the Iranian demand that the council acknowledge its failure to condemn the Iraqi invasion. Far more important was the fact that the process of consultation had led the permanent members to act as a group. If not an absolute first in UN practice, participants knew it was an unusual departure.

After this one episode the permanent members went their separate ways. On 14 March the State Department spokesman said, "We have stressed that expansion of the conflict elsewhere in the Gulf Region would be a major threat to U.S. interests." The next day UK Minister of State for Foreign Affairs Timothy Renton announced, "Kuwait knows that were she to ask for specific military equipment or military assistance we would consider such a request quickly and sympathetically." In May and June France and Iran held talks aimed at normalizing relations; following Iranian pressure, Iranian dissident Massoud Rajavi left Paris for Baghdad. In August Iran announced an agreement to resume shipment of natural gas to the Soviet Union; ten days later the Iranian navy stopped the Soviet freighter *Pytor Yemtsov* in the gulf and escorted it to Bandar Abbas, only to release it after determining it carried no war matériel. In August the United States criticized China for supplying arms to Iran, including MiG-21 planes. Surely there was as yet no pattern of policy coordination.

On 21 August the *New York Times* editorialized: "What is striking about this conflict is that both superpowers are reduced to hoping that neither side wins. . . . For the most part, the United Nations has been irrelevant. Its peacemaking attempts are scorned by Iran, and its non-aligned members cannot bring themselves to denounce butchery among their own number. Washington and Moscow, the twin satans of Iranian demonology, are also on the sidelines."

Pérez de Cuéllar

Javier Pérez de Cuéllar was born in Lima, Peru, on 19 January 1920. His father, a well-to-do businessman, was a member of the educated rather than the landholding upper class. He died when Javier was four. Javier had a French governess,[18] attended Roman Catholic schools, and earned a doctorate of laws at the Catholic University in Lima. In 1940, while still at university, he began working at the Foreign Ministry for the salary of $50 per month. In 1944 he signed on as a diplomat.[19]

Pérez de Cuéllar's early diplomatic work included tours as embassy secretary in Paris, London, La Paz, and Rio de Janeiro. In 1946 he was a member of the Peruvian delegation to the first General Assembly. He maintained an interest in international law, teaching at the Peruvian diplomatic academy and writing a book, published in 1964, entitled *Manual de Derecho Diplomático*. The same year he was appointed Peru's ambassador to Switzerland.[20]

From 1966 to 1969 he was permanent under secretary and secretary-general of the Foreign Ministry in Lima. He was credited with promoting Peru's full membership in the nonaligned movement and normalizing relations with Moscow.[21] In 1969 he became Peru's ambassador to Moscow, with simultaneous accreditation to Warsaw.

In 1971 Pérez de Cuéllar became Peru's permanent representative at the United Nations, and two years later Peru won election to a coveted seat on the Security Council. There he gained invaluable experience dealing with the Arab-Israeli war of October 1973 and then the reintroduction of peacekeeping forces in the Sinai and on the Golan. In 1974 Secretary-General Waldheim appointed him special representative for Cyprus, a difficult post that he held for three years. Years later, when elected sectetary-general, he still considered his main accomplishment getting the two Cypriot sides to talk in 1976, even if the conflict had not been settled. He explained, "This is what happens with the U.N. You have an improvement in the atmosphere. You are so close to a solution. Then you are frustrated."[22]

In 1979 Waldheim appointed Pérez de Cuéllar under secretary-general for special political affairs. While holding this position, his most important assignment was as the secretary-general's personal representative for Afghanistan. The *Times* of London commented, "It has been Señor Pérez de Cuéllar's fate to be chosen to mediate in disputes where the two sides could hardly be further apart."[23] Undeterred by the difficulties facing him, he set up the framework for talks that ultimately produced the Geneva Accords on Afghanistan in 1988. Discussing Pérez de Cuéllar's character as a mediator, Pakistan's ambassador said he had an ability "to go to the heart of the matter, to listen to both sides."[24]

For two months during the fall of 1981 council members were deadlocked over the contest for the secreatry-general's office between Kurt Waldheim, seeking a third term, and Salim Salim of Tanzania. China insisted that the new secretary-general come from the Third World and thus opposed Waldheim. The United States opposed Salim Salim. Pérez de Cuéllar, who had just retired from the Peruvian diplomatic service, let it be known that he would not be a candidate unless Waldheim and Salim withdrew. When they did so in December, the council turned to Pérez de Cuéllar.

Although by the time of his election Pérez de Cuéllar had been a diplomat for forty years and active at the UN for the last ten, he remained an enigma to some colleagues. "He's such a quiet person, it's hard to assess what his performance will be like in a public job," a senior UN officer commented. "Nobody knows whether he has a cutting edge."[25] He was known for his interest in music and literature, especially the novels of Argentina's Jorge Luis Borges and Colombia's Gabriel Garcia Marquez. "It was apparent," commented a British observer, "that he would bring a literary and philosophical approach to the United Nations that has been absent since the tenure of Mr. Dag Hammarskjöld."[26]

On 15 December the president of the General Assembly, Ismat Kittani, administered the oath of office to Pérez de Cuéllar. The new secretary-general spoke briefly:

The United Nations is a body of States gathered together for purposes and ends which go beyond and above purely national motives. Hence this House symbolizes an entity that is conceptually different from the component parts. It is almost possible to say, paraphrasing Darwin, that, being a more complex entity, the Organization is a more advanced evolutionary form, since it represents a kind of community life that is higher than what would prevail if it did not exist. We have to arm ourselves not only with courage but also with the feeling of reality which is necessary so as not to be overcome by discouragement, like the mythological character who was forever pushing a rock uphill.[27]

The new secretary-general was right that his first term would be a time of troubles for the United Nations. The deepening rift in U.S.-Soviet relations ruled out serious cooperation on matters affecting international peace and security; the problems of Afghanistan, Cyprus, Lebanon, the Arab-Israeli conflict, the Iran-Iraq war, Cambodia, Nicaragua, the western Sahara, and southern Africa all seemed to get worse. The United States, unsatisfied with the UN's financial and administrative practices, threatened to reduce its payments for the assessed budget. Before looking for successes, Pérez de Cuéllar needed to keep the situation of the United Nations from worsening.

In his first annual report Pérez de Cuéllar challenged the drift away from the charter concept of collective security. "Without such a system, the world community will remain powerless to deal with military adventures which threaten the very fabric of international peace, and the danger of the widening and escalation of local conflicts will be correspondingly greater."[28] "The Council must be primarily used for the prevention of armed conflict and the search for solutions," he argued the next year. "If such an analysis seems Utopian, it is certainly preferable to a course of action which risks, through partisanship, the elevating of a local conflict into a world confrontation. Indeed the habit of adopting a concerted approach to problems of international peace and security might lead to the statesmanlike co-operation which will be essential in bridging the great present divisions of our international society and in turning the tide in crucial matters such as disarmament and arms control."[29]

Pérez de Cuéllar developed his ideas in three main themes, which he repeated throughout his ten years as secretary-general. "First, the permanent members of the Security Council, especially the two most powerful, must perceive that, notwithstanding bilateral differences and distrust, it is in their national interest to co-operate within the Security Council and, within this framework, to apply their collective influence to the resolution of regional disputes."[30] He appealed to the permanent members to maintain adequate working relations so that they could fulfill their obligations as members of the council,[31] to give questions of peace and security priority over bilateral controversies and the clash of ideologies, and to make a concerted effort, using all the possibilities of the charter, to solve at least one or two problems on the council's agenda.[32]

He addressed the second theme more widely. "All Member States must perceive in far greater measure that the existence of an authoritative and representative international organ capable of maintaining peace and security is in their individual as well as the common interest and that, therefore, its decisions must be respected."[33] Governments have a responsibility to follow up resolutions with support and action.[34] The adoption of a resolution should not be the antithesis of action by governments, nor a substitute for it.[35] "Decisions of the various organs should be the beginning, not the end, of governmental concern and action. A continuous effort to contribute to the implementation of United Nations decisions should be an integral part of the foreign policy of Member States to a far greater extent than it is at the present time."[36]

Third, he emphasized, again and again, the need for the secretary-general and the Security Council to work in tandem. Both the exercise of traditional diplomacy by the secretary-general, such as third-party efforts to assist with dispute resolution, and newer techniques, including both resolutions and concerted action through bilateral policies of council members, were needed to realize the UN's potential.[37] When the council gave the secretary-general the task of following up on implementation of a resolution, his efforts needed diplomatic and other support by member states to have a fair chance of bearing fruit.[38] Ritualistic support for the secretary-general without practical support for his efforts did not exonerate members from performance of their charter obligations. "To express full confidence in the Secretary-General while failing to give the necessary support to the Security Council or to work constructively in the General Assembly to bring conflicting positions into greater consonance is fundamentally contradictory."[39]

At Oxford University in 1986 Pérez de Cuéllar spoke on the secretary-general's role and his relationship to the Security Council, especially in the difficult situations when council members were divided, or when they failed to support a resolution, or when one of the parties rejected it. These problems, frequent for most of the UN's history, laid the basis for the "leave it to Dag" tendency during Hammarskjöld's tenure. Pérez de Cuéllar insisted that member states could not discharge their own responsibilities simply by passing them on to him:

> We must cling to the Charter concept of collective action for peace and security, and we must do nothing to weaken the chances of eventually putting it into practice. . . . No authority delegated to the Secretary-General, and no exercise by him of this authority, can fill the existing vacuum in collective security. This vacuum is due to dissension among the Permanent Members of the Security Council, to the failure of member states to resort to the Charter's mechanisms for the settlement of disputes, and to their lack of respect for the decisions of the Security Council."[40]

Pérez de Cuéllar offered guidance for a secretary-general to follow in any good-offices mission:

- The Secretary-General must not only be impartial but must be perceived to be so.
- He cannot shoulder the burden of his office without unlimited patience, and an unfailing sense of justice and humanity.
- If a third party is to succeed in resolving the conflict, he has to address the fears of each with empathy and imagination.
- Sometimes the leadership of a state takes a stubborn stand and seems immune to rational persuasion. In such a case, the Secretary-General should go on as far as the point at which further exercise of his good offices can only disguise the reality: he should then state the facts plainly, without denunciation but without hiding the facts.[41]

Reelection

Pérez de Cuéllar's discreet diplomacy pleased the major powers, but he had his critics. "While there is no denying that the Secretary-General is a supreme diplomatic technician, able to come up with brilliant blueprints and work out intricate formulas for solving the most intractable disputes, he is faulted for lacking the political drive that is often necessary to give negotiations that final push. As one diplomat put it: 'He is no good at knocking heads,'" reported the *Times* of London. "Many observers believe the Secretary-General may well preside over the collapse of the United Nations."[42]

In April 1986 he told a British correspondent he wanted to leave office at the end of the year.[43] In July, because of chest pains, he canceled a planned trip to Africa and returned from Europe. On 24 July he underwent quadruple bypass surgery at New York's Mount Sinai Medical Center. The operation went well, and he was expected to return to work in a few weeks.

At the beginning of September the British, French, and U.S. delegations consulted each other on the upcoming election. London, Paris, and Washington were ready to support a second term for Pérez de Cuéllar; they thought it likely Beijing and Moscow would feel the same way. Would the permanent members this time cooperate to avoid deadlock over the election? During September the Cold War atmosphere returned to the United Nations; when the United States arrested a Soviet UN employee on spy charges, Soviet authorities arrested U.S. journalist Nicolas Daniloff in Moscow, and the United States forced a major reduction in the size of the Soviet UN mission.

Diplomats representing Britain, France, and the United States nevertheless approached their Chinese and Soviet colleagues to propose that their ambassadors together call on Pérez de Cuéllar to inform him that their governments supported his reelection. The Chinese and Soviet ambassadors agreed to seek instructions. Previously the Soviet Union had joined with Britain, France, and the United States to make joint demarches on a limited number of questions, in particular the UN's budget and proposals for revising the UN Charter. China had not joined in such demarches. Beijing and Moscow agreed to the proposal to tell the secretary-general of their governments' support for his reelection. This time, unlike in the previous February, the permanent members were acting together on their own initiative. This was the second crucial step toward instituting a process for cooperation among the permanent members.

On 2 October, the permanent representatives of Britain, China, France, the Soviet Union, and the United States called on the secretary-general to ask him to stand for reelection and to assure him of the support of their governments. The secretary-general asked for two assurances. First, he wanted from Washington support on the question of UN finances, already strained by Washington's decision not to pay $100 million of its assessed contribution. Second, he wanted improved superpower relations, at least inside the United Nations.[44]

On 10 October the General Assembly, acting on the unanimous recommendation of the Security Council, reelected Pérez de Cuéllar secretary-general. "To decline in such circumstances would have been tantamount to abandoning a moral duty to the United Nations, with which I have been linked for many years and in whose permanent validity I have unshakable faith," the secretary-general told delegates after the voting. "It would also have meant ignoring the creative opportunity for renewal and reform which the current crisis may provide."[45]

Then, speaking with the experience of five difficult years behind him, he made demands on member states.

> It is my hope that the consensus both in the Security Council and in the General Assembly on the appointment of the Secretary-General will serve to encourage a sense of common intent in the working of this Organization. The Office of the Secretary-General is an integral part of the United Nations and not something separate and discreet. It is, to my mind, of highest importance that the same harmonization of wills and viewpoints should be achieved in relation to the great substantive issues on the agenda of the Organization. We need to act with unity and resolve to accelerate the solution of some of the long-enduring conflicts which threaten international peace and security.[46]

Policies Change

When in March 1985 Mikhail Gorbachev became general secretary of the Communist party and Eduard Shevardnadze became Soviet foreign minister, it seemed possible that new thinking might bring change to Soviet foreign policy. A month earlier on 19 and 20 February in Vienna, for the first time since the 1977 U.S.-USSR joint statement on the Middle East, the U.S. assistant secretary of state for the region, Richard Murphy, met with his Soviet counterpart, Vladimir Polyakov. "The meeting was probably a mistake as far as Mideast diplomacy was concerned," a State Department official told the *New York Times*, "but a success in terms of Soviet-American relations."[47] In June 1986 Murphy and Polyakov met again, this time in Stockholm.[48] Even if these meetings only improved U.S.-Soviet relations, they might open the way to eventual cooperation on Afghanistan, the Iran-Iraq war, or the Arab-Israeli conflict.

Arab statesmen, who for years had opposed the involvement of outside powers in their region, were changing their point of view. When Iran captured the Fao peninsula, the firing of artillery at the front could be heard in Kuwait City, only twenty-five miles away. The Arab League's Committee of Seven now wanted the permanent members to move from expressions of concern to "adequate pressure" on the belligerent party. As the league's secretary-general, Chadli Klibi, told the council in February, "The big Powers have not given the Iran-Iraq conflict its due importance, commensurate with the danger it represents, so much so that we must wonder whether . . . they really want the war to stop."[49]

One reason why Iraq had initiated the expansion of the tanker war was that by 1986 its enlarged network of oil pipelines allowed it to overcome the loss of its oil terminals on the gulf. Between 1983 and 1986 Iraq doubled oil exports to 1.8 million barrels a day (mbd), approximately the same level as Iran.[50] Iraq increased the capacity of its pipeline through Turkey to the Mediterranean to 1.7 mbd and tied into the pipeline network through Kuwait and Saudi Arabia to gulf ports (.6 mbd).[51] In August, September, and October 1986 Iraqi production levels topped those of Iran for the first time since the beginning of the war.[52] Iraq, in a major improvement of its strategic situation, had adjusted to being landlocked.[53]

Attacks on tankers more than doubled from 47 in 1985 to 107 in 1986, with both sides becoming more active. Previously most Iranian attacks had been conducted by the Iranian navy, which operated mainly in the southern gulf. Now seaborne units of the Revolutionary Guards, stationed further north, were equipped with Boghammer speed boats capable of attacks against shipping in the narrow waters of the northern gulf. Iranian leaders did not consider Kuwaiti policy, which included financial support for Iraq and transshipment of goods and matériel through Kuwait, to be neutral, and their statements suggested Kuwait should no longer be treated as a neutral nonbelligerent. Iran targeted neutral shipping calling at Kuwait's ports.[54]

At the start of the General Assembly in September 1986, when many foreign ministers were in town, Ambassador Kittani asked the Security Council to meet on the war. Iran boycotted the proceedings. The secretary-general warned: "The international community has a legitimate concern over the dangers of the expansion of the boundaries of the conflict, which could bring unpredictable and perhaps uncontrollable consequences. . . . The sharp escalation in attacks on commercial vessels from third countries and the widening area in which they occur are perceived by neighboring states in particular as threats to security in their region, with potential repercussions which could draw in Powers from beyond."[55] He called on the council to establish a basis for negotiation acceptable to both sides, the unfulfilled goal of the nonaligned effort of the previous February.

Resolution 588 (1986), adopted unanimously on 8 October, broke no new ground. In explaining the U.S. vote Ambassador Vernon Walters echoed the secretary-general's warning: "The heightened tempo of the fighting and the heightened danger that this fighting will spill over to other countries have increased the risk to the security of the entire region. The war continues to be a threat to neutral shipping. As my delegation has said on other occasions, the United States would view an expansion of the war to neutral third parties as a major threat to our interests."[56]

The United States, through Operation Staunch, was trying to restrict arms sales to Iran. "We have intensified our efforts to discourage our friends from selling arms to Iran with significant, but not complete, success," Secretary George Shultz explained to the press when describing his two weeks of meetings with other foreign ministers who were in New York for the start of the General Assembly. "We and Soviet officials agreed that we share a common interest in seeing an end to the Iran-Iraq war." But Shultz criticized the Soviet Union for not working to cut off the supply of arms to Iran.[57]

Shultz hosted a lunch for GCC foreign ministers in the comforting surroundings of a private club in Manhattan. He emphasized that the United States was determined to cut off the flow of arms to Iran. According to an Arab participant, the GCC ministers expected that the United States, as a great power, would always maintain some relations with Iran, including perhaps the shipment of a limited amount of arms. But because of Shultz's evident personal sincerity, he convinced the ministers the United States was doing all it could to cut off arms to Iran.

On 3 November *Ash Shiraa,* a magazine in Beirut with pro-Shiite tendencies, published the bombshell story of a secret U.S. diplomatic mission to Tehran the previous May. The story was evidently leaked by supporters of Mehdi Hashemi, an activist of the Iranian revolution who had been arrested by the Iranian government after an attempt to smuggle arms to Saudi Arabia during the Hajj in 1986. Hashemi was a partisan of the faction that believed Iran's priority should be to export its revolution to other countries in the region.[58] Parliament Speaker Rafsanjani, whose rival faction favored more pragmatic policies and who was the target of the U.S. mission, confirmed on 4 November that the mission had taken place. Hashemi would later be executed.

As more information came out, the story of the Iran-Contra scandal, now documented by a literature of its own, eliminated the credibility of the U.S. policy of cutting off arms to Iran. The immediate goal of the operation had been to secure release of U.S. citizens held hostage by radical Shiite groups in Lebanon by trading arms to Iran.[59] Briefly, there were initial contacts in 1985, and hostage Benjamin Weir was released that year on 15 September. On 18 February 1986, one week after Iranian forces had captured the Fao peninsula and while diplomats in New York were negotiating the text of resolution 582, five hundred U.S. TOW antitank missiles were delivered to the port of Bandar Abbas in Iran. After meetings in Frankfurt on 24–27 February between Lt. Col. Oliver North and his Iranian contacts, another five hundred TOWs were delivered to Bandar Abbas on 27 February.[60] A "rogue" operation in the White House was working at cross-purposes to the State Department's Operation Staunch.

On 25 May a delegation headed by former National Security Adviser Robert McFarlane arrived in Tehran. The plane carried one pallet of Hawk missile spare parts, which McFarlane's hosts removed. On 26 May he cabled to Admiral John Poindexter at the White House that "the incompetence of the Iranian government to do business requires a rethinking on our part of why there have been so many frustrating failures to deliver on their part."[61] McFarlane set a deadline for all of the hostages to be released by 6:30 A.M. 28 May. When the deadline passed with no releases, the U.S. delegation departed Tehran. Two months later on 26 July Father Lawrence Jenco was released.

In September 1986 terrorists in Beirut seized two more U.S. hostages, Frank Reed and Joseph Cicippio. On 5–7 October Colonel North met with Iranian contacts in Frankfurt, a meeting at which North presented a Bible inscribed by President Reagan. Incredibly, there are indications that at the same time CIA Director William Casey was meeting with Tariq Aziz to ask if the Iraqi military was satisfied with the intelligence provided by the United States and to urge Iraq to bomb economic targets deep inside Iran.[62] Another U.S. hostage, Edward Tracey, was seized on 21 October. Then another meeting was held in Frankfurt on 26–28 October to arrange payment and delivery schedules for more TOW missiles and an unspecified number of Hawk missiles. Five hundred TOWs were delivered to Iran on 29 October.[63] All told, from August 1985 to November 1986 Iran received five separate covert shipments from the United States that included 2008 TOW missiles, 235 other missiles, Hawk parts, and other spare parts.[64]

The U.S. initiative, despite the arguably defensible motives of securing the release of the hostages and providing an opening to Iran, had few defenders and only negative consequences. "It involved the wrong people (McFarlane, North, Teicher) advised by the wrong 'experts' (Ledeen, Ghorbanifar) supported by the wrong allies (Israel); they went to the wrong place (Tehran) at the wrong time (during the month of Ramadan and after the United States had tilted to the Iraqi side in the gulf war) carrying the wrong tactical plan," according to James A. Bill, a leading scholar of relations between the United States and Iran. "The unprofessional and uninformed nature of this adventure jeopardized the credibility and political survival of both American and Iranian leaders, dealt another serious blow to the fading credibility of the United States in the international arena, and, in the process, threatened to freeze Iranian-American relations for another decade."[65]

The "opening" to Iran had major repercussions. Dealing with the consequences at home presented the most severe challenge to President Reagan during his eight years in office. In an article in *Foreign Affairs*, former Secretary of Defense James Schlesinger wrote, "The consequences need hardly to be spelled out. The nation is in an uproar. The Administration is in disarray. Its energies will be directed in large degree, at least until October 1, 1987 (when the Senate says it will finish its investigation), toward attempting to control the damage. It has lost control over the national agenda. Public confidence in the President has been seriously eroded. The question remains whether the Administration can partially recover or whether it will be permanently crippled."[66]

Because Iran's Ayatollah Khomeini damned efforts to improve relations with the United States as "satan-oriented,"[67] there was no U.S.-Iranian rapprochement. The arms sales had hurt Iraq most by helping Iran to restore Hawk surface-to-air missiles to operation and thus offset one of Iraq's main military advantages, its superior air power.[68] Revelations of these dealings shook Iraq's confidence in its new relationship with the United States, but Baghdad's reaction, after initial public criticism, was to encourage the United States to correct its errors.

The "opening to Iran" troubled the GCC states. Their foreign ministers had been confident of U.S. policy because both sides had an interest in maintaining an open market for oil and freedom of navigation in the gulf; protecting these interests meant preventing an Iranian victory. Secretary Shultz had not only promised that the United States was working to restrict Iranian access to the international arms market, he had convinced GCC states that this was so. A report to the Senate Committee on Foreign Relations asked, "How could the United States ever decide to sell weapons to Khomeini's radically aggressive regime, whose military victory over Iraq would so clearly injure Western interests throughout the region?"[69] U.S. ambassadors found that their credibility had plummeted. However, because fundamental interests of the GCC states and the United States converged, these governments still wanted close cooperation with the United States, including over-the-horizon defense protection.

As early as September 1986 Kuwait, the GCC state with the most at risk in the tanker war, approached both the Soviet Union and the United States to seek the protection of their flags for its shipping.[70] On 10 December the Kuwait Oil Tanker Company (KOTC) asked the U.S. Coast Guard to provide information on U.S. reflagging requirements, and the Coast Guard responded in the following weeks. On 13 January 1987 Kuwait asked the U.S. embassy if reflagged vessels would receive U.S. Navy protection. At the same time the United States learned that the Soviet Union had already agreed to charter Soviet tankers to Kuwait or to provide protection to Kuwaiti tankers sailing under the Soviet flag.[71] The Kuwaiti request for reflagging and protection would be on the agenda of the mid-January 1987 White House meeting set to review policy toward Iran and the war.

Kuwait's move implied much more than protecting tankers or keeping down insurance rates on shipping. By engaging the superpowers Kuwait had made it harder for them to ignore the war and leave Iran and Iraq battering away at each other and threatening other states in the region. Kuwait's request increased the dangers of superpower rivalry in the gulf and the risk that, as the theater of war spread, one or both superpowers could become engaged in hostilities. All along, the war had been dangerous for Kuwait; now it would be increasingly dangerous for others. Might these growing risks, according to the logic of diplomacy, induce the superpowers to engage in a serious effort to end the war?

The Final Offensive

During the fall of 1986 Iran recruited and gave rudimentary training to up to 100,000 new Basij troops. On the night of 23–24 December the "Division of the Prophet Mohammed" led an attacking force of up to 60,000 Pasdaran and Basij in Operation Kerbala IV toward the Shatt; another force of 15,000 tried to secure the gulf islands of Umm al Rassas, Umm Babi, Qate, and Shoail. Massed infantry assaults were launched at prepared Iraqi positions. Dug-in Iraqi forces repulsed the attack with up to 12,000 Iranian deaths.[72] By 26 December Iraqi forces had pushed the Iranians back to their starting positions.

Kerbala V, launched days later on 6 January in the area south of Basra, threatened Iraqi defenses more seriously. The attacking force included 120,000 of the 200,000 Iranian troops on the southern front, mostly Pasdaran and Basij units. The attack against Iraqi positions guarding the approach to Basra began shortly after midnight, and the Iranians crossed the border and moved along the eastern bank of the Shatt, south of the Fish Lake water barrier that Iraq had constructed. The Iranians came to within twelve miles of the outer suburbs of Basra.

Iraq repelled the invaders with difficulty. Massive artillery exchanges took place between the two sides. Iraq suffered heavy tank losses, possibly to the U.S.-supplied TOW missiles.[73] At least 30,000 Iranians held positions inside Iraq near Fish Lake, and after ten days of fighting the U.S. government estimated that there had been approximately 40,000 Iranian and 10,000 Iraqi casualties.[74] The *New York Times* on 20 January reported speculation that there was an even chance that Basra would fall to the Iranians[75] and over the coming weeks printed pessimistic views on Iraq's military situation.[76]

On 8 January the Soviet Union issued a major statement criticizing the Iranian offensive and calling for a peaceful solution: "Military methods only make the final settlement more distant. . . . Despite the complex and acute nature of the problems and disputes existing between Iraq and Iran, there are no insurmountable obstacles for the cessation of war and the establishment of peace." At a press conference Alexandr Belonogov, the Soviet Union's permanent representative in New York, drew attention to the statement. Highlighting the criticism of Iran, he pointed out that the Soviet Union "does not support materially or in any other form the party that is on the offensive, and I think this is of some importance."[77]

7

Pérez de Cuéllar's Move

The Secretary-General Invites Action

When starting his second term in office, Pérez de Cuéllar told a press conference on 13 January 1987 that Security Council members needed to reach a "meeting of the minds" on ending the Iran-Iraq war. "The Security Council at the highest possible level has to understand that it must do something in order to stop a conflict which not only is extremely costly in human lives but also has the potential to be extended to the whole area." When a journalist expressed doubts that the Soviet Union and United States would work together, Pérez de Cuéllar rejected this skepticism:

> I think that the leaders of both countries are conscious of their obligations and must realize that in a meeting of minds, which is what I have in mind, they have to do something, that they have obligations under the Charter and obligations to the international community. They are the two most powerful countries; they have to show that they can deal with problems where the Security Council has a role to play. If I assume that they are not going to agree on something, what is the use of having a Security Council? The five permanent members have an obligation to try to reach agreement on the solution of problems related to peace and security. That is their duty. Of course, they could start by having differences, but they have to work until they agree on a solution to international problems. That is why they have the veto power. It is not something given to them generously by the membership of the United Nations. The veto power implies that they have to work in order to reach agreement for the peaceful solution of international problems.[1]

Another journalist pointed out that, because Iran boycotted the council, "it would seem to be a strange choice for the body that would pursue peace in the Iran-Iraq war." Pérez de Cuéllar, modifying the position he had taken earlier that the council needed to define a basis for action acceptable to both sides, said council members should not start out looking for positions to satisfy the parties. First, "the Security Council has both the right and the obligation to express its views on the problem, in a very clear-cut way . . . then, they must express their views in such a way as to let the parties know their position on the present problem."[2]

On 15 January Pérez de Cuéllar invited the permanent members' ambassadors, plus the council president, Venezuela's ambassador Andries Aguillar, to meet with him over a cup of tea in his office on the thirty-eighth floor of the secretariat building. Their meeting the next afternoon was informal and kept off the secretary-general's calendar posted for the press. Pérez de Cuéllar asked the ambassadors to reflect on his request that the Security Council find a common line for dealing with the war. The ambassadors might meet privately and informally, keeping their discussions off the council's agenda until they had explored all possibilities for a meeting of minds. Should the council agree on a new basis for action, perhaps it should meet at the level of foreign ministers to signify the importance of this step. He asked that the same group meet again before his departure in a week for the summit in Kuwait of the Organization of the Islamic Conference. The ambassadors agreed, adding that the week would give them time to consult their governments on the secretary-general's request.

Late in the afternoon of the twenty-third the ambassadors of the permanent members returned to Pérez de Cuéllar's office. All had received authorization to begin informal, exploratory talks along the lines suggested by the secretary-general. U.S. Ambassador Vernon Walters put on the table a proposal for a resolution to determine that there was a threat to international peace and security, to invoke the full authority of chapter VII, and to issue a mandatory cease-fire order; if one of the parties failed to comply, the council could institute an arms embargo. Without discussion of any specific proposal, the ambassadors concurred with the general idea of new, meaningful action by the Security Council that members would back up by concerted actions through their bilateral policies.

The secretary-general then fleshed out his own ideas. An informal exchange of views among Security Council members, particularly its permanent members, should begin the process, with the goal of preparing for a council meeting at the level of foreign ministers. Discussion should aim at producing concrete actions that members could implement at the bilateral level; the validity of proposals should not be tested by their acceptability to the parties. An agreement on practical steps, formalized at a high political level, would also strengthen the Security Council.

The secretary-general shared a number of points that the permanent members might want to include in their discussions:

- Should the council consider setting up an ad hoc body to investigate the responsibility for starting the war?
- Is it conceptually feasible and politically realistic to provide international protection for freedom of navigation and merchant shipping in the gulf?
- Could action be taken to counter the risk that continued use of chemical weapons would irreparably weaken the 1925 Geneva Protocol?
- Could the council and individual major suppliers demonstrate to the belligerents that they are determined to close the supply of arms?

- How could such steps be advanced to the stage of truce or cease-fire, leading to withdrawal of troops to the line of status quo ante?
- Would the issues of reparations and reconstruction also have to be faced?

Pérez de Cuéllar reemphasized that the goal should be an agenda for action in terms of concerted policies. Ideas should be produced and explored to define concrete actions for council members to implement in the context of bilateral relations. Although a formal council meeting should legitimize this agenda, Pérez de Cuéllar did not want the council to adopt another resolution that the parties could ignore. The five ambassadors concurred that consultations should go forward on this basis.

The secretary-general uncovered no favorable omens during his visit to Kuwait. The prelude to the conference included Iran's offensive, bombing incidents in Baghdad, threats against planes flying to Kuwait, Iranian artillery hitting Kuwait's Failaka Island, and the kidnapping in Beirut of Terry Waite. Iran refused to attend the conference. Pérez de Cuéllar called in his speech for new efforts toward peace, and on the margins of the conference he met with other leaders. The summit's meager result was a call for Iran and Iraq to stop fighting and for the Security Council to bear its responsibility for peace and security. The summit broke no new ground.

A New Game for New York Diplomacy

The secrtetary-general's gambit was to become the catalyst for the kind of diplomatic process among the permanent members that on their own they had never managed to initiate. He brought together the five ambassadors, established a constructive ambiance for negotiation, encouraged them to seek agreement on parallel actions, and articulated a rationale to justify this collaboration.[3]

UN diplomats are constantly engaged in corridor conversations that usually lead nowhere, and the idea that the permanent members should cooperate to end the Iran-Iraq war had been bruited about for some time. Only Pérez de Cuéllar, as secretary-general, was in a position to be the catalyst for realizing this idea.[4] Had the invitation to action been made by one of the five ambassadors, it would not have appeared impartial; for the same reason the talks could not be located in one of the five capitals. He asked the permanent members to make good on their pledges of support for his second term in office. As secretary-general, Pérez de Cuéllar used the argument that each permanent member had a special interest and responsibility for the work of the Security Council.

Having given legitimacy to the initiative by calling for it in public, he purused it in private. Pérez de Cuéllar's suggested approach, which built on the experience of the permanent members' collaboration during the negotiation of resolution 582 and the reelection of the secretary-general, would later become standard operating procedure for the permanent members: private and informal meetings, unrestricted talks to find a meeting of minds, and no prior commitments except to the process of making the effort.

At the time the permanent members were well disposed. All five agreed there should be neither a victor nor a vanquished in the Iran-Iraq war, and for different reasons they were now ready to engage in New York. The United States was casting about for a diplomatic road to recovery from the debacle of the Iran-Contra scandal. The Soviet Union wanted to avoid defeat for its Iraqi client and to try out the Security Council as a forum for liquidating regional conflicts. Britain and France saw that this process would enhance the value of their positions as permanent members and perhaps rein in the risk of U.S. unilateral actions taken with little regard for the interests of allies. China reluctantly engaged.

Pérez de Cuéllar was using his authority as secretary-general to modify the rules of the game for Security Council negotiations.[5] For the permanent members to cooperate they would have to understand their respective national interests, recognize that restraint on unilateral actions could be mutually advantageous, and be willing to commit to jointly defined policies.[6] Because they had no track record to suggest that such negotiations would succeed, the mix of optimism and skepticism among participants was heavily weighted toward the latter.

Pérez de Cuéllar had emphasized the informality of the process. When diplomats engage in informal negotiations, they avoid green baize-covered banquet tables and sit in chairs around a coffee table. They speak in conversational tones, and, as their object is a give-and-take, they can probe with tentative positions, withdraw concessions, or put partial agreements on hold. Everything is *ad referendum* to capitals. Personal relations are very important in facilitating this type of exchange.[7]

Because these five governments had so far used the council mainly to wrangle in public, their ambassadors had doubts whether the rules for an informal process would be followed. No one wanted to be the first to risk trusting the others, but all knew they just might be facing a rare opportunity to obtain a qualitative change in the diplomatic process, one that could benefit both the work of the Security Council and bilateral relations among the permanent members. Fred Iklé described the purpose of rules of accommodation as "the equivalent in diplomacy of Kant's imperative in ethics."[8] The permanent members are almost always involved in negotiations with each other, and if they could expect reciprocity in style, each would have a reason to adopt those methods which they would like to see adopted generally.

There were reasons to suppose such cooperation could take hold. Since the UN's establishment New York has been a major diplomatic capital. Over 150 permanent missions maintain contact with the secretariat, negotiate decisions to be taken by intergovernmental bodies, and represent governments in UN meetings. Diplomats use the United Nations as a listening post for information on regional conflicts: in the constant exchange of information diplomats learn the views and intentions of other governments; they put on record those of their own government for others to report back home. The diplomatic corps is large and well informed, but often underemployed.

The missions of Britain, China, France, the Soviet Union, and the United States shared several similarities. They were large, usually with more than one ambassador and several senior counselors covering political, legal, economic, and social affairs, plus experts on the different regions. This structure easily accommodated parallel discussions among counselors on technical issues and among ambassadors on policy aspects. These missions were all closely instructed, meaning that capitals, not the ambassadors, had the final word on important points of substance. Precisely because the ambassadors were on a short leash, reporting discussions in detail and asking for instructions, they could use the process of consultation with capitals to become a central link in concerting policies with other governments. In addition, because these five governments had real interests in the gulf area and policies toward the region, any step toward policy coordination could go beyond declaratory policy and have a significant impact.

Extraordinary and talented diplomats headed the missions of the permanent members. In 1987 Sir John Thompson represented Britain. A career diplomat from a distinguished academic family, he had entered the Foreign Office in 1950 after taking a degree at Trinity College, Cambridge. He had served in Jeddah, Damascus, and Washington and then in several positions in London. In 1977 he had become the British high commissioner in New Delhi, a post he had held until becoming Britain's UN representative in 1982. While in New York he encouraged increased attention to the Iran-Iraq war by the Security Council, but when the chance came, he was just three months short of the mandatory retirement age of sixty for British diplomats.[9]

Sir Crispin Tickell succeeded Thompson. A first-class honors graduate in modern history at Christ Church, Oxford, Sir Crispin had served in The Hague, Mexico City, and Paris before becoming private secretary to the chancellor responsible for the negotiations for the UK entry into the European Community. While a fellow at Harvard's Center for International Affairs in 1975, he had written *Climate Change and World Affairs*, an influential book still in print a decade later. Next he had been chef de cabinet for Roy Jenkins during his presidency of the EC Commission. Sir Crispin had been ambassador to Mexico and then head of Britain's overseas development program before coming to New York in 1987.[10]

Li Luye was China's ambassador. In addition to posts inside China, he had served in Sri Lanka and, just before coming to New York, as permanent representative to the United Nations in Geneva.[11] Relaxed and avuncular in manner, he paid close attention to Third World attitudes.

In January 1987 Claude de Kemoularia represented France. A financial expert with close ties to the Socialist party, he had been in and out of government since 1945. From 1957 to 1961 he had been a personal assistant to Dag Hammarskjöld. After working for the PARIBAS bank from 1968 to 1982, he had become France's ambassador to the Netherlands, and in 1984 permanent representative in New York.[12] A strong personality, he deserved his reputation for making things happen.

Pierre-Louis Blanc, a career diplomat with ties to the Gaullists, replaced de Kemoularia in the spring of 1987. His early career had taken him to Morocco, Switzerland, Japan, Spain, and London, after which he had been director of the prestigious Ecole Nationale d'Administration for seven years. A one-time aide to General De Gaulle, he had written a book on the general's last years. He had been ambassador to Sweden and then Greece before coming to New York.[13]

In 1986 Moscow sent Alexandr M. Belonogov, then its ambassador in Cairo, to New York. Earlier assignments had included five years in London, plus work in the departments of the Foreign Ministry responsible for legal affairs and for international economic organizations.[14] *Forbes*, the capitalist tool, announced, "Russia's New U.N. Ambassador Is Impressive," and explained that he seemed to be "really wired" to Gorbachev. "Belonogov talked to a small group of American businessmen with candor as unexpected as it was amazing."[15]

General Vernon A. Walters, already a figure of legend, became the U.S. permanent representative in 1985. During early school years in France and England he had become truly fluent in French, Spanish, Portuguese, German, and Italian, as well as able to decipher the hieroglyphics on the victory column in the Place de la Concorde. When his father, an insurance executive, had suffered setbacks in the Great Depression, Vernon had worked as an insurance adjuster in New York. In 1941 he had enlisted in the U.S. Army, had been selected for officer training, and had become an intelligence officer. During the war he had served in Morocco, where he had met the young Prince Hassan, and in Italy, where he had been General Mark Clark's aide. After the war he had been aide and interpreter for General George Marshall, Averell Harriman (including during his talks with Iran's Mohammed Mossadegh), and President Harry Truman.

From 1956 to 1960 Walters had been staff assistant to President Eisenhower. He had been with Vice President Richard Nixon in Caracas when the vice president's car had been attacked, cementing a lifetime relationship. He had gone on to be defense attaché in Brazil, Italy, and then in Paris during the 1968 upheavals. While in Paris he had arranged Henry Kissinger's secret talks with the Vietnamese. He had been deputy director of the CIA during the Watergate years and George Bush's time as director. He had come out of retirement in 1981 to be ambassador-at-large for Ronald Reagan, and in four years this inveterate traveler and subway explorer had visited 108 countries on official missions.[16] A lifelong bachelor, Walters was known for his raconteurship, bonhomie, and love of chocolate.

These ambassadors agreed to take on a role not normally played by UN missions—not just negotiating on a UN decision, but seeking to develop convergences in their governments' policies toward ending the Iran-Iraq war. In consultation with London the British delegation began to draft a mandatory resolution, as proposed earlier by Ambassador Walters, to order a cease-fire and withdrawal of forces. In Washington the National Security Council met in mid-January to map a new policy toward Iran and the war, a policy that included reflagging Kuwaiti tankers, a renewed commitment to Operation Staunch, and working at the United Nations to secure a resolution under chapter VII ordering an end to the fighting and, if the fighting continued, an arms embargo.

Proceedings

In the beginning of February 1987 the ambassadors launched the process of negotiations that changed the way diplomacy is practiced in the Security Council. Throughout the coming months the ambassadors met every few weeks at the British ambassador's residence on Beekman Place, conveniently close to the United Nations. In this informal and private setting, each ambassador accompanied by one counselor, they reviewed the work being done by the counselors' group, framed questions on which to seek guidance from capitals, shared the responses received, and renewed the mandate of the counselors' group. The ambassadors retained responsibility for managing the process of negotiation. They also determined what questions to raise with the secretary-general and the procedure for consulting other delegations.

When the counselors first met in mid-February, the secretary-general's office had provided for them a package with the secretary-general's Eight Points of 1985, plus two additional points requested by Iraq, the talking points the secretary-general had used during his meeting with ambassadors on 23 January, and a table indicating elements included in Security Council resolutions 479, 514, 522, 540, 552, 582, and 588. To keep the tone of their meetings informal, the counselors agreed to postpone any decision whether they were preparing a short, simple resolution or a comprehensive one and to explore all options.

For reasons of convenience the counselors met at the U.S. Mission, directly across First Avenue from United Nations headquarters. The five counselors were all professional diplomats with long experience, which for several included more than one posting at the United Nations. At times the British, French, and U.S. counselors were accompanied by lower-ranking colleagues; the Chinese and Soviet counselors always came alone. Meeting over coffee and cookies in late morning or midafternoon, once or twice a week they shared information from capitals and from their other contacts in New York. Then, in successive *tours de table*, they sought answers to their ambassadors' questions. How might the parties be engaged in a process of negotiation? What were the positions of the parties on the elements already included in UN resolutions, or on other elements that had been proposed? Could the permanent members agree on a formula for invoking the mandatory powers of chapter VII? Should the council first adopt a "simple" cease-fire resolution, or would it be better to have a comprehensive resolution including guidelines for a settlement? Under what circumstances and how could a resolution be enforced?

Because the counselors operated at the technical level, they could "brainstorm," that is explore options, without any implication of commitment. All understood that the counselors lacked power to commit their governments; that the ambassadors had authority to commit on questions of process but not of substance; and that capitals retained the power to commit on substance. After an initial discussion, the counselors would draft a "nonpaper" (a diplomatic working paper without attribution or commitment). They might produce the initial draft by writing down and then refining the comments made orally; U.S. delegation staff often served as the secretariat for this purpose. At other times one counselor would circulate a draft for comment, with this paper becoming the basis for discussion. The counselors did their drafting work by modifying a single text, not by trying to reconcile competing drafts.

One early discussion considered how to engage the parties in a peace process. During the first round, ideas put forward included

- requesting each side to express views on possible regional security arrangements;
- using the Security Council to encourage the mediation efforts of the secretary-general;
- seeking to have prolonged or made permanent the agreed moratorium on attacks on civilian targets;
- dispatching a fact-finding mission; and
- engaging the parties in discussion of practical arrangements for peacekeeping or security guarantees.

Either the secretary-general, the Security Council or its president, or the permanent members could take the lead in implementing these measures. After review most of these ideas were put aside, but others, such as regional security arrangements and peacekeeping, were retained as possible steps in an action-oriented agenda.

By early March the counselors sent forward to their ambassadors a nonpaper analyzing elements from earlier resolutions and elements proposed by the parties. The elements acceptable to both sides included investigation of the question of responsibility for the conflict (although the two sides had very different interpretations of what that meant), mutual assurances of nonaggression and of respect for international obligations, and reconstruction efforts. Footnotes to the list explained the parties' conflicting interpretations; Iraq insisted that a cease-fire and withdrawal precede a settlement and Iran that they should not. The paper identified elements sought by Iran but unacceptable to Iraq, such as reparations, and Iraq's request, unacceptable to Iran, that resolution 582 be implemented in an interconnected way according to a precise timetable (a way of demanding early withdrawal).[17] The counselors framed two questions for their ambassadors to ask the secretary-general: Did he prefer support by council members for his mediation efforts to be private or public? And, if public, should the council's statement or resolution be comprehensive and include other elements?

In March, after Iran's winter offensive had spent its force, the counselors continued to meet periodically but with diminished urgency. As they explored options, they grew accustomed to meeting informally, under the ground rules blessed by their ambassadors: First, the permanent members would not call for Security Council action unless they agreed on doing something meaningful. Second, they would concentrate on ending the war, not on pressuring the parties to respect international humanitarian law or reducing the risk to third parties while the war went on. Third, they would explore the option of a mandatory resolution under chapter VII ordering a cease-fire and a withdrawal of forces. Fourth, understanding that a mandatory resolution implied the willingness to adopt enforcement measures if required, they would examine the issue of sanctions. Fifth, they would seek to produce a comprehensive draft that included a framework for an ongoing diplomatic process to resolve the conflict, not merely to stop the fighting.

In April the counselors began to review a working draft that the British delegation had prepared. Although skeletal in form, it contained those points that survived examination in the brainstorming sessions: a mandatory cease-fire and withdrawal of forces, release and repatriation of prisoners of war, support for the secretary-general's mediation, a call on other states to exercise the utmost restraint, a request for looking into the question of establishing an impartial body to investigate the responsibility for the war, a recognition of the need for reconstruction efforts, an examination of measures for regional security, and a decision to consider measures (sanctions) to ensure compliance.[18]

This nonpaper, after several revisions, became the basis on which the five ambassadors asked for revised instructions. Two issues became paramount. First, the United States wanted a "tie-in": no agreement on a comprehensive, mandatory resolution would be final before the permanent members made a firm commitment in principle on the conditions under which sanctions would be adopted and the nature of those sanctions. Second, without new instructions the counselors could not agree on the proper form for indicating that the resolution was in fact mandatory. Need the text be entirely explicit on this point, determining that there was a threat to international peace and security in the language of article 39, as the British insisted? Or, would the use of such explicit language, as China and the Soviet Union argued, tend to weaken the authority of other Security Council resolutions not explicitly adopted under chapter VII by implying that states were under no obligation to comply with them? Was this a technical problem that could be solved in additional drafting sessions, or did it reflect fundamentally different views on invoking the authority of chapter VII of the charter?

Pressures in Capitals

Back in the five capitals the reports from the ambassadors represented only one aspect of the five governments' national policies toward the war. Kuwait's requests to the Soviet Union and the United States for shipping protection raised the specter of direct superpower competition in the gulf, and a massive redeployment of U.S. naval vessels to the area was in preparation. Meanwhile the Soviet Union and the United States had begun to improve their bilateral relations, an effort launched by Reagan and Gorbachev that included, in addition to arms control issues, regular discussions on regional crises, such as the Iran-Iraq war. Iran's unfalteringly bellicose rejections of peace feelers, topped by ruptures in relations with Britain and France, reduced Iran's ability to influence the diplomatic process. On Iraq's side the Arab League pushed in each of the five capitals for joint action to end the war. All of these developments raised the value of agreement in New York.

In Washington the mid-January White House policy meetings had considered both general policy toward the war and Kuwait's request for shipping protection. On 23 January President Reagan issued a statement defining U.S. policy toward both:

> As I have emphasized many times, we are determined to help bring the war to the promptest possible negotiated end, without victor or vanquished, leaving intact the sovereignty and territorial integrity of both Iran and Iraq. We cannot but condemn Iranian seizure and occupation of Iraqi territory, and we again call upon the Government of Iran to join the Government of Iraq in seeking a rapid negotiated solution to the conflict.
>
> We share the concern of our friends in the gulf region that the war could spill over and threaten their security. We would regard any such expansion of the war as a major threat to our interests as well as to those of our friends in the region. We remain determined to ensure the free flow of oil through the Strait of Hormuz. We also remain strongly committed to supporting the individual and collective self-defense of our friends in the gulf, with whom we have deep and longstanding ties.[19]

In February White House meetings looked at diplomatic options and the implications of reflagging. During the month Iran successfully test-fired a Chinese HY-2 Silkworm missile, designed for use against shipping, from a site on Qeshm Island (near the Strait of Hormuz), and the United States learned that the Soviet Union had responded favorably to Kuwait's request for reflagging and protection of five tankers. On 25 February President Reagan reaffirmed his 23 January statement but added that he had asked "Secretary of State George Shultz to take the lead in an international effort to bring Iran into negotiations."[20] He expressed full support for Operation Staunch and called for "an immediate cessation of hostilities [and for] negotiations and withdrawal to borders." He urged the international community to cooperate to this end.

In March Kuwait and the United States negotiated over arrangements to protect shipping. To eliminate a direct Soviet role, the United States offered to protect all eleven tankers in question; on 10 March Kuwait accepted. A week later the chairman of the Joint Chiefs of Staff, Adm. William Crowe, visited Kuwait and reaffirmed the agreement.[21] The administration explained that its decision supported two interests: "First, to help Kuwait counter immediate intimidation and thereby discourage Iran from similar attempts against the other moderate gulf states; and, second, to limit, to the extent possible, an increase in Soviet military presence and influence in the gulf."[22] Meanwhile Kuwait took out diplomatic reinsurance by chartering three Soviet tankers and approaching Britain, China, and France on the question of protection for Kuwait shipping. The arrangement for Kuwait to charter Soviet vessels rather than to hoist the Soviet flag over their own made it less likely that the Soviet Navy would have access to gulf ports and facilities.

These arrangements to protect shipping pressured the Reagan administration to register concrete progress on the diplomatic track. The reflagging of Kuwaiti tankers raised U.S. exposure in the area, and the only practical way to limit those risks was to end the war. The administration, already vulnerable to domestic critics over the Iran-Contra scandal, would have to overcome congressional resistance to the decision to reflag and protect Kuwaiti tankers. While all permanent members saw that a joint effort to end the war could help keep events from spinning out of control, for the United States a credible diplomatic effort would also be a source of legitimacy for the more unilateral and military aspects of its policy. In contrast, the other permanent members thought that an active diplomatic track at the United Nations might allow them to restrain U.S. unilateralism. The Soviet Union voiced concern over growing U.S. naval deployments.

Surveying the challenges to U.S. policy, the *New York Times* recommended, "One choice is for the West, possibly in consultation with Moscow, to try, with additional diplomatic and military efforts, to end the war."[23] Joseph Twinam, a former senior State Department officer with long experience in the area, published an analysis pointing out that the realistic goals of both superpowers in the area were in fact limited and not inherently in conflict: "In sum, could the superpowers come to see the Gulf as a delicate place of great importance to the world at large in which cooperation rather than competition would better serve both Soviet and Western interests?"[24]

Moscow was becoming more active diplomatically. In December 1986 a Soviet delegation had visited Tehran for the first meeting of the joint Soviet-Iranian economic commission in six years. In January, as already mentioned, the Kremlin criticizied Iran's offensive and asked for an end to the war. On 13 February Iranian foreign minister Ali Akbar Velayati went to Moscow. While the two sides signed an agreement that called in general terms for greater economic cooperation, Andrei Gromyko, then president of the Soviet Union, took a tough line with Velayati over Afghanistan. *Pravda* characterized the talks as "frank and businesslike."[25]

Moscow, looking at ways to cut the costs of its foreign policy, was taking a more favorable view of the United Nations. After all, the United Nations was managing the negotiations regarding Afghanistan and would play a significant role in any agreement leading to Soviet withdrawal. Perhaps arrangements involving the United Nations could help the Soviet Union liquidate the costs of involvement in other regional conflicts. For example, an agreement under UN aegis that provided for Angolan security from the South African military in Namibia could ease termination of support for the Cuban military presence in Angola. In short, better use of the United Nations might reduce the demands of unilateral Soviet policies.

In April Deputy Foreign Minister Vladimir Petrovsky, an advocate of new-style Soviet diplomacy who had been a UN official and was responsible within the Foreign Ministry for the United Nations, visited Kuwait, Oman, and the United Arab Emirates. He asserted that Moscow and Washington had agreed to take (unspecified) "joint steps" to bring an end to the war[26] and then tried to drum up support for proposals aimed at demilitarizing the gulf and condemning the growing U.S. naval presence.[27]

Arab League foreign ministers meeting in Tunis agreed unanimously that the war had to be brought to an early, negotiated end, that Iran was the intransigent party, and that the flow of arms to Iran had to be stopped. The league sent delegations to Beijing, London, Moscow, Paris, and Washington to pressure those governments for joint action at the United Nations. On 30 April, when Moscow was considering the proposal worked up by the ambassadors in New York, a delegation including Tariq Aziz visited to lobby for Soviet support.

When an Arab League delegation visited Washington on 7 May, Secretary of State Shultz told them that the United States would work to block arms to Iran and to secure a UN resolution to end the war. If Tehran rejected the UN plan, the United States might back appropriate enforcement measures.[28] At the same time Assistant Secretary of State Richard Murphy visited Iraq and the gulf states; he was the first high-ranking U.S. official to do so since the Iran-Contra scandal broke. While he was traveling, the spokesman for the State Department announced that the United States had begun an effort at the United Nations to secure a worldwide arms embargo against Iran.[29] The *Times* of London reported that Murphy's talks in Baghdad had concentrated on how the United States could play a role in bringing about the earliest possible end to the war.[30] Before early May there had been, surprisingly, no hints in the press of the New York discussions among the permanent members that were already laying the basis for fundamental change in the way the Security Council operates.

Going Forward

While waiting for the capitals to respond to their joint proposal, the ambassadors told their counselors to brainstorm questions that would arise in implementing a resolution along the lines proposed and in applying sanctions in case one or both parties failed to comply with the cease-fire. In a series of meetings the counselors first discussed key points, then U.S. mission staff produced notes of the discussions, and in a third step the counselors reviewed the notes to produce, through several revisions, a nonpaper for their ambassadors. To record that no commitments had been made on the substance of an initiative, the paper was labeled with a caveat: "The purpose of this paper is to explore questions in connection with a Security Council resolution ordering a cease-fire which would be binding under Article 25 of the Charter (i.e., not necessarily under Chapter VII)."[31]

In drafting this paper, which never became the basis for a Security Council decision, the counselors were looking in two directions at once—how to secure a cease-fire and, if this effort failed, how to apply sanctions.

Under the broad heading "Acceptance of a cease-fire by both parties" the counselors listed points dealing with the military and diplomatic consequences of a cease-fire. Here came questions concerning what a cease-fire actually would mean on the ground, whether simply an end to fighting or that plus greater restrictions on military movements. Regarding the supervision of a cease-fire, the paper left open whether there should be UN observers, how a cease-fire violation would be defined, and what the consequences should be for a violation. The paper also included a point on "A Special Representative of the Secretary-General"; eleven months later the Soviets would raise this idea not as a way to manage implementing a cease-fire but as a way to induce the parties to agree to one.

The subheading on disengagement listed measures often implemented by UN peacekeeping forces, such as establishment of cease-fire lines and exchanges of prisoners of war, and it raised the question whether a peacekeeping operation would have to be established at some point. The last military item mentioned was "withdrawal to international borders." Although the paper questioned whether a withdrawal would "automatically" follow a cease-fire or whether it would be but one of a number of measures directed toward peace negotiations, it ignored the existence of any dispute as to what the international borders might be. Although this was a key issue for the parties, especially along the Shatt, the permanent members had little interest in the exact boundary and would be satisfied if forces were withdrawn to either side of the river.

The paper then listed points dealing with the diplomatic consequences of a cease-fire. What role, if any, should the Security Council play either in making recommendations to bring about a comprehensive settlement or in facilitating its implementation? And what role should the secretary-general be encouraged to play? This section noted that there were questions of process, specifically whether the various measures should be tied together in a set time frame and whether council members should reach agreement on how to implement a cease-fire resolution before they moved to adopt it.

These questions had predictable answers. The cease-fire resolution would contain general guidelines for a settlement, but once a cease-fire was in place and the threat to international peace and security was diminished, questions of implementation would be left to the secretary-general and the parties. Consistent with the idea that the permanent members were designing a process for ending the war, not a precise plan for doing so, the Security Council could adopt a resolution without knowing beforehand precisely how it would be implemented.

The second half of this paper, under the broad heading "non-compliance by one or both parties with the cease-fire," raised questions that would have to be addressed by any decision to "enforce" a resolution through sanctions. The preparation of these questions revealed that among the permanent members there was only a tentative understanding that by adopting one mandatory resolution they were embarking on a process that implied a willingness later to adopt sanctions. In equivocal language that the ambassadors knew had different meanings for different capitals and thus covered potential disagreement with ambiguity, the paper neither ruled in nor ruled out the U.S. request that the permanent members commit themselves on sanctions before the Security Council adopted a mandatory resolution.

If an outside observer looked in on one of the counselors' drafting sessions, they would have seen that the style of negotiations fit in with the rules used by friendly countries: no unambiguous lies, no breaking of explicit promises, no invective or threats, and no blatant backtracing on agreements in principle and mutual understandings.[32] Rather than addressing each other's positions, they kept the focus on the questions that the ambassadors had asked them to examine. The counselors spoke to the point and kept repetitions and distortions to the minimum. Furthermore, they maintained maximum discretion in briefing other delegations, not sharing information that would embarrass their negotiating partners. The style of negotiation raised the value of unity among the permanent members, a unity that, although not a block to unilateral actions, would be needed to minimize misunderstandings and miscalculations during the process of implementation of an agreed course of action.

During the first half of 1987 the permanent members came to perceive an overlap in their separate interests and policies, making possible an understanding on limiting the risks of the Iran-Iraq war to international peace and security. By improved working relations among the delegations in New York, by quiet examination of the issues, and by avoiding premature commitments to specific actions, they developed a proposal for a mandatory, comprehensive resolution that could, in different ways, serve the interests of all.

For the first time since the founding of the United Nations the permanent members had discussed together how to use the powers of chapter VII and even exchanged ideas on how to enforce a mandatory resolution by sanctions if one of the parties failed to comply. Whatever course these governments decided to follow in the immediate case, they were building up a shared understanding of how the provisions of chapter VII might be applied in practice. Now their ambassadors asked for new instructions authorizing them to open consultations with other council members.

Improved working relations among the permanent members could benefit other cases. Namibia was one example, and Cambodia another. Some permanent members wanted the new style of collaboration to lead to work on the Middle East, at least to private discussions among the permanent members. The five permanent members began to sense that, when they took a unified position, they could wrest initiative in the council from the nonaligned caucus. Rather than being reactive, they could shape the agenda.

8

A Meeting of the Minds

Informing Others

When the five ambassadors received authorization to proceed, the time had come for them to enlist the support of the other ten council members for their approach. In early May the secretary-general reported to the council the findings of a team of experts he had sent, on his own authority but in response to an Iranian request, to investigate allegations that Iraq had used chemical weapons. His report informed the council of evidence found by the team, including descriptions of injuries suffered by soldiers whom the team had examined in Iranian hospitals. The report stimulated the interest of nonpermanent members in reactivating the council on the subject of the war. After four months of working just among themselves, the permanent members now moved to open up the process of negotiation.

China's ambassador Li Luye was council president for the month. He told his political counselor to draft a presidential statement, the form of response used in the past when the secretary-general had reported on the use of chemical weapons. But the nonpermanent council members, not only the nonaligned but also Germany, Italy, and Japan, who by this time were all aware that the permanent members had been working among themselves, considered asking for a debate in the council on the war as a way to force the permanent members to open up their negotiations to the entire council. To head off such a request, the permanent members decided to present during informal consultations of the council a preliminary briefing on their work.

On 14 May, the same day that the council approved a presidential statement condemning the repeated use of chemical weapons and prolongation of the war, Ambassador Li read a brief statement during informal consultations. Speaking in English, he said he was acting on behalf of the delegations of Britain, China, France, the Soviet Union, and the United States. Those five delegations had been following up on the secretary-general's call for a serious effort by the Security Council to find a meeting of minds regarding the war by conducting discussions among themselves. The five felt their effort was nearing a point at which they would be able to inform other members of the council of the results of their work, and they looked forward to doing so.

Ambassador Li's simple statement was extraordinary. It marked another significant step away from the confrontations of the Cold War era toward businesslike cooperation. The permanent representative of China read in English from a text approved in Beijing, London, Moscow, Paris, and Washington and spoke explicitly on behalf of those five governments. The substance of the statement was vague, but its message was clear. Whatever the differences among the five, they would present themselves to the other members of the council as a single group for the purpose of responding to the secretary-general's invitation. Li's statement put off suggestions that the council should become active on this subject, but it stumulated press interest on the collaboration among the permanent members.

For the next two weeks New York delegations of the permament members refined the text of their draft resolution, adding preambular paragraphs and making technical adjustments elsewhere in response to instructions from capitals.

During this critical period Iran further damaged its relations with the Soviet Union and Britain. On 7 May during daylight hours, speedboats under control of Iran's Revolutionary Guards attacked the Soviet freighter *Ivan Korotoyev* off the coast of Dubai, in what the *Washington Post* interpreted as an apparent warning to the Soviets to keep their ships out of the gulf.[1] On 16 May the tanker *Marshal Chuykov,* one of the three Soviet vessels leased to Kuwait, was damaged by a mine in waters off Kuwait. Iranian prime minister Hussein Moussavi, reacting to both U.S. and Soviet plans to protect Kuwaiti shipping, warned the superpowers "not to enter these quicksands."[2]

In mid-May British officials arrested an Iranian vice consul in Manchester on a charge of shoplifting, and within days Iranian officials arrested Edward Chaplin, a British diplomat in Tehran, on charges of corruption. The two sides then played tit-for-tat, with Britain expelling five Iranian diplomats on 4 June and Iran retaliating on 7 June. When the series of expulsions and recallings ended on 18 June, each was left with only one diplomatic representative in the other's capital. The staff of Iran's office in London that managed Iran's efforts to procure arms on international markets was not affected.

In contrast to the treatment accorded Iran's actions, Iraq benefited from an apparent predisposition by the United States not to impute negative intentions to its actions. On 17 May an Iraqi plane fired two Exocet missiles that ripped through the USS *Stark,* then operating in international waters. The reaction by the United States to this incident, ironically, increased cooperation between the United States and Iraq and support by the United States for the shipping of GCC states. This outcome was made possible by the U.S. determination that the attack was "inadvertent," by adroit Iraqi diplomacy (including a rare statement from Saddam Hussein regretting the loss of life), and by the agreement between the two sides to investigate the incident, to set up procedures to prevent its recurrence, and for Iraq to pay damages (albeit with Saudi money).

Two days after the attack on the *Stark* the Reagan administration announced it had reached agreement with Kuwait on the reflagging operation. Within forty-eight hours the Senate voted ninety-one to five to require a detailed report on security precautions before the operation could begin. Although the attack on the *Stark* did not deter the administration, it underlined just how dangerous an environment the Persian Gulf had become. To protect itself from these dangers and from congressional criticism, which would surely flare up in the aftermath of any further incident, the Pentagon expanded the size of the protection force for the reflagged tankers. Thus the attack on the *Stark* deepened the U.S. commitment in the area, and because it would have more assets at risk if the war went on, the United States was more determined to establish a diplomatic track for ending the war.

Secretary of Defense Weinberger raised the question of the Persian Gulf at the NATO ministerial meeting on 26 and 27 May. The Persian Gulf, beyond the geographic scope of the North Atlantic Treaty, was considered an "out of area" question not normally a matter for allied cooperation within the NATO framework. The press reported that Weinberger asked NATO allies to support the planned U.S. role in the gulf and that they turned down his request. Some allies objected to dealing with an out-of-area question at a NATO meeting; others, such as the Federal Republic of Germany, were more sympathetic than Washington to Iranian concerns.[3] Undeterred by lukewarm allied support, on 29 May President Reagan warned, "The use of the vital sea lanes of the Persian Gulf will not be dictated by the Iranians. These lanes will not be allowed to come under the control of the Soviet Union. The Persian Gulf will remain open to navigation by the nations of the world."[4]

Later that day the five permanent members' ambassadors met with the secretary-general. They informed him they had concluded the first phase of the work, seeking a meeting of minds among their governments. Next they would engage other council members. Pérez de Cuéllar thanked them for the work done, pointing to the importance of the new process of consultation among the permanent members aimed at producing unity of action. Since it had taken almost five months to get the process to this point, the ambassadors said they wanted to give other council members adequate time to consult their governments on the text. Although they did not indicate any set time frame, for tactical reasons the ambassadors preferred not having final negotiations on the text until France assumed the council presidency on 1 July.

On 31 May Iranian Revolutionary Guards, using Boghammer speedboats capable of fifty-five miles per hour, seized seven Kuwaiti speedboats in waters off Bubiyan Island.

Opening the Negotiations

While the permanent members' counselors were completing work on a package of agreed papers and talking points for their ambassadors to use in presenting the permanent members' initiative to other council members, elsewhere on the diplomatic circuit the main issue was the role of foreign fleets in the gulf. Before leaving Moscow in mid-June on a trip to the area, Soviet Deputy Foreign Minister Yuli Vorontsov, contradicting a *Washington Post* report that the Soviet Union had sent three minesweepers to join two frigates that had been in the gulf since 1986, said the Soviet Union would not augment its fleet there.[5] During his stop in Tehran, where his hosts demanded the evacuation of Soviet troops from Afghanistan, Vorontsov emphasized that the Soviet Union and the United States did not have parallel interests in the gulf, that the Soviet Union opposed the presence of foreign forces in the area, and that the United States was aiming to damage the interests of both Iran and the Soviet Union in the area.[6] He then visited Baghdad. He invited both sides to come to Moscow for a conference on resolving the war, an invitation at variance with the joint diplomatic approach being developed in New York with the other permanent members. On 1 July Iran rejected Vorontsov's invitation.[7] This Soviet diplomatic tactic, offering services as a mediator to help the parties escape pressure applied at the level of the Security Council, would be tried again later, again without success.

The fulcrum for the issue of foreign forces was in Kuwait. Kuwait's agreements with the United States and the Soviet Union for protection of its shipping, even without an explicit superpower military commitment, gave Iran a message about the dangers of attacking Kuwaiti tankers. These arrangements were apparently accepted by Iraq, which was deeply suspicious of the growing U.S. role.[8] For Kuwait these arrangements served an additional political objective, putting pressure on the superpowers to find a way to end the war. A Western diplomat in Kuwait, reflecting on the situation caused by the requests to the Soviet Union and the United States for protection of shipping, commented, "I don't think it has anything to do with shipping. The goal is to get the superpowers involved."[9]

President Reagan wanted the seven industrialized countries at their Economic Summit on 8 and 9 June to declare support for the U.S. decision to protect shipping in the gulf and for diplomatic activity at the United Nations aiming at ending the war, including the imposition of a UN arms embargo if need be. The summit participants agreed to a statement that urged new and concerted international action to end the war, endorsed strong action by the Security Council, and declared that the flow of oil and other traffic must continue unimpeded through the Strait of Hormuz. Their statement did not offer explicit support for U.S. naval deployments or for a UN arms embargo, should a mandatory cease-fire not be implemented.

In mid-June the Reagan administration reported to Congress its plans for reflagging. Under Secretary of State Michael Armacost, in testimony to the Senate Foreign Relations Committee on 16 June, admitted that the United States would prefer a Western protective regime, rather than a unilateral U.S. force, for shipping in the gulf, but not an international regime that would permit the Soviet Union to legitimize a long-term military presence in the area.[10] A report by Secretary of Defense Weinberger was more explicit:

> The United States seeks to minimize Soviet political and military inroads in the region and does not want to legitimize Soviet naval presence in the Gulf as a participant in an international shipping protection plan, but we are not adverse to working with the USSR in multilateral efforts to end the war. Ending the threat of conflict will benefit both countries, as well as the entire region. The United States notes the declaratory Soviet support for freedom of navigation in the Gulf but believes that, rather than engaging the Soviets in formal arrangements in the Gulf, efforts should focus on ending the war so that the question of shipping protection need not arise. We have worked well with the Soviets so far at the UN.[11]

In New York by 12 June the permanent members had agreed on a process for consulting with other council members. Even though the draft text of a resolution was ready, they decided to open consultations using a less specific "elements" paper, accurately listing all of the operative points in the draft but not including its preambular elements. For example, they saw no benefit in drawing early attention to the decision to resolve their differences on the mandatory character of Security Council resolutions by stating that the resolution fell under articles 39 and 40 (authority for determining existence of a threat to the peace and for adopting provisional measures), rather than under chapter VII as a whole (which would have covered the enforcement measures of articles 41 and 42 as well). They reasoned that it would be better to focus the attention of other council members on the ideas being presented in order to encourage first a discussion of the general approach, as the permanent members had done in their own meetings. An elements paper might offer the additional tactical advantage of allowing the permanent members to retain more control over the process of negotiation.

The approach used in the draft showed that the permanent members aimed to end the war rather than simply to repeat council exhortations for the belligerents to bring their conduct of the war into line with international law on such points as chemical weapons and freedom of navigation. Thus there was a legally binding "demand" for a cease-fire and withdrawal of forces. On the issue of boundaries they settled on the phrase "the internationally recognized boundaries," which the council had already used and which allowed council members to avoid taking positions on what the boundaries were. There were several provisions for the secretary-general, acting as the council's diplomatic agent, to assist negotiations on the issues dividing the parties. Thus one provision directed the secretary-general to consult with the parties to set up an international panel to look into responsibility for the war (an equivocal formula that avoided choosing between Iran's and Iraq's proposals on this point). Picking up an Iranian idea, the text asked the secretary-general to consult with Iran, Iraq, and other states in the region on regional security measures. It called on other states to exercise the utmost retraint. It also recognized the need for reconstruction efforts, with "appropriate" international assistance.

The five ambassadors decided to use the format of informal consultations to present the paper to other members. One of the ambassadors would act as spokesman for all five. The counselors prepared a speaking note describing the elements of the draft.[12] If asked about sponsorship of the draft, the spokesman would state that this remained to be determined but that the five would welcome the sponsorship of all council members. He would invite other members to present their comments to any of the permanent members in whatever manner they chose. According to the procedure agreed to in advance, the counselors would then prepare joint responses to comments and questions from other delegations.

On 23 June Sir Crispin Tickell used the agreed speaking note to brief the other council members. Delegations of the permanent members, conscious of the months of effort they had taken to reach this point, felt the significance of presenting as a group the fruits of their collaboration. The reaction from the other members was muted. Because the permanent members had presented an elements paper rather than a full text to which one could propose specific drafting changes, other members felt they had been handed the short end of the stick. They wondered if the agreement among the permanent members was fragile or solid, and how receptive the permanent members would be to amendments. In any case, the elements paper, although reported home to capitals, failed to lead to a general discussion of the approach suggested. Other members wanted the full draft of a resolution, a text that they could amend.

Lobbying for a Tie-in

On 1 July, his first day as council president, French ambassador Pierre-Louis Blanc convened informal consultations so that the permanent members could present their draft resolution. In the ten days since receiving the elements paper, none of the other council members had made substantive comments, giving the reasonable explanation that their governments would respond when presented an actual text. The text distributed on 1 July did not differ at all from the elements paper in substance; the format was changed, and preambular paragraphs were added. While over the next three weeks the ten other council members would ask for amendments to many provisions, the only entirely new provision added concerned peacekeeping.

Once the text had been distributed and forwarded to capitals, activity slowed down in New York. The nonpermanent members took several days to consult with capitals and then among themselves before seeking further contacts with the permanent members. Meanwhile counselors of the permanent members were working out positions for responding to expected proposals to amend the draft and a scenario for the meeting of the Security Council at the level of foreign ministers in which the resolution would be adopted. At the insistence of the United States, they began drafting an enforcement resolution, specifying an arms embargo, to be ready for use if one of the two parties refused the cease-fire demand.

Developments elsewhere overshadowed the activity in New York. In Washington during the first week of July, Lieutenant Colonel North testified in the congressional hearings on the Iran-Contra scandal. The hearings were set to continue throughout the month, with Secretary Shultz to testify on 22 July. Simultaneously the process of reflagging Kuwaiti tankers, positioning U.S. naval vessels in the Persian Gulf and the Gulf of Oman to protect these ships, and moving the whole program past the risks of congressional opposition was coming to a head. For the Reagan administration, passage of a suitable Security Council resolution could generate badly needed political support by showing that, whatever the past shortcomings of its policies, the administration now had opened a credible diplomatic track that enjoyed broad international support and merited equally firm support at home.

In Paris, French authorities had surrounded the Iranian embassy in an effort to arrest Wahid Gordji, an embassy employee, for questioning in connection with a series of bombings. Authorities in Tehran confined twenty-eight French nationals to the French embassy, and ten days into the crisis two Iranian gunboats attacked a French ship. On 16 July Iran threatened to break relations unless France immediately removed the forces surrounding its embassy in Paris;[13] in Tehran the authorities summoned a French diplomat to court on espionage charges. France immediately broke diplomatic relations, suggesting that the two sides evacuate their embassies within five days.[14] By the end of July France took steps to increase security precautions at its embassies and publicly rejected an Iranian demand that French arms exports to Iraq be ended before any French hostages in Lebanon could be released.[15]

The United States remained keen that the permanent members prepare for the "second step"—adoption by the Security Council of sanctions should one or both of the parties refuse to accept the demand for a cease-fire. The United States recalled what had happened when, eight years earlier, Ambassador Donald McHenry had sold President Carter on a two-step process in the case of the hostages held by Iran: first, a resolution warning Iran, then a resolution imposing economic sanctions (which the Soviet Union vetoed). What the United States wanted, and indeed had stated it required since the beginning of the negotiations in January, was a "tie-in": agreement among the permanent members to tie in to the agreement on the cease-fire resolution a firm and specific commitment to adopt an arms embargo. While a tie-in expands the area of agreement, governments engaged in a negotiating process often prefer to keep open options by limiting their commitments to the minimum needed to keep the process going.

The Department of State instructed the U.S. delegation in New York to insist that, before the first resolution ordering the cease-fire could be adopted, the permanent members had to commit themselves to a resolution imposing sanctions, if need be, within a limited period of time, perhaps as short as two weeks. During July the counselors worked on a draft for a sanctions resolution, but without any commitment to the tie-in demanded by the United States.

General Walters, who had already scheduled a visit to Moscow to consult on UN matters, prepared to raise this question there, as well as in Beijing and Tokyo. On 2 July, following a meeting with Deputy Foreign Minister Petrovsky, Walters, responding to a reporter's question, said he had seen no difference between the U.S. and Soviet positions regarding the need for Security Council action in support of achieving a cease-fire in the war.[16] No doubt Petrovsky had listened carefully to Walter's presentation and agreed on the need for Security Council action, but on the crucial point, whether the cease-fire resolution should quickly be enforced by sanctions, Petrovsky gave no commitment.

On 3 July, two days after Iran had turned down Vorontsov's invitation to Iran and Iraq to come to Moscow for a Soviet mediation aimed at ending the war, an official TASS statement supported the need for the Security Council to adopt the draft already before the council. The same statement openly criticized U.S. naval deployments to the gulf and gave no suggestion that the Soviet Union would support a sanctions resolution. "Pseudo-measures supposedly motivated by concern for the safety of shipping are now being undertaken by the United States, which would want to exploit the present alarming situation to achieve its long-harbored plans of establishing military-political hegemony in this strategically important area."[17] Although Moscow was ready to cooperate with the United States for the adoption of the resolution before the council, it seemed to prefer the tactical advantages of gaining influence in Iran and of opposing U.S. naval deployments to adopting an arms embargo.[18]

In Tokyo Walters briefed Vice Minister Ryohei Murata on his discussions in Moscow before boarding a U.S. military aircraft for the flight to Beijing. Walters told Murata that overt support for sanctions was needed to back up the mandatory resolution already before the Security Council. Without such support Iran could be expected to reject the council cease-fire order. Japan had important trade ties to both Iran and Iraq, and earlier it offered to mediate between them. Now Japan was a member of the Security Council. Walters emphasized that the sanction under consideration was limited to an arms embargo, but Murata cautioned that before moving to any kind of sanctions the Security Council should give ample time for the secretary-general to reopen the diplomatic track toward a cease-fire.

The Japanese view was shared by the Federal Republic of Germany and Italy, the other Western nonpermanent members of the council. While Britain, France, and the United States were locked in consultations with the Soviets and Chinese and because the other council members belonged to the nonaligned caucus, these three delegations reviewed drafts together to develop joint positions. All three maintained ties to Tehran. Thus it was natural that they, more than Britain, France, and the United States, insisted on more time for talking with Iran rather than on moving quickly to an arms embargo.

Walters, accompanied by a small staff, flew to Beijing. During a late afternoon meeting with Deputy Foreign Minister Qian Qichen at the Daiyoutai Guest House, the two sides were arrayed on either side of a large banquet table covered in green felt. Walters was flanked by Winston Lord, U.S. ambassador in Beijing, and Qian Qichen by Li Luye, Walters's counterpart in New York. For two hours they lumbered through formalities and generalities to the main point—what to do should either Iran or Iraq not respond favorably to the demand for a cease-fire. Although Qian Qichen did not rebut Walters's argument in favor of an immediate move to sanctions, his response—that China would consider follow-on action and not use its veto to block action agreed upon by the other fourteen members of the council—was not encouraging.

After this formal session ended and before the banquet for the two delegations, Walters registered quietly Washington's long-standing concern about the Silkworm missiles sold by China to Iran. The Silkworms (HY-2) were positioned in several areas, including near the Straits of Hormuz, where they threatened shipping in the Persian Gulf. During Walters's stay in Beijing an Iranian group was in China to receive training to operate the Silkworms. The issue of Chinese arms sales, important to China's military industries but destabilizing in terms of regional security, was a constant irritant to U.S.-Chinese cooperation in the area.

The next morning Walters met with Foreign Minister Wu Xueqian in an even more formal setting at the Foreign Ministry. Their conversation, for which Walters had prepared through the talks of the previous evening, was more abbreviated and general, with the emphasis on activity at the United Nations. China would stay fully engaged with the other permanent members, but it was not committed on the question of sanctions.

Negotiations in New York

While Walters was off in Moscow, Tokyo, and Beijing drumming up support for a sanctions resolution, New York negotiators were working on the draft resolution already presented by the permanent members. At this point the Iranians, who had shunned the Security Council since 1980, entered the scene.

In late June, once the permanent members had agreed on a text, officials in the Foreign Ministry in Tehran prepared a counterdraft, patterned on the New York text. But the Iranian draft ordered neither a cease-fire nor a withdrawal of forces. It called for negotiations between the parties and gave added prominence to the call on other states to remain neutral and to exercise the utmost restraint. While this draft suggested a plausible diplomatic process, it cleverly avoided any provision that might contradict the actual Iranian policy of continuing the war.[19]

The Iranians, deciding not to be involved in negotiations in New York, injected their thinking into the negotiating process by giving this text to the German, Italian, and Japanese embassies in Tehran. In this way the Iranian Foreign Ministry shared these thoughts "informally" with selected council members but maintained that the text was merely an informal, internal working paper without any status. The Iranians surely expected these delegations to share this privileged information with Britain, France, and the United States. The Iranian tactic, by introducing a new and uncertain variable, might impede or complicate the negotiations on the permanent members' text. After all, was it not a major step forward that the Iranians were now contemplating being engaged in Security Council negotiations aimed at structuring a process for ending the war?

Iran's effort to exert influence over the negotiations flopped. The cause of this failure was Iran's isolation since the Islamic revolution. The extent of this phenomenon was well described at the time by an expert comparing the economic situations of Iran and Iraq:

> The critical difference in economic terms between the two sides is the reliability each enjoys in its external relations. Iran, during the revolution, turned its back on much of the world. It gratuitously offended the USA and the USSR and did little to endear itself to Western Europe. Iraq has gone out of its way to establish a comprehensive network of economic relations with both the Comecon group and with OECD states. Iran's access, in consequence, to the international market for arms, civil commodities and technology has been extremely limited. In many ways, Iranian industrial, agricultural and petroleum sectors suffer from a high degree of isolation from developments elsewhere and have done so since 1979. The same has been true in intellectual terms—a consideration which may have a more inchoate but nonetheless profound effect on Iran's capacity to cope with the war.[20]

By the second week of July capitals had instructed delegations of council members how to respond to the permanent members' draft. The nonaligned caucus met to prepare a group position. Germany, Italy, and Japan discussed the draft among themselves, but they did not develop a group position. The permanent members, through bilateral contacts at the ambassadorial level, received comments and suggestions for amendment;

their counselors worked up responses. Because the permanent members wanted to widen the circle of support for their draft, making it the off-spring of the entire council, they incorporated, to the extent possible, all suggestions consistent with their text.[21]

Some suggestions added elements from earlier resolutions referring to the outbreak of the war and the obligation to respect international law on the conduct of armed conflict. The permanent members had omitted these provisions on the assumption that the parties would stop the fighting as demanded by the resolution and therefore it would be unnecessary or even inconsistent to include such points. The additions included the third and fourth preambular paragraphs:

> Deploring the initiation and continuation of the conflict,
> [and,]
> Deploring also the bombing of purely civilian population centres, attacks on neutral shipping or civilian aircraft, the violation of international humanitarian law and other laws of armed conflict, and, in particular, the use of chemical weapons contrary to obligations under the 1925 Geneva Protocol.

The permanent members included a proposal from Ghana to provide for peacekeeping. During the original drafting they had discussed such a provision but decided not to include it only because a subsequent, specific resolution would in any case be needed to create a force. This proposal became operative paragraph 2:

> Requests the Secretary-General to dispatch a team of United Nations Observers to verify, confirm and supervise the cease-fire and withdrawal and further requests the Secretary-General to make the necessary arrangements in consultation with the Parties and to submit a report thereon to the Security Council.

Three other changes addressed the nature of the negotiating process for going from a cease-fire to a peaceful resolution of the conflict between the parties. These changes included addition of a preambular paragraph—"Convinced that a comprehensive, just, honourable and durable settlement should be achieved between Iran and Iraq"; adding to the first operative paragraph the point that the cease-fire was a first step "towards a negotiated settlement"; and including a request that the secretary-general assign a team of experts to study the question of reconstruction (operative paragraph 7).

The only difficult negotiations concerned the mandatory provisions of operative paragraph 1. The text as drafted demanded an immediate cease-fire and a withdrawal of all forces to the international boundaries "without delay." Should the forces of one party occupying the territory of the other at the time of the cease-fire be required to depart unconditionally? Or could the occupying forces stay put while political questions were settled? At the beginning of this exercise the secretary-general had advised the

permanent members not to consider the demands of the parties as constraints on their work, and they came at this question with his advice in
mind. The argument in favor of keeping a close link between the obligation
to end the fighting and that to withdraw was based on a preference to
counter the natural desire of an occupying power to draw out occupation
until benefits were received at the negotiating table. Since the basic theory
of this paragraph was a return to the status quo ante, use of prolonged
occupation as a bargaining lever was to be resisted. The phrase "without
delay" was meant to provide adequate time for necessary military measures but not permission to draw out this period for political purposes.

The counterargument, put forward by the German delegation among
others, was that the phrase "without delay" made the resolution unrealistic. Because the avowed purpose of the resolution was to establish a basis
for a political solution, preferably without applying sanctions, the text had
to take fair account of Iran's position. The phrase "without delay" should
be replaced by "subsequently" or other wording that would permit the
initiation of a political process before withdrawal. The counselors of the
permanent members went back and forth over this question, including
"subsequently" in at least one of their internal working papers. Then,
just hours before Foreign Minister Tariq Aziz made a vigorous demarche
insisting on the phrase "without delay," they decided to stick with the
original wording.

Several ambiguous phrases in the text went unchallenged during these
negotiations. Not one delegation wanted a clearer description of the border
than the phrase "internationally recognized boundaries." Despite earlier
attention to the possible role of an impartial body to determine responsibility for the conflict, there was no modification to wording merely asking
the secretary-general to explore this question with the parties. Equally abstract terms were accepted without change for provisions on damages,
reconstruction, and regional security measures.

Resolution 598 Adopted

When in January 1987 the secretary-general urged the permanent members
to seek a meeting of the minds, he recommended that they solemnify their
work at a formal meeting of the Security Council, perhaps at the level of
foreign ministers. By the third week of July council members had agreed
on the text. Now there remained only three questions of form: Who would
present the draft to the council? Who would attend the meeting? And
what would be the scenario?

The permanent members wanted the president of the council, acting on
behalf of all its members, to present the draft. The alternative would have
been for the permanent members, perhaps joined by other members of
the council, to introduce the draft as cosponsors. After pleas for council
unity, Ghana, considered sympathetic to Iranian views, concurred in the
decision to give authority to the council president to present the draft.

The State Department instructed the U.S. delegation and embassies in capitals to lobby for foreign ministers to attend. Secretary Shultz was scheduled to testify in the congressional hearings on the Iran-Contra scandal on 22 July, and a rare council meeting at the level of ministers just two days earlier might create a better atmosphere for his testimony. French foreign minister Roland Dumas would preside over the session, and ministers from Argentina, Britain, Germany, Italy, the United Arab Emirates, and the United States would attend. The Soviet Union and China declined to send their ministers, as did Bulgaria, Congo, Ghana, Japan, Venezuela, and Zambia.

Informal consultations carefully scripted a scenario for the meeting. There would be no debate. Delegations could explain their vote before or after the adoption of the resolution, a procedure that seemed to convey the maximum sense of solemnity and unity.

On the afternoon of 20 July the action went forward as scripted. Foreign Minister Dumas called the council to order. Members agreed to vote on the resolution without debate. Then Secretary of State Shultz spoke. He described the need to end the war, the provisions of the resolution, and the nature of relations between the United States and the governments of Iran and Iraq. Shultz, a former professor and student of negotiations, spoke about the process of diplomacy that led to this meeting: "The secretary-general played a crucial role in catalyzing the unprecedented process that led to the adoption of this resolution under the terms of Chapter VII of the United Nations Charter. He called upon the Permanent Members of the Security Council to shoulder their special responsibilities. This we have done; and, the Council as a whole has functioned in the collegial spirit envisioned by the founders of the United Nations at its creation." He stressed the U.S. insistence that the council be ready to back up its demand for a cease-fire. "We also support the decisive application of enforcement measures should either or both parties reject the call of this body."[22] In his memoirs, Shultz wrote that he was "proud to be the representative of the United States on this dramatic occasion."[23]

Next, council members raised their hands in favor of the draft before them, and Dumas announced that resolution 598 (1987) had been adopted by a vote of fifteen in favor, none opposed, and no abstentions. The secretary-general asked to speak.

In order to end the war, he said, "It is necessary that the national policies and actions of all Member States are harmonized with the declared will of the Council." He cited the specific obligation of all states to refrain from any act that might lead to further escalation of the conflict.[24] Because the United States had already announced that it would send the first convoy of reflagged tankers into the gulf within forty-eight hours, his comment seemed directed at the United States.

Pérez de Cuéllar, referring to the other points in the resolution, indicated how he intended to engage the parties in a process of negotiation and implementation. He emphasized that as a first step the belligerents would have to establish a cease-fire. After the meeting he would immediately begin consultations with the parties, and he emphasized the need for full cooperation by Iran and Iraq in order to make possible the achievement of a comprehensive, just, and honorable settlement. He addressed his concluding comment to council members, making the point that moving the negotiations forward required that the council stay engaged and maintain support for his efforts. "I shall not be able to fulfil the mission assigned to me by the Council without the firm and sustained support of its members."[25]

Soviet Ambassador Belonogov, like the secretary-general, emphasized the paragraph of resolution 598 that called on all states to exercise the utmost restraint and avoid actions that might lead to further escalation. Although he deleted from his comments Moscow's suggestion that he cite the United States by name because of its growing naval presence, he asserted simply that "everybody knows to whom [paragraph 5] is primarily addressed."[26] Actually Belonogov, somewhat like Pérez de Cuéllar before him, was reading into the resolution what he wanted to see there. The text of paragraph 5 was lifted from resolution 582 (1986), a good indication it was not drafted with the specific intent of addressing U.S. naval deployments a year and a half later.

At the meeting, foreign ministers presented a tableau of council unity behind the new resolution. Two important precedents had been set: the permanent members had worked together as a group to lead the council, and the council had decided to use the powers of chapter VII to address an ongoing threat to international peace and security.

The situation was far from static. Within days Iran and Iraq were expected to give their official reactions to the resolution, and the secretary-general intended to renew negotiations with the parties and to prepare for peacekeeping forces to monitor the cease-fire and withdrawal. If Iran and Iraq did not agree to a cease-fire, outside naval deployments in the area and the possibility of sanctions would be on the agenda. On 21 July the first convoy of reflagged Kuwaiti tankers entered the gulf, and three days later the reflagged tanker *Bridgeton,* traveling in a convoy organized by the U.S. Navy, hit a mine while approaching Kuwait.

9

Making It Work

Deepening Iranian Isolation

Iran's ambassador in New York, Said Rajaie-Khorassani, immediately denounced resolution 598 as a "vicious American diplomatic manoeuver." The official Iranian news agency simply said the resolution was "null and void."[1] For the coming months Iranian diplomacy would stay on the same tack—no formal rejection of 598 but no cease-fire.

On 23 July 1987 Tariq Aziz sent Pérez de Cuéllar a letter to welcome 598 and offer Iraq's cooperation in its implementation. He added caveats and conditions: Iran would have to state its readiness to fulfill its obligations under the resolution, the resolution must be considered an integral and indivisible whole, the phrase "without delay" should mean that withdrawal would be completed within ten days from the start of the cease-fire, prisoners of war would have to be released and repatriated within eight weeks of the cease-fire, and the overall implementation of the resolution would "be short so as to prevent any procrastination or delay from any quarter whatsoever."[2] Iran did not reply to the secretary-general until 11 August.

Meanwhile Security Council members, in their own ways, were following up on the resolution. When Foreign Minister Velayati visited Bonn, Foreign Minister Hans Dietrich Genscher told him Iran should accept a cease-fire and begin negotiations as the best way to promote Iran's interests.[3] In Washington George Shultz asked Tariq Aziz for a commitment to end Iraqi attacks on shipping in the gulf, whether or not Iran immediately accepted the resolution. Although Tariq Aziz rejected any "de facto cease-fire" as too beneficial to Iran, Iraq did suspend attacks on shipping.[4] On 4 August Deputy Foreign Minister Vorontsov returned to Tehran, causing speculation about deals on railroads, pipelines, and refineries.[5] A week later Britain and France announced that they would each send minesweepers to the gulf, primarily to assist their own vessels.

The main event, however, was mayhem at the Grand Mosque in Mecca. On 31 July Iranian Shiite pilgrims performing the Hajj clashed with Saudi security authorities. Four hundred died. Pilgrims shouted, "Death to America. Death to the Soviet Union. Death to Israel."[6] The demonstrations, animated by Iranian resentments over Saudi support for Iraq in the war, were seen as an attack against the legitimacy of the Saudi royal house. After the mayhem in Mecca, a Tehran mob went on a rampage, attacking the Kuwaiti, Saudi, and French embassies. On 2 August, officially designated in Iran as a "day of hate," Iranian officials called for the "uprooting" of the Saudi royal family. The incident deepened animosity between Iran and the gulf states, and because other Muslims thought Iranian demonstrations at Mecca profaned one of Islam's holiest shrines, Iran lost sympathy throughout the Muslim world. Iran was driving itself into deeper isolation.

On 11 August Iran sent its "detailed and official" response to the secretary-general: "Resolution 598 (1987) has been formulated and adopted by the United States with the explicit intention of intervention in the Persian Gulf and the region, mustering support for Iraq and its supporters in the war, and the diversion of public opinion from the home front. None of these objectives correspond to the legitimate objective of seeking a just solution to the conflict."[7] The letter leveled eight scattershot charges at the Security Council and 598: It was drafted without consulting Iran; "Iran, as the victim of aggression, is the main party to determine how the war can be terminated"; the Security Council must explain why it determined a breach of the peace only after seven years of war; in resolution 479 (1980) the Security Council called on Iran "to practically submit to aggression"; the Security Council, by adopting the resolution submitted by the United States, had made itself a party to the conflict; this resolution immediately led to an expansion of tension, evident in increased U.S. naval deployments and the events at Mecca; U.S. military provocations in the Persian Gulf made the United States the first violator of the resolution; and, by seeking a sanctions resolution against Iran, the United States was preparing grounds for its own confrontation with Iran.

Iran wanted the crisis in the Persian Gulf separated from the war and given priority for solution, with particular attention to U.S. naval deployments and to the need to stop attacks on shipping. Iraq should be named the aggressor and held responsible for war reparations. Iran was ready to cooperate with the secretary-general on chemical weapons, prisoners of war, his 1985 eight-point plan, and "in the framework of his independent efforts and initiatives." As for the Security Council a "clear-cut" identification of Iraq as responsible for the conflict remained the most important action the council could take.[8]

Pérez de Cuéllar briefed council members on the responses. The next day he met with ambassadors of the permanent members to solicit guidance from the council on how to proceed. In contrast to his approach in 1985, he now intended to have the explicit backing of the council for his dealings with the parties. He viewed 598 as an integrated whole, the elements of which should not be opened up or selected for independent implementation. He suggested telling Iran he was prepared to discuss all the points in 598, but only if Iran accepted that a cease-fire would be the first step in implementation. Fighting would have to stop before action would be taken to identify responsibility for the conflict. He did not intend to conduct discussions that could be seen as an excuse for continuing the war.

Council members consulted for ten days before approving guidance for the secretary-general. At stake was the framework both to support the secretary-general's talks with the parties and to determine when the council should find a party not in compliance and adopt sanctions. Council members were convinced of the utmost need to maintain their unity in support of 598. They agreed with the secretary-general that 598 should be implemented urgently as an integrated whole. They urged him to proceed "on the basis of the opinion he has made available to the members of the Council" (i.e., the points explained initially to the permanent members).

Tensions were mounting again. On 29 August Iraq ended its moratorium on attacking Iranian shipping and bombed Iranian offshore oil installations. After the State Department protested the attacks to Iraqi ambassador Hamdoon, he told the press Iraq would continue to attack Iranian shipping and oil installations.[9] In the last weeks of August the U.S. Navy deployed forty-six ships to the area, and Britain and France announced they would send additional naval forces.[10]

Iraq negotiated with the expectation of receiving broad diplomatic support. Since 1982 Iraq had asked for a cease-fire, offered to settle disputes peacefully, withdrawn from occupied territory, opened relations with the United States, expanded relations with France, repaired relations with the Soviet Union, and developed trade with China. Support from the GCC states gave Iraq strategic depth politically and economically.

What about Iran, which garnered no support for its demand that the aggressor be punished? It remained isolated, with its foreign policy decisions strongly influenced by domestic politics. It threatened neighbors and violated normal rules of diplomacy. Rather than seek the benefits of diplomatic relations with countries whose policies it opposed, it broke relations. Its main diplomatic asset was simply that other governments still valued the prize of friendship with Iran.

On 4 September Pérez de Cuéllar told council members he would visit Tehran on 12 and 13 September and Baghdad on the fourteenth and fifteenth. To focus the talks on a neutral, single text and to suggest a time frame for implementing 598, the secretary-general's staff developed an "outline implementation plan." This plan assumed that, as a practical matter, both sides would want understandings on the process for implementing other parts of the resolution before putting the "immediate" cease-fire into effect.

The key to the plan was the date (D-Day) the parties would pick for starting the cease-fire. On that day a team of UN observers would begin to verify, confirm, and supervise the cease-fire and subsequent withdrawal of forces, and the secretary-general would begin negotiations to settle all outstanding issues. Other steps (withdrawal of forces, release and repatriation of prisoners of war, the inquiry by an impartial body into responsibility for the war, and discussions on the question of regional security) would begin on the same day or later, as agreed by the parties. At some point after D-Day the impartial body would conclude its work, and the secretary-general would send experts to consider reconstruction.

Pérez de Cuéllar planned to use this outline to engage the parties in designing the process of implementation and in building a shared understanding of how that process would go forward. His immediate aim was to get agreement on a date for D-Day and then before D-Day on the other points. If the parties did not agree on other points, he would ask them to respect his own decisions in this regard.

"I am acting with a kind of straitjacket," Pérez de Cuéllar announced on arrival in Tehran, emphasizing that he worked within the framework of 598.[11] Foreign Minister Velayati said Iran would refuse a cease-fire unless Iraq was identified as the aggressor.[12] On the second day of the visit Parliament Speaker Rafsanjani reiterated that, even if there was no explicit promise of punishment, Iran would only accept the cease-fire when the United Nations identified Iraq as the aggressor.[13]

In Baghdad Pérez de Cuéllar was reminded that Iraq accepted resolution 598, as Tariq Aziz had already written. Saddam Hussein now asked that the Security Council take "punitive" measures against Iran for its failure to agree to a cease-fire and withdrawal of forces.[14]

On 16 September Pérez de Cuéllar told council members the Iranians had emphasized the need to identify the aggressor, followed by punishment and reparations. The Iranians had been careful not to reject any part of the resolution, but they wanted to shuffle the order of implementation by starting with an informal cease-fire, then identification of the aggressor, followed by a formal cease-fire. Iraq insisted that implementation of the paragraphs of 598 strictly follow the sequence in that resolution. Baghdad refused to start the implementation process with the work of an impartial body and argued that Iran's demand to do so constituted a clear rejection of the resolution.

The United States reacted to the secretary-general's report two days later: "It is our preliminary conclusion that Iran has neither indicated its clear acceptance of 598, nor does it appear ready to implement the resolution without conditions."[15] The State Department's spokesman called on Iran's President, Ali Khamenei, to pledge before the General Assembly Iran's unconditional acceptance of 598 and readiness to implement it in all of its parts.[16] Without such a statement Washington wanted the council to move rapidly to adopt enforcement measures.

On 20 September the war entered its eighth year. Iran wanted to block the threat of sanctions by dissuading the Soviet Union and China from agreeing to this step.[17] The United States wanted the secretary-general to announce that Iran would not comply with 598's order for a cease-fire, an announcement that could trigger the adoption by the Security Council of an arms embargo against Iran.

The UN's Busy Season

Before the General Assembly on Monday, 21 September, President Reagan called on President Khamenei to announce Iran's acceptance of a cease-fire. If Iran did not do so, Reagan said the Security Council should adopt sanctions. Events in the gulf seemed to confirm the need for Reagan's tough stance. On the day he spoke Iran attacked a British tanker, the *Gentle Breeze*, igniting a fire and killing one of the crew. In response Britain closed down Iran's London office that effectively coordinated Iranian arms purchases throughout Europe. Within twenty-four hours of Reagan's address a U.S. naval helicopter detected the Iranian vessel *Iran Ajr* laying mines in a shipping channel used by American ships. U.S. forces seized the Iranian vessel, killing three Iranian sailors and capturing twenty-six. The U.S. Navy seized ten mines aboard the *Iran Ajr*.

When Khamenei spoke to the General Assembly later on the twenty-second, he first explained the aims of the Islamic revolution and the need to purge Iranian society of the corruption of the Shah's regime. Then he turned to the war. "What Iraq anticipated as a reward for this invasion, apart from the stabilizing of its internal situation, was to emerge as the dominant Power in the region or at least in the Arab sphere. This would have been a lot for the nonentities ruling Iraq. Access to a considerable coastal border in the very important Persian Gulf region was certainly another motive."[18] The Iranian people "decided not only to liberate the occupied territories and seek war compensation—to both of which they are unambiguously entitled, despite the fact that they could not be compensated for a great part of the damages—but also, as a more important goal, to punish and remove the aggressor."[19] Citing favorably the consequences of the Nuremberg Trials, he warned "the kind of peace approved by the Iraqi regime today would, after a few years or whenever it suspected itself to be in a strong position, evaporate in a moment, and another war would engulf the region. The only guarantee for the future is punishment of the aggressor."[20]

Khamenei gave the Security Council short shrift: "Why has the Security Council of the United Nations, as an organ that was created primarily to safeguard international security and oppose aggression, totally ignored its obligations and even acted in defiance of its duty?"[21] At the outset of war the council failed to condemn Iraqi aggression or demand Iraqi withdrawal from Iranian territory. Throughout the war the council ignored Iranian demands for justice. In contrast the secretary-general's initiatives, even recent ones regarding resolution 598, were useful and instructive. "Our feeling is that the Security Council has been pushed into this indecent, condemnable position by the will of some big Powers, particularly the United States."[22]

Goaded by the *Iran Ajr* incident, Khamenei directed his most heated remarks at the United States. The "arch-satan's" navy had turned the region into a powder keg, and the United States would have to bear responsibility for the bitter consequences. He accused the United States of complicity in the crimes of the Shah. His final charge was that the United States had played an "influential part" in the killing of four hundred pilgrims at Mecca.

On 25 September Tariq Aziz rehearsed the opposite history of the war: When the war began, "in the field of external relations the objectives of Iraqi foreign policy included the achievement of stability in the region, non-intervention in the internal affairs of neighboring countries, and the settlement of differences by peaceful means."[23] Iraq suffered Iranian threats with great patience, but finally Iraq had no choice but to recognize that Iran's violations had rendered the Algiers agreement null and void. "The measures taken by the Iraqi Government since 4 September 1980 to counter the Iranian aggression are consistent with the right of legitimate self-defence because they met the conditions of necessity and reasonableness established by international law for the legitimate exercise of this right."[24] Iran used "blackmail and a game of deception" in its dealings with the Security Council.[25] Iraq was ready to cooperate with the secretary-general in implementing 598. Iran was not. Tariq Aziz asked the Security Council to back up its resolution, to reject Iranian deception, and to use "means provided by the Charter," meaning sanctions, to establish a durable peace.

Pérez de Cuéllar met separately with Khamenei and later with Tariq Aziz. Khamenei told the secretary-general that implementation should begin with informal observance of a cease-fire and establishment of an impartial body of inquiry. That body could quickly complete its first task, identification of the aggressor, and then move on to determine the consequences. When asked if Iran would accept the findings of the body, whatever they were, Khamenei said there was no one who did not know who the aggressor was. If the judgment of the body were not correct, how could it have been impartial?

Tariq Aziz hammered on the need for the "sequential approach," implementing the resolution's paragraphs in strict order, putting the work of an impartial body far back in the implementation process. When briefing the Security Council Pérez de Cuéllar said this divergence raised a fundamental question for the council—whether the terms of the resolution would permit an impartial investigation to be conducted simultaneously with an informal cease-fire.

The first week of the assembly's general debate is an efficient venue for foreign ministers to meet. On 24 September Shultz urged Foreign Minister Shevardnadze and Foreign Minister Wu Xueqian to support an arms embargo against Iran. Although they agreed on the need for "unity" among the permanent members, Shultz made "no headway" in persuading them that the time had already come to adopt sanctions.[26] Shultz later said both were willing to support an arms embargo if further diplomatic efforts by the secretary-general failed to produce a cease-fire.[27]

Each year during this week the secretary-general hosts a luncheon for the foreign ministers of the permanent members. Until 1987 the luncheon was mostly a protocol event, but this year the ministers discussed the Iran-Iraq war. After two hours they authorized the secretary-general, acting on their behalf, to present a statement to the press. This statement was another important sign of diplomatic change, showing that the permanent members intended to work together and to support the secretary-general on this issue. In it the permanent members expressed determination to bring the war to an end and to support 598 as the sole basis for a settlement. They commended the secretary-general for his efforts. Finally they expressed determination to continue cooperation within the Security Council and to work on further steps to ensure compliance with 598.[28]

The Detailed Outline Plan

On 15 October council members, divided on whether and when to adopt sanctions, sidestepped this issue in a paper designed to give guidance for the secretary-general. The paper simply noted "that the outline plan of the Secretary-General envisages on D-day, which should be agreed upon as soon as possible, the observance of the cease-fire and the setting into motion of other necessary elements of the resolution."[29] To prepare for renewed contacts with Iran and Iraq the secretary-general's staff fleshed out the outline plan's suggested time frames and described how provisions of 598 might be implemented. On the key issue of an impartial body, options included entrusting this task to an existing body or to an ad hoc body, for which there were additional questions to settle before it could be set up. Pérez de Cuéllar handed his detailed outline plan, designed to avoid an early deadlock caused by contrary views on timing, to the Iranian and Iraqi ambassadors, and he asked for written responses by 1 November.

From this point on Pérez de Cuéllar had to contend with U.S. pressure that he clarify Iran's position so that there would quickly be either a cease-fire or sanctions against Iran. The Soviet Union countered that repeated clashes between U.S. and Iranian naval forces underscored the need for the United Nations to take over protecting shipping in the gulf.

Iranian forces challenged the U.S. protective regime for Kuwaiti shipping. On 15 October an Iranian missile hit an American-owned tanker in Kuwaiti waters, causing a massive explosion and fire; U.S. officials ruled out retaliation because the vessel was not flying the U.S. flag and was not in international waters.[30] The next day an Iranian missile struck a U.S. flagged vessel in Kuwaiti waters, injuring eighteen crew members. Secretary Shultz urged Kuwait to circulate a letter at the United Nations to report the incident without requesting a meeting of the Security Council.[31] Then, on 19 October, U.S. forces struck back by using naval gunfire to destroy three offshore oil platforms in the lower Persian Gulf that Iran had used as communications and logistic bases for gunboats. Twenty minutes before the shelling, Iranians on the platforms were warned to evacuate. Iran threatened to deliver a "crushing blow" to avenge the shelling.[32]

On 22 October another missile fired from Iranian positions on the Fao peninsula caused heavy damage to Kuwait's main offshore oil terminal. Because China had supplied Iran with Silkworm missiles, the Reagan administration put curbs on the transfer of high technology products to China.[33] When China denied it still sold arms to Iran, the Reagan administration countered that China had recently sent Iran artillery pieces and shells.[34] On 3 November Under Secretary of State Armacost announced that China had told the United States it would try to stop its arms from reaching Iran.[35]

The escalation of tension between the United States and Iran again raised Soviet concerns that the United States might use the collective approach of 598 as a cover for its unilateral military activities. When Secretary of State Shultz visited Moscow in late October to prepare for the December summit in Washington, a TASS report expressed anxiety over the situation ensuing from the attacks on Kuwait.[36] By 31 October Soviet deputy foreign minister Vorontsov, on yet another "peace mission" to Iran and Iraq, criticized the presence of the U.S. Navy, saying that one nation acting alone could not bring about a cease-fire between Iran and Iraq.[37] If the permanent members were "unified" in support of 598, they were still divided over how to induce the parties to implement it.

After receiving the secretary-general's detailed outline plan, Iraq moved to counter what it saw as a pro-Iranian tendency among the secretary-general's staff. On 20 October the *International Herald Tribune* reported that the United Nations was investigating a charge that Iqbal Riza, the UN's senior expert on the Iran-Iraq war, had arranged a meeting at which military information had been passed to two Iranian officials. This information involved computer-enhanced pictures of the border area, including Iraqi fortifications, produced by a company called Ocean Earth Resources. This company had previously tried to sell its product to the United Nations for peacekeeping operations, but the United Nations never entered into an agreement. The meeting between Iranian officials and the company took place in a UN meeting room, without any UN official present.[38] Because this information was based on publicly available satellite pictures and commercially available computer programs, it contained no sensitive military information that Iran could not acquire by other means. Nevertheless, following these allegations, an in-house investigation, and vigorous Iraqi protests, Riza was moved laterally to another job.

On 28 October Tariq Aziz, responding to the detailed outline plan, wrote to the secretary-general. He insisted that the positions of the parties should be judged by their fidelity to the letter and spirit of 598, including the sequence of the paragraphs as a guide to implementation, and stated, "If we review closely the behavior of the Iranian government since the adoption of the resolution on 20 July 1987, we will find, beyond any shadow of doubt, strong indications of Iran's intention to subvert the peace process."

Tariq Aziz developed the Iraqi insistence on a sequential approach. Not only did the paragraphs have to be implemented in order, but the cease-fire and withdrawal would have to take place before other issues could even be discussed: "When the first paragraph has been implemented, discussion can be entered into on the other operative paragraphs in the resolution and how to implement them." He objected to the plan's description of the cease-fire as "a preliminary and provisional step, providing a breathing space for negotiations of more lasting agreements." Iraq insisted that a cease-fire had to be conclusive and lead to a withdrawal completed within ten days. The letter showed impatience that in the three months since 598 was adopted there had been no progress toward a cease-fire.

Velayati's letter of 30 October had a patient tone. The naming of Iraq as the aggressor would be the first step toward a just peace. A date for a cease-fire could be set once there was reasonable progress in the overall negotiations. Withdrawal of forces should be delayed, because Iraq's nullification of the Algiers agreement meant that "internationally recognized boundaries" had to be determined, and withdrawal had to be contingent on payment of reparations and on security guarantees for Iran. It was imperative that the secretary-general include plans to implement operative paragraph 5, the call on other states to avoid actions that might increase tensions. In closing Velayati emphasized that Iran wanted to negotiate on the basis of the secretary-general's plan. "Iran declares its readiness to continue its cooperation and negotiations with Your Excellency. To envisage a D-Day as soon as possible, it is best to try to reach an agreement on the first two steps relating to the responsibility of [sic] the conflict and observance of the cease-fire based upon the understanding with the Secretary-General and proceed with implementation of these two major steps while negotiations continue on other provisions."

While Iraq insisted on a strict, rigid interpretation of 598, Iran was trying to move the negotiations away from 598, with its implied threat of sanctions, toward less structured negotiations over the secretary-general's plan. On 2 November the secretary-general briefed the permanent members, then later briefed the full council in the consultation room. After being encouraged to continue contacts with the parties, Pérez de Cuéllar invited both sides to send emissaries to New York in early December.

Building to a Summit

With no movement toward either a cease-fire or sanctions, the diplomatic process was stalling. On 1 November Speaker Rafsanjani, after criticizing U.S. military and diplomatic activities, said the United Nations was cheating with its own resolution and favoring Iraq.[39] In New York the permanent members' activity had been reduced to consultations among their counselors and with the secretariat staff in search of ideas on how the diplomatic process might recover momentum. Any new impetus would have to come from outside events.

In early November the conservative French paper *Le Figaro* published a Defense Ministry report on arms sales to Iran by the French firm Luchaire in violation of France's arms embargo against Iran. The report's main political victims were President François Mitterrand and Defense Minister Charles Hernu. It alleged that between 1983 and 1986 Luchaire had sold Iran over half a million artillery shells, that Hernu had accepted over $500,000 to look the other way, and that Mitterrand, although he learned of the sales in 1984, did nothing to stop them.[40] On 16 November Mitterrand acknowledged he had been told of the sales in 1984 but said he had tried to stop them. He explained he could not be faulted if they had then continued without his knowledge.[41] Whatever happened in 1984, the impact of the scandal pushed French policy in the same direction as the Iran-Contra scandal pushed U.S. policy—Paris, like Washington, now ardently advocated a UN arms embargo against Iran.

Simultaneously Prime Minister Chirac sponsored negotiations that led to the release of two French hostages in Lebanon on 25 November. The group making the release, the Organization of Revolutionary Justice, claimed France would change its policy of supporting Iraq in the war.[42] Two days later Paris allowed the departure of Wahid Gordji, the translator at the Iranian embassy in Paris.[43] Within a week France expelled seventeen members of the People's Mujahidin, an Iraqi-sponsored Iranian leftist group that opposed Khomeini.[44] President Mitterrand criticized Chirac's government and asked, because France had earlier granted asylum, that the expulsions be justified. Strong British and American criticism followed. Whatever Chirac's deal was with Tehran, French support for an arms embargo against Iran did not flag.

The Arab Summit in Amman from 8 to 11 November condemned Iran for occupying Iraqi territory and for delaying acceptance of 598. The summit declaration "called upon Iran to accept the resolution and to implement it in accordance with the sequence of its operative paragraphs."[45] The declaration supported measures by Saudi Arabia to "ensure a fitting atmosphere in which pilgrims to the Holy Kaaba might perform the rites of the Pilgrimage" and by Kuwait to protect its security. It appealed to the international community to take appropriate measures against Iran (that is to adopt sanctions).

In the weeks leading up to the December Reagan-Gorbachev summit, Washington pressed Moscow on the sanctions issue. Without Moscow's support there was no chance the Security Council would enact an arms embargo against Iran. On 2 November Secretary of Defense Frank C. Carlucci said the United States was disappointed that the Soviet Union was not yet willing to move ahead with an arms embargo.[46] He recalled that on 24 September Shultz and Shevardnadze had agreed on a two-track approach, with action through both the secretary-general's negotiations and the preparation of an arms embargo. Carlucci said that Shevardnadze told Shultz when they met in October that the U.S. naval presence in the gulf violated 598 and caused tensions to rise in the area.[47]

On 25 November Pérez de Cuéllar told council members he was frustrated by delays in arranging talks with Iranian and Iraqi envoys, especially by the delayed arrival of the Iranian side. The next day the *New York Times* reported that Britain, France, and the United States were convinced that Iran was only temporizing and had no intention of agreeing to a date for a cease-fire and that they wanted the secretary-general to say so in order to trigger a Security Council decision to adopt sanctions.[48] The secretary-general's spokesman confirmed Pérez de Cuéllar's sense of frustration over the delay but said he would persevere in his efforts to bring peace.[49]

On 2 and 3 December Pérez de Cuéllar met with the Iranian team led by Deputy Foreign Minister Javad Larijani. The secretary-general asked that discussion concentrate on four elements that could form part of an agreed package: determination of a date for D-Day, achievement of a cease-fire, arrangements for withdrawal, and commencement of the work of the impartial body. There was no "progress" in Iran's position. Iran would cooperate with the secretary-general on the basis of his outline plan (not explicitly accepting 598). The work of the impartial body and an informal cease-fire should begin simultaneously. The impartial body had first to identify the aggressor, a political decision to be taken quickly; then it should determine the consequences, including reparations, a judicial process that could take longer. Because the identity of the aggressor was a known fact, the secretary-general could determine the composition of the impartial body. As for withdrawal, first the borders would have to be determined, which could be done after reparations had been settled. Finally, Iran asked the secretary-general to ensure respect for paragraph 5, which called on outside parties to practice the utmost restraint.

Shortly after these talks the secretary-general briefed the U.S. and Soviet ambassadors so that they could inform ministers making final preparations for the Washington summit, at which senior officials would discuss regional conflicts, including Afghanistan and the Iran-Iraq war, before similar discussions between Reagan and Gorbachev. In Moscow's first reaction President Gromyko told the Iranian ambassador, "You as an ambassador and the Iranian leadership made a great number of statements about the wish to end the war. But the war goes on. Iran is practically not carrying matters toward ending the war." Then, after citing resolution 598, Gromyko warned that the question of enforcing 598 might be put on the Security Council's agenda.[50]

On 7 and 8 December Pérez de Cuéllar met an Iraqi delegation headed by Tariq Aziz and Ambassador Kittani. Tariq Aziz insisted that 598 be accepted both as an integrated whole and in its separate parts without equivocation, reservation, or condition. Implementation should be sequential, especially of the first three paragraphs. On the question of withdrawal, the boundaries were adequately settled by the treaties, agreements, and protocols of 1847, 1913, 1937, and 1975. Apparently, for Tariq Aziz the land boundaries were adequately defined; whether the boundary was in the *thalweg* or on the eastern bank of the Shatt would have no impact on lines for withdrawal.

On 10 December the secretary-general briefed council members. After the council's consultations he told the press:

> I will just direct to you a statement which actually contains the gist of what I have told to the Security Council after having given to them in a very precise, detailed manner, the positions of the two sides. Well, what I can tell you is that I have just informed the Members of the Security Council of my recent discussions with Iranian and Iraqi officials. My conclusion is, that at the moment a fresh and resolute impulse by the Council is needed. . . . I said also that I was ready to work together with the Council on this. The determination of the Security Council to stand by its own resolution is essential if respect is to be maintained for the authority of the Council on which the repute of the Organization and the well-being of the international community depend.

The Moment Slips Away

Although Reagan and Gorbachev discussed regional conflicts, particularly Afghanistan, at the Washington summit, there was no agreement on sanctions against Iran. The final communiqué characterized these discussions as "frank and businesslike."

> The two leaders noted the increasing importance of settling regional conflicts to reduce international tensions and to improve East-West relations. They agreed that the goal of the dialogue between the United States and the Soviet Union on these issues should be to help the parties to regional conflicts find peaceful solutions that advance their independence, freedom and security. Both leaders emphasized the importance of enhancing the capacity of the United Nations to contribute to the resolution of regional conflicts.[51]

Reagan made a special point of these talks in his departure remarks.

> The General Secretary and I expressed different points of view—we did so bluntly—and for that reason alone, our talks have been useful in this area. . . . The door has been opened and it will stay open to serious discussion of ending these regional conflicts.[52]

After the summit Assistant Secretary Murphy spoke at the Middle East Institute in Washington. He explained that a key element of U.S. strategy toward the war was to preserve the unity of the Security Council, particularly its permanent members, because a "successful effort by the Five to end this war would have far-reaching implications for crisis management around the world." U.S. patience, however, was limited. "We need to move now to maintain the credibility of the United Nations and its role in promoting world peace. The Soviets proclaim their desire that the United Nations assume a more central role in world affairs. This argues for joining together, now, to enforce the Council's mandate and help restore a measure of peace to this critical area of the world, where tensions are rising."

Murphy criticized Soviet diplomacy:

> Some have pointed to the Soviet Union's diplomatic activities with both parties, and concluded that the U.S. has been shunted off to the side. This is a facile and erroneous interpretation of events. As they pursue their diplomacy in Tehran and Baghdad, the Soviets mix cooperation and political gain. Regrettably, they have sought to exploit the situation in the Gulf by asserting that our presence in the region violates the terms of Resolution 598. The problem is the Iran-Iraq war, not our naval presence in the Gulf. Afghanistan and the Gulf war are high priority regional issues we confront together with the Soviets. We want to work in a cooperative manner. But it simply does not accord with the facts to seek to identify the U.S. as the catalyst for tensions in the Gulf.

Murphy confirmed that discussions at the Summit were inconclusive:

> The Soviet position did not develop beyond contentions that Iran deserves more time, that voluntary compliance by Iran with 598 remains possible, and that a "real" force should be established by the UN to implement 598. We believe these Soviet positions reflect continuing Soviet efforts to play this issue both ways: avoiding actions in the UN which would sour Soviet-Iranian relations while doing just enough to blunt the increasing criticism of the Arab states directed at Moscow. . . . Iran's unwillingness last week to accept 598 as drafted should make clear to those who said they needed more evidence that now is the time to move on the second resolution. The President has emphasized this point to General Secretary Gorbachev.

Murphy torpedoed the preferred Soviet project for follow-on action to 598, setting up a UN Naval force. "The Soviets have championed a UN naval presence—alleging that U.S. and allied navies are somehow the cause of tensions in the area. We, like the Arab states and most members of the Council, understand that the Iran-Iraq war, not foreign navies in the Gulf, is at the root of tensions. Debating the pros and cons of UN reflagging or protection only serves to divert attention from the real need of the hour, early passage of a follow-on enforcement resolution."

As for China, Murphy said Under Secretary of State Armacost, in his recent visit to Beijing, had stressed that Iranian use of the Chinese Silkworm missiles could affect the bilateral relations between the United States and China, after which China had taken measures to strictly control the export of Silkworms. "The Chinese leadership is aware of how serious a matter it is when Chinese-supplied missiles are used to attack U.S. flag ships and otherwise to threaten the freedom of navigation in a vital waterway."

A week after the summit Moscow answered the U.S. request for support of a UN arms embargo against Iran. The Soviet Union attached considerable importance to maintaining the unity of the permanent members of the Security Council as the most important element in the UN efforts to achieve a settlement of the war. Therefore Ambassador Belonogov, now the Security Council president, would seek council approval of a statement in response to the secretary-general's call for "a fresh and resolute impulse." Moscow would authorize Belonogov to discuss with other permanent members provisions to include in a resolution imposing an arms embargo. While not a commitment to support adoption of an arms embargo, for the first time since July the Soviet side was willing to discuss this subject.

Ambassador Belonogov's consultations for a council statement were unhurried. On 24 December he read out a text expressing "concern over the slow pace and lack of real progress" in the negotiations with Iran and Iraq. In declaring council members' determination to consider steps to ensure compliance with 598 his text merely hinted that the permanent members would start negotiations on an arms embargo. Belonogov insisted to ambassadors of the other permanent members that their talks include parallel consideration of both a UN naval force, as proposed by the Soviet Union, and an arms embargo, as desired by Britain, France, and the United States.

10

Peacekeeping or Sanctions

New Thinking

The work on resolution 598 generated a rebirth of interest in the United Nations and led naturally to proposals for a UN force to protect international civilian shipping in the gulf. As early as June 1987, the *New York Times* published a letter from Representative Tom Downey of New York proposing that the United Nations play such a role, permitting the United States to avoid a unilateral commitment to do so. In the next three months Cyrus R. Vance, former secretary of state, and Elliot L. Richardson, former secretary of defense, developed these ideas, which were then espoused by the Soviet Union.

During the first half of 1987 the Reagan administration had justified the growing U.S. naval presence in the gulf on two grounds: to help Kuwait counter Iranian intimidation and discourage attempts against other GCC members; and "to limit, to the extent possible, an increase in Soviet military presence and influence in the Gulf."[1] Thus in a 15 June 1987 report, Secretary of Defense Weinberger stated, "During the past four years . . . the Soviets have skillfully exploited opportunities to play on the anxieties of these moderate states and to press for increased diplomatic, commercial and military relations. They have steadily pursued an irresponsible campaign of propaganda, contending that the United States seeks only to establish a permanent military presence in the Gulf, creating doubts about our commitment to the stability of the regional states and about our objectives in the region."[2]

When Under Secretary of State Armacost testified before the Senate Foreign Relations Committee on 16 June, he warned that the Iran-Iraq war had created opportunities for the Soviet Union to play on the anxieties of the GCC states to press for commercial, diplomatic, and military relations. He rejected an "international regime" to protect shipping because it could provide cover for the Soviet Union to legitimize a long-term military presence in the gulf. "The best way for the United States and the U.S.S.R. to collaborate in our stated common interest to end the war is through the work currently being undertaken in the Security Council. We challenge the Soviets to work with us in this important endeavor."[3]

U.S. allies made parallel deployments on a national basis. In August 1987, after Iran mined the Gulf of Oman, Britain announced it would send four 615-ton Hunt class minesweepers to join a destroyer, two frigates, and a supply ship. France said it would send three minesweepers and a support ship to join the carrier *Clemenceau* and two destroyers and a supply ship just outside the gulf.[4] On 3 September Italy decided to send ships on a national basis, after which Belgium and the Netherlands announced they would each send two minesweepers.[5] The Italian group of eight ships sailed on 15 September. By early October the Europeans had announced deployment of thirty-five ships. On 27 October Kuwait announced the registration of three of its shuttle tankers under the British flag.[6] Although allied navies officially operated under national commands, in practice they relied on their experience at coordinated operations gained while working together during NATO exercises.

The Soviet Navy had escorted Soviet merchant vessels since the boarding of a Soviet ship by Iranian forces in September 1986. Since 1 April 1987, when Kuwait and the Soviet Union agreed on a formal charter arrangement that covered three tankers plus two that could be available on short notice,[7] Iranian forces had attacked the *Ivan Korotoyev,* a cargo ship en route from Kuwait to Saudi Arabia via Dubai, on 7 May; and on 16 May an Iranian mine had hit the *Marshal Chuykov,* one of the three leased tankers, in what appeared to be a deliberate, planned attack.[8] Alexander Ivanov, head of the gulf section of the Soviet Foreign Ministry, warned that the Soviet Union would respond with all means available under international law in response to any attack on a Soviet vessel, particularly in international waters.[9] In June 1987 the Soviet presence included (in the gulf, northern Arabian Sea, Gulf of Aden, and southern Red Sea) a Kara cruiser, a Kashin class destroyer, three minesweepers, and several support ships.[10]

On 8 July Vance and Richardson published in the *New York Times* an article entitled "Let the U.N. Reflag Gulf Vessels."[11] They argued that their proposal would "achieve the aim of protecting innocent passage while substantially reducing the risk of stumbling into an unwanted war." For the Soviet Union it would reduce the dangers of increased U.S. deployments and pressure by the United States for bases. The authors thought Kuwait would benefit from international protection without overt dependence on either the United States or the Soviet Union, that Iran would cooperate because its shipping could be protected, and that Iraq would go along because the United Nations offered the best opportunity of bringing the war to an end.

Vance and Richardson suggested a Security Council resolution to "authorize seafaring United Nations peace-keepers to place a United Nations flag on vessels entering the Gulf that asked a United Nations guarantee of safe passage and that submitted to United Nations inspection to insure that no war materiel was on board." Ships flying the UN flag could ask for an escort from either an unarmed UN patrol boat or a naval vessel from a state authorized by the Security Council. "The guiding principle of the United Nations reflagging plan is diplomatic deterrence, which is likely to be more effective than military deterrence furnished by a nervous super-power."

A week later Vance and Richardson discussed their proposal with Secretary Shultz. Taking into account the mandatory cease-fire order to be included in resolution 598, they explained that their proposal was consistent with U.S. strategy. In addition, UN observers could monitor a cease-fire and inspect vessels to ensure no military cargoes were being shipped through the gulf, and the reflagging proposal could be implemented simultaneously. Shultz answered politely that, if the United Nations helped resolve the gulf war, its success could lead to positive steps elsewhere.

On 14 August Vance wrote to Pérez de Cuéllar. The adoption on 20 July of 598, with its implicit threat of sanctions, had changed the situation. Vance now said that among the goals of the proposal were to lessen risks of an Iranian-American confrontation, to spur the peace process aimed at ending the war, and to make it easier for commercial vessels to transit the gulf. The key lay in connecting the effects of a cease-fire on land (favored by Iraq) with that of a cease-fire at sea (favored by Iran):

- The UN reflagging service could be limited to vessels going to or from nonbelligerent ports or ports of a belligerent in compliance with the cease-fire provision of 598.
- If the United Nations adopted an arms embargo against a party not complying with the cease-fire order of 598, whether on land or at sea, the UN inspectors could check vessels bound for the belligerents or their neighbors for war materiel.
- Because any UN peacekeeping role at sea would be vulnerable in the absence of progress toward an end to the war, the Security Council should have to review the mandate frequently.

Vance wrote to Secretary of Defense Weinberger to explain that, following traditional UN practice, neither U.S. nor Soviet forces would directly participate in the peacekeeping operation, thus avoiding an opening for an enlarged Soviet presence. Addressing Weinberger's concerns, Vance warned that one potential result of the large-scale U.S. naval deployment could be to provide a pretext for a larger Soviet presence and expanded Soviet economic and political ties with Iran. Vance urged, as he had with the secretary-general, that efforts to secure a cease-fire at sea were needed to balance the emphasis on a cease-fire on land.

In each explanation the fundamental concept was from the model of peacekeeping—an operation based on the consent of the parties responsible for maintaining a cease-fire. It would not require invoking the mandatory authorities of chapter VII. Vance and Richardson expressed confidence that, even without a general cease-fire, the parties would hesitate to attack vessels enjoying UN diplomatic protection. Obviously, they were counting on unspoken, implicit consent from Iran and Iraq to be enough of a basis for the operation. Deterrence was the essence of this proposal; that of the U.S. reflagging operation was deterrence plus protection.

On 17 September 1987 the Soviet press published an article signed by Gorbachev entitled "Reality and Safeguards for a Secure World."[12] Gorbachev laid out the new Soviet thinking on the United Nations and its role in the international system, setting the parameters for Soviet diplomacy at the United Nations.

The contrast with Soviet policy and performance from the Azerbaijan crisis to the recent past was startling. Now, "the world community cannot stand aside from inter-State conflicts."[13] Wider use should be made of UN peacekeeping forces both to separate troops involved in fighting and to monitor cease-fires and truce agreements. The permanent members should act as "guarantors" of regional security and pledge themselves to refrain from "the use or threat of force and from conspicuous displays of military strength."[14] Citing the extensive powers given by the charter to the Security Council, most of which had never been used, he asked for efforts to ensure that these powers could be used effectively. "A sensible step for this purpose would be to hold, when the next session of the General Assembly opens, a meeting of the Security Council at the level of ministers for foreign affairs to review the international situation and engage in a joint search for effective ways of improving it."[15]

On 23 September Foreign Minister Shevardnadze developed these themes before the General Assembly: "Peace should be ensured exclusively by the United Nations and its Security Council on the basis of strict observance of the principles and provisions of its Charter."[16] Turning to the Persian Gulf, Shevardnadze warned of the dangers of a massive foreign military presence. "The greater the military presence, the higher the probability of yet another conflict and the involvement in it of a State not belonging to the region."[17]

On 16 December Secretary Shultz offered his own thinking on a UN naval force. When a journalist asked about reports that the Soviet Union had linked agreement on sanctions against Iran to creation of a UN naval force, Shultz responded that he had heard there was now a readiness to work on a mandatory embargo of arms shipments to Iran. After acknowledging that the Soviet position included a parallel resolution on enforcement of the embargo, apparently by a naval force, Shultz said the place to start was with the embargo. If, in accordance with a mandatory embargo, all states refused to ship arms to Iran, and particularly if the permanent members of the Security Council persuaded their friends and allies to work for an effective embargo, it would be effective.[18]

Shultz distinguished a peacekeeping force from a force overseeing an arms embargo. A peacekeeping force would be appropriate if both parties had accepted 598 and were committed to a cease-fire. It would be deployed on the land border; probably not much of a naval presence would be required for peacekeeping, and naval forces in the area would decline. But as long as Iran rejected resolution 598, Shultz insisted that the concept of a peacekeeping force was not relevant. There was simply no basis of consent for peacekeeping. As for the idea of a naval blockade to enforce an arms embargo, "you would have to have a land blockade as well as a naval blockade." After ruling this out Shultz repeated that the way to start was by agreeing on mandatory sanctions.

The Soviet Proposal for a UN Naval Force

By January 1988, months had passed since interest had peaked in Washington over reflagging and the Vance-Richardson proposals. When the Soviet proposal came, it was too little, too late.

When the permanent members regrouped to resume discussions on sanctions, Shevardnadze had already insisted with Shultz that the talks follow "parallel tracks." The Soviet delegation would consider an arms embargo if the other permanent members engaged in talks of equal status on a UN naval force. This dual agenda was agreed on. Because France, Britain, and the United States rejected any implication that agreement on a UN naval force was needed before action on an arms embargo, they insisted that discussion of the two items be totally separate. The counselors would meet first to discuss either the arms embargo or the naval force, then adjourn for ten minutes and reconvene to discuss the other item in a "separate" meeting.

Because the Soviet Union was the only permanent member that wanted to establish a UN naval force, the Soviet delegation had to put forward ideas for discussion. Other delegations merely reacted. In comparison with the enormously complicated practical arrangements such a force would require, the preliminary points put forward by the Soviets were surprisingly sketchy. Their proposal, unlike that of Vance and Richardson but like that for U.S. forces, assumed the force would include combat vessels and operate in a hostile environment. Britain, France, and the United States maneuvered to kill this proposal by insisting on answers to difficult but necessary questions. China took no active role in the discussions.

The Soviet proposal described the mission of a UN naval force as ensuring the safety of commercial navigation in international waters and passage to gulf state ports. The Soviet counselor offered no answers to the questions and doubts expressed, nor did Moscow provide responses for subsequent meetings. Would all commercial vessels be protected, even those of belligerents? Would a belligerent who refused the cease-fire of 598 still receive protection? Would all ships be protected, without regard to their cargo? Would the protection regime cover ships in the "exclusion zones" declared by Iran and Iraq? Would all Iranian ports be covered? How could the United Nations ensure safety of passage to Iraqi ports, including Basra,

Fao, and Umm Qasr? Would the Shatt be considered an international waterway for the purposes of this force?

The proposal was vague on the composition of the force, whether its units would be more like the unarmed patrol boats flying the UN flag to escort commercial vessels of the Vance-Richardson proposal or more like the Western navies, using combat vessels. The force would be comprised of "naval" vessels provided by interested states; the number would be reasonably sufficient to carry out its assigned mission; and the vessels would be of types suitable for escorting ships and carrying out other necessary operations, such as minesweeping. Would the permanent members, some of whom normally did not contribute forces to UN peacekeeping operations, participate? If not, how many other states could provide the vessels required?

The Soviet proposal grappled unsuccessfully with the question of financing. Peacekeeping forces, except for the operation on Cyprus, are paid for by all member states through assessed contributions. There are no special charges on the countries where the forces operate or on those who benefit from the operation. To keep down costs the United Nations pays a flat rate per soldier, whether from a high-cost or low-cost country; and equipment (which does not include high-technology items) is leased at a set rate from troop contributors. Naval vessels, especially modern ones capable of operating in a hostile environment, are enormously more expensive than motorized patrols and soldiers for observation posts. The Soviets suggested that costs be borne by the states providing the escort vessels and by charges on users of the sea routes, including states, commercial shipping companies, and insurers. They had no estimate of the required size or composition of the force or of its cost. Nor had they any scheme to demonstrate the consequences of apportioning costs as they proposed.

The most difficult aspects of operating a UN naval force would be, first, command and control, and second, rules of engagement. A national force has established patterns for command and control; peacekeeping forces operate in basically nonhostile environments where command-and-control structures are rarely under great pressure. A naval force operating in a hostile environment needs a system of command and control able to respond to such threats as being locked onto by a missile radar system. Units from different navies would have to act in coordination, but various national units might speak different languages and have incompatible communications gear. The secretary-general would have to name a commander and provide him with a staff able to carry out necessary coordination.

On the crucial question of rules of engagement the Soviet proposal indicated only that the UN naval force would have the right to self-defense. As evident from two cases involving the U.S. Navy—the attack on the USS *Stark* and the later downing of the civilian airliner Iran Air 655—even a unified national force can interpret specific rules of engagement differently on separate occasions. The final, inadequate Soviet response to British,

French, and U.S. questions was simply an additional point stating that the Security Council would resolve these questions.

The Soviet Union dropped its proposal for a UN naval force by March 1988, but it still opposed the U.S. naval presence in the gulf. A year later, on 25 February 1989, during a trip to Cairo, Shevardnadze said, "We have few ships there and are ready to withdraw them as of tomorrow and hope the Americans will follow suit." By that time the number of U.S. naval vessels in the gulf area had dropped to fourteen.[19]

Aiming for an Arms Embargo

From the start of talks among the permanent members in January 1987, the United States had wanted the Security Council to impose an arms embargo against Iran. The first step would be a mandatory resolution under chapter VII ordering a cease-fire and withdrawal. If Iran did not comply, the council should then take enforcement action. Before the council adopted 598, General Walters was unable to secure from the other permanent members a commitment to move quickly to an arms embargo; but soon afterward, in July and August 1987, the counselors reviewed drafts for an arms embargo resolution.

These drafts prepared the ground for the resumption of negotiations at the start of 1988. One July draft would have simply decided in its first operative paragraph that all states stop all trade in arms and related materials of all types with the sanctioned country. This version contained optional provisions in brackets to set up a Security Council committee to monitor compliance with the embargo. The definition of the embargo's scope borrowed from the language in Security Council resolution 418 (barring arms trade with South Africa), and the monitoring committee came from resolution 421 (set up to monitor the South African arms embargo).

A second July draft added three provisions. First, to specify the relationship between the cease-fire order and the enforcement action, a second operative paragraph began with the determination that "I—" had failed to comply with resolution 598. Another provision indicated that the embargo would apply "notwithstanding" previous contractual obligations. The British delegation insisted on the third change. During the endgame in the Rhodesian negotiations, Prime Minister Thatcher's cabinet had worried that, even if the Lancaster House talks between Her Majesty's government and the Rhodesian parties were successful, one permanent member (perhaps the Soviet Union) could block repeal of Rhodesian sanctions by a Security Council veto. Thus a new bracketed provision stated that, unless 598 was complied with sooner, the sanctions would remain in force for an initial period of one year, subject to renewal by the Security Council.

The next working paper, from early August, identified Iran as not complying with 598. Otherwise it repeated the July draft, merely expanding the embargo's scope to include licensing or other support for manufactur-

ing arms and military supplies and adding a paragraph barring cooperation in the manufacture and development of nuclear weapons (to parallel
a similar provision enacted against South Africa).

To restart negotiations the British produced an "elements paper" based
on the July and August texts. The British paper stated that an arms embargo would be applied against the party (unspecified) not complying with
598. Explanatory points indicated that the resolution should follow the
precedent of the South African arms embargo wherever possible; that the
embargo should cover arms and military equipment, plus technology or
equipment used to manufacture arms; and that military training could be
barred. There were provisions for a ban on cooperation that might assist
development of nuclear weapons, for a committee to monitor compliance,
and for a time limit on the sanctions, subject to renewal.

Negotiations

Pérez de Cuéllar's 10 December statement calling on the council to provide
a "fresh and resolute impulse" had in effect declared time out for his own
efforts in order to put pressure on council members to break the diplomatic
deadlock. On 4 January 1988 he met with Iraqi ambassador Kittani and on
5 January with Iranian ambassador Mohammad Ja'afar Mahallati. While he
wanted to maintain close contact with both, he told them he did not intend
to undertake another round of talks without assurances that consultations
would produce progress. He appealed to both for flexibility to overcome
the impasse he had described to the council on 10 December.

By the second week of January the counselors were alternating discussions between an arms embargo resolution and the Soviet proposal for a
UN naval force. By 17 January they prepared an elements paper to inform
their ambassadors. This paper had no formal backing from capitals and
therefore implied no commitment on the substance.

On 19 January Ambassador Mahallati, just back from Tehran, gave Pérez
de Cuéllar a letter from Foreign Minister Velayati. Velayati criticized the
secretary-general's 10 December statement because it failed to indicate that
"it is indeed Iraq which has presented unreasonable demands in an effort
to impede further progress in the negotiations. Iraq's insistence on implementing only the first three paragraphs without giving credence to the
essential [operative paragraphs] contradicts the 'integrated whole' character of the Resolution and rejects the foundations of the proposed outline
plan."[20] Velayati claimed that almost all council members rejected Iraq's
sabotage and procrastination.

Velayati said Iran accepted the position endorsed by the Security Council—that implementation of the resolution could begin with a cease-fire
and the beginning of work of the impartial body. The slow pace in progress
toward implementation of the plan was a consequence of Iraq's position.
"Only negative and destructive attitudes towards your implementation

plan should establish the criteria for further measures by the Council," he argued.[21] Iran was ready to meet with the secretary-general at any time and place. In conclusion, Velayati said the intervention of foreign naval forces in the gulf made the situation worse and hindered prospects for an early settlement based on the secretary-general's plan. Iran would welcome any proposal to guarantee the safety of all civilian and commercial shipping in the gulf.

On 20 January Sir Crispin Tickell, then council president but still serving as ambassadorial coordinator for the permanent members and their spokesman, briefed the council on the permanent members' discussions. He reported that, after the presidential statement of 24 December, one permanent member had proposed elements for a draft resolution to impose an arms embargo on the party not complying with 598. Such a resolution would define the scope of the embargo, provide for a monitoring committee, and suggest a time limit.[22] Among points made by other permanent members (i.e., not Britain), he said, were the need to specify now that Iran was the party not in compliance and to call again for efforts to seek a political settlement within the framework of 598. As a separate matter he reported that one permanent member proposed the creation of a UN naval force. Its task would be to ensure the safety of commercial shipping by escorting commercial ships of nonbelligerents and by minesweeping. Vessels for the force could be provided by interested states. Other elements included the number and type of vessels and the means of financing the force. Sir Crispin solicited no reaction to his statement.

On 23 January Iraqi foreign minister Tariq Aziz sent a letter to the secretary-general. He explained that Iraq welcomed resolution 598 and treated it as a binding resolution not subject to "bargaining, fragmentation, or selective application."[23] He pointed out that members of the Security Council knew that Iran had rejected the resolutions of the Security Council and heaped abuse on the council, indulging in prevarication since 598 was adopted, and that Iran had selected the paragraphs out of order and had given to them interpretations not in accordance with the customs of the United Nations. While reaffirming Iraq's readiness to cooperate in good faith to implement the resolution, he warned that Iraq could not accept arrangements inconsistent with the text and spirit of the resolution that would only give Iran opportunities to continue the war.

On 25 January Pérez de Cuéllar met separately with Mahallati and Kittani to ask if their governments wanted to share with him any additional views before he would brief the council in a few days. Three days later Ambassador Mahallati came back with a message: Iran would like to receive, from both the secretary-general and the Security Council, a clear indication of what was expected from it and what Iran could expect in return. Iran had already shown considerable flexibility on 598, and apart from insisting that the cease-fire and the process for determining responsibility for the aggression begin at the same time, Iran had no rigid position on Pérez de Cuéllar's plan. Since the presidential statement on 24 December Iran had shown flexibility; but Iraq, he said, had shown only intransigence, insisting on sequential implementation of 598, a point unacceptable to Iran. The attempt by some members to have the council adopt enforcement measures could cut off the ability of the secretary-general to explore Iran's flexibility. Iran believed the criteria for considering enforcement measures should be the attitudes of the two sides toward the secretary-general's plan.

On 29 January the secretary-general briefed the council. He would study the contacts he already had and keep open channels of communication with the two sides, keeping the council president informed. In other words he still wanted the council to produce its own resolute step before he resumed negotiations.

General Walters became council president on 1 February. Washington wanted Walters to use his presidency to move the arms embargo resolution forward. The council presidency confers on an ambassador numerous tactical advantages, such as proposing the format, timing, and agenda for meetings. The president learns firsthand the positions of the parties, the intentions of the secretary-general, and the views of council members. However, when acting as president, an ambassador removes his national "hat" and acts officially on behalf of the council's membership. Despite many advantages, he needs members' support to make anything happen. Throughout February, Moscow kept a sanctions resolution off the council's agenda.

Ambassador Kittani maintained the practice of meeting at the beginning of each month with the council president to exchange views and to register Iraqi concerns. By 1988 the Iranian ambassadors had adopted a similar practice, even though Iran still boycotted council meetings; but Ambassador Mahallati would not meet with a U.S. ambassador serving as council president. General Walters, who throughout a long career earned a reputation as a diplomat adept at maintaining contact with all sides, considered Ambassador Mahallati's refusal to meet with him, even after other council members urged Mahallati to do so, not just a breach of diplomatic etiquette but also an affront to the role of the council. Walters saw this refusal to be consistent with Iran's picking and choosing which actions of the council to approve and which to reject. As council president and U.S. ambassador, Walters insisted 598 was a comprehensive basis for resolving the dispute, the provisions of which could not be selected à la carte.

On 1 February Kittani's deputy, Ambassador Ali Sumaida, sent to the secretary-general a riposte to Iran's latest position. Sumaida said there was no doubt that Iraq accepted 598 and the secretary-general's plan, on the understanding that it followed the sequence of the operative paragraphs of 598. Iran was practicing trickery in trying to separate 598 from the implementation plan in order to obscure Iran's categorical rejection of 598. By demanding to know what the council expects of Iran and what Iran can expect in return, Iran showed that it did not accept 598 as binding. Before the secretary-general initiated new contacts, Sumaida suggested the Security Council send a letter to Iran asking that an authoritative official provide a direct answer to the question "Does Iran unreservedly and unconditionally accept Security Council resolution 598?"[24]

There seemed to be some change in the Soviet position. In January Secretary Shultz had criticized the Soviets for stalling on an arms embargo resolution, in part by insisting on parallel action to set up a UN naval force.[25] The Saudi foreign minister, Prince Saud al-Faisal, visited Moscow with Prince Bandar ibn Sultan, the Saudi ambassador in Washington; they met with President Gromyko and Foreign Minister Shevardnadze.[26] By the end of January, the discussions of a UN naval force had already come up against the complications that would soon bring these talks to an unproductive halt.[27] On 6 February an official of the Supreme Soviet, Gaibnazar Pallayev, on a visit to Baghdad, said the representative of the Soviet Union at the United Nations would work to impose an arms embargo on the party that did not agree to end the war.[28]

During the first half of February the counselors' group turned the January elements paper into a sanctions resolution ready to present to other council members. Working from a British draft, by the third week of the month they produced a full text, still without commitments from capitals. The draft included a determination that Iran had failed to comply with resolution 598, provisions for an embargo and monitoring committee, and a two-year period of validity for the sanctions. On 20 February the permanent members shared this text with other council members. Britain, France, and the United States wanted, following the procedure used with resolution 598, to present the draft as an agreed initiative, to open consultations, to elicit the views of others, to amend the draft as required to secure the broadest possible support, and to put the revised text to a vote. China and the Soviet Union were willing to have the text given to others, but without any implication that their governments endorsed it. The text was shared, but with the introduction that it represented the current stage of the permanent members' discussions, that they wanted to inform others of the text, and that they would welcome comments. Other members quickly understood there was no agreement, and not one of them provided substantive comments. Again the effort stalled.

Shultz was in Moscow from 21 to 23 February. He discussed the Iran-Iraq war with Shevardnadze, with Gorbachev, and again with Shevardnadze in a tête-à-tête. By the end of Shultz's visit it was understood that the Soviets in New York would cooperate to secure adoption of an arms embargo against Iran during the remaining week of February. But Shevardnadze asked, and Shultz agreed, that the draft have two amendments. The coming into force of the embargo should be delayed for a period of thirty to sixty days from the date the resolution was adopted. If diplomacy were able to achieve compliance with 598 during this period, the sanctions would not come into effect. An unusual provision for a UN resolution, the delay mechanism was consistent with the theory that sanctions served only to back up diplomatic efforts to secure compliance rather than to punish Iran.

The second provision created more difficulty. Shevardnadze wanted a special emissary, appointed by the secretary-general, who would devote his full energies to achieving a cease-fire. Pérez de Cuéllar had reason to be cool toward this idea. It implied the impasse to date was due, at least in part, to the fact that the secretary-general did not devote himself full-time to talks with Iran and Iraq either because he had other duties or because he had decided to interrupt his efforts to spur the Security Council to consider sanctions. There was no evidence to suggest that more meetings with the parties would have produced more progress.

The immediate impact of appointing a special emissary would have been to block consideration of sanctions. Moreover, any special emissary would want a fair chance to succeed, and this would require time. He would oppose actions, such as the enforcement of sanctions, that might complicate an already difficult task. Pérez de Cuéllar, who had already determined that, unless the parties were more flexible, diplomatic contacts alone would not bear fruit, would have to support a more active diplomatic process than he thought appropriate. Some council members, inclined to defer any action that might complicate efforts of a new special representative, could be counted on to oppose sanctions as long as there was any diplomatic activity.

Endgame

On 28 February, before the deal struck in Moscow became a text in New York, Foreign Minister Velayati wrote again to the secretary-general. He said Iraq's insistence on sequential implementation was evidence that Iraq had rejected the secretary-general's efforts to implement 598. In contrast, Iran's acceptance of his plan was "tantamount to the acceptance of Resolution 598 for which the 'outline plan' remains the only available avenue of implementation."[29] Iran concurred with the secretary-general that the key to implementation was the cease-fire and determination of responsibility for aggression, and Velayati urged the secretary-general to put forth his own concrete formula on these points now.

Velayati said the Security Council should have taken binding punitive measures against Iraq when it committed aggression against Iran. Now it should concern itself with Iraqi intransigence and procrastination. Efforts to engage the council in actions against Iran would only sabotage the secretary-general's efforts. Instead the international community should be reminded that Iraq launched the first major military operation after the adoption of 598 and that Iraq had recently resumed attacks against purely residential areas in Iran.

Late on 3 March, Ambassador Mahallati met with Yugoslav ambassador

Dragoslav Pejic, the next council president, to ask that he inform the council of Iran's position, which he wrote down on an unsigned note. The note said: "You are well-aware of our flexibility for the implementation of Resolution 598. The recent letter of the Foreign Minister removed the last excuse for preventing the implementation of the plan of the Secretary General. The letter of Foreign Minister Velayati explicitly declares that Iran has accepted Resolution 598." The United States considered that this statement was a further ploy to block an embargo; the Soviet Union considered it a significant justification for not imposing an arms embargo.[30]

Meanwhile the political counselors, working from the February arms embargo text already shared with council members, added a clause expressing support for having the secretary-general appoint a special representative. Another addition asked the secretary-general to undertake urgent consultations with the parties and to report by 30 March. A third amendment indicated that the embargo would go into effect on 1 April. Taken together, these three changes reflected the agreement reached by Shultz and Shevardnadze.[31]

The February and March texts were the closest the United States would get to agreement on a UN arms embargo against Iran. From time to time the counselors would review the draft, and after the 1 April deadline passed, they dropped the thirty-day trigger mechanism. Driven by the impact of new Iraqi initiatives on the battlefield, the tide began to run out on the effort to use the powers of chapter VII to secure a cease-fire.

PART THREE

A New Era

IN THE SPRING OF 1988 it became evident the Security Council would not adopt sanctions against Iran, despite its refusal to comply with the mandatory cease-fire of resolution 598. Iraq renewed air attacks against Iranian cities, drove Iranian forces out of the Fao peninsula, and used chemical weapons—all actions that made sanctions against Iran seem less necessary or justified to many council members. In several clashes the U.S. Navy destroyed Iran's navy. The Soviet Union sidetracked the permanent members' preparation of an enforcement resolution, and then China, after a clash with the United States over Chinese arms sales, announced it would not support sanctions. Without any action by the council to enforce resolution 598, the secretary-general's negotiations with Iran and Iraq made no progress.

On 3 July the USS *Vincennes* shot down an Iranian civilian airliner. Iran, for the first time since the Iran-Iraq war began, brought a complaint to the Security Council. Pérez de Cuéllar urged both sides not to use the public debate to sharpen the sense of conflict, and in the debate both Foreign Minister Velayati and Vice President Bush avoided polemics. While the council president was brokering a resolution with both sides, Iran, pressed by the Iraqi army advancing into Iranian territory, accepted a cease-fire. Before the guns fell silent Pérez de Cuéllar had to secure agreements on a peacekeeping force and on the format for negotiations to implement other provisions of 598. Even if the council had not taken enforcement measures to back up its own resolution, the procedures for collaboration among the permanent members had proved their worth.

Over the next two years the permanent members practiced this new habit of cooperation. Their foreign ministers used the annual meeting with the secretary-general for frank discussions on resolving regional conflicts. After the United States, with support from the Soviet Union, arranged for agreements to prepare the way for Namibia's independence, the permanent members worked together in negotiations to launch the UN operation in Namibia, maintaining their cohesion even when confronting the council's nonaligned caucus. They cooperated in the Central American peace process. They began a long and difficult process to end the civil war in Cambodia. They gave little attention, however, to the unfinished business between

Iran and Iraq, and in the first half of 1990 Iraq opened direct bilateral talks with Iran, diminishing the secretary-general's role.

The Security Council's reaction to Iraq's invasion of Kuwait on 2 August 1990 showed just how much diplomacy had changed. Led by the permanent members, the council in quick succession adopted mandatory resolutions demanding Iraqi withdrawal, establishing comprehensive sanctions, and authorizing the use of force to enforce the sanctions. Close contacts between the United States and the Soviet Union, including a summit between Presidents Bush and Gorbachev, paved the way. The Security Council finally used the range of authorities given to it by the charter's chapter VII to manage a collective response to aggression.

When on 29 November 1990 the Security Council authorized the use of force to end Iraqi occupation of Kuwait, limitations on the role of the council were evident. Secretary of State James Baker negotiated the text through trips to capitals, not through ambassadors in New York. Ultimate decisions on war or peace still lay with national leaders. Secretary Baker, rather than the secretary-general, would conduct the final negotiations with Iraq.

Even so, the successful invocation of the charter's provisions for collective security marked how far United Nations diplomacy had been transformed. While changed relations between the Soviet Union and the United States were the basis for this development, the new diplomatic process of consultation among the permanent members, aimed at generating collective action to counter threats to the peace, had nurtured its growth since January 1987. After forty-five years the United Nations enjoyed a new beginning.

11

Diplomacy Yields to War

War of the Cities

On 27 February 1988 Iraq carried out a major air attack on a refinery in Tehran, and Iran, vowing to retaliate, fired off three SCUD missiles that landed south of Baghdad's city center. This attack, the first such since November,[1] reignited the "war of the cities." Iraq, having extended the range of its Soviet SCUD-B missiles to twice their normal range of 190 miles, fired back. By 6 March Iraq had hit Tehran thirty-three times and Qom three times, killing nearly sixty people. By 10 March Iraq had shot off approximately fifty missiles and Iran, because it had fewer missiles in its inventory and could not keep up the pace, only twenty-five. While both attacked with airplanes, the Iranian air force managed only a few sorties. Iran used artillery attacks on Basra to compensate for its air inferiority. Iraq offered a cease-fire to end this round in the war of the cities, on condition that it got the last shot. A cease-fire went into effect on 11 March.

The repercussions reached the permanent members in New York. Because the missiles landing on Tehran were originally of Soviet making, Iranians attacked the Soviet embassy in Tehran with rocks and firebombs and tried to break into the compound; evidently, there was also an attack on the Soviet consulate in Isfahan.[2] The rage abated when Rafsanjani publicly accepted the Soviet explanation that the missiles were short-range but the Iraqis had modified their range with the help of Western countries.[3] In New York Ambassador Belonogov received new instructions.

After fifteen months of working together to develop a meeting of the minds on dealing with the war, Moscow now felt a particular urgency to stop the renewed war of the cities. During a morning meeting at Sir Crispin's Beekman Place apartment overlooking the East River, Belonogov proposed to surprised colleagues a resolution that would call for an end to missile attacks on civilian areas and request the secretary-general to appoint a special representative for negotiations with the parties.[4] Belonogov's news that the Soviet Union had decided to move unilaterally took the other ambassadors aback. There was no mention of enforcement measures to back up resolution 598. This new Soviet approach differed from the work of the permanent members over the past year because it was presented as a unilateral initiative and because it would have been apart from the comprehensive framework for UN efforts established by resolution 598. The unity of the permanent members in dealing with the Iran-Iraq war was in jeopardy.

Meanwhile Pérez de Cuéllar had appealed publicly on 1 March for an end to attacks on civilian targets. He was able to arrange the cease-fire covering such attacks that went into effect on 11 March, eliminating the urgency behind the Soviet draft.

In the days immediately following, the council president, Yugoslavia's ambassador Pejic, negotiated agreement on a council statement. The statement expressed grave concern over the war, particularly the recent attacks on cities, and called for rapid implementation of 598. It encouraged the secretary-general to proceed with another round of talks and asked him to report to the council within three weeks. It repeated, once again, the veiled threat that the council would consider enforcement measures, if there were no progress.[5] The cease-fire arranged by the secretary-general and this statement sidelined the Soviet draft and its threat to the unity of the permanent members. The secretary-general's resumed negotiations, even without either "a fresh and resolute impulse" from the council or signs of flexibility from the parties, deferred action on both the U.S. proposal for an arms embargo and the Soviet request for appointment of a special representative.

On 18 March Pérez de Cuéllar wrote to the presidents of Iran and Iraq, asking them to send special emissaries to New York for urgent consultations. He wanted to obtain clear-cut positions on 598 and to examine possibilities for implementing it. He proposed talks with Iran on 30 and 31 March and with Iraq on 4 and 5 April. He appealed to both to refrain from all acts that could lead to an escalation of the conflict and to end all attacks on civilian targets. He repeated this appeal four days later.

Iran's response was dilatory. On 30 March Ambassador Mahallati told the secretary-general that Iran's special emissary could be in New York on 6 and 7 April, after the dates proposed for talks with Iraq. Iraq, not willing to be leapfrogged, then set its own dates for 11 and 12 April.

When Pérez de Cuéllar met with Iranian deputy foreign minister Javad Larijani and then with Wissam Al-Zahawie, Iraq's senior under secretary in the Ministry of Foreign Affairs, there was little chance to make progress. On the table were the secretary-general's four points from the previous December (determination of the date to begin implementation, cease-fire, withdrawal of forces, and beginning of the work of an impartial body). If the parties could not agree on certain points, perhaps they would entrust them to the secretary-general, for example setting the dates for a cease-fire and withdrawal. As had been expected,[6] this round of talks, the last before renewed fighting completely changed the situation on the ground, registered no progress. Larijani and Al-Zahawie merely permitted Pérez de Cuéllar to relay their positions to the Security Council.

Iran's main points were that justice, the cardinal point for any lasting settlement, required determination of responsibility for the conflict and that Iran would cooperate with the secretary-general on the basis of his outline plan. Iran saw the observance of a cease-fire and the determination of responsibility as the two pillars of the outline plan. Discussion of other elements, including withdrawal, should take place within an established time frame. Iran believed that the renewed attacks against cities and the use of chemical weapons had seriously affected the atmosphere for UN efforts and that immediate action by the Security Council on these issues would indicate that it was prepared to discharge its charter obligations for the settlement of international disputes. In other words the council still had to overcome its fault of inaction at the beginning of the war.[7]

Iraq's position had hardened. Al-Zahawie delivered a letter from Tariq Aziz, which indicated that, once the Security Council had obtained Iran's explicit, documented, and unconditional acceptance of 598, Iraq would be ready to enter into discussions with Iran, under the auspices of the secretary-general, to implement the resolution. Already Iraq was signaling its preference for direct talks rather than indirect talks through the secretary-general. After checking again with Baghdad at Pérez de Cuéllar's request, Al-Zahawie confirmed that Iraq could not discuss details in the absence of an official document signed by the highest authorities in Iran accepting resolution 598 explicitly and unconditionally.

Pérez de Cuéllar did not propose any way forward. The strength of 598 was based on the unity and resolve of the members of the council. No doubt they would want to reflect on the responses of Iran and Iraq and to weigh them carefully. It seemed the diplomatic track had turned into a dead end.

Chemical Weapons

Charges that Iraq had used chemical weapons brought another test to the permanent members' initiative and unity. On 17 March Ambassador Mahallati sent the secretary-general a letter reporting that, on the day before, Iraqi warplanes had bombarded Shiraz and Bakhtaran, causing numerous deaths and injuries. "The criminal and savage Iraqi regime also deployed chemical weapons in the operational theatre of Valfajr on the said date; several civilians were martyred and injured."[8] A second letter the same day reported that chemical weapons had been used against Iraqi Kurdish areas. Iran called on the Security Council to uphold the 1925 Geneva Protocol for the Prohibition of the Use in War of Poisonous, Asphyxiating and Other Gases and to compel Iraq to stop using chemical weapons, thus relieving Iran "of the agony of considering retaliatory measures."[9] Mahallati asked the secretary-general to dispatch an expert team to investigate.[10]

Iranian foreign minister Velayati wrote to the secretary-general to regret that in the past, despite unambiguous evidence, the Security Council had done nothing to stop Iraqi use of chemical weapons. "This irresponsible and indifferent attitude of the Security Council had indeed encouraged and emboldened Iraq to employ chemical weapons even against innocent Iraqi civilians."[11] Velayati reported that on 18 March Iraqi use of chemical weapons in the Halabcheh area had killed more than five thousand Iraqi Kurdish civilians and wounded four thousand more. He asked if this clear evidence was not enough for the United Nations and the Security Council to understand the real nature of the Iraqi regime. "What is the effect of these crimes on the one hand and the silence of the United Nations on the other?"[12]

Mahallati repeated Iran's request for a UN investigation in letters of 21 March[13] and 25 March:[14]

> The history of the use of chemical weapons by the war criminals in Baghdad clearly illustrates the fact that the inaction of the United Nations—caused by political expediency—has only emboldened the Iraqi rulers to increase the intensity and gravity of their crimes. The recent systematic and large-scale use of chemical weapons against civilians is the most unfortunate illustration of the effects of past inaction on the part of the international community. . . . It is horrifying even to speculate how the Iraqi war criminals would interpret this message in planning and carrying out their future acts of genocide and other crimes against humanity.[15]

At this point the secretary-general sent a medical specialist to Iran to investigate. Dr. Manuel Dominguez, a colonel in the Spanish Army Medical Corps and professor of preventive medicine, had participated as an expert on chemical weapons injuries in all previous UN missions sent to Iran and Iraq to investigate the use of chemical weapons. A senior secretariat official accompanied Dominguez. When Iraq complained on 5 April that Iran had used chemical weapons and requested an investigation, Pérez de Cuéllar sent Dr. Dominguez to Baghdad.

During his investigations in Iran from 28 to 31 March Dr. Dominguez examined randomly selected patients in medical institutions in Tehran and Bakhtaran. The patients suffered injuries caused by two types of chemical weapons: yperite (mustard gas) and a neurotoxic agent (nerve gas). The patients said they had been injured as a result of attacks in the Halabcheh area of Kurdish Iraq between 16 and 18 March or in the Marivan-Nowdoshe-Sanandaj area of Iran between 17 and 27 March. Testimony indicated that the chemicals had been released from bombs. "During our brief stay in the Islamic Republic of Iran we became aware of widespread concern among Iranians, officials as well as the average citizen, over the possible use of chemical weapons against their cities."[16] Dominguez concluded that "compared with previous years, there has been an increase in the intensity of the attacks with chemical agents, in terms of both the number of victims and . . . the severity of injuries sustained. Furthermore, there appeared to be a higher proportion of civilians among those affected than in previous investigations."[17]

During his visit to Iraq from 8 to 11 April Dr. Dominguez examined thirty-nine patients, all soldiers or officers, in the Al Rasheed Military Hospital at Baghdad. They testified they had been injured, also in the Halabcheh area, on 30 and 31 March by chemical agents delivered either by aerial bombs or artillery shells. According to Iraqi military authorities, all had been stationed in mountain-top positions north of Halabcheh at the time of the attack. Dr. Dominguez concluded that all thirty-nine patients had been exposed to yperite, and four may have been exposed to another chemical agent in small concentrations.[18]

In his letter transmitting these findings to the secretary-general, Dr. Dominguez wrote that, despite repeated appeals by the United Nations, chemical weapons continued to be used, apparently on a more intensive scale than before. "The continued use of such weapons in the present conflict increases the risk of their use in future conflicts. This awesome prospect may become reality unless concrete steps are taken to redress the current trends, which appear all the more disturbing if we consider that there has been an apparent increase in the number of civilian casualties, primarily with yperite (mustard gas)."[19]

Pérez de Cuéllar attached an introductory note to the report and sent it to the Security Council. He recalled that following a similar investigation in 1987 the expert team had concluded there was little more experts could do to assist the United Nations in preventing the use of chemical weapons—only concerted efforts at the political level could prevent the irreparable weakening of the Geneva Protocol.[20] He expressed a deep sense of dismay and foreboding at the continued use of chemical weapons and the apparent increase in the number of civilian casualties, a turn of events that could seriously undermine the Geneva Protocol, "a document which for 60 years has been a hopeful symbol of mankind's desire and its ability to mitigate the effects of war through universal adherence to humanitarian concerns."[21] Referring to this as an awesome prospect, Pérez de Cuéllar called for a concerted exercise of political will to prevent it from becoming reality.

The council president in April 1988 was Algeria's ambassador Hocine Djoudi. Algeria, like other nonaligned members, had little desire to take the lead on a report drawing attention to the use of chemical weapons by two members of the nonaligned movement. The permanent members, none of whom objected to council action on this subject, were busy trying to maintain their unity as they struggled over a possible arms embargo against Iran. Because other council members resented the degree to which the permanent members acted as a directorate guiding council action on the Iran-Iraq war, it seemed natural inside the council that Germany, joined by Italy and Japan, would take the lead in preparing and negotiating a draft resolution.

Outside the council it also seemed natural. At the time neither Britain, France, nor the United States, all of whom had taken strong positions against the use of chemical weapons and now supported preparation of a resolution, had relations with Iran. Germany, Italy, and Japan maintained significant commercial ties to Iran. By taking the lead the German government might counter criticism that its lax enforcement of German law had allowed German firms, in violation of German law, to be in the forefront of commercial partners of the Iraqi chemical weapons effort.[22]

It took two weeks for this diplomatic effort to bear fruit. On 9 May the council adopted resolution 612 (1988), which affirmed the need to observe the Geneva Protocol, condemned the continued use of chemical weapons, expected both sides to refrain from the use of chemical weapons, and called on all states to control strictly the export to the parties of products serving for the production of chemical weapons. For the first time the council responded to a report on chemical weapons use with a resolution rather than a statement, but the text was neither vigorous nor indignant. In deference to the uneasiness of some council members, it was agreed neither to have a debate nor to explain votes when the council adopted the resolution. The meeting lasted only five minutes.[23]

The End of Negotiations on Sanctions

In the spring of 1988 two developments overcame the U.S. effort to secure a UN arms embargo against Iran: Chinese opposition to an embargo and the failure of Iranian arms.

Enter the China connection. China was the only permanent member to maintain a significant arms supply relationship with Iran. The sale by China of Silkworm missiles to Iran created an additional risk for U.S. naval vessels operating in the gulf. Throughout 1987, against the backdrop of a policy review in Washington whether or not to ease restrictions on the export of high technology items to China, U.S. and Chinese diplomats discussed the problem of Silkworm missiles. At the end of his November trip to Beijing, Under Secretary Armacost said the issue had been resolved.

When Foreign Minister Wu Xueqian met with President Reagan on 8 March 1988, he said China would support a UN arms embargo against Iran if it were supported by the "overwhelming majority" of the Security Council. Wu's position was in line with what he had told General Walters the previous July, but for the first time the Chinese position was public. The catch was that the United States, with no help from the Chinese, had to secure the support of the council's "overwhelming majority." The White House spokesman told the press that "to the best of our information" China had stopped the export of Silkworm missiles to Iran but still had a substantial trade in conventional arms with Iran.[24]

The next day Wu Xueqian told a National Press Club luncheon there was no direct arms trade between China and Iran. "Since the adoption of

U.N. Security Council resolution 598 last year, China has adopted strict measures to prevent what you call the Silkworm missiles from flowing into Iran through the international arms market."[25] Meanwhile the departments of State, Defense, and Commerce were reviewing the restrictions on the sale of high-technology weapons to China, and U.S. officials indicated that in 1987 China may have sold Iran $1 billion in arms, earning valuable foreign exchange and confirming China's role as a major arms supplier to the Third World. Even if the problem of Silkworm missile sales were resolved to Washington's satisfaction, the strains Chinese arms sales were putting on U.S.-Chinese relations remained.[26]

By the end of March bilateral tension over Chinese arms sales rose again, this time over missiles sold to Saudi Arabia. On 30 March a spokesman for the State Department announced that Ambassador Hume A. Horan, then visiting Washington, would not be returning to Riyadh.[27] State Department spokesmen denied that the recall of Horan was directly tied to the question of Chinese missiles.[28] However, Horan's recall came at the time of a major dispute between the United States and Saudi Arabia over the deployment of Chinese missiles, and a bipartisan group of senators signed a letter calling on the United States to suspend all arms sales to Saudi Arabia until the missiles were withdrawn. Before traveling to Washington Horan had, on instructions, raised the issue of the Chinese missiles with King Fahd.

During the third week of April, after clashes between U.S. and Iranian naval forces, the United States appealed to other council members to support adoption of a UN arms embargo to end the war. Then, on 22 April a State Department official said, "China has told us that because of recent developments in the war, it would complicate matters to pass an arms embargo resolution and that this was not the way to bring the war to an end. . . . It's a clear example of how the clashes are being used as an excuse to delay action on the embargo."[29] When China pulled the plug on the U.S. campaign for a UN arms embargo, it could find refuge in the circumstances—U.S.-Iranian clashes, Iraq's use of chemical weapons, Iraq's advances in the war, and reluctance by other council members, including the Soviet Union. Beijing also had a particularly Chinese reason for its decision—the U.S. effort to shut off Saudi Arabia as well as Iran as a market for Chinese arms.

Chinese vice foreign minister Qi Huai Yuan, in an interview with American journalist Flora Lewis, argued that the missile sales to Saudi Arabia were welcomed by the Arab states and contributed to regional security. Qi flatly rejected the idea that China, as a major power, had to be drawn into international consultations on arms escalation in dangerous regions.[30] With its military industries under pressure of a tight budget squeeze but able to earn profits from foreign sales, it was natural that China insist on a unilateral right to decide on arms sales. China, the only permanent member with significant arms sales to Iran, must have been relieved at how events had helped it to deflect pressure for a UN arms embargo against Iran.

The second development to overcome consideration of sanctions was the collapse of Iran's military effort. When clashes in April between the U.S. and Iranian navies ended, the Iranian navy had been swept from the seas. On 14 April the U.S. frigate *Samuel F. Roberts* hit a mine in waters off Qatar, sustaining serious damage to the vessel and injuries to ten crewmen. Washington blamed Iran.

The U.S. Navy struck back in carefully planned actions on 18 April. The U.S. naval vessels *Merrill, McCormick,* and *Trenton* ordered Iranians to abandon the Sassan oil platform; after shelling with naval guns, Marines boarded the platform, set explosive charges, and detonated the explosives. The U.S. vessels *Wainwright, Simpson,* and *Bagley* ordered Iranians to abandon a platform near Sirri Island and then shelled it, destroying it by fire. The Iranian fast attack craft *Joshan* was destroyed during an attack on the *Wainwright.* The Iranian frigate *Sahand* fired on U.S. ships and was severely damaged by Harpoon missiles and laser-guided bombs. The Iranian frigate *Sabalan* fired on U.S. ships and was badly damaged by a laser-guided bomb. When the smoke had cleared, the Iranian Navy had lost nearly half of its major operational ships.[31]

The White House explained that these actions were taken to deter further Iranian mining of gulf waters. "They represent a measured response to Iran's unlawful use of force against the United States and to Iran's numerous violations of the rights of other non-belligerents. And they constitute a lawful exercise of the United States' inherent right of self-defense under Article 51 of the United Nations Charter."[32] Within a day Washington was considering expanding the role of the U.S. fleet in the gulf, and on 22 April the Reagan administration informed Congress that in some circumstances U.S. naval vessels would come to the assistance of neutral shipping.[33] As announced later by Secretary of Defense Frank Carlucci, if a vessel under attack requested assistance, a U.S. warship would respond positively if it were in the vicinity and its mission permitted such assistance. The new rule covered "friendly, innocent, neutral vessels, flying a nonbelligerent flag, outside declared war exclusion zones, that are not carrying contraband or resisting legitimate visit and search by a Persian Gulf belligerent."[34] The first time an American vessel defended a neutral ship was on 2 July, when the frigate USS *Montgomery* assisted a Danish tanker being fired on by Iranian boats. After warning shots by the *Montgomery,* the Iranians fled.

Iranian fortunes in land fighting were even worse. Battles in April, May, and June forced Iranian forces to withdraw from Iraq and caused the destruction or disintegration of forward Iranian units. Inside Iran, for the first time since the war began eight years earlier, the government's uncompromising war policy became a political liability.

On 17 April Iraq achieved tactical surprise in an attack against Iranian positions on the Fao peninsula. Divisions of the Seventh Corps attacked south along a line parallel to the Shatt Al-Arab; an armored attack carried out by the Presidential Guards Division of the Republican Guards, Iraq's strategic reserve corps, moved east across marshes and salt flats northwest of the Iranian defenses. Iranian forces, numbering from thirty thousand to fifty thousand, broke under the weight of the combined attack. On 18 April an Iraqi communiqué indicated that the last pockets of enemy resistance at Fao were being eliminated. "Your sons have entered the dear town of Fao, liberating its soil from the filth of the invaders."[35]

The recapture of Fao was of great military and psychological significance. By pushing Iranian forces east of the Shatt, it shortened the line of Iraqi defensive positions in the Basra area, making it possible to shift many of the forty thousand troops stationed there to participate in attacks elsewhere. It showed that the Iraqi army, which had been on the defensive since 1980, could conduct a major offensive operation with success. The victory at Fao fueled Iraqi military confidence and growing despondency in Iran over the course and costs of the war.

A month later Iraqi forces conducted another successful offensive to recapture Iraqi territory, this time in the Shalamcheh area south and east of Basra. All along the front Iranian forces, inferior in the air and now crippled at sea, were for the first time since 1980 thrown on the defensive in the land war.

On 25 June, in an operation to the north of Basra, Iraqi forces ousted Iranian troops from the last significant piece of Iraqi territory that they held. This area contains one of the world's largest oil fields, centered on Majnoon Island, with reserves estimated at up to thirty billion barrels. The main assault was again conducted by the Republican Guards, this time with the Third Army Corps. During June, Iraqi forces attacked Iranian positions in Kurdish villages in the northern mountains of Iraq and Mehran, an Iranian border town in the central sector. Iraq handed over Mehran to the Mujahidin Khalq, an Iranian opposition group backed by Iraq.

Although it took the Iraqi forces only eight hours to end the three-year Iranian occupation of Majnoon, Saddam Hussein publicly charged that the United States had supplied Iran with information on Iraq's plans to attack. A senior Iraqi diplomat in Paris elaborated, "It is a continuation of the Iran-contra affair on a bigger scale, with France, Britain, Canada and the United States all trying to endear themselves to Rafsanjani." A senior State Department official dismissed this charge as "absolutely ridiculous."[36]

The accumulation of military losses was starting to force a change in Iran's war policy. Iraq controlled the skies and could attack Iranian cities with relative impunity. The Iranian navy had lost half of its major surface combatants in one day of fighting with the U.S. Navy. Iraq's superiority in armor, by as much as a ten-to-one ratio at times, drove Iranian forces to defeat at Fao, Shalamcheh, and Majnoon Island. Iraq's use of chemical weapons demoralized Iranian soldiers. On the home front shortages, inflation, and unemployment were the problems, and voters in the spring elections supported candidates calling for nationalizations and redistribution of agricultural land. If at the beginning of the year the Iranian people had wondered if war was the right policy, by June they were openly asking for the war to end.

On 2 June two signs of change came to Tehran. Ayatollah Khomeini appointed Parliament Speaker Rafsanjani to be commander of Iran's armed forces. The appointment of Rafsanjani, considered a moderate and a pragmatist on foreign policy, was in response to frustration over the recent military setbacks.[37] The same day Mehdi Bazargan, the first prime minister appointed by Khomeini, sent the Ayatollah a letter accusing him of "a despotism worthy of the pharaohs." "You have denounced the policy of the United States, and they are now installed solidly at our gates in the Persian Gulf. You have spoken of the failure of Iraq and the crumbling of its regime, but thanks to your misguided policies, Iraq has fortified itself, its economy has not collapsed, and it is we who are on the verge of bankruptcy."[38]

The debate over Iranian policies on the war was now openly engaged, but in fact since March there had been contradictory trends in Iran's foreign policy. In April Iranian deputy foreign minister Larijani asked the secretary-general to pass a message to the United States indicating a desire to open a direct dialogue.[39] Secretary Shultz confirmed that the United States went back through third parties with a message: "We are willing to establish a channel, a single authoritative channel, and this is an official message, so name one."[40] After the April clash between the U.S. and Iranian navies, Iran did not respond positively.

On 26 April Saudi Arabia announced it was breaking diplomatic relations with Iran, and King Fahd said Saudi Arabia would not hesitate to use its Chinese missiles in defense against Iran. Saudi officials announced, because of the riots caused by Iranian pilgrims in Mecca the previous year, that they had decided to cut the number of Iranian pilgrims to forty-five thousand, approximately one-third of the 1987 figure. Rafsanjani denounced the move as "flagrant treachery that serves the interest of the United States."[41]

In the weeks before the French presidential election on 8 May, Prime Minister Chirac's government tried through contacts with the Iranian government to arrange for the release of three French hostages in Lebanon. Three days before the election Chirac welcomed the released hostages at Villacoublay air base outside Paris. He thanked "the Iranian Government for various interventions that permitted the liberation of our compatriots" and announced that "the re-establishment of normal relations between France and Iran can be envisaged in keeping with our conception of what should be the relations among states."[42] French spokesmen insisted that the only concessions made to Iran were to repay the remaining amount due on a $1 billion loan made by the Shah's government and to agree in principle to reestablish diplomatic relations. Foreign Minister Jean-Bernard Raimond briefed the ambassadors of the United States, Britain, West Germany, and Italy. After the election the new prime minister, Michel Rocard, confirmed that the deal would be kept. On 15 June France and Iran announced they would reestablish relations the next day, a move that a spokesman for the Quai d'Orsay stressed did not imply any change in French policies toward the region.[43]

Iran wanted to improve its relations with the West. Iranian officials complained that the military setbacks of the previous months were due to Iran's international isolation and military and economic embargoes applied against Iran. The Iranian government was negotiating with Britain a compensation package for damage to the British embassy in Tehran and to the Iranian embassy in London, and Iran's desire to restore relations impressed a British parliamentary delegation visiting Tehran.[44] Iran launched an effort to reopen ties with Canada.[45]

Iran did not, however, soften its attitude toward the United States. On 2 July Rafsanjani said a priority of Iranian foreign policy had to be to make friends abroad, but not with the United States. "One of the wrong things we did in the revolutionary atmosphere was to constantly make enemies. . . . We pushed those who could be neutral into hostility and did not do anything to attract those who could become friends. It is part of the new plan that in foreign policy we should behave in a way not to needlessly leave ground to the enemy."[46]

Unfinished Business

At the end of April Pérez de Cuéllar proposed to Velayati and Tariq Aziz that a technical-level team from the secretariat meet with both sides for a round of talks, after which he would propose a calendar for implementing 598. He stipulated that any acceptance of this invitation would have to be based on a readiness to implement 598 in all of its aspects. "This is the last chance to stop Resolution 598 going the same way as Resolutions 435 and 242," commented a senior secretariat official, referring to the landmark Security Council decisions for resolving the dispute over Namibia and the Arab-Israeli conflict.[47] Neither had been implemented since their adoption ten and twenty years earlier.

Iraq replied two weeks later that, although it had accepted 598 in good faith, Iran had not done so but had instead resorted to maneuvers to avoid accepting the resolution and to create obstacles to its implementation. Iraq insisted that the first efforts must be to obtain Iran's express, official, and unconditional acceptance of that resolution at the highest level in Tehran, after which talks should be conducted at that level, and in no case lower than the level of foreign minister. Until that time, there was no reason to conduct talks of a "technical" nature. Iran accepted the secretary-general's proposal on 31 May but insisted that the first step had to be the beginning of the work of the body charged with determining the aggressor.

The inflexibility of these answers showed the extent to which, a year and a half after its beginning, the diplomatic process that produced resolution 598 had run out of steam. Whether out of a concern for security or a demand for justice, neither side was ready to take risks to implement 598. Mutual distrust, plus hard experience, convinced both to pursue the military option.

By the end of June 1988, what had resolution 598 accomplished? It had not ended the war, nor helped to protect shipping, nor led to imposition of UN sanctions. It had, however, begun to change the way governments looked at the potential for Security Council diplomacy.

The secretary-general had been the catalyst for starting the new process of consultations among the permanent members. Pérez de Cuéllar's analysis that a meeting of minds among Security Council members would reinforce the secretary-general's hand as mediator was correct; but then the council failed to respond to his public request for "a fresh and resolute impulse." Thereafter, although resolution 598 was mandatory under the provisions of the charter's chapter VII, the parties responded to his mediation as if it were conducted within the limited, recommendatory powers of chapter VI.

Resolution 598 did not lead to adoption of measures for naval peacekeeping. The permanent members used unilateral measures, such as naval deployments, as the most forceful expressions of their policies. One ambassador directly involved claimed this outcome could have been different if only the United States, following the adoption of 598 in July 1987, had put a hold on its operation to reflag Kuwaiti tankers and to protect them with naval vessels.[48] Could the United States, by delaying its unilateral measures, have made 598 and the prospect of collective measures more central? Considering the engagement already made to Kuwait, the military prepreparations undertaken, and the domestic opposition overcome, the mere possibility that the Security Council would move quickly to enforce 598 was hardly enough to delay the momentum behind the reflagging operation. No convincing case can be made that there was ever an open window of opportunity for collective action on either naval peacekeeping or an arms embargo.

Even after China announced its opposition, the United States maintained its determination to secure a UN arms embargo against Iran. After the counselors' group stopped work on an arms embargo resolution, the U.S. and Soviet delegations negotiated a text for the others to review. The "consolidated negotiating text" worked out in May and June recorded growing disagreement. The first operative paragraph, which at one point had been agreed upon, now existed in four different versions—determining that Iran had failed to comply with 598, that it had refused to comply with 598, that it had refused to indicate its readiness to comply with 598, and that the position of Iran warranted resorting to enforcement actions. As late as the first week of July the State Department was preparing a round of demarches to secure support by council members for an arms embargo.

Resolution 598 nevertheless produced a framework, like resolutions 242 for the Arab-Israeli conflict and 435 for Namibia, that acquired extraordinary legitimacy in defining the path to a settlement. As a guide for and expression of the foreign policies of other nations, resolution 598 subjected Iran and Iraq to pressure to end the war.[49] Despite their differences over naval peacekeeping and an arms embargo, the permanent members were unified in calling for a settlement within the terms of 598.

The most important accomplishment of the process that led to the adoption of 598 was that the permanent members kept talking. During negotiations the options are to agree, to disagree, or to keep talking.[50] Even when discussing their conflicting positions over protection of shipping in the gulf or the need for an arms embargo against Iran, the Soviet Union and the United States both showed that they placed a higher value than previously on their bilateral relationship. "We now have something which we haven't had for a very long time: a Soviet-American dialogue, not just on disarmament, but on all the problems," said Soviet spokesman Gennadi Gerasimov in April 1988. "This includes regional conflicts. There are many problems made more difficult by our rivalry that we can solve together."[51]

Other permanent members, particularly Britain and France, welcomed the new Soviet and American attitudes toward Security Council diplomacy. They had something to gain from always being at the table at which negotiations were taking place. To the extent that the Security Council became a place for the major powers to find a meeting of the minds on issues of collective security, it could function as the United Nations' founders had intended.

12

From Tragedy to Cease-Fire

Tragedy

On 3 July the cruiser USS *Vincennes* shot down Iran Air 655, an Iranian civilian Airbus en route from Bandar Abbas to Dubai, killing all 290 people on board. Shortly before, the *Vincennes* and the *Montgomery*, operating in the Strait of Hormuz, had responded to an attack by Iranian boats on a helicopter from the *Vincennes*. In an area crowded with commercial shipping and air traffic, the crew on the *Vincennes* made a tragic mistake. President Reagan immediately expressed sympathy and condolences to the victims and their families, regretted any loss of life, and affirmed that "the only U.S. interest in the Persian Gulf is peace, and this reinforces the need to achieve that goal with all possible speed."[1]

Reactions in Iran fueled the debate launched by Rafsanjani over foreign policy. "We will not leave the crimes of America unanswered," warned Iranian radio. "We will resist the plots of the Great Satan and avenge the blood of our martyrs from criminal mercenaries."[2] Ayatollah Montazeri called for revolutionary forces to target American interests. In a funeral oration for the victims, President Khamenei said the U.S. presence in the gulf was not acceptable and "the Iranian nation and officials assert that they reserve the right to take revenge in any manner and at any place, and, God willing, they will exact revenge with force."[3]

Not all Iranian reactions were so bellicose. Rafsanjani, while retaining for Iran the right of revenge, said "the timing is up to us, not America."[4] Foreign Minister Velayati, without threatening revenge, warned that "the United States is responsible for the consequences of its barbaric massacre of innocent passengers."[5] Sirous Nasseri, the Iranian ambassador to the United Nations in Geneva and a key player on Rafsanjani's diplomatic team, told U.S. television he hoped the episode would "ease itself down through a proper approach to the matter, that is the condemnation of the act by the United States and putting those people who are responsible on trial and making compensation."[6]

This incident caused great international concern. Prime Minister Thatcher expressed profound regret. France viewed the incident with consternation. Foreign Minister Genscher expressed great shock, and the Italian prime minister called it an "atrocious episode." China's official statement said, "We condemn this action and express our condolences for the victims. . . . We reiterate that the Chinese Government is opposed to big-power military involvement in the gulf region. Such involvement is not conducive to peace and stability in the region."[7]

The statement issued by TASS suggested the Soviet Union might try to stir up the Iranian reaction against the United States. "The tragedy, responsibility for which is wholly with the American command, has been far from accidental. It has been, in effect, a direct corollary of United States actions over the past year to increase its military presence in the Gulf." TASS called for the removal of the U.S. fleet from the gulf. Deputy Foreign Minister Yuli Vorontsov, who for over a year had been offering to mediate between Iran and Iraq, met with the Iranian ambassador to discuss Soviet-Iranian relations.[8] Despite these efforts to ingratiate itself with Tehran, other signs suggested Moscow would refrain from the temptation to be opportunistic in denouncing the United States. As Soviet deputy foreign minister Petrovsky had said the day before the incident, "We are working very hard to overcome this enemy image which was created on both sides."[9]

On 5 July Ambassador Mahallati asked the president of the Security Council, Ambassador Paulo Nogueira-Batista of Brazil, for an urgent meeting of the council to consider "the massacre of 290 innocent civilian passengers of Iran Air flight 655 by the naval forces of the United States."[10] Mahallati told a press conference Iran's attitude toward resolution 598 was a separate matter. "I think the minimum we can expect from the Security Council is an unequivocal and direct condemnation of the United States, and a call on the United States to immediately withdraw its forces from the Persian Gulf to terminate this sort of barbarism."[11] This possibility had already been discounted by a U.S. official, who pointed out that council members would see that, because its attacks in the gulf had heightened tensions, Iran bore a share of responsibility.[12]

Nogueira-Batista had to decide how to proceed. The accumulated wisdom of earlier council presidents suggested some guidelines: to make initial soundings with the parties and important delegations, keeping consultations as informal as possible and talking with the parties on a practical level; to anticipate how council members would line up on the issues in conflict; to conduct further individual bilateral consultations with the parties and council members, rallying support for a specific course of action; then, using a president's draft or one produced by another council member, to guide negotiations in the direction of some kind of practical outcome.[13] The extremes he would want to avoid were either a failure by the council to give Iran satisfaction that it had received a fair hearing or a veto by the United States of a condemnatory resolution. In between lay the practical outcomes.

Security Council: The Public Side

Pérez de Cuéllar, concerned that this incident came at a sensitive time in Iran's debate over the war, urged restraint and caution. He made this point to Deputy Foreign Minister Larijani and then to Foreign Minister Velayati, as well as to Ambassador Vernon Walters.[14] He told Velayati that, if Iran insisted on condemnation by the Security Council, the United States, probably joined by Britain and France, would veto the resolution. He suggested to Walters that it was in the U.S. interest that Iran get a fair hearing, so as not to reinforce Iranian suspicions of Security Council bias and thus to set back the effort to have Iran accept 598.

Ambassador Nogueira-Batista had the difficult task of designing a constructive scenario. The Iranian and U.S. debate statements would surely defend national positions, but they should not inflame passions, complicating negotiations on a resolution or making it more difficult for Iran to accept 598. Nogueira-Batista's initial consultations confirmed how important a factor was Iran's extreme diplomatic isolation. Iran's refusal to accept 598 hobbled its ability to find allies on the council. Meanwhile Iraq was lobbying the nonaligned members of the council (Algeria, Argentina, Nepal, Senegal, Yugoslavia, and Zambia), who would normally present a resolution on Iran's behalf, not to do so. U.S. allies (France, the Federal Republic of Germany, Italy, Japan, and the United Kingdom) would not take Iran's side. Neither the Soviet Union nor China would take the lead. By default, it was left to Nogueira-Batista, as president, to take charge of drafting and negotiations.

The United States took three steps before negotiations began. On 11 July the White House announced *ex gratia* payments to families of the victims. Such payments, technically called *solatia*, are unlike reparations in that they imply no admission of guilt or liability. The White House emphasized Iran had "a particularly heavy burden of responsibility" because it had continued the war.[15] The next day the White House announced that Vice President Bush would speak for the United States in the Security Council debate. "One of the main things we want to do is direct the debate," explained a senior official, "so that it doesn't end up being totally focused on 'What a terrible thing to shoot down an Iran Air flight' but rather to point to the issues behind it."[16]

On the eve of the debate, delayed by Nogueira-Batista until 14 July, European diplomats wanted to move negotiations in the direction of a resolution that would mollify public opinion in Iran as a step to Iranian acceptance of 598. "We've got Iran like a fish on a line, and we don't want them to wiggle off."[17] They thought that the best possible outcome might be for the United States to abstain on a resolution that gave Iran some satisfaction. "We're serene here," said a U.S. diplomat. "We've expressed regret, and we don't have to lie."[18] Nogueira-Batista postponed negotiation of a resolution until after Velayati and Bush spoke.

the debate. All expressed grief at the incident, and most cited positively the U.S. decision to offer *ex gratia* payments to the victims' families. Withholding judgment on responsibility for the incident, all insisted it demonstrated, if additional proof were needed, that there should be a cease-fire in the war and that 598 should be implemented. Only two speakers expressed support for Iran's requests to condemn the U.S. action and to demand the withdrawal of the U.S. fleet from the area.

The two exceptions were the Soviet Union and China. Ambassador Valentin V. Lozinskiy, quoting from TASS, said the United States had full responsibility for the incident. "The Soviet Union emphasizes the urgent need to reduce the acute tension [in the region], to withdraw the United States fleet from the Gulf, and to resolve the problem of security in that waterway by using United Nations naval forces."[25] Ambassador Li of China said the "United States Government has unshirkable responsibility for this incident."[26] Recalling Chinese opposition to the presence of foreign naval fleets in the area, he asked for the withdrawal of the "big-Power military presence."

Security Council: The Private Side

Nogueira-Batista was now ready to conduct negotiations for a draft resolution. Members' statements in the debate suggested that any resolution should call again for implementation of 598. Members wanted to deplore, in some form, the tragedy of the shooting down of Iran Air 655, but the United States rejected any condemnation, direct or indirect, of its actions. As for the Iranian demand that the council call for the withdrawal of foreign forces from the gulf, only the Soviet Union and China supported this position.

In Montreal the International Civil Aviation Organization (ICAO) had just concluded negotiations on a resolution reacting to the incident. Its resolution deplored the use of weapons against a civilian aircraft and set up an investigation, but it did not condemn the U.S. action. "The United States does have its influence, its power," complained Iranian ambassador Nasseri. "It is not easy for member countries to speak openly, frankly, decisively against the United States, even when the United States commits a very serious crime."[27] In Montreal the United States had been able to hold the line without the veto power it has in the Security Council.

As diplomats often aspire to be deal-makers, there was no lack of would-be intermediaries between the U.S. and Iranian delegations. Ambassador Walters, however, would deal only through Nogueira-Batista. To further reduce the temptation for third parties to influence the negotiations, Walters took an unusual step. He let it be known that, because the United States was directly involved, it would work for a resolution it could vote for; if it had to, it would vote against a draft, but it would not abstain. Several European diplomats resented Walters's "hard-ball" diplomacy, be-

At 11:00 A.M. on 14 July Nogueira-Batista welcomed Vice President Bush and Foreign Minister Velayati to the Security Council and called on Velayati to speak.

Velayati, dressed in a dark suit and collarless shirt, spoke in Farsi for more than an hour. To prove the shooting down of the Airbus could not have been an accident, he read into the record the transcript of communications between the Iran Air plane and air traffic controllers. He cited and rebutted official U.S. descriptions of the incident. "The evidence presented by American officials themselves clearly suggests that the United States forces initiated hostilities on 2 and 3 July 1988 with the clear intention of carrying out unprovoked aggression against the territorial integrity of the Islamic Republic of Iran."[19] The attack, Velayati said, was a criminal act and a flagrant violation of the principles of international law. "Therefore, the Security Council cannot but condemn the United States for its unjustified shooting down of the civilian airliner of the Islamic Republic of Iran. Anything less than such a clear position of condemnation would be a clear show of disrespect for human life."[20]

Velayati made a broader case against any presence of the U.S. fleet in the Persian Gulf. U.S. policy, he explained, was to allow one side, under U.S. protection, to attack the merchant shipping of the other side, while denying to that side—Iran—the right to defend its vital interests. "The massive United States military presence has brought the peoples of the region nothing but insecurity, death, destruction, lawlessness, intervention and tension."[21] While expressing doubt that the Security Council would deal objectively with acts of aggression already committed, Velayati said, "It is time that the Security Council took a more serious and objective look at this grave threat to international peace and security, and compelled the United States and other foreign forces to leave the Persian Gulf. Anything less would be a further evasion of responsibility by the Security Council."[22]

He said nothing about the war going on between Iran and Iraq.

Vice President Bush was the only other speaker that morning. He emphasized, from beginning to end of his twenty-minute statement, that "the critical issue confronting this body is not the how and why of Iran Air 655, which I will discuss. It is the continuing refusal of the Government of the Islamic Republic of Iran to comply with Resolution 598 (1987), to negotiate an end to the war with Iraq and to cease its acts of aggression against neutral shipping in the Persian Gulf."[23] Bush made a special appeal to stop the use of chemical weapons, asserted that the USS *Vincennes* acted in self-defense, and expressed the grief of the American people at this tragedy. On the U.S. naval presence he said, "The implementation of resolution 598 (1987) would enable the United States to return to the modest naval presence in the Gulf we have maintained for more than 40 years, with the support of the Gulf States. We look forward to that day."[24]

When other council members spoke the next day, two themes dominated cause he ruled out the possibility of a draft that Iran would accept and they would support, but on which the United States would abstain. Walters's tactic, by increasing U.S. leverage in the negotiation, made it more likely that the permanent members, although they had explained their positions differently, would find themselves voting together in favor of the draft.

Nogueira-Batista took very personal control of the negotiations. He limited initial contacts to the U.S. and Iranian delegations, and, contrary to the usual practice, he dealt only with Ambassadors Walters and Mahallati, without aides or notetakers. At several points he held meetings with Walters or Mahallati late in the evening, over a cup of Brazilian coffee, at his residence on Fifth Avenue. When he briefed the other council members on the progress of his talks, he invited only the ambassadors to consultations in the office he used as council president, not in the room for informal consultations. Ambassadors had to squeeze into the office, without aides, notetakers, or translation services. Naturally some resented that they could not speak in their preferred languages but had to use English. Nogueira-Batista's approach, even if idiosyncratic, made sense because the United States and Iran were the two parties to the dispute. If they both accepted the same text, then other council members could be expected to do likewise.

Nogueira-Batista's negotiations were soon overshadowed by events on the ground. The Iraqi army, continuing its series of offensives, occupied the Iranian city of Dehloran in the central sector. On 17 July, the twentieth anniversary of Baath party rule in Iraq, Saddam Hussein claimed that Iraq had inflicted "material and moral ruin" on Khomeini's government and now stood "at the edge of victory."[28] Unlike eight years earlier, this time the Iraqi government did not want to retain Iranian territory indefinitely. "We will not give the Iranians this card to play with in mobilizing their population," said Nizar Hamdoon, now Iraq's deputy foreign minister. "If they want to continue the war, they will have to explain to their people why they are attacking us because we are stopping at the international border."[29]

On 18 July Iranian President Khamenei wrote to Pérez de Cuéllar that "the Islamic Republic of Iran—because of the importance it attaches to saving the lives of human beings and the establishment of justice and regional and international peace and security—accepts Security Council Resolution 598."[30] Khamenei explained the aggression against Iran had "now gained unprecedented dimensions, bringing other countries into the war and even engulfing innocent civilians." He cited the shooting down by U.S. warships of the Iranian civilian aircraft. Speaker Rafsanjani, then acting commander in chief of the armed forces, said the decision had been made by Ayatollah Khomeini. "This decision is based on many reasons, but since Imam Khomeini is aware of many political and military secrets, he cannot give more explanations at the moment."[31] Two days later Khomeini confirmed the decision in a public statement, saying that it was like "taking poison."[32]

The Iranian decision resulted from an accumulation of factors: the inability of the Iranian military to overcome losses suffered during the failed attack on Basra at the end of 1986; the Iraqi advantage in the tanker war, especially after the U.S. entry into the gulf; the demoralizing impact of Iraqi attacks on civilian targets during the war of the cities; the fear in the Iranian army that Iraq would again use chemical weapons; the destruction of the Iranian navy; the recent defeats of the Iranian army at Fao, Shalamcheh, Majnoon, and Dehloran; and the nearly ten-to-one advantage that Iraq now had in battle tanks. Despite the weight of these substantial factors, Iranian officials ascribed the decision to two other causes.

In public, Iranian officials said the immediate catalyst for this decision was the shooting down of Iran Air 655. Rafsanjani said Iran did not begin serious debate over its war policy until the tragedy of 3 July, which he said Iran saw as a warning that the United States would perpetrate "immense crimes" if Iran did not end the war.[33] As reflected in Khamenei's letter to Pérez de Cuéllar, this interpretation was used to explain the decision to Iranians: by shifting the focus of discussion to the 3 July incident, attention would be diverted from military setbacks inflicted by Iraq.[34] But the fundamental reason for this shift by the Iranian leadership must have been concern for domestic politics and the future of the Islamic revolution. This concern had driven Iranian policies during the hostage crisis in 1979, created the tensions that produced cross-border incidents before the Iraqi attack in 1980, alienated Iran's other neighbors in the gulf, caused Iran's extreme diplomatic isolation, and sustained Iran's war policy through eight years of immense human and material losses. With its military in retreat, its economy a shambles, and its civilian population demoralized, the future of the revolution required change.

Nogueira-Batista's negotiations, on which so much had seemed to depend, became anticlimatic once Iran accepted a cease-fire. By 19 July he had brokered a text that expressed deep distress at the downing of the plane and sincere condolences to the families of the victims. It welcomed the decision taken by ICAO to conduct a fact-finding investigation and urged all parties to observe international rules and practices concerning the safety of civil aviation. Finally, it stressed the need for full and rapid implementation of resolution 598, a point Iran no longer opposed.

The council met on 20 July to adopt resolution 616 (1988). Nogueira-Batista presented the draft as a chairman's text. Shortly after the meeting opened, Ambassador Mahallati thanked the president for his efforts. He said that Iran had not started the war and the hostilities in the gulf, indeed that Iran had more to gain than anyone else from peace in the gulf. In bringing the case on the downing of its civilian airliner to the Security Council, Iran was "aware that the culprit would also be the ultimate judge."[35] Nevertheless Iran would comply with the draft resolution and called for "an end once and for all to further loss of life in Iran and Iraq."[36] All council members voted for the resolution. Before the meeting ended Ambassador Walters reaffirmed the U.S. commitment to peace in the area. "Once tensions decrease and the threat to Western interests dissipates in the area, then the level of our naval presence will naturally be reduced."[37] The diplomatic aspects of the Iran Air 655 incident closed with a degree of success that was hardly foreseen on 3 July.

Achieving a Cease-Fire

Iraq's reaction to the Iranian acceptance of 598 was to emphasize that the war had not ended. In Baghdad, Tariq Aziz said the Iranian statement was a deception, Iraq would be cautious about Iranian intentions, and the war was still going on.[38] Ambassador Kittani met on 19 July with Pérez de Cuéllar to present him a letter from Tariq Aziz proposing five "practical steps" to the United Nations and Iran: (1) holding a meeting in New York, to be followed by meetings in Baghdad and Tehran, under the secretary-general's auspices, for direct talks between the two sides aimed at implementation of 598 "in accordance with the sequence of its operative paragraphs"; (2) clearing of the Shatt Al-Arab by UN agencies for the two sides' shipping; (3) an immediate guarantee of Iraq's right of free navigation in the gulf and Strait of Hormuz; (4) while hoping to reach a direct understanding between the two sides, retention by the secretary-general and the Security Council of their role in taking effective decisions, whenever that is deemed necessary; and (5) noninterference by Iran with shipping on the high seas and in the Straits of Hormuz.[39]

During a press conference Pérez de Cuéllar appealed to Iran and Iraq to avoid any act that might endanger his efforts to arrange a cease-fire. He announced that he would send Lt. Gen. Martin Vadset of Norway, commander of the United Nations Truce Supervisory Organization (UN-TSO) in Jerusalem, to lead a team of military experts to suggest arrangements for UN observers to supervise a cease-fire and withdrawal. He wanted to set a firm date for termination of all hostilities in about a week, when the military team was expected to report.[40]

On 21 July, aware that Iraq's demand for direct talks had neither been accepted by Iran nor endorsed by the secretary-general, Saddam Hussein repeated the demand on Iraqi television. While Iraq had a profound desire for peace, Saddam said, it wanted a durable peace, not "a temporary formula to freeze certain war activities or a cease-fire only."[41] Kittani repeated to a New York press conference that Iraq wanted Pérez de Cuéllar to invite Iran and Iraq immediately to send representatives to New York for direct talks, to be followed by direct talks in Baghdad and Tehran. "Iran says it accepts 598 and wants a cease-fire but it will not even talk with Iraq."[42] Because resolution 598 did not require direct talks, Ambassador Mahallati accused Iraq of sabotaging UN efforts.

While the Iraqi army kept driving for military victory, diplomatic efforts aimed to achieve a cease-fire. In a major offensive in the central sector, Iraqi mechanized forces captured large numbers of prisoners and weapons, but Iraq repeated that its forces would withdraw from all captured territory. After informal discussions all Security Council members, including France and the Soviet Union, Iraq's main arms suppliers, agreed to bring to bear what leverage they had to persuade Iraq to accept the cease-fire. There were indications that Saudi Arabia and other GCC members would urge Baghdad to accept cease-fire talks.[43] On 22 July Pérez de Cuéllar invited both sides to send emissaries to New York, leaving open the possibility of the direct talks desired by Baghdad. Both accepted the invitation for meetings the week of 25 July. "Whatever the Secretary-General deems necessary for implementing Resolution 598 we will go along with," said Ambassador Mahallati when announcing the planned arrival of Foreign Minister Velayati.[44]

On 26 July Velayati met with Nogueira-Batista in the council president's office and then with Pérez de Cuéllar. Velayati did not agree to a direct meeting with Tariq Aziz, who still insisted on such talks: "It is absolutely incorrect to be hasty in taking any step before knowing the intentions of the Iranian side very accurately and comprehensively and before confirming them with tangible steps."[45] Nogueira-Batista predicted that the two would meet together later in the negotiations.[46]

The next day Tariq Aziz insisted with Pérez de Cuéllar that "the first step for constructive work is face-to-face negotiations between the two parties under the auspices of the UN Secretary-General."[47] Pérez de Cuéllar recessed talks for a day of reflection. In Baghdad, ambassadors representing Britain, China, France, the Soviet Union, and the United States urged Iraq to show flexibility. Prince Bandar ibn Sultan, Saudi Arabia's ambassador to Washington, at this point paid a call on the secretary-general amid reports that King Fahd might be willing to play a role in easing Saddam Hussein's insistence on direct talks before any cease-fire.[48] Bandar "emphatically" denied these reports.[49] The New York talks adjourned for the weekend.

On Monday, after two hours with Velayati, Pérez de Cuéllar told the press that General Vadset's military team would report to him on Thursday, that he would study the report, and that he would then set the date for the cease-fire. His decision would not depend on the parties, and he hoped to begin direct talks very soon after the cease-fire was declared.[50]

Iraq rejected this solution. "We demand face-to-face talks in the interest of real peace, rather than a temporary truce . . . we will not accept a *fait accompli*, no matter from which quarter it comes."[51] Sir Crispin Tickell, speaking on behalf of the permanent members, assured both Velayati and Tariq Aziz that the governments of the permanent members were committed to full implementation of 598, not simply to a cease-fire. On Friday

Tariq Aziz, for the first time in a week, met with Pérez de Cuéllar. He did not budge from Iraq's insistence on direct talks.[52]

On 6 August, after the secretary-general had conducted over a dozen separate meetings with the two ministers,[53] Saddam Hussein announced in Baghdad that Iraq would accept a cease-fire if Iran agreed that direct talks would take place immediately after a cease-fire took hold. "Invoking what is blessed by God, we extend a hand of friendship and peace to the people of Iran in spite of the bitterness we feel deep inside us for the aggression that has afflicted us."[54] When Iran accepted, the secretary-general told council members during informal consultations that on Monday, 8 August, he would announce the date for the cease-fire. After the meeting, Sir Crispin expressed the "common hope that all military activity between them will cease now."[55]

On 8 August the secretary-general announced to a formal meeting of the council that the cease-fire would begin on 20 August. Iraq and Iran had both agreed that UN observers could be deployed before the date of the cease-fire. On 25 August representatives of Iran and Iraq would meet with the secretary-general in Geneva for direct talks.[56] The president of the council, speaking on behalf of the members, endorsed the secretary-general's statement and promised him support.

Pérez de Cuéllar had to organize a peacekeeping force. In a report issued on 7 August he recommended to the Security Council that it set up a United Nations Iran-Iraq Military Observer Group (UNIIMOG). UNIIMOG's mandate would be to establish the cease-fire line, monitor compliance, investigate violations, confirm the withdrawal of forces, and seek agreement of the parties for other arrangements to help reduce tensions. Based on General Vadset's reports, UNIIMOG would need up to 350 military observers and would "be under the command of the United Nations, vested in the Secretary-General, under the authority of the Security Council."[57]

Pérez de Cuéllar recalled four essential conditions for peacekeeping operations: the backing of the Security Council, the consent and cooperation of the parties, the ability to function as an effective military unit, and adequate financial arrangements. Unlike UN peacekeeping forces in Cyprus and the Golan Heights, UNIIMOG would not be responsible for holding any ground between the two sides. The ability of 350 unarmed observers to monitor the long line between the two sides depended on active cooperation from the Iranian and Iraqi military. Even such a small force would, however, be able to reduce tensions and resolve incidents before they escalated. On 11 August the Security Council unanimously adopted resolution 619 (1988) to authorize UNIIMOG.

Pérez de Cuéllar also had to launch a process of negotiations aimed at achieving implementation of other points in 598—withdrawal of forces, release and repatriation of prisoners of war, and settlement of other aspects of the dispute. To launch this process he had assured Iraq that Iran would enter into direct negotiations. On 8 August he sent identical letters to Mahallati and Kittani:

> In pursuance of the official contacts I had with Iraq and the Islamic Republic of Iran, I should like to inform you that both governments have agreed that direct talks between their Foreign Ministers shall be held under my auspices, immediately after the establishment of the cease-fire, in order to reach a common understanding of the other provisions of Security Council Resolution 598 and the procedures and timings for their implementation.

Securing the Cease-Fire

On 25 August in Geneva the secretary-general opened talks with both foreign ministers. "Your presence here clearly indicates your governments are quite prepared to pursue the path to peace," he told the two. "Against the background of the cease-fire, our discussions will be businesslike, constructive, and indeed productive."[58] Pérez de Cuéllar and his aides sat at a head table; to his left and right at separate tables the Iraqi and Iranian delegations faced each other. The secretary-general aimed immediately to set a time frame for implementation of 598. Iraq, wanting the parties, not the mediator, to play the leading role, rejected the idea that the two sides allow him to set the timetable.

The next day Tariq Aziz insisted that Iran recognize Iraq's claim to full sovereignty over the Shatt. He refused to agree to any timetable unless Iran pledged not to interfere with Iraqi efforts to clear the Shatt and reopen it for shipping. To square this position with Iraq's earlier insistence on strict sequential implementation of 598, Iraqi diplomats explained that understandings on sovereignty over the Shatt and shipping rights in the gulf were needed to implement a cease-fire, and thus had to precede talk about the mandatory withdrawal provision of the first operative paragraph of 598.

Velayati did not reject the idea of reopening the Shatt, but he insisted that any permanent settlement be based on the 1975 Algiers agreement, in other words that the boundary would be the *thalweg*.[59] Iraq had dug in around a position that, even if politically significant, in a military sense was "inherently absurd," because shifting the boundary would not have made its access to the sea any less vulnerable to modern air power and missiles. According to an eminent student of the war, "The issues are now strategically meaningless to the point of military absurdity. It is equally hard to conceive, however, that either Iraq or Iran will easily accept this reality."[60]

On the third day of talks Iraq released a statement by Saddoun Hammadi, the acting foreign minister, that the Shatt had been "a river of Iraqi sovereignty through all stages of history. . . . Any attempt to minimize the full sovereignty of Iraq over this vital lane would be faced with categorical rejection from our side."[61] Velayati countered that treaties cannot be abrogated by unilateral action and that "border treaties are permanent, unchangeable, and decisive."[62] Pérez de Cuéllar, admitting the talks had run into difficulties, took two moves to get them back on track. He spoke with the Geneva ambassadors of the permanent members to ask that their governments support his efforts to bridge the gap between the two sides. He prepared an initiative suggesting that Iran would guarantee the right of Iraqi vessels to sail unhindered in the gulf and through the Strait of Hormuz and that Iraq would agree to withdraw its forces from Iranian territory.[63] In addition the United Nations would conduct a feasibility study of the work that needed to be done to reopen the Shatt.[64] Both foreign ministers remained in Geneva, but there were no more joint meetings.

On 1 September Pérez de Cuéllar announced he was departing Geneva for vacation and appointing Swedish ambassador Jan Eliasson as his personal representative for the talks. Eliasson, then Sweden's permanent representative in New York, had previously been under secretary for political affairs at the Foreign Ministry in Stockholm and before that foreign policy adviser to Olof Palme. He had worked with Palme during his mediation in the Iran-Iraq war. Earlier in his career Eliasson had served in Bonn, Washington, and Paris.[65] After one more session on 10 September, the talks were effectively in recess.

At the end of August Pérez de Cuéllar had tried to involve the permanent members in his negotiations, but they demurred. With the cease-fire in effect, the immediate threat to their interests had passed, and they were not eager to become reinvolved. In September Pérez de Cuéllar proposed that the talks be moved from Geneva to New York, which would in effect bring them back closer to the Security Council. Iraq, now that it had prevailed on the battlefield, wanted the negotiations kept away from the council. On 25 September Ismat Kittani told the secretary-general that Tariq Aziz accepted his invitation to talks in New York, but only for a single meeting with Velayati on Saturday, 1 October. Any further talks would have to be held in Geneva. Kittani specified that the only purpose of the Saturday meeting should be to set a date for talks to resume in Geneva. Other signs suggested the secretary-general might try to prolong talks in New York through a series of consultations with both sides.[66]

On 28 September the foreign ministers of the permanent members met with the secretary-general for their annual meeting. Their collaboration, which had been so improbable during the United Nations' first four decades, had produced its first significant success after less than two years of effort. Could the same procedure be used with success on other issues?

This year, for the first time, the five foreign ministers issued a formal, detailed communiqué.[67] The text emphasized regional issues, the improved international atmosphere, and the role of the United Nations. Regarding the Iran-Iraq war the ministers welcomed the cease-fire and the start of direct talks under the auspices of the secretary-general; they called on both sides to show restraint and flexibility in the talks. The only other point specifically referring to a regional conflict was a reaffirmation of their commitment to the sovereignty, independence, and territorial integrity of Lebanon. Now that the conflict between Iran and Iraq had been contained and seemed on the way to solution, the ministers spent more time on other regional conflicts and discussed, and differed on, the possibilities for dealing with the Arab-Israeli conflict in the Security Council. Namibia and Cambodia would be put on the agenda of their ambassadors in New York in the coming months.

On Friday, 30 September, Pérez de Cuéllar met separately with Tariq Aziz and Ali Akbar Velayati to present new proposals. He suggested that initial steps include an Iranian guarantee for Iraqi shipping in the Persian Gulf and Strait of Hormuz, an Iraqi withdrawal from Iranian territory, release and repatriation of prisoners of war, and postponement of discussion of the Shatt al-Arab.[68] The Saturday meeting lasted for over four hours, with agreement being reached only to renew the talks in Geneva on 26 October. Two days later Velayati reaffirmed Iran's attachment to the 1975 Algiers agreement and vowed that Iran would "never permit the Iraqi Government to achieve its aggressive designs by its resort to destructive ploys in the peace talks."[69]

Talks in Geneva resumed on 31 October. For the first time the two delegations, during one of the breaks, accepted an invitation to take refreshments together. Otherwise the only progress was an agreement on a partial exchange of sick and wounded prisoners of war: 411 Iranians held in Iraq and 1,115 Iraqis held in Iran. Later in the month, Iran suspended the planned ten-day prisoner exchange process after only three days because the exchange was uneven.[70]

The two sides met with the secretary-general and Ambassador Eliasson in December, without forward progress. Pérez de Cuéllar soon followed the advice he had given as part of his 1986 Oxford lecture—mediators, when confronted with an inability to modify the positions of the parties through rational arguments, should explain the factual situation accurately and dispassionately. He explained:

At present, the parties continue to hold divergent views on what constitutes a cease-fire. They have different views also on when the withdrawal of forces to the internationally recognized boundaries should begin. On the question of the restoration of the Shatt al-Arab to navigation, the parties have different positions as to the context and manner in which that matter should be addressed. These divergences emerge in the context of a disagreement on the wider issue of the framework for the conduct of the direct talks. The divergent views of the parties illustrate the necessity of creating trust and confidence between them.[71]

The negotiations had settled into a pattern. Now that a cease-fire was in place, the permanent members no longer treated the Iran-Iraq conflict as a subject for their joint action. The secretary-general, with Ambassador Eliasson, was on his own to coax and cajole the parties forward in the peace process. There was no progress. The peacekeeping force of UNII-MOG, despite logistical difficulties, monitored the cease-fire, resolved local incidents, investigated violations, and worked with the parties to solidify the cease-fire.

13

The Permanent Members
Working Together

A Maturing Institution

In the two years that followed the August 1988 cease-fire the permanent members expanded their new pattern of collaboration. Made possible by improved relations between the Soviet Union and the United States, change could be seen in the annual meetings of foreign ministers; in the now-regular consultations among both the ambassadors and counselors of the permanent members; and in the way these gradually institutionalized practices accommodated the natural rotation of ambassadors.

When the foreign ministers of the permanent members had their annual luncheon with the secretary-general on 28 September 1988, the discussion, as noted, centered on regional conflicts. After reaffirming support for Pérez de Cuéllar's diplomacy with Iran and Iraq,[1] they talked about the Middle East. Since the founding of the United Nations, year in and year out, more than half of the meetings of the Security Council have dealt with one aspect or another of the Arab-Israeli conflict. Britain, China, France, and the Soviet Union supported the idea for an international conference on the Arab-Israeli conflict, with the participation of the permanent members and of the Palestinian Liberation Organization "on an equal footing." France and the Soviet Union wanted the Security Council, in particular its permanent members, to act as a preparatory committee for the conference. To one extent or another these governments wanted the Arab-Israeli conflict on the agenda for talks among the New York ambassadors of the permanent members. George Shultz would have none of it. For the next year, except for one stiff exchange of positions at the ambassadorial level, the Arab-Israeli conflict was not on the agenda.

The communiqué issued after the ministers' 29 September 1989 meeting showed evidence of change. This time the communiqué went beyond regional crises to include points on terrorism, narcotic drugs, peacekeeping, and an expression of "satisfaction at the improved working relations within the Council and with the Secretary-General." But the bulk of the communiqué again concerned regional conflicts, in the order of Namibia, the

Middle East (including Lebanon, Iran, and Iraq), Central America, and Cambodia. The point on the Middle East avoided new commitments: "Having reviewed developments in the Middle East, the ministers reaffirmed their support for an active peace process in which all relevant parties would participate, leading to a comprehensive, just and lasting peace in the region."[2] Aides drafted the communiqué beforehand, and during two hours not all these crises could be discussed in depth, but one can assume the four other ministers again pressed Secretary of State Baker to agree to discussions of the Middle East among the permanent members.

In 1989 and 1990, new permanent representatives took over leadership of the U.S., Soviet, Chinese, and British delegations in New York. In March 1989 Thomas R. Pickering replaced General Walters. Pickering, who held the personal rank of career ambassador, the highest in the U.S. Foreign Service, was only the second career officer to hold this position. He had previously been ambassador to Jordan, to Nigeria, to El Salvador, and most recently to Israel.[3] Pickering was once called "an unfriendly ambassador of a friendly country" by a parliamentary member of Israeli Prime Minister Shamir's party when he served there, and when he was moved to the New York post, King Hussein said Pickering was the best American ambassador he had worked with during his long reign.

President Bush, who twenty years before had been the U.S. ambassador in New York, decided that Pickering, unlike his predecessors, would not have cabinet rank. Bush chose the consummate professional for the job, and he wanted the work done at the highest professional level. Pickering, known among colleagues for inexhaustible energy and restless creativity, was a man to master the details in every brief: "I've always believed that if you like your job and enjoy it, you ought to do it with some verve."[4] A *New York Times* profile said Pickering had "a self-effacing wit and the professional diplomat's ability to listen, or at least give the impression of listening, to another's point of view."[5] He was naturally relaxed and approachable, a key to his success with colleagues from over 150 countries.

In early 1990 Yuli Mikhailovich Vorontsov presented his credentials to the secretary-general as the new permanent representative of the Soviet Union. From 1966 to 1977 Vorontsov had served first as counselor, then as minister-counselor, at the Soviet embassy in Washington. He had been ambassador to India from 1977 to 1983, and to France from 1983 to 1986. From 1986 until 1990 Vorontsov had been first deputy foreign minister in Moscow, and, as seen, had repeatedly visited Tehran and Baghdad, offering to help the two sides find a better way to resolve their problems. From 1988 to 1989, while retaining his position in Moscow, Vorontsov had been concurrently the Soviet ambassador in Kabul, a sure sign that he had Gorbachev's and Shevardnadze's utmost confidence.[6] Almost always wearing a conservative dark blue suit, Vorontsov conveyed the impression that he truly enjoyed the games of power politics.

Li Daoyu, the new permanent representative of China, presented his credentials on 12 June 1990. Li had entered the foreign service in 1952 at the age of twenty. In Beijing he had held various posts in the Department of International Organizations and Conferences, and from 1983 to 1984 he had been China's deputy permanent representative to the United Nations office in Geneva. He had returned to Beijing to become director of the Department of International Organizations and then assistant foreign minister.[7] Able to switch to English whenever the translating seemed unsatisfactory, he conveyed an impression of mental discipline and matter-of-fact realism and merited his reputation of being tough, canny, and agile.

Sir David Hannay became Britain's permanent representative in September 1990. Sir David had begun his diplomatic career in 1959 with Persian language study and a tour in Tehran. From 1965 to 1977 he had served in Brussels, first with the British delegation to the European Community and then as chef de cabinet to Sir Christopher Soames at the EC Commission. He had then held various posts in the Foreign and Commonwealth Office, including head of the Middle East Department. He had spent little more than a year as minister at the British Embassy in Washington before becoming Britain's ambassador to the European Community in Brussels.[8] Members of his own staff in New York released the rumor that Sir David had been the model for Sir Humphrey, the manipulative senior civil servant in the British TV satire "Yes, Minister."

Experience modified the way the permanent members worked as a group. They changed the practice of the British always hosting the ambassadors and the Americans the counselors for a quarterly rotation with the same delegation hosting both groups. In addition to the annual meetings of ministers and the working sessions of ambassadors and counselors in New York, senior officials from capitals began to meet periodically, specifically on the question of Cambodia.

As the permanent members gained experience in coordinating their diplomacy on an expanding number of subjects, collegiality, more than unity of views, remained characteristic of their work. Even though other delegations, including the nonaligned, wanted the permanent members to maintain good working relations, they worried that these five delegations would work together to maximize their influence, limiting the ability of other members to influence the council's agenda.

Confirmation of Change

In the two years that followed the cease-fire between Iran and Iraq the permanent members used their process of consultations within the framework of the Security Council to help resolve conflicts in Namibia, Central America, and Cambodia. This work confirmed the process of change in Security Council diplomacy, and it emphasized the growing connection between the bilateral policies of the permanent members and the work in New York.

At UN Headquarters on 22 December 1988 Secretary of State Shultz presided over the ceremony at which the foreign ministers of Angola, Cuba, and South Africa signed agreements for South Africa's withdrawal from Namibia, for implementation of the UN plan for Namibian independence (resolution 435), and for the departure of Cuban troops from Angola. Getting to this point had taken a decade of tough diplomacy.[9] Now the Security Council had to activate the arrangements approved a decade earlier to oversee the end of South African administration of Namibia and to provide a UN peacekeeping force, the United Nations Transition Assistance Group (UNTAG).

Council members were divided over the arrangements to implement 435. The United States and the Soviet Union wanted UNTAG cut substantially to reduce the estimated price tag of $600–$700 million,[10] and the other permanent members agreed to cooperate.[11] On 20 December they urged the secretary-general to reexamine the issue. African front-line states, led by Zimbabwe's ambassador, determined the position of the African group and therefore that of the nonaligned caucus. On 21 December a nonaligned delegation told the secretary-general that, "if anything, there was a need for an increase in the military component of UNTAG."[12]

Ambassadors of the permanent members and of the nonaligned caucus agreed that their counselors would negotiate to reach agreement over the size and cost of UNTAG. One European ambassador noted that this was the first time the permanent members and the nonaligned caucus would negotiate together, and he hoped this could become a new model for Security Council cooperation.

From the start the meetings went poorly. From the week before Christmas until New Year's Day, long negotiating sessions revealed a clash of diplomatic cultures. Counselors of the permanent members went through the issues point by point, based on detailed instructions from capitals. The nonaligned team argued against any reduction. Whenever several hours of negotiation resulted in a modified text, the nonaligned asked for time out to consult front-line delegations, after which few compromises survived. On New Year's Eve the council president, Japan's ambassador, consulted widely and proposed a compromise. The effort failed. Britain's Ambassador Tickell called the deadlock "a great tragedy" and explained, "We couldn't enter into new negotiations on points we had already discussed at length."[13]

On 16 January the council adopted resolution 629 (1989), which asked the secretary-general to identify, "wherever possible, cost-saving measures," in effect shifting the burden of decision-making to Pérez de Cuéllar. Both sides pressed their views on the secretary-general. Zimbabwe's ambassador called the demands of the permanent members "unacceptable" and threatened to delay Namibian independence if the size of the UN forces were reduced.[14] On 23 January the secretary-general recommended cuts in the size of the military component of the peacekeeping force and a budget of $416 million. He stated that, should a real need for additional military personnel become apparent, he would deploy as many as needed (subject to no objection from the Security Council) and hoped that the permanent members would provide a free airlift to transport any additional troops.[15]

Neither side was satisfied. Nonaligned delegations resented the secretary-general's cutting the force under duress; the permanent members bridled at the idea that he might expand its size unless the council objected. On 16 February the council approved the secretary-general's report. According to Paul Lewis of the *New York Times,* "Diplomats said the action of the permanent Council members marked the first time in the United Nations that the Soviet Union and China have allied themselves firmly with the United States on such a sensitive matter in opposition to the third world."[16] The power shift within the council was evident: the size of the operation was cut and its cost kept under $400 million.

The first foreign policy issue confronted by the new Bush administration was the conflict in Nicaragua. After the February 1989 Tesoro Beach Accord among Central American governments, President Bush called on the Soviet Union to abandon "old thinking" and to cut support for the Nicaraguan armed forces: "The Soviet Union has no legitimate security interests in Central America; and the United States has many. We reject any doctrine of equivalence of interest in this region as a basis for negotiations." During the coming months the Soviet Union shifted policy by restricting aid to Nicaragua, both directly and through Cuba. In September 1989 Foreign Minister Shevardnadze told Secretary Baker the Soviet Union would work to cut the flow of weapons from Nicaragua into El Salvador. "We combined a U.S. diplomatic approach toward Nicaragua with limits on Soviet arms shipments to give the people of that wounded nation a chance to determine their own future," Baker later explained. "The Soviets joined us in a commitment to respect both the electoral process and its result. Peace and democracy were the outcome."[17] The U.S. and Soviet delegations in the Security Council then worked together to authorize arrangements proposed by the secretary-general to support the regional peace process.

On 27 February 1989, after a year of indications that the war in Cambodia might be ended, delegations of the permanent members put Cambodia on their agenda in New York. The member states of the Association of South East Asian Nations (ASEAN) wanted to keep the United States and other Western powers engaged on Cambodia so that they would not be left alone to deal with de facto Vietnamese hegemony in Cambodia. The Soviets wanted a graceful way to unload the burden of supporting Vietnam. China insisted that Vietnamese withdrawal must be subject to international verification. France, with its historical connections with Southeast Asia, wanted to promote its special role as cochairman with Indonesia of the Conference on Indochina. Britain and the United States were looking for information on Chinese and Soviet views and for openings to influence events.

Starting in May 1989 the five counselors looked for areas of convergence. They identified the functions for an international control mechanism that would monitor the withdrawal of Vietnamese troops, a cease-fire, the cessation of arms shipments, cantonment of armed forces, demobilization, repatriation, human rights protection, and elections. In June France proposed to host a conference on Cambodia, with the starting date of 30 July. The counselors now served as a preparatory committee, producing conference papers (formally unattributed but known to come from the permanent members) on military arrangements, human rights, international guarantees, and elections. The UN secretariat provided papers on repatriation and reconstruction. The French circulated these papers along with points on the complete withdrawal of foreign forces, a suitable control mechanism, the ending of external assistance, elections, genocide, international recognition and guarantees, the return of refugees, and reconstruction.[18]

The Paris conference, meeting through August, achieved less than hoped for. It foundered on the issue of power-sharing among the Cambodians, who could not overcome their animosity and agree on any interim formula. Four unresolved problems were (1) defining an interim authority for power-sharing in Phnom Penh, (2) designing UN or international auspices for the settlement, (3) deciding how the genocidal policies of the Khmer Rouge would be condemned, and (4) the issue of Vietnamese settlers in Cambodia. After a month of committee work French foreign minister Roland Dumas held a meeting to prepare for the closing ministerial session planned for 28–30 August. Secretary of State Baker, through his representative, announced that he "was not prepared to participate in a hazardous exercise."[19] Neither were the Soviet or Chinese ministers. The final communiqué claimed progress but acknowledged "that it was not yet possible to achieve a comprehensive settlement."[20]

On 5 January 1990 Secretary of State Baker told the secretary-general he had invited the permanent members to meet at the level of Asia directors to identify key issues vis-à-vis a Cambodian transition process. His aim was to reach consensus, to move the process along, and to reconvene the Paris Conference later in the year. The Asia directors began that month a series of meetings to define the conditions for an enhanced UN role. This initiative represented a change in procedure for the work of the permanent members: for the first time the key players were officials from capitals, and after each session they issued joint communiqués.

During the first seven months of 1990 they held five such meetings:

• On 15 and 16 January in Paris they stated that their aim was to facilitate a political process leading to free and fair elections, and they agreed on

a set of principles and on supporting efforts by regional parties to reconvene the Paris Conference.[21]

- On 11 and 12 February in New York they defined conditions for successful peacekeeping (withdrawal of foreign forces, cease-fire, end of external
  military assistance, and cantonment of local forces in designated areas).
  They discussed options for establishing a Supreme National Council in
  which sovereignty would repose during the transitional period.[22]
- On 12 and 13 March in Paris they issued principles for the election process, invited the Cambodian parties to agree on setting up the Supreme
  National Council, and defined the role for a United Nations Transitional
  Authority in Cambodia (UNTAC) as exercising all powers during the
  transitional period necessary to assure the Cambodians that they would
  be free from intimidation, to provide them with protection from economic and social discrimination, and to guarantee their human and
  civil rights.[23]
- After meeting in New York on 25 and 26 May their communiqué stated
  the "Five" had discussed transitional arrangements, including the authority to be exercised by a Supreme National Council and the role to
  be played by the United Nations. The Five would prepare documents
  for discussion with the Cambodian parties.[24]
- On 16 and 17 July in Paris the Five registered further progress on transitional and military arrangements. They affirmed their intention to speed
  up work on elections, human rights, and international guarantees, and
  they called on the Cambodian parties to return to the negotiating table.[25]

On 28 August the Five issued the framework agreement that, after endorsement by the Security Council and the General Assembly, became the
basis for reconvening the Paris Conference.[26]

Despite the two innovations that marked this process, the role of senior
officials from capitals and the use of communiqués to keep other parties
and the Security Council informed, in essence this diplomatic process was
the same as that suggested by the secretary-general in early 1987 for work
on Iran-Iraq—a general discussion aimed at producing a meeting of minds
that could then be reflected both in the Security Council and in the bilateral
policies of its permanent members.

Choices

Since the permanent members had begun to work together, the kind of
diplomacy practiced in the Security Council had shifted from public confrontations toward confidential negotiations. At the same time the bond
had grown between diplomacy at the Security Council and the bilateral
policies of the major powers, reinforcing both. However, despite the reference in resolution 598 to articles 39 and 40 of the charter, the council later
took no action to invoke the powers providing for sanctions or the use of

force. The permanent members had studied the use of sanctions at length, but they had examined military issues only superficially in their discussion of the proposal for a UN naval force.

If the council were asked to authorize the use of force, what choices would council members have? There are three possibilities in chapter VII—the authority in article 40 used as the basis for peacekeeping, the authority in article 43 for members to make military forces available to the Security Council, and the authority in article 51 recognizing the inherent right of individual or collective self-defense.

Article 40 provides authority for provisional measures that are "without prejudice to the rights, claims, or position of the parties concerned" to be taken "to prevent an aggravation of the situation." Peacekeeping operations, as Pérez de Cuéllar had explained in his report on setting up UNII-MOG, depend on four essential conditions: the backing of the Security Council, the consent and cooperation of the parties, the ability to function as an effective military unit, and adequate financial arrangements. In order for any of these conditions to be met there must be a well-defined, practical mandate for the peacekeeping force. Because the cooperation and the consent of the parties has been considered an essential requirement, peacekeepers have not been authorized to use force except in self-defense, and then under restrictive guidelines. The chain of command for peacekeepers goes to the secretary-general.

It is logical to assume that a peacekeeping force given a mandate to enforce the peace must be prepared to operate without the consent and cooperation of at least one of the parties. In some circumstances such a mandate might both "aggravate the situation" and prejudice the position of one party. The other conditions stated by Pérez de Cuéllar would consequently become more difficult to meet: any decision to use force would be likely to provoke dissent from some members of the council; many governments that willingly provide soldiers for peacekeeping could not be counted on to send their troops to a combat situation, and it is far more difficult for a military unit to be effective under combat conditions than during peaceful patrols; and costs would rise exponentially. How many national armed forces are equipped to serve in combat situations far from home?

The second option would be to activate the arrangement in article 43:1, which states, "All Members of the United Nations, in order to contribute to the maintenance of international peace and security, undertake to make available to the Security Council and on its call and in accordance with a special agreement or agreements, armed forces, assistance and facilities, including rights of passage, necessary for the purpose of maintaining international peace and security." Subsequent provisions give the Security Council important functions: to take the initiative in negotiating such agreements; to invite members supplying forces to participate in decisions regarding the use of those forces; and to plan for the application of armed force with the assistance of the Military Staff Committee, which in turn would be "responsible under the Security Council for the strategic direction of any armed forces placed at the disposal of the Security Council." While the chain of command for such forces seems to go through the Military Staff Committee to the Security Council, article 47:3 states that "questions relating to the command of such forces shall be worked out subsequently."

Before 1989 the Security Council had never taken the initiative to negotiate such agreements, so these provisions were inoperative for practical purposes. Any series of negotiations to make these provisions operative would be long and complicated. In short, these provisions could not be activated to meet the needs of a crisis situation unless a series of agreements for members to make military units available to the Security Council were already in place.

Nor had the permanent members even discussed the merits of activating these provisions.

The third option for the use of force under chapter VII would be to rely on the authority of article 51, which recognizes the inherent right of individual or collective self-defense. One benefit of this provision is that it leaves decision-making in the hands of those national leaders having command of the military forces involved; action can be taken in a crisis. Naturally, strong states with the ability to project military power beyond their borders view recourse to this provision more favorably than do weaker states. One detriment is that, by acting unilaterally or with a group of governments outside the context of the Security Council, it is more difficult to meet the criteria of international law for the legitimate use of force.

In any future crisis in which council members saw a need for force to be used to meet the needs of the situation, they would have to consider these choices. Rather than relying on these provisions separately, could they come up with a general formula giving legitimate authorization for the use of force for a specific purpose?

Iran and Iraq on Their Own

One issue the permanent members did not discuss together after 1988 was the Iran-Iraq conflict. Despite frequent meetings with the parties throughout 1989, the secretary-general and Ambassador Eliasson made no progress toward implementing 598. In February Pérez de Cuéllar met with both foreign ministers and then held a joint plenary meeting. In March and April Eliasson conducted separate talks with both sides, followed by a round of joint plenary meetings chaired by the secretary-general. In July Pérez de Cuéllar again met with both ministers. In September, at the Non-Aligned Summit in Belgrade, he met again with both sides. On 29 September he met with Velayati in New York, and on 4 October he met with

Tariq Aziz. During two weeks in November Eliasson visited Baghdad and Tehran, meeting with both President Hussein and now President Rafsanjani (elected in July 1989, following the June death of Ayatollah Khomeini). In mid-December Pérez de Cuéllar met twice with Tariq Aziz and twice with Velayati.

In September 1989 the secretary-general explained to the Security Council that Iraq insisted on direct talks with Iran, but Iran simply wanted the mandatory withdrawal of 598 implemented:

> In essence Iraq stresses that resolution 598 (1987) should be fully implemented as a peace plan. It affirms that it bases its position on the resolution and my letter to the parties of 8 August 1988, of which the Council has been informed. Its main concern is the implementation of the other provisions of the resolution, once the withdrawal to the internationally recognized boundaries has been carried out. Iraq maintains that the direct talks it had envisaged to reach a common understanding of the provisions of the resolution as a whole have yet to take place. Iran, on the other hand, maintains that the withdrawal to the internationally recognized boundaries is a mandatory provision of the resolution which should be carried out without delay or pre-conditions. It asserts that the withdrawal should be implemented as a first step, together with the cease-fire, in accordance with paragraph 1 of the resolution. However, Iran can accept a limited package within the framework of my 1 October 1988 presentation.[27]

Tariq Aziz and Velayati explained their differences in starker terms. As Tariq Aziz complained, rather than the direct meetings promised in the 8 August 1988 letter of the secretary-general, there were "merely meetings during which the Iranians avoided any direct and serious discussions on the important issues." He further asserted, "When Iran recognizes Iraq's historical and legal rights to the Shatt al-Arab waterway, there will be no problem regarding our forces' withdrawal from the small territorial spots on which they had been present when the cease-fire came into effect."[28] Velayati countered, "Iraq should accept present common borders between the two countries and the water border in the Arvand river within the framework of the 1975 accord."[29]

As a way around this deadlock Iraq pursued direct contacts with Iran. The contact points were the ambassadors of the two sides at the UN headquarters in Geneva: Iraq's Barzan al-Takriti was a half-brother to Saddam Hussein; Iran's Sirous Nasseri was well connected to President Rafsanjani. On 5 January 1990, during an address to the nation on the sixty-ninth anniversary of the Iraqi army, Saddam Hussein made public another offer for direct talks. He said representatives of both sides should meet alternatively in Baghdad and Tehran, under UN auspices, over the next three months to develop a common understanding of the provisions of 598. He proposed an immediate exchange of sick and wounded prisoners of war and of all prisoners captured before 4 September 1982, as well as an exchange of organized religious visits by peoples of both countries.[30] Iran rejected this initiative, calling it "a new campaign of public deception to undermine Resolution 598."[31] Within a month the parties resumed public bickering.

To salvage the situation, Pérez de Cuéllar in March proposed to the ambassadors of both sides a draft agenda for resumed direct talks.[32] In May Saddam Hussein sent Rafsanjani a letter offering "an opportunity for a comprehensive settlement to the border conflict," and Rafsanjani characterized the letter as a "signal" of good intentions in Baghdad.[33]

On 3 July Ali Akbar Velayati and Tariq Aziz met at Geneva's Palais des Nations under the auspices of the secretary-general. Pérez des Cuéllar said: "The meeting was sending to the two peoples, the Iranians and the Iraqis, the right message, that both Governments are really committed to finding a peaceful solution to the problem as soon as possible. . . . I think it is a breakthrough in the sense that it is the first face-to-face meeting of the two Ministers since the cease-fire. The two have never met alone with me. On previous occasions, the foreign ministers talked to me and did not address each other. It is the first time that they will be together with me and exchange views. Psychologically, this is very important."[34] Tariq Aziz described the meeting as "cordial and constructive," but he claimed its aim was to arrange a summit meeting between Presidents Hussein and Rafsanjani.[35] Velayati gave a different slant, saying that, if agreement were reached on prisoners of war and borders, implementation of other points in the resolution would be facilitated. He emphasized that Iran was very firm about the provisions of the 1975 treaty and that this was the most important criteria for future talks.[36]

On 30 July Saddam Hussein wrote to Rafsanjani. He offered a package deal to begin with a meeting of the two heads of state. The aim would be a comprehensive settlement within the framework of 598. Withdrawal of forces would take place within two months of the conclusion of a comprehensive agreement, as would full release and repatriation of prisoners of war. But Iran would have to accept full Iraqi sovereignty over the Shatt, in exchange for either navigation rights up to the *thalweq* or arbitration. Saddam demanded agreement to drop the requirement for an impartial body to investigate responsibility for the war, "finally to set it aside, because it obstructs rather than promotes progress towards peace." He concluded his offer, "Everything is thus made clear, leaving no room for any contrary interpretation: what we see is a genuine, comprehensive and rapid peace."[37]

Perhaps a breakthrough was near.

14

Opening the New Era

Invasion

On the evening of 1 August, the Pickerings were guests at a dinner at the Carlyle Hotel given by former U.S. Ambassador Thomas Enders and his wife. The Tickells were the only other guests. At 10:00 P.M. the phone right outside the restaurant kitchen rang; it was a call from Under Secretary of State Robert M. Kimmitt for Ambassador Pickering. Kimmitt explained that Iraq had invaded Kuwait, and Pickering was soon on his way back to work. Using his car phone, Pickering called Ambassador Aurel-Dragos Munteanu of Romania, who had just taken over as Security Council president, and then tried to locate the permanent representative of Kuwait, Mohamed Abulhasan. After several calls he traced Abulhasan with the help of the Bahraini ambassador's daughter, who explained that the GCC ambassadors had all gathered at the Russian Tea Room for a farewell dinner in honor of her father.

Pickering called the restaurant, and when Abulhasan came to the phone, he shared with the shocked Kuwaiti ambassador news from Washington that Iraqi forces had invaded Kuwait. Pickering said Washington wanted the Security Council to meet immediately to pass a resolution condemning the invasion. After expressing personal regret, Pickering said he was already en route to his office and suggested that the U.S. and Kuwaiti delegations prepare for a Security Council meeting within a few hours. Abulhasan shared the news with his colleagues at the restaurant and returned to his office.

Pickering called Kimmitt back to confirm that Kuwait was ready to take the lead with the United States in asking for an immediate Security Council meeting. Next they discussed points to put in a resolution condemning the Iraqi invasion, and Kimmitt said the State Department would quickly fax up a draft to use with other delegations. Then Pickering called Sir Crispin, bringing him abreast of events and talking over what the U.S. and British delegations should do to get the resolution adopted without delay. There was another call to the Romanian ambassador to tell him Kuwait and the United States would ask for an immediate meeting of the council

188 *A New Era*

and to the secretariat so that necessary staff would return to work later that night.

It was after midnight before council consultations were announced for 1:30 A.M. By this time the U.S. and Kuwaiti delegations had sent in letters asking for an immediate meeting and agreed on a draft for a resolution, explicitly under chapter VII's articles 39 and 40, condemning the invasion and demanding Iraqi withdrawal. In 1987 it had taken six months of negotiations to secure agreement to take action under these provisions; now the response was immediate. Pickering and Abulhasan made initial contacts with other council members so that they would get in touch with their capitals and receive instructions to support the resolution and preferably to cosponsor it. Before leaving the U.S. Mission for the Security Council, Pickering and his small staff could feel comfortable that Britain, Canada, Finland, and France would cosponsor. China and the Soviet Union would likely support the resolution but not cosponsor. The challenge was to get nonaligned cosponsors.

It was a night of "frenzied negotiations,"[1] with delegates taking turns at the phone booths in the consultations area to stay in contact with capitals. Gradually Abulhasan and Pickering made progress in getting others to see that what was at stake was a rule of law, embodied in the UN charter, that should give weak, small states protection against the ambitions of stronger, larger neighbors. Malaysia's representative, after checking with Kuala Lumpur, agreed to cosponsor. He explained in the formal meeting, "We are against acts of external interference, aggression and the use of force and the threat of force in inter-State relations without exception. This is particularly important to protect the sovereignty of small states."[2]

The Ethiopian delegation could not get through on the telephone to Addis Ababa. After a few hours of trying, Ethiopian Permanent Representative Tesfaye Tadesse acted on his own. Ethiopia would cosponsor the resolution. A week later Tadesse restated Ethiopia's point of view: "What we are watching before our very eyes is an act of utter lawlessness, a sad re-enactment of the tragic events of the 1930s when might made right. We all recall where that led. . . . It is with this conviction that Ethiopia, which itself was a victim of such aggression in the past, condemns Iraq's aggression."[3] Canada, Colombia, Côte d'Ivoire, Ethiopia, Finland, France, Malaysia, the United Kingdom, and the United States—but not the Soviet Union or China—cosponsored the resolution.

Shortly after five o'clock that morning Munteanu called the Security Council to order. Kuwait's Abulhasan, using permissible exaggeration, warned the council that, if it did not deter Iraq in a decisive manner, "no country will be safe after this, and the security, sovereignty and territorial integrity of every State will be jeopardized."[4] Claiming that the council was responsible for protecting Kuwait, Abulhasan said, "This is a test for and the responsibility of the Council *vis-à-vis* peace and security in that vital area of the world and towards all small nations that are defenseless and helpless."[5] Iraq's representative rebutted weakly, arguing that, because there was a new government in Kuwait, "the person in the seat of Kuwait here represents no one, and his statement lacks credence" and that Iraq rejected "the flagrant intervention of the United States in these events."[6]

"The United States has made it clear that it will stand shoulder to shoulder with Kuwait in this time of crisis," Pickering told the council. Putting the crisis into its larger historical context, he said, "The Security Council has seldom faced a more blatant use of force. . . . It is the time for peace and diplomacy, not the time for war and aggression. The world is now watching what we do here and will not be satisfied with vacillation or procrastination."[7]

Sir Crispin characterized the crisis as "an ugly moment in world affairs," and said, "I want to express not just a sense of dismay but also a sense of disgust that this kind of thing can still happen in 1990 in the world community in which we all live and breathe."[8]

After the brief debate the ambassador of Yemen, Abdalla Al-Ashtal, announced that Yemen would not participate in the voting because his delegation had no instructions. The council adopted resolution 660 (1990) with fourteen votes in favor, none opposed, and Yemen not participating. The meeting adjourned shortly after six o'clock.[9]

Secretary of State Baker was then in the Soviet Union for meetings with Foreign Minister Shevardnadze. In the months ahead their cooperation was crucial to the diplomatic process centered in the Security Council. On 2 August, the Soviet Union announced an embargo on arms to Iraq, and President Bush signed an executive order banning all trade with Iraq and freezing the assets of both Iraq and Kuwait. The next day Baker and Shevardnadze issued a joint statement condemning Iraq's invasion. After describing the Iraqi invasion as a "blatant transgression of the basic norms of civilized conduct," the statement said the two sides believed the "international community must not only condemn this action, but also take practical steps in response to it. . . . Governments that engage in blatant aggression must know that the international community cannot and will not acquiesce in or facilitate aggression."[10]

Meanwhile European Community governments, Japan, and Canada were moving to impose their own sanctions against Iraq. On the afternoon of Friday, 4 August, the U.S. delegation in New York faxed to other council members the text of a resolution that would impose against Iraq comprehensive economic sanctions, excepting only medicine and food in humanitarian circumstances. A committee of Security Council members would monitor the sanctions regime. After adoption of resolution 598 on the Iran-Iraq conflict, the permanent members had negotiated, inconclusively, for twelve months on a comparable but much simpler text intended to impose an arms embargo only. Although this would be only the third time that the Security Council had used the authority of article 41 to impose sanctions (the other cases being the Rhodesian trade embargo and the arms embargo against South Africa), Pickering again asked for immediate action. By Sunday, just two days later, after informal consultations of the council, he told the press that the council was "strongly in favor of moving ahead to a vote" the next day.[11]

After further consultations on Monday morning, nine delegations (Canada, Colombia, Côte d'Ivoire, Ethiopia, Finland, France, Malaysia, the United Kingdom, the United States, and Zaire—but not the Soviet Union or China) asked for the council to meet and vote on their draft resolution imposing sanctions. When the council meeting started at 1:30 P.M., Abulhasan spoke first and then Iraq's Ambassador Abdul Amir Al-Anbari. Al-Anbari complained that, because the draft was prepared by a single state which then lobbied others to support it, "that makes the draft resolution null and void, because anything imposed by force and threat is not legitimate under the principles of the Charter."[12] A superpower, he claimed, was trying to use the Security Council as if it were simply its foreign ministry.

Pickering turned Al-Anbari's rhetoric against him, pointing out that he was insulting other council members by dismissing their determination on this issue with the charge that the council had somehow become the U.S. foreign ministry. "By this draft resolution, we declare to Iraq that we will use the means available to us provided in chapter VII," added Pickering. "Iraq must learn that its disregard for international law will have crippling political and economic costs, including, but not limited to, arms cut-offs. Our concerted resolve will demonstrate that the international community does not—and will not—accept Baghdad's preference for the use of force, coercion and intimidation."[13]

Sir Crispin chose to emphasize two points: "The first is that the draft resolution will remain in effect only so long as resolution 660 (1990) is not complied with. Secondly, economic sanctions should not be regarded as a prelude to anything else. Here I obviously refer to military action." The council was acting as originally intended, he explained, and it should set a precedent for management of world order based on respect for law, sovereignty, and territorial integrity. He continued, "It must succeed this time where the League of Nations failed and where it itself has faltered in the past."[14]

Soviet Ambassador Lozinskiy's statement showed the Soviet Union was making hard choices, choices it had avoided making two years earlier when the issue was enforcing resolution 598. After Iraq's invasion of Kuwait, the Soviet Union had halted the delivery of arms to Iraq and had taken "the unusual step" of issuing a joint appeal to other states asking them to do likewise. The Soviet Union "actively facilitated" the adoption of resolution 660 condemning Iraq's invasion of Kuwait. Now the Soviet Union would vote for a resolution to impose sanctions against Iraq. "It was a difficult decision," said Lozinskiy, "because the draft resolution directly affects a whole set of relationships between us and Iraq that have been developing over many years now."[15] With other interests at stake, the relationship with Baghdad was expendable.

The council adopted resolution 661 (1990) by thirteen votes in favor, with Cuba and Yemen abstaining. After the meeting adjourned the director of the secretariat staff assigned to the Security Council noted that "this is the first time we have skipped lunch—certainly in the past 15 years."[16]

Events moved quickly over the next three days. On 6 August, after King Fahd invited friendly forces to Saudi Arabia to reinforce its defenses, President Bush ordered a squadron of F-15 fighters to a Saudi air base along with the 82d Airborne Division. The same day Saddam Hussein claimed his seizure of Kuwait was "irreversible." On 7 August Saudi Arabia and Turkey shut down the oil pipelines through which Iraq exported its petroleum to Red Sea and Mediterranean ports. On the eighth, President Bush announced in a televised speech the deployment of U.S. troops to the Middle East and stressed that four principles guided U.S. policy: the demand for the withdrawal of Iraqi forces from Kuwait; restoration of the legitimate government of Kuwait; the U.S. commitment to peace and stability in the gulf; and protection of American lives in the region. Iraq proclaimed the annexation of Kuwait, and the United Kingdom sent additional air and naval units to defend Saudi Arabia.

As soon as Iraq proclaimed its annexation of Kuwait, Ambassador Abulhasan asked for a Security Council meeting. The next morning, 9 August, the council adopted unanimously a draft resolution prepared in the course of prior consultations. The key paragraph in resolution 662 (1990) expressed the council's decision "that annexation of Kuwait by Iraq under any form and whatever pretext has no legal validity, and is considered null and void."

The statements that followed adoption of the resolution were remarkable for the degree to which they prefigured discussions on the legitimate basis for using force to reverse Iraq's aggression. Pickering took the lead in asserting that the increased U.S. military presence to help protect Saudi Arabia was in conformity with article 51 of the charter, which protects the inherent right of individual or collective self-defense when an armed attack occurs against a member of the United Nations. He cited the provision in resolution 661 stating that article 51 applied in this case. Then, after insisting "we" cannot allow sovereign states to be swallowed up, Pickering hinted that the United States would seek to avoid unilateral military action to this end. "The United States stands ready to return to the Council as circumstances warrant to seek further Council action to implement resolution 660 (1990)."[17]

Ambassador Blanc said France would look with favor on subsequent decisions taken to ensure the implementation of resolutions 660, 661, and 662. Ambassador Lozinskiy, after repeating how hard and bitter it was for the Soviet Union to criticize Iraq, given the long friendship between the two countries, stated twice, "The Soviet Union is against reliance on force and against unilateral decisions."[18] Sir Crispin reported the British decision to send forces for the collective defense of Saudi Arabia in accordance with article 51: "The presence of British forces, particularly naval forces, in the area will be of added advantage in the context of securing the effective implementation of resolution 661 (1990). . . . We see the close monitoring of maritime traffic as a key element in making the embargo effective."[19]

The ambassadors of Cuba and Iraq argued that the introduction of foreign forces into the area was the result of unilateral decisions and without the legitimacy of collective actions taken properly under the provisions of the charter. They did not agree that U.S. and British military deployments could be justified under article 51. Operating on a different tack, Ambassador Abulhasan said that the motive for Iraq's aggression became clear through its annexation of Kuwait. "This brings us back to the law of the jungle."[20]

A senior official in Washington, speaking on condition he not be identified, said that the United States preferred that any military operations in the gulf be "wrapped in the U.N. flag."[21] Following the Security Council meeting, Ambassador Pickering was asked about the possibility of a UN force. He answered, "Those are all decisions that President Bush will have to make, and the President has said nothing is ruled in and nothing is ruled out."[22]

The Iraqi Diplomatic Offensive

In mid-August Saddam Hussein launched a three-part diplomatic offensive. The first operation succeeded in part at considerable cost, the second fizzled, and the third backfired.

On 8 August President Rafsanjani answered Saddam Hussein's 30 July offer to settle the Iran-Iraq conflict within the framework of 598. Rafsanjani rejected the proposal that he meet with Saddam Hussein, pointing out that a meeting would be effective only if all the key issues had already been sorted out. He rejected Saddam's proposal for settling the boundary in the "Arvand Rood" (the Persian name for the Shatt) and insisted on the terms of the 1975 Algiers agreement recognizing Iranian sovereignty up to the *thalweg*. Recalling that the secretary-general had proposed a two-week period for withdrawal of forces, he rejected Saddam's suggestion of a two-month period. Rafsanjani criticized the Iraqi occupation of Kuwait, which led to "extensive presence of foreign forces in the region, disturbing peace and tranquility, creating problems for Muslim people." "No doubt, while peace talks are in process between the two countries, unexpected aggression against a neighbor country without the slightest notice, and accompanied by all its grave consequences for us," Rafsanjani noted in an understatement, "could weaken our trust and create serious doubt in the motives of the past few months' talks."[23]

Within a week Saddam folded his position on the boundary in the Shatt. On 14 August he sent back a letter agreeing to the Iranian proposal that the 1975 agreement would be the basis for settling the dispute. The Iraqi withdrawal would begin on Friday the seventeenth, and on the same date an immediate and complete exchange of prisoners of war should begin. Saddam stated, "With this decision of ours all has become clear, and thus all that you have desired and all that you have stressed has been achieved. . . . Each of us will respect the rights of the other, we shall dismiss from our shores those who fish in troubled waters, and we shall perchance co-operate in ensuring that the Gulf remains a lake of peace and safety, free of foreign fleets and the forces of the foreigner which lie in ambush to our misfortune."[24]

The release and repatriation of prisoners of war began on 17 August, and the withdrawal of Iraqi forces was completed on 21 August.[25] For the rest of the crisis, Iran neither helped nor hurt Iraq. Thus ended the cycle of conflict that began with Iraq's invasion of Iran in September 1980.

Saddam's second diplomatic initiative was aimed at the Arab world. On 12 August, with Islamic rhetoric, he attacked the United States, "its despicable ally, Israel," and their lackeys in the Middle East. His initiative was an improbable offer to withdraw from Kuwait if Israel withdrew from territories occupied during the 1967 war and from southern Lebanon. The conditions and limitations attached to the offer made it a sham. Israel would have to withdraw "unconditionally" from all those territories; Syria would have to withdraw from Lebanon; Iraq and Iran would have to withdraw from each other's territory; and, *then* the situation in Kuwait would be settled taking into account "the historic rights of Iraq to its territory and the choice of the people of Kuwait."[26] For good measure Saddam added that all the measures taken by the Security Council against Iraq (comprehensive sanctions) had to be "applied to all who do not respect or comply with this arrangement."[27]

Saddam then said U.S. and foreign forces had to be withdrawn from Saudi Arabia, to be replaced by Arab forces agreed to by both Iraq and Saudi Arabia. He explicitly disqualified Egypt because of its close relations with the United States. While this plan was being implemented, there would be "an immediate freeze of all decisions relating to the boycott and blockade against Iraq."[28] He continued, "If the United States and its allies and lackeys fail to respond positively to our initiative, we shall oppose their evil inclinations with force, assisted by the worthy sons of the Arab nations and the great Iraqi people, and we shall triumph with the help of God, causing the forces of evil, who will be routed and forced to leave the region defeated, vanquished, damned and humiliated, to regret their acts. God is great and woe unto the vanquished."[29]

Tariq Aziz followed up by publicly affirming to the secretary-general that Iraq "has no intention of initiating any military action against the Kingdom of Saudi Arabia."[30] Next he accused the United States of intending to use the trade embargo to starve and intimidate the people of Iraq. On 16 August Saddam sent an "open letter" to President Bush, but his intended audience must have been the populace in Arab countries, whom he directly addresses at some points. The letter was a mixture of bluster and threat. The Arabs, he claimed, were those who would sweep from power "he who does not resist your shameful designs against the Arab nations and Moslem holy shrines, and through which you demonstrated how much you hate Arabs and how much you belittle their will and the will and views of Moslems."[31] Already Saddam's thoughts were turning to the prospects for war: "We will continue to pray to God that the two sides will not clash, because if they do thousands of Americans whom you have pushed into this dark tunnel will go home shrouded in sad coffins. The gates of heaven are now open to you, Arabs. You now have the chance of living a noble life. Your turn, Moslem believers, has come and the road of holy war which infuriated the outrageous Bush is now open."[32]

Except among Palestinians Saddam had little success in his attempt to whip up Arab support and thus to discredit the international coalition arrayed against Iraq. Saddam's themes were more popular than he was personally. Powerful leaders in Egypt, Syria, and the Arab gulf were part of the multinational coalition opposing Iraq. Saddam's biggest problem may well have been simply that, from early on, it seemed too improbable that Iraq could prevail against the forces called into play by its occupation of Kuwait.

Saddam's third diplomatic initiative, aimed at the United States and other Western states, backfired. On 16 August Saddam threatened to intern all four thousand Britons and two thousand Americans in Kuwait; Iraq had already on 10 August ordered all embassies in Kuwait to close. On the seventeenth the speaker of Iraq's parliament announced that citizens of "aggressive" nations would not be released until the threat of war against Iraq ended.

On Saturday the eighteenth, France's Ambassador Blanc, who throughout this period was the coordinator for the meetings of the permanent members, arranged for the five ambassadors, accompanied by counselors, to meet in the conference room of the French Mission. On the table for discussion was a draft resolution, again under chapter VII of the charter, demanding that Iraq permit and facilitate the immediate departure from Kuwait and Iraq of third-country nationals and to grant consular access to such individuals. After a brief discussion the ambassadors agreed to ask the council president to convene consultations later in the day with the idea of getting agreement on the draft from all fifteen members and then proceeding to adopt it at a formal meeting.

The secretariat faxed the draft to all fifteen members, who throughout the afternoon and early evening consulted with each other and with capitals. By 10:30 P.M. agreement was reached in informal consultations on a text that all council members would support.

The meeting quickly adopted resolution 664 (1990), with most delegations strongly denouncing Iraq's decision to hold innocent civilians hostage and to place some as "human shields" at strategic sites. Taking note of President Bush's order to the U.S. Navy to intercept shipping to or from Iraq and Kuwait (a measure also being taken by the Royal Navy), speeches that night sharpened the debate over the use of force to ensure compliance with the council's mandatory resolutions. Yemen's Ambassador Al-Ashtal made the initial criticism of the unilateral decision to set up a naval blockade without taking into account the role of the Security Council or asking for its explicit authorization.

Cuban Ambassador Alarcón, as was his custom, spoke at length. He argued that the U.S. claim that it was acting under article 51 and the right to self-defense was invalid, because that article authorized self-defense "until the Security Council has taken measures necessary to maintain international peace and security." Alarcón said the United States was twisting the terms of the charter, infringing on the authority of the Security Council to legitimize its own unilateral actions.[33] Pickering immediately shot back that the United States was acting correctly under article 51, as reaffirmed by resolution 661. When Iraqi Ambassador Al-Anbari repeated Alarcón's argument, Pickering suggested that having Iraq interpret Security Council resolutions was like "setting the fox to watch the hen house."[34]

The next day Saddam released an open letter to families of foreigners detained in Iraq. Its tone was slightly hysterical to Western ears. Saddam, already encircled by the multinational coalition, offered a deal: he would permit the foreigners to leave if the Security Council undertook to guarantee either an agreement by the United States to withdraw its forces from the region or more generally peace and security in accordance with Saddam's 12 August initiative. Alternatively Saddam offered to let the foreigners depart if President Bush announced, "clearly, unequivocally and in writing," that U.S. and allied forces would withdraw from the region and not use force against Iraq; in addition President Bush would have to lift the embargo against Iraq and "work together with Iraq on a basis of mutual respect, equality and a commitment not to damage each other's interests."[35] As for Kuwait, that question would have to be left to the Arabs and addressed as an Arab issue.

Following Saddam's hostage ploy, France ordered its fleet in the gulf region to ensure compliance with UN sanctions against Iraq. Saddam's television talk with British hostages in Baghdad on 23 August generated further adverse reaction in Western public opinion.

Authorizing the Use of Force

On 10 August Secretary of State Baker told a meeting of the North Atlantic Treaty Organization that resolution 661 gave the United States the right to use force to prevent other countries from trading with Iraq and Kuwait:

"It is the view of some of us that we have the legal authority necessary to institute such an embargo or blockade, provided that the request comes from the legitimate Government of Kuwait."[36] In New York at this point, other council members disagreed with this view, maintaining that resolution 661 might allow foreign naval vessels to monitor ship movements and report to the Security Council but not to use force.

On 12 August, backing up Baker's assertion, the White House press spokesman made a statement reporting a request from the Emir of Kuwait for the United States to take steps to ensure that the UN sanctions against Iraq and Kuwait be effectively implemented: "In view of the Emir's request, the President has decided that the United States will do whatever is necessary to see that relevant UN sanctions are enforced. The President stressed that these efforts will complement, not substitute for, individual and collective compliance that has been highly successful thus far. The United States will coordinate its efforts with the governments of other nations to whom the Kuwaiti Government has made similar requests."[37]

"For the first time since the beginning of the crisis," cabled home one UN ambassador, "the United States looked isolated."[38] On Monday, 13 August, when the council members met in informal consultations, ambassadors from Canada, Cuba, France, Malaysia, and the Soviet Union raised questions about the U.S. announcement that it would use force to turn ships away from Iraq and Kuwait.[39] They criticized the U.S. decision, in part because it was unilateral and reached without discussion in the Security Council. As a TASS statement had explained the previous week, the Soviet Union opposed unilateral military action by Britain or the United States, wanted "full use of UN mechanisms," and was "prepared to enter into immediate consultations within the framework of the Military Staff Committee."[40]

"I tried to make the point that Canada is Washington's best friend on the Council, and that if your best friend can't bring you bad news, who can?" explained Ambassador Yves Fortier. "I said that these are uncharted waters, that there are no precedents, so why not play it as the framers of the Charter had envisioned it?"[41] The framers of the charter had provided in articles 43 to 47 for agreements to be concluded between states and the United Nations, at the initiative of the Security Council, putting armed forces at the disposal of the Security Council, and for a Military Staff Committee to advise and assist the council on military questions. The trouble was that no such agreements had ever been concluded, and thus the council had no forces at its disposal. In effect those provisions were inoperative.

"What we are seeing is that in agreement with the governments of Saudi Arabia and Kuwait, some decisions have been taken . . . but not in the context of the UN resolutions," explained Pérez de Cuéllar.[42] "Only the United Nations, through its Security Council resolutions, can really decide about a blockade."[43] While Secretary Baker thought resolution 661, when coupled with a request from Kuwait for help with self-defense, gave implicit, indirect authorization for a blockade, the secretary-general thought explicit, direct authorization was needed.

On Tuesday, 14 August, Under Secretary of State Kimmitt called in the British, Chinese, French, and Soviet ambassadors in Washington to discuss putting the naval operation in the gulf under UN auspices. The two options under discussion were a more concrete proposal, initially by the Soviet Union, to set up a joint command of naval vessels in the gulf under Security Council auspices (similar to the UN naval force proposal of two years earlier) and a vaguer arrangement to give the warships the protection of the UN flag (the U.S. preference).[44]

According to one participant, "The Americans threw the Soviets the bone they wanted"[45]—an agreement that the ambassadors of the permanent members in New York would meet together with their military staff officers, following the format of the political discussions of the last two and a half years. On 17 August the ambassadors met. At Chinese and U.S. insistence they agreed that meetings with military officers would be informal, kept separate from the Military Staff Committee, and for the purpose of briefing the Security Council president. When military advisers joined the meeting, Admiral Kelly gave a briefing on U.S. plans for a conference of naval commanders in the gulf in ten days to help with practical measures to coordinate activities. Others present pointed out that the naval forces were present in the area on a national basis, that such a conference should not set up a force outside the UN framework, but that information from the conference could be passed to the Military Staff Committee. The meeting ended with an agreement to inform the Security Council president that the members of the Military Staff Committee had met informally to exchange information and established procedures for future informal meetings.

By Sunday, 19 August, the military issue was no longer academic. U.S. warships were tracking two Iraqi tankers: the *Khanaqin* was in the Gulf of Oman heading toward Yemen, and the *Baba Gurgur* was in the Strait of Hormuz. "It's not a question of if we are going to stop these tankers," said a senior official in Washington. "It's a question of when."[46] In New York the permanent members met throughout the day at the level of both ambassadors and counselors, hoping to work out differences over how to put teeth in the embargo before asking for a council meeting.

On Monday evening Ambassador Pickering was instructed to ask for an urgent Security Council meeting and to keep the council in session however long it took to get a resolution passed authorizing the use of force. He argued that the council should act before 6:00 A.M. the next morning, New York time, when the *Khanaqin* would reach Yemeni waters. Seeking a UN seal of approval but not a UN command, the United States wanted the council to "put a UN umbrella but not a UN flag" over its naval operations.[47] Such a resolution, while necessarily involving the potential use of force and thus under chapter VII of the charter, could not cite any of the articles with specific provisions for the UN military force, because it had never been constituted. As consultations went on late into the night, other diplomats resented that the United States had forced the issue in order to give an international character to naval interdiction measures it had decided to take in any case.[48] The standoff ended at 1:00 A.M., when Yemen's Al-Ashtal announced that his government would not permit the *Khaniqin* to be unloaded.[49]

The respite was only temporary. On Tuesday the twenty-first the ambassadors of the permanent members met for two hours to consider a U.S. draft. "Everyone reaffirmed the importance of the five and the Council as the mechanism to see that sanctions are enforced," Sir Crispin told the press.[50] In Moscow Foreign Ministry spokesman Yuri Gremitskikh said Foreign Minister Shevardnadze had sent a message to Secretary of State Baker: "We have to maximize the potential of political measures which have already been taken. In considering the use of force, we must avoid hasty decisions." Gremitskikh said, "It's hard for me to predict whether we will abstain or use our veto."[51]

Baker, who was vacationing in Wyoming, spoke on the phone with Shevardnadze on Wednesday. Shevardnadze said he had made a strong appeal to Iraq's deputy prime minister Saddoun Hammadi to release foreign nationals and to withdraw from Kuwait. Shevardnadze agreed to an enforcement resolution[52] but asked for forty-eight hours to give Saddam Hussein time to respond. "My colleagues and I are concerned that it is more difficult to build a relationship with a country than to break it up," said Col. Valentin Ogurtsov, a senior official in the Soviet Defense Ministry. "The Iraqi actions have been condemned by the international community and the United Nations. But it is not easy for us to move from full-fledged relations to zero."[53] In Washington, policy makers said that Soviet officials felt the United States was moving too fast on this issue and that they wanted convincing evidence that sanctions were being evaded.

On Thursday the permanent members referred to their capitals a revised draft presented by the United States. The U.S. draft, citing the authority of chapter VII, called on member states deploying maritime forces to the area "to use such minimum force as may be necessary under the authority of the Security Council to halt all inward and outward maritime shipping . . ." Concerning the Military Staff Committee, the draft asked states concerned to use as appropriate the mechanisms of the committee to submit reports.[54] In the evening Pickering presented to the Sanctions Committee evidence, including maps showing the locations of oil tankers, of Iraqi efforts to evade sanctions; Sir Crispin offered evidence of Libyan help in arranging the transshipment of military equipment to Iraq.[55]

Friday the twenty-fourth was a long day. In Moscow Alexandr Belonogov, now deputy foreign minister, summoned U.S. ambassador Jack Matlock to approve the U.S. draft, with two changes. One change emphasized the need for the maximum use of political and diplomatic measures; the other replaced the phrase "minimum force" with the vaguer "measures commensurate to the specific circumstances."[56] The same day President Gorbachev warned Saddam Hussein to abide by the Security Council's resolutions: "Sidestepping these demands will inevitably prompt the Security Council to adopt appropriate additional measures." TASS described Gorbachev's warning as an "urgent personal message."[57] Throughout the day the Bush administration, through a presidential message to Chinese leaders and meetings in Washington, Beijing, and New York, stressed that it would be unthinkable for China to veto the draft, especially since the Soviet amendment removed the explicit reference to force that had been unacceptable to China.[58] U.S. ambassadors in all Security Council capitals were lobbying hard to secure support for the draft.

Through the evening Pickering picked up cosponsors: Britain, Canada, Côte d'Ivoire, Finland, France, and Zaire. Pickering, Sir Crispin, and Lozinskiy presented the draft to a meeting of the nonaligned caucus. The ambassadors of Colombia and Malaysia expressed reservations. While delegations shuttled between consultations and telephone calls to capitals, a particular effort was made to bring China along. When his colleagues, including some nonaligned ambassadors, told China's permanent representative that, as a permanent member, China had no business abstaining, Li Daoyu listened but gave nothing away.

Ambassador Munteanu called the Security Council to order at 3:15 A.M. Saturday, 25 August. After initial formalities, Ambassadors Al-Ashtal, Alarcón, and Enrique Peñalosa (Colombia) explained that the draft moved too quickly to the use of force, gave unclear powers without a definition of the Security Council's role, and was acting only to give color of legality to a U.S. decision to use force.[59]

When the vote came, thirteen members voted in favor of resolution 665 (1990), including Li Daoyu, whose vote surprised many of those present. Only Cuba and Yemen abstained.

Pickering put on record the U.S. understanding of the resolution. Resolution 665 granted authority permitting the use of armed force, if required; U.S. naval forces would use minimum force to enforce sanctions strictly. The resolution did not, however, impair the legal authority of Kuwait or other states to exercise their inherent right of self-defense.[60] Sir Crispin emphasized that article 51 and the Kuwaiti request already provided sufficient legal authority for the use of force to enforce the embargo.[61]

There were two disclaimers. Li Daoyu, in a statement that could have been written to explain why China opposed resolution 665, said that the text did not contain the concept of using force and, based on that understanding, China supported it.[62] The second disclaimer came in a letter the next day from Shevardnadze, in which he emphasized that the resolution "consolidates the Council's control over measures to implement the sanctions and provides for a coordinating role for the Military Staff Committee."[63]

Four weeks into the crisis, the *Wall Street Journal* assessed the impact of UN diplomacy.

The U.N. has emerged as an invaluable tool. President Bush, himself a former U.N. delegate, understood the potential of the organization for providing cover and legitimacy for his response to Iraq's invasion of Kuwait. Without the prospect of U.N. support, he might not have been able to persuade Saudi Arabia to accept U.S. troops. Without U.N. action, it would have been more difficult for an Islamic state such as Turkey to close its oil pipelines. Without the U.N., the likelihood of Soviet involvement in international action was slim; from the outset, Moscow made it clear that it would not move without the U.N. The administration has at some points in the current crisis moved at a slower pace, or shown more caution, than officials would have preferred—specifically in order to keep the five permanent members of the Security Council moving in unison. For instance, Mr. Bush held off on unilaterally enforcing the embargo. That was a deliberate strategy chosen in hopes that the crisis could set a precedent in which the Security Council showed it would take concerted action against international aggressors, something it has seldom done in the past.[64]

Consolidating New Positions

Presidents Bush and Gorbachev consolidated these new positions in Helsinki on 9 September. During the previous week Foreign Minister Shevardnadze gave a speech in which he talked about the "complex set of problems involving the Arab-Israeli conflict, the fate of the Palestinians and the tragedy in Lebanon" and concluded, "We have to step up pressure for an international conference on the Middle East without deferring for a subsequent period the efforts to bring about a comprehensive settlement under the aegis of the United Nations."[65] But a few days later, after a meeting between Gorbachev and Tariq Aziz, the official Soviet spokesman played down the idea of linking the Kuwait crisis with other problems in the region.[66]

The joint statement issued by the two presidents after the summit stressed their determination to end Iraq's occupation of Kuwait. In cautious diplomatic language it addressed the difficult issues of using military force and of working together to solve other conflicts in the area. First, the statement said, "Our preference is to resolve the crisis peacefully, and we will be united against Iraq's aggression as long as the crisis exists. However, we are determined to see this aggression end, and if the current steps fail to end it, we are prepared to consider additional ones consistent with the U.N. Charter. We must demonstrate beyond any doubt that aggression cannot and will not pay." Second, as soon as that goal had been achieved:

"The Presidents direct their foreign ministers to work with countries in the region and outside it to develop regional security structures and measures to promote peace and stability. It is essential to work actively to resolve all remaining conflicts in the Middle East and Persian Gulf . . . at the proper time."[67]

In the press conference that followed, Bush said he supported, under certain circumstances, the proposal for an international conference on the Middle East, but he rejected any link between the Kuwait crisis and such a conference. Gorbachev, after noting that the joint statement emphasized the need for the two sides to cooperate on the Middle East, said, "There is a link here because the failure to find a solution in the Middle East at large also has a bearing on the acuteness of the particular conflict we've been talking about here."[68] Commenting on the shift toward U.S.-Soviet cooperation on the Middle East, a U.S. official said, "There is no blueprint here, but there is a recognition that Soviet foreign policy toward regional disputes is changing and that their new thinking deserves to be matched by new thinking here."[69]

While Gorbachev and Bush were meeting, a naval commanders' conference to coordinate national procedures ("in view of Resolution 665") was taking place in Bahrain. The aim of the conference was to coordinate interception operations, including timing of deployments and areas of operation, logistics, communications, and sharing of information. Under Kuwaiti chairmanship the participants (from Australia, Bahrain, Belgium, Canada, Denmark, France, Greece, Italy, The Netherlands, Norway, Oman, Pakistan, Portugal, Qatar, Saudi Arabia, Spain, Turkey, the United Arab Emirates, the United Kingdom, and the United States) agreed to divide the area into four zones and to use communication procedures following standard U.S. practice.

On 18 September the political counselors and military officers of the permanent members met at the French Mission in New York. U.S. and French officers provided briefings respectively on the Bahrain conference and on a meeting of the Western European Union in Paris on 14 September. Western diplomats saw the meeting as the bone with which to satisfy the Soviet demand that the Military Staff Committee become more involved in coordinating enforcement action; Soviet diplomats, who wanted to be involved in contingency planning, were not satisfied with simply receiving briefings.[70]

Filling in the gaps in the framework designed to counter Iraq's occupation of Kuwait, the Security council adopted four more resolutions before the end of September. Resolution 666 (1990) aimed to settle an argument of interpretation: under what circumstances could foodstuffs and medical supplies be sent through the embargo? A decision on the issue had been triggered by a request from the government of India to the Sanctions Committee asking permission for an Indian cargo vessel to sail to an Iraqi port to unload food for South Asian residents of Kuwait. When the council met late in the evening of 13 September, first it voted on a draft submitted by Cuba that would totally exempt foodstuffs and medical supplies from the embargo. This draft failed because only China, Cuba, and Yemen voted in favor. A second draft, submitted by Canada, Finland, France, the Soviet Union, the United Kingdom, and the United States, set out provisions for delivery of foodstuffs and medical supplies to Iraq and Kuwait through the United Nations in cooperation with the International Committee of the Red Cross or other humanitarian agencies. As Ambassador Pickering explained, these safeguards had been made essential because the council could not "count on the good faith of the Iraqi Government."[71] The Sanctions Committee had already approved the sailing of the Indian ship. Thirteen members of the council voted for the resolution; Cuba and Yemen voted against. Within days Iraq refused any cooperation with the United Nations or humanitarian agencies as provided for in resolution 666.[72]

On Sunday, 16 September, the council unanimously adopted resolution 667 (1990) to condemn Iraqi aggression against diplomatic personnel in Kuwait and to demand the release of third-country nationals. Two days earlier Iraqi soldiers had forcibly entered the French ambassador's residence in Kuwait and detained the French military attaché and three other French nationals. Similar violations occurred at the Belgian, Canadian, and Dutch embassies.[73] By the third week of September the permanent members began drafting in earnest a resolution to extend sanctions to include air transport of cargoes to Iraq; the resulting draft was adopted by the meeting chaired by Foreign Minister Shevardnadze on 25 September as resolution 670 (1990).

Meanwhile the Sanctions Committee had received requests for assistance from states hard hit by losses in carrying out sanctions against Iraq. Article 50 of the charter provides that, if enforcement actions ordered by the council cause a state "special economic problems," that state "shall have the right to consult the Security Council with regard to a solution of those problems." Resolution 669, adopted unanimously on 24 September, entrusted the Sanctions Committee with responsibility to examine such requests and to make recommendations to the president of the Security Council.

15

Into the Future

Changing with the End of the Cold War

The Kuwait crisis transformed and redefined the UN's usefulness as an instrument for collective security. Only two years earlier, after the permanent members reached the milestone of resolution 598 on the Iran-Iraq cease-fire, they could not agree on an arms embargo to enforce it nor on an international effort to protect shipping in the gulf. UN officials called the Security Council's activity during August 1990, from the resolution demanding Iraqi withdrawal from Kuwait to the approval of measures necessary to enforce sanctions, "what the World War II allies had in mind during the final days of the war when they began drafting the charter of an organization that would be able, in the new atomic age, to prevent regional conflicts from growing to global proportions."[1] Statesmen and citizens of the permanent members could look at this change with favor, hoping that by staying together on the Kuwait crisis they might be able to do so as well in other troubled areas.[2] Not all, however, shared these hopes.

The transition to a post Cold War era, with the permanent members acquiring power by working together, reduced the diplomatic influence of the Third World majority at the United Nations. The UN's "center of gravity," which during the Cold War had passed to the General Assembly dominated by the majority of Third World states, was now shifting back to a Security Council led by its permanent members. Even within the Security Council, resentment grew over the role played by the permanent members, whom another council member accused of serving "precooked dinners we are supposed to swallow and be grateful for."[3] "I've been around the U.N. for twenty years, but never thought I'd see it approving such sanctions," reflected Yemen's Ambassador Al-Ashtal. "In the General Assembly, we shout and we condemn, and it doesn't matter."[4]

In the assembly's general debate, foreign ministers voiced different opinions on these changes. Eduard Shevardnadze spoke of the beginning of the rebirth of the United Nations "according to the blueprints of 1945. Wiping off the grime left by the 'cold war,' we see a work of collective wisdom. The United Nations was conceived as an instrument of action. Henceforth, we must all ensure that our words are bound to joint—and I emphasize 'joint'—actions."[5] Iran's foreign minister Velayati recalled the world's indifference to Iraq's invasion of Iran, and, while not objecting to action against Iraq, was less positive: "All of a sudden, the major Powers in the Security Council, in particular the United States, rose to the defence of the Charter in an unprecedented manner, claiming that they would not allow any tampering with cardinal and universally recognized principles of international law. . . . A spectacular public [display] of international solidarity to corner the aggressor was painted in front of the unbelieving eyes of the world public."[6]

Britain's foreign secretary Douglas Hurd reminded the assembly that when the great Chinese statesman Chou En-Lai was asked what he thought of the French Revolution, he replied, "It is too soon to tell."[7] Hurd insisted on a sober analysis of international relations, stating, "The basic unit in the system, the basic unit in this Hall, the basic unit in our Organization will continue to be the nation state. . . . It is not a perfect system; no one here would claim that. But it has proved enduring and it has been supplemented by regional groupings. Where these groupings are successful they smooth the rough edges between nation states."[8] Implicit in Hurd's analysis was the belief that the United Nations, when successful, could supplement the system based on nation states but could not supplant it.

The crucial policy question facing the major powers was deciding when to move beyond economic sanctions to military action to compel implementation of the Security Council's decision ordering Iraqi withdrawal from Kuwait.

The argument in favor of not moving beyond sanctions to military action was essentially that, in time, sanctions would be effective at lower cost. As explained by Zbigniew Brzezinski, the costs of the military option "could prove to be prohibitive, its success is not easy to define in terms of the time involved and the scope of the required effort, and its dynamic consequences could have a regionally destructive ripple effect." Even if "the peaceful strategy of sustained pressure suffers from obvious limitations and has its costs," Brzezinski advised, patience and prudence were to be preferred "over the leap into the abyss of warfare."[9] In hindsight, Saddam's ability to withstand several years of embargo after coalition forces defeated his army is conclusive proof that he would have withstood years of the embargo without the use of force.

The argument in favor of military action was that, even if the sanctions worked, there was still the danger that they would only get Saddam to the negotiating table, at which point international pressure would mount to save his face, handing him a gain that would amount to a defeat for the United States and its coalition partners. At some point the policies of sanctions and of military action would become mutually exclusive. President Bush would have to decide how long to wait for sanctions to work and how far he was prepared to go without unanimous international support. If he waited long enough to determine conclusively that sanctions alone would not get Iraq out of Kuwait, he might no longer be able to secure political backing for the military option. As Henry Kissinger pointed out in late September, "Foreign policy is remembered for its end games, not the opening moves. And the most difficult decisions remain to be made."[10]

When the United States made its choice whether or not to ask the Security Council to approve the use of force, would it be able to keep together a coalition ready to join in its lead?

Enter the Arab-Israeli Conflict

Saddam had tried in August to use the Arab-Israeli conflict to split the coalition opposing Iraq's occupation of Kuwait. On 1 October, President Bush told the General Assembly that after Iraq's unconditional departure from Kuwait there could be opportunities "for all the States and peoples of the region to settle the conflict that divides the Arabs from Israel."[11] The next day Saudi foreign minister Saud Al-Faisal, whose government resented deeply that in Saudi Arabia's moment of need Yasser Arafat had repaid decades of Saudi support by expressing sympathy for Iraq, agreed with Bush's priorities. The principal Arab cause, Prince Saud said, was the Palestinian cause, but Iraq's adventure had diverted attention from the search for a just solution to the Palestinian cause. He continued, "It is for the sake of Palestine that Iraq should withdraw from Kuwait; it is for the sake of Palestine that it should abide by the dictates of international legitimacy so that we may move international legality to achieve for the people of Palestine what, God willing, will be achieved for the people of Kuwait."[12] This sense of priorities was then adopted on 4 October by nonaligned foreign ministers.[13]

On 8 October clashes took place on Jerusalem's Temple Mount that threatened to put the Arab-Israeli conflict back at the top of the agenda. The causes for the incident were unclear, with Israeli authorities and Palestinians giving conflicting opinions as to what provoked the conflict, but between 17 and 21 Palestinians were killed and more than 150 wounded by Israeli security forces; upwards of 20 Israeli civilians and police were wounded by Palestinians.[14] Within hours the Security Council was meeting in emergency session to hear a Palestinian plea for international intervention: "We do not understand how oil in the Gulf can be valued more highly by you than Palestinian blood and Moslem rights and shrines; we do not understand how the Security Council can ignore our plea for protection when it is prepared to send troops to fight a war in the Gulf region."[15] Zehdi Labib Terzi, the PLO's representative, complained that Israel was permitted to run things the way it thought best because it counted on support from a permanent member. Israel's ambassador charged that the PLO caused the incident to draw attention away from Iraq's aggression.

Other speakers then deplored or condemned the shooting by Israeli security forces and called on the council to reactivate a UN role in the peace process. Soviet ambassador Vorontsov made the key statement. After condemning Israel's use of force and recalling traditional Soviet positions relating to a Middle East settlement, he quoted the joint statement issued ten days earlier by the foreign ministers of the permanent members. That statement expressed concern at tensions in the Middle East, "determination to support an active negotiating process," and agreement "that negotiations should be based on resolutions 242 (1967) and 338 (1973)," but it did not suggest any active role for the UN.[16]

For the next four days there was a tug-of-war over the text of a resolution. Pulling on one side were nonaligned members, working from a PLO position that they had turned into a draft resolution; on the other side was the United States. Washington threatened to veto any draft suggesting that the United Nations should provide protection for Palestinians in the occupied territories, the main point of the PLO-originated draft. Underlining the U.S. isolation in this negotiation, the Foreign Office in London announced that Foreign Secretary Hurd had called Secretary Baker to warn him that another U.S. veto in favor of Israel would damage efforts to reverse Iraq's occupation of Kuwait. Arab members of the anti-Iraq coalition were telling Washington that a veto would be "very harmful, very dangerous." Secretary Baker phoned Foreign Minister Shevardnadze to keep U.S. and Soviet diplomacy from working at cross-purposes, and Prince Saud al-Faisal went to Paris to urge the French to move negotiations toward a text the United States would not veto.[17]

By the fourth day attention had shifted to a draft by the council president, Britain's Sir David Hannay. This draft removed the proposal regarding protection of Palestinian civilians from the resolution and put it in a statement by the council president, a less authoritative form of decision. Washington accepted a condemnation of the use of violence by Israeli forces but rejected movement in the direction of a Security Council role in the Arab-Israeli peace process, in part because it did not want the Security Council sidetracked from its focus on the Kuwait crisis.[18] Egypt and Saudi Arabia, eager to avoid a U.S. veto, worked on other council members to bring them around to accepting the version that the United States would support.[19]

Late on Friday, 12 October, the tug-of-war ended when the council adopted resolution 672 (1990) unanimously. Most ambassadors, including those from the closest allies of the United States, called for the Security Council to become active in the Arab-Israeli peace process. Prime Minister Shamir criticized both the Security Council and the United States for questioning anything that Israel did in Jerusalem. "If Israel rejects the Security Council decision," Secretary Baker warned in a letter to Shamir, "there will be some who compare you, even though it is not justified, to Saddam Hussein and his rejection of Security Council decisions."[20] President Bush told reporters, "We want to see that U.N. resolution fully implemented."[21] A senior Israeli official, looking back at the diplomacy of the previous week, said, "We are not prepared to be the sacrificial lamb of the anti-Saddam coalition."[22]

Israel rejected the secretary-general's request that a UN investigatory mission visit Jerusalem. On 24 October, with the United States voting in favor, the council adopted a resolution deploring Israel's refusal to cooperate. Although the secretary-general submitted his report on 31 October and the issue stayed on the agenda, the crisis passed. The United States, if supported by its key Arab allies in the anti-Saddam coalition, could block an Iraqi-backed move to give the Arab-Israeli conflict star billing on the council's agenda.

Naturally Iraq took its case against U.S. policy to the General Assembly, where it would be harder for the United States to control the agenda. On 5 November Iraqi Ambassador Al-Anbari asked that the assembly add to its agenda an item entitled "United States military concentrations in the Gulf region: threats to Arab and international peace and security."[23] But article 12 of the charter states that, when the Security Council is dealing with a dispute, the General Assembly should not take any action on it. Although this rule had rarely been followed, Pickering told the assembly's steering committee, "On very rare occasions there are requests so improper, so ill-founded, so mendacious and so tendentious that it is simply impossible to recommend that the General Assembly deal with them. The item requested by Iraq is such a case."[24] The other twenty-eight members of the committee agreed, approving without a vote a Canadian motion to take no action on the Iraqi request. The assembly might be a place susceptible to control by the Third World majority, but Iraq was totally isolated and without any hope of a majority.

The Gang of Four

On 29 October, after several weeks of negotiations, the Security Council adopted a resolution that was a "marriage" of two separate proposals. One proposal, put forward a few weeks earlier by Cuba and Yemen with support from Colombia and Malaysia, was to entrust the secretary-general with launching a negotiating track with Iraq, a course intended to halt the drift toward war. This idea was tacked on as the last two paragraphs of resolution 674 (1990). The other eleven paragraphs, provided by the British and U.S. delegations, were designed to press Iraq to permit departure of third country nationals, to establish a basis for Kuwaiti claims against Iraq, and to seek evidence of human rights abuses.

Unsatisfied with this outcome, the delegations of Colombia, Cuba, Malaysia, and Yemen, led by Colombia's ambassador Enrique Peñalosa, prepared a second peace initiative. They feared that, unless a diplomatic negotiating channel were opened, the situation would drift toward war. To open such a channel they wanted to signal to Iraq that, if it withdrew from Kuwait, sanctions would be lifted and its underlying claims against

Kuwait would be settled. These four delegations wanted to wrest the initiative in the Security Council away from the permanent members. Peñalosa
wanted to keep his ideas from being submerged in another resolution put
forward by the permanent members. To circumvent their control of the
situation in the council, he decided to take his proposal to the General
Assembly, which he expected would be a more favorable forum.

The substance of Peñalosa's proposal bore an uncanny resemblance to
work that had been done at Harvard's Program on Negotiation. On 15
October Professor Roger Fisher, head of the program, published in the
Christian Science Monitor an op-ed piece entitled "For Saddam, Where's the
Carrot?" Fisher argued that "if sanctions are to have a chance of working
we need to provide Saddam with a way out." Although emphasizing that
Saddam should get no more than he was entitled to under international
law, bargaining points could include

> a transitional Arab peacekeeping force in Kuwait to follow Iraqi withdrawal;
> an invited Soviet presence in Iraq under UN auspices to guarantee Iraq against
> attack; President Bush's reassurance that the U.S. will leave the Gulf when the
> area is stable; arms control negotiations among Iraq, the U.S., and Saudi Ara-
> bia to reduce Iraqi military potential in exchange for U.S. withdrawals; appoint-
> ing a distinguished Arab mediator to work on the Iraq-Kuwait disputes over
> the Ramaila oil field and Iraq's Gulf access; establishing a procedure for dealing
> with all financial issues over frozen assets, debts, and claims for compensation;
> and [an] invitation from Kuwait for Arab assistance in moving toward internal
> democratization consistent with Islamic values.[25]

If the United Nations could offer Saddam a package of terms more attrac-
tive than ongoing sanctions, Saddam's perceptions and choices might
change, with the sanctions finally generating effective pressure for Iraqi
withdrawal.

On 6 November, after Peñalosa and his Cuban, Malaysian, and Yemeni
partners had consulted with selected Third World delegations, they faxed
to seventeen European missions a note introducing their working paper.
"You will note that this is the first comprehensive draft resolution that
covers all the aspects considered necessary to bring about a peaceful settlement of the current crisis in the Gulf," the note explained. "The timing of
this initiative is considered crucial as there is now rather feverish talk of
the war option appearing in the media. . . . A diplomatic initiative of this
kind is needed to avert the outbreak of war." The four ambassadors invited
the note's recipients, none of whom were members of the Security Council,
to meet the same afternoon. The sponsors of the initiative wanted "to
canvass the support of countries outside the Council . . . before consultations are held within the Security Council."

The ten operative paragraphs in the attached draft resolution tracked all
of the points in Fisher's article, with the sole addition of a final paragraph
expressing determination to ensure prompt compliance with Security

Council resolutions relating to the conflict in the Middle East, "in particular, the Palestinian question."

Besides trying to circumvent the process of collegial consultations within the Security Council, over which the permanent members were now exercising decisive influence, the four ambassadors wanted to work around the Arab and Western delegations at the core of the anti-Saddam coalition. The Saudi Arabian mission, perceiving a direct threat to its own interests, prepared, and the same afternoon faxed out, a counterdraft with "killer" amendments aimed to bring this initiative back into line with the course taken by the Security Council. Peñalosa and his colleagues found that most delegations hesitated to oppose those states most immediately involved and preferred to let the Security Council carry on, even if imperfectly, rather than to work around it. The four ambassadors found little support.

On 16 November Peñalosa, in the name of the four ambassadors, sent out a second paper explaining that their approach toward defining a process for postwithdrawal negotiations would make sanctions more effective without offering appeasement for Saddam. Support was still scant, for few delegations wanted a debate and decision in the General Assembly that might conflict with the Security Council's work, pitting the two sides of the body against each other. In the following weeks, while the Security Council was preparing to authorize the use of force to eject Iraq from Kuwait, Peñalosa reworked this approach, circulating a final working paper with a letter dated 5 December.[26] The Gang of Four's initiative fell flat.

Secretary Baker's Resolution

By the end of October it became necessary to seek answers to two questions: at what point to use force to compel Iraqi withdrawal from Kuwait, rather than rely on sanctions; and how to involve the United Nations in that decision. President Bush gave a partial answer to the first question on 8 November when he announced his decision to increase the size of the U.S. forces committed to Desert Shield "to ensure that the coalition has an adequate offensive military option should that be necessary."[27] The additional forces to be sent included 3⅓ Army divisions, 3 aircraft carriers, 1 battleship, 30,000 Marines, and more Air Force units, which would raise the total U.S. forces committed in the area from 230,000 to approximately 400,000. Offensive capacity would be improved by the arrival of 1,200 M-1 tanks. The deployment would take until January, and military specialists warned it would be better to fight before the hot weather that would arrive in the spring. It looked as if Saddam Hussein might enjoy another two to three months of further undisturbed possession of Kuwait.

At his press conference President Bush was asked if he thought the United States was free to take offensive action without a UN resolution authorizing it. "Yes, we have the authority," Bush answered. "But we've been great believers in going to the United Nations. And I think one of the major successes has been the ability to have world opinion totally on our side because of UN action."[28] In short, UN authorization might be preferable but was not required.

Abraham D. Sofaer, who had been the State Department's legal adviser until a few months earlier, laid out the policy arguments in an article titled "Asking the U.N. Is Asking for Trouble" in the 5 November *Wall Street Journal*. Sofaer argued that the self-defense authorization of article 51 remained effective after the council had taken a measure, however ineffectual: "It is absurd to contend that Kuwait should have less authority to defend itself after the Council has upheld its legal and moral position than it would have had before the Council acted." Asking for Security Council backing would require overcoming likely Soviet and Chinese opposition to the use of force, and to maintain unity of command it would be essential to avoid a restriction on the authorization that would require use of the Military Staff Committee apparatus. Sofaer warned that further reliance on the Security Council was likely to undermine its usefulness as an instrument of peace. If "the Council authorizes the use of force in a manner that ensures its effectiveness, so much the better; . . . but the U.S. must not make the Council's approval a precondition for action by the multinational force, nor should it agree to a role for the Military Staff Committee under circumstances apparently intended to obstruct the effective use of force."[29]

The problem of the Military Staff Committee had already been taken care of. On 29 October, using the August format of meeting outside UN Headquarters not as the committee itself but as representatives of members of the committee, the ambassadors of the permanent members were joined at the French Mission by Vice Adm. Alain Coatanea (director of France's Joint Military Staff), Col. Gen. Bronislav A. Omelichev (first deputy chief of general staff, Soviet Armed Forces), Maj. Gen. Edwin H. A. Beckett (British defense attaché in Washington), Maj. Gen. Du Kuanyi (China), and Lt. Gen. Michael Carns (director of the Joint Staff at the Pentagon). The agenda covered a review of the military situation in the area, action to support the naval and air embargoes, and the efficacy of sanctions. There was no response to the Soviet proposal to activate the Military Staff Committee to investigate incidents or to plan for use of force. "I'd lead you away from the idea that we're spending lots of time dreaming up ways to make the Military Staff Committee a focal point of military operations," a State Department official commented.[30]

On 3 November Secretary Baker set out on a marathon trip to consult with allies in the anti-Iraq coalition and to round up support from Security Council members for a resolution granting authorization for the use of force to compel Iraq's withdrawal from Kuwait. His first stops were Saudi Arabia and Bahrain, then Egypt. In Cairo on 6 November he met with Chinese foreign minister Qian Qichen, who said at the opening of their meeting: "The UN resolutions are intended to increase the pressure on

Iraq for a peaceful solution. All of the armed forces have two roles to play. One is to fight a war, the other is to seek peace." After the meeting a U.S. official said China would not use its veto to block a resolution authorizing the use of force.[31]

The next day Prime Minister Thatcher told the Commons, "Time is running out for Saddam Hussein. . . . Either he gets out of Kuwait soon or we and our allies will remove him by force and he will go down to defeat with all its consequences. He has been warned."[32] But other allies were telling Baker that he needed UN authorization for the use of force, and U.S. officials saw that UN authorization would make the military threat more credible and, even while insisting that article 51 gave sufficient legal authority for a military strike,[33] add legitimacy to any use of force.[34] A senior official traveling with the secretary acknowledged a desire "to maintain the international consensus to the extent possible and certainly further United Nations action would be a good measure of that continued international support." The idea was to secure action during November, when the United States held the presidency of the Security Council.[35]

On 8 November Baker was in Moscow, where he met first with Shevardnadze for six hours. In the afternoon President Gorbachev told Baker, according to an official's notes, "If we pass a resolution authorizing force, and if Saddam does not move, you will have to use force. If you do it, you have to use it. Are you really ready to do that now?"[36] Gorbachev suggested a two-step approach, with one resolution in November authorizing the use of force and a second one, after a pause of six weeks or so for diplomacy, giving the green light.[37]

Briefing the press, Shevardnadze said, "Whether or not use of force could be ruled out—well, probably this could not be ruled out, . . . but I still think that any decision should be taken in the framework of the Security Council. . . . We should not doubt the ability of the Security Council to take wise and mature decisions. So I would advise against looking for some differences in the positions between the Soviet Union and the United States." Baker said he had still to consult with a number of countries before decisions would be made.[38] Later he explained, "What we are seeking to do is solicit the views and opinions of each of the countries in the coalition, give them our views, and then come up with a consensus position."[39] Brief stops in Paris and London confirmed French and British support.

By mid-November Baker had the assurances of the permanent members that they would not vote against a resolution authorizing the use of force. Bush sent Gorbachev a cable indicating he wanted to secure agreement on a resolution at their upcoming meeting in Paris on 19 November.[40] To avoid the problem of the ambassadors in the Security Council acting at variance with commitments made by ministers, Baker decided to negotiate directly with the ministers, whom he would then invite to New York for a vote before the end of November.[41] In Geneva on Saturday, 17 November, Baker met Foreign Ministers Tesfaye Dinka of Ethiopia, Simeon Ake of Côte d'Ivoire, and Kalimba Wakatana Mushobekwa of Zaire, who said, "We support it," when asked about a resolution authorizing the use of force.[42]

Before Baker met with Shevardnadze late on Sunday the eighteenth in Paris, he had firmed up support with other council members. Canada looked favorably on the proposal for a resolution; Foreign Minister Adrian Nastase of Romania said he favored a peaceful solution but was ready to consider a military option in a constructive way; Foreign Minister Pertti Paasio of Finland said the decision was mainly for the permanent members.[43] Although Baker had yet to consult the Gang of Four, so far he had found no entrenched opposition. After their Sunday meeting Shevardnadze said no decision had been reached, and Baker advised, "Stay tuned and you'll get an answer tomorrow."[44]

Bush and Gorbachev dined together in Paris on Monday, 19 November, at the U.S. ambassador's residence. Gorbachev accepted the U.S. proposal for a single resolution, and Bush agreed to incorporate the Soviet idea of a grace period for diplomacy.[45] Gorbachev asked Bush not to make their agreement public until he had consulted with Beijing and Baghdad. "We all need patience, but that does not mean we are going to weaken, that we are going to retreat," Gorbachev said. "No, we are going forward in a very resolute way. And the fact that we are working together—not only the Soviet Union and the United States, but the United Nations as a whole are acting together—allows me to expect that in this very difficult crisis resolutions will be found."[46]

After meeting Shevardnadze the next day, Baker said they had not done any drafting but were "unified with respect to the goal and objective of full implementation of the UN Security Council resolutions." Shevardnadze said the main point was that the council's resolutions had not been implemented and aggression had not been stopped. "Now, our task is to consult with each other as to how that essential element can be implemented."[47]

When leaving Paris on 21 November, Bush said he thought action should be taken in the United Nations before 30 November, and Baker said he was pleased with the progress to date.[48] Baker went to Sanaa, where he received no assurances concerning Yemen's position. Next he was in Bogotá. On the twenty-third Shevardnadze met for three hours with Qian Qichen in the Chinese border city of Urumqi, and Qian Qichen called Baker to say he would come to New York for a council meeting, a further sign that the Chinese would not use their veto.[49] French foreign minister Dumas suggested it might take another three weeks to come up with a resolution, but Soviet ambassador Vorontsov announced that Shevardnadze would be in New York the next week to vote for the resolution, stating, "This is not comedy hour in the Security Council."[50] The final stage-setting came on 27 November, when the State Department announced that, despite restrictions on high-level exchanges, Qian Qichen had been invited to visit Washington on 30 November, the day after the planned meeting in New York.[51]

On Thursday, 29 November, Secretary Baker presided over the Security Council meeting that adopted resolution 678 (1990). Canada, Britain, the Soviet Union, and the United States sponsored the resolution. Like resolution 665, it avoided reference to specific articles of the charter by generally citing chapter VII, and it authorized member states cooperating with the government of Kuwait "to use all necessary means to uphold and implement resolution 660 (1990) and all subsequent relevant resolutions and to restore international peace and security in the area." Twelve members of the council voted in favor, China abstained, and Cuba and Yemen voted against.

"With the cold war behind us, we now have the chance to build the world which was envisioned . . . by the founders of the United Nations," Baker said at the opening of the meeting. "We have the chance to make this Security Council and this United Nations true instruments for peace and for justice across the globe."[52] Iraq thought this resolution was the wrong way to begin a new era, Third World governments were apprehensive, and the permanent members were cautious. The only line they agreed on was that ultimate power still resided with nation states, not the United Nations.

Iraqi Ambassador Al-Anbari argued, as he had when resolution 665 was adopted, that the draft violated the charter because it authorized states to use force neither in self-defense (which no longer applied, he said, because the council had already acted on the conflict), nor through article 43's mechanisms for a UN force, nor through the transitional arrangements of article 106, intended for use in the UN's early days. While Iraq advocated peace, the United States imposed an embargo, "a brazen violation of the principle of equality between the countries and peoples of the world."[53] Because small states do not have veto power, they could find no one to protect them from superpower permanent members and sanctions under chapter VII of the charter. "Where is that new international order?" Al-Anbari asked. "Is it the massing of American forces and their deployment in the Gulf region? Is it the threats of the invasion and destruction of Iraq?"[54]

The speeches of Yemen, Colombia, and Cuba criticized aspects of the new world order which others were sighting on the horizon. Ambassador Al-Ashtal said Yemen did not like the draft because it left up to states with military forces in the area the decision of when to use force, and the Security Council would have no control over those forces. It would be better for the council to stick with sanctions and give the secretary-general a free hand to mediate than to begin a new world order based on the war option. Foreign Minister Bernardo Jaramillo of Colombia attacked the use of the veto power during the Cold War and recalled that Colombia had always emphasized the negative effect of the veto power.[55] Cuban foreign minister

Isidóro Malmierca said the United Nations should democratize itself and abandon the practices of privilege adopted at its founding. Cuba opposed a resolution that would give "the United States and its allies *carte blanche*" and violate the charter by "authorizing some States to use military force in total disregard of the procedures established by the Charter."[56]

The permanent members showed caution and optimism. China's Qian Qichen, after claiming that "China does not have, nor does it wish to seek, any self-serving interests in the Gulf region," said China would not vote for the resolution because it moved prematurely to permit member states to use military force against another member state.[57] France's Roland Dumas said the goal in the final analysis was that law must prevail: "This is in the interest of all our States; at stake is the future of relations among States in the building of a more secure and stable world."[58] In a world of nation states, said Britain's Douglas Hurd, the obliteration of one state by another undermined and threatened the whole structure of international order, threatening the safety of all.[59] "We are giving preference to the law, to action under the authority of the Charter and of the Security Council, and to collective efforts," said Shevardnadze. "We have just become aware of the universal value of freedom and democracy for man, for society and for international relations. They must be protected and upheld. Only on the basis of those values can we build a new, just world order and move towards equitable, mutually respectful and mutually beneficial relations among States and peoples."[60]

Secretary Baker summed up. Since 2 August many nations had worked together to prove that aggression must not be rewarded. "The result is a new fact: a newly effective United Nations Security Council, free of the constraints of the cold war." The council had just authorized the use of force and a pause for peace, inviting Saddam Hussein to respect the will of the international community. "We meet at the hinge of history. We can use the end of the cold war to get beyond the whole pattern of settling conflicts by force, or we can slip back into ever more savage regional conflicts in which might alone makes right."[61]

Questions for a New Era

In 1946 the first meetings of the Security Council quickly settled into a pattern of division among the permanent members, with the Cold War's public rhetoric displacing quieter diplomacy. After 1985 the erosion of this pattern gained momentum, and by the summer of 1990 Iraq's invasion of Kuwait triggered a reaction that revealed a new pattern already in place. Change in the Soviet Union had made possible the new pattern. The way had been prepared by cooperation among the permanent members on other regional conflicts, starting with their effort to end the Iran-Iraq war within a UN framework. Saddam Hussein's direct defiance of the nation-state system by claiming to obliterate Kuwait presented the firmest possible grounds for council action. In just four months, from August to November 1990, the Security Council had for the first time, after forty-five years, moved through the progressive steps specified in chapter VII and authorized the use of force. As recently as 1988 such action had not been possible, and at many points in 1990 it seemed most unlikely.

Over the previous two years the Soviet Union had shown how important its willingness to cooperate within the Security Council could be. But already by 1990 the capacity of the Soviet Union to participate in the anti-Iraq coalition was limited to political activity; at no point was there any question that Moscow would play a military role.[62] In August 1990 Secretary Baker asked Saudi Ambassador Prince Bandar about the acceptability of possible Soviet participation in the multinational force; after phoning King Fahd, Bandar said this would not be a problem. The Soviets, however, declined.[63] When Shevardnadze later resigned, on 20 December 1990, the first issue he cited was the charge that he planned to send Soviet troops to the Persian Gulf: "I explained that there are no such plans. They do not exist. Nobody is going to send a single military man, or even a single representative of the Soviet armed forces there."[64] Would Saddam have reacted differently to the Security Council's decisions if Soviet forces had participated in the multilateral force?

Was resolution 678, Security Council authorization for national decisions to use force, the most full use of chapter VII one can realistically aim for? Or, should arrangements provided in article 43 of the charter for creation of a UN force be activated, with the aim of enabling the Security Council to decide to use force?[65] Whatever the answers to this question may be in future, in 1990, as in 1945, it was a world of nation states; and because the United Nations had no existence apart from its member states, national leaders controlled the armed forces in the field and the ultimate decision to use force.

The belief that the United Nations has an independent personality, embodied in the secretariat and led by the secretary-general, is wrong. Member states constitute the United Nations. In the 1950s it was useful for Dag Hammarskjöld to develop a capacity for independent executive action when the major powers were deadlocked. The thawing of the Cold War pulled the capacity for leadership on questions of peace and security back where the charter placed it, to the Security Council and its permanent members in particular. When the Security Council began to work as a place for states to concert their policies, it reduced the room remaining for the secretary-general to display leadership.[66] Secretary Baker, not Secretary-General Pérez de Cuéllar, held the diplomatic lead in the period from 1 December 1990 to 15 January 1991. The responsibility for political leadership lies with nation states.

In January 1987, Pérez de Cuéllar had invited the permanent members to create a "meeting of minds" that would permit them to concert their policies with the aim of ending the Iran-Iraq war. They did, and the importance of their new practice of collaboration was soon evident. In the ensuing four years, they used the mechanism of the Security Council to concert policies toward ending conflicts in the Persian Gulf, Namibia, Central America, Cambodia, and again the Persian Gulf. This trend favored a shift of attention away from the General Assembly, which is more a sounding board for a world town meeting, and toward the Security Council. The council, with restricted membership and advantages for permanent members, served to encourage a meeting of the minds and to legitimize the resulting decisions. But even the council is a body of member states, not a corporation with an independent personality, and member states retain the responsibility to implement its decisions.

Forty-five years after the United Nations was founded, it seemed closer to achieving its first purpose, "To maintain international peace and security, and to that end: to take effective collective measures for the prevention and removal of threats to the peace, and for the suppression of acts of aggression." Collaboration among the permanent members gave new vitality to the work of the Security Council. The series of decisions culminating in resolution 678 solidified the coalition the United States put together to counter Iraq's invasion of Kuwait. Although the UN forces envisaged in the charter had not been created and national forces had to be marshaled, the coalition used force within the framework of the charter and with the Security Council's approval. By defeating Iraq's aggression, will the Security Council and its members gain credibility to deter aggression elsewhere?

Documentary Annex

Charter of the United Nations, Chapters VI and VII

Chapter VI: Pacific settlement of disputes

Article 33. 1. The parties to any dispute, the continuance of which is likely to endanger the maintenance of international peace and security, shall, first of all, seek a solution by negotiation, enquiry, mediation, conciliation, arbitration, judicial settlement, resort to regional agencies or arrangements, or other peaceful means of their own choice.

2. The Security Council shall, when it deems necessary, call upon the parties to settle their dispute by such means.

Article 34. The Security Council may investigate any dispute, or any situation which might lead to international friction or give rise to a dispute, in order to determine whether the continuance of the dispute or situation is likely to endanger the maintenance of international peace and security.

Article 35. 1. Any Member of the United Nations may bring any dispute, or any situation of the nature referred to in Article 34, to the attention of the Security Council or of the General Assembly.

2. A State which is not a Member of the United Nations may bring to the attention of the Security Council or of the General Assembly any dispute to which it is a party if it accepts in advance, for the purposes of the dispute, the obligations of pacific settlement provided in the present Charter.

3. The proceedings of the General Assembly in respect of matters brought to its attention under this Article will be subject to the provisions of Articles 11 and 12.

Article 36. 1. The Security Council may, at any stage of a dispute of the nature referred to in Article 33 or of a situation of like nature, recommend appropriate procedures or methods of adjustment.

2. The Security Council should take into consideration any procedures for the settlement of the dispute which have already been adopted by the parties.

3. In making recommendations under this Article the Security Council should also take into consideration that legal disputes should as a general rule be referred by the parties to the International Court of Justice in accordance with the provisions of the Statute of the Court.

Article 37. 1. Should the parties to a dispute of the nature referred to in Article 33 fail to settle it by the means indicated in that Article, they shall refer it to the Security Council.

2. If the Security Council deems that the continuance of the dispute is in fact likely to endanger the maintenance of international peace and security, it shall decide whether to take action under Article 36 or to recommend such terms of settlement as it may consider appropriate.

Article 38. Without prejudice to the provisions of Articles 33 to 37, the Security Council may, if all the parties to any dispute so request, make recommendations to the parties with a view to a pacific settlement of the dispute.

Chapter VII: Action with respect to threats to the peace,
breaches of the peace, and acts of aggression

Article 39.   The Security Council shall determine the existence of any threat to the peace, breach of the peace, or act of aggression and shall make recommendations, or decide what measures shall be taken in accordance with Articles 41 and 42, to maintain or restore international peace and security.

Article 40.   In order to prevent an aggravation of the situation, the Security Council may, before making the recommendations or deciding upon the measures provided for in Article 39, call upon the parties concerned to comply with such provisional measures as it deems necessary or desirable. Such provisional measures shall be without prejudice to the rights, claims, or position of the parties concerned. The Security Council shall duly take account of failure to comply with such provisional measures.

Article 41.   The Security Council may decide what measures not involving the use of armed force are to be employed to give effect to its decisions, and it may call upon the Members of the United Nations to apply such measures. These may include complete or partial interruption of economic relations and of rail, sea, air, postal, telegraphic, radio, and other means of communication, and the severance of diplomatic relations.

Article 42.   Should the Security Council consider that measures provided for in Article 41 would be inadequate or have proved to be inadequate, it may take such action by air, sea, or land forces as may be necessary to maintain or restore international peace and security. Such action may include demonstrations, blockade, and other operations by air, sea, or land forces of Members of the United Nations.

Article 43.   1. All Members of the United Nations, in order to contribute to the maintenance of international peace and security, undertake to make available to the Security Council, on its call and in accordance with a special agreement or agreements, armed forces, assistance, and facilities, including rights of passage, necessary for the purpose of maintaining international peace and security.
2. Such agreement or agreements shall govern the numbers and types of forces, their degree of readiness and general location, and the nature of the facilities and assistance to be provided.
3. The agreement or agreements shall be negotiated as soon as possible on the initiative of the Security Council. They shall be concluded between the Security Council and Members or between the Security Council and groups of Members and shall be subject to ratification by the signatory States in accordance with their respective constitutional processes.

Article 44.   When the Security Council has decided to use force it shall, before calling upon a Member not represented on it to provide armed forces in fulfilment of the obligations assumed under Article 43, invite that Member, if the Member so desires, to participate in the decisions of the Security Council concerning the employment of contingents of that Member's armed forces.

Article 45.   In order to enable the United Nations to take urgent military measures, Members shall hold immediately available national airforce contingents for combined international enforcement action. The strength and degree of readiness of these contingents and plans for their combined action shall be determined, within the limits laid down in the special agreement or agreements referred to in Article 43, by the Security Council with the assistance of the Military Staff Committee.

Article 46. Plans for the application of armed force shall be made by the Security Council with the assistance of the Military Staff Committee.

Article 47. 1. There shall be established a Military Staff Committee to advise and assist the Security Council on all questions relating to the Security Council's military requirements for the maintenance of international peace and security, the employment and command of forces placed at its disposal, the regulation of armaments, and possible disarmanent.

2. The Military Staff Committee shall consist of the Chiefs of Staff of the permanent members of the Security Council or their representatives. Any Member of the United Nations not permanently represented on the Committee shall be invited by the Committee to be associated with it when the efficient discharge of the Committee's responsibilities requires the participation of that Member in its work.

3. The Military Staff Committee shall be responsible under the Security Council for the strategic direction of any armed forces placed at the disposal of the Security Council. Questions relating to the command of such forces shall be worked out subsequently.

4. The Military Staff Committee, with the authorization of the Security Council and after consultation with appropriate regional agencies, may establish regional sub-committees.

Article 48. 1. The action required to carry out the decisions of the Security Council for the maintenance of international peace and security shall be taken by all the Members of the United Nations or by some of them, as the Security Council may determine.

2. Such decisions shall be carried out by the Members of the United Nations directly and through their action in the appropriate international agencies of which they are members.

Article 49. The Members of the United Nations shall join in affording mutual assistance in carrying out the measures decided upon by the Security Council.

Article 50. If preventive or enforcement measures against any State are taken by the Security Council, any other State, whether a Member of the United Nations or not, which finds itself confronted with special economic problems arising from the carrying out of those measures shall have the right to consult the Security Council with regard to a solution of those problems.

Article 51. Nothing in the present Charter shall impair the inherent right of individual or collective self-defence if an armed attack occurs against a Member of the United Nations, until the Security Council has taken measures necessary to maintain international peace and security. Measures taken by Members in the exercise of this right of self-defence shall be immediately reported to the Security Council and shall not in any way affect the authority and responsibility of the Security Council under the present Charter to take at any time such action as it deems necessary in order to maintain or restore international peace and security.

Negotiating Texts, 1987 and 1988

The following are unpublished negotiating documents referred to in the text. They are from the author's personal files.

March 1987: Nonpaper Used to Brainstorm

Elements Acceptable to Both Sides (1)
1. Respect for Geneva Protocol of 1925 on Chemical Weapons. (2)
2. Cessation of attacks on civilian population centers and aircraft. (2)
3. Cessation of attacks on neutral shipping. (2)
4. Cessation of attacks on ports and oil-export facilities. (2)
5. Cease-fire and withdrawal to international borders in the context of a settlement. (3)
6. Exchange of prisoners of war.
7. Investigation of the question of responsibility for the conflict. (4 & 5)
8. Mutual assurances of nonaggression and of respect for international obligations. (5)
9. Reconstruction efforts. (5)

Elements Sought by Iran but Unacceptable to Iraq
1. Condemnation of Iraq as aggressor.
2. Reparations.
3. Condemnation of Iraqi use of chemical weapons and attacks against civilian population centers.
4. Regional security arrangements. (6)

Element Sought by Iraq but Unacceptable to Iran
Balanced and interconnected implementation of resolution 582 according to a precise and reasonable timetable.

Notes:
(1) Acceptable to Iraq only in the context of a comprehensive settlement.
(2) These elements are linked and would be subsumed in an overall cease-fire resolution.
(3) Iraq insists that a cease-fire and withdrawal must precede a settlement, while Iran insists that they should not.
(4) Iran emphasizes the "initiation" of the conflict, while Iraq emphasizes the "prolongation" of the conflict.
(5) Elements not contained in existing resolutions of the Council.
(6) Iraqi position unknown.

April 1987: Nonpaper Used to Brainstorm

The purpose of this paper is to explore questions in connection with a Security Council resolution ordering a cease-fire which would be binding under Article 25 of the Charter.

I. Acceptance of a cease-fire by both parties

   —What does a cease-fire imply on the ground? Simple halt in firing or prevention of any forward military movements? Assurances of no military action against third parties?

   A. Mechanisms for supervising a cease-fire
      1. Observers
      —Are they necessary?
      If so:
      —Should they be provided under terms of SC resolution 514 (12 July 1982), which was not accepted and not implemented?
      —Should they be provided under terms similar to resolution 514 but by way of a new SC decision?
      —Should a somewhat different mechanism such as United Nations Truce Supervisory Organization (UNTSO) be utilized?
      2. A Special Representative of the Secretary-General
      3. Incidental violation of cease-fire
      —How defined?
      —What does the Council do about it?

   B. Disengagement measures
      —What should be done to reinforce a cease-fire?
      Should a cease-fire line be established?
      —Should cease-fire be replaced by a truce (including exchange of wounded, partial exchange of POWs, formal disengagement arrangements)?
      —Will creation of peacekeeping or disengagement observer force be necessary or desirable at some point?

   C. Withdrawal to international borders
      —Does withdrawal automatically follow a cease-fire?
      —Should it be treated as one of a number of measures directed toward peace negotiations?

   D. Measures to bring about just and comprehensive settlement of the conflict
      —Are specific recommendations to this end by SC necessary?
      How would any such recommendations relate to previous resolutions?
      —Should the Security Council form a subsidiary organ to prepare or facilitate the implementation of such recommendations?

   E. What role should the Secretary-General be encouraged to play?

   F. In what time frame should the above steps be taken?

   G. Do we need prior agreement on all or some of the above measures before voting a cease-fire resolution?

II. Noncompliance by one or both parties with the cease-fire—actions to obtain compliance from noncomplying party or parties

   A. Overt rejection by one or both parties
      1. Are there intermediate actions short of enforcement that SC needs to consider (e.g., warning from SC, dispatch of mission to area, unilateral or joint demarches)?
      2. What measures may be needed to give effect to SC resolution?
      —Should voluntary measures be resorted to first? Or should SC resort immediately to mandatory measures?
      —Should we assume that both voluntary and mandatory measures will be drawn from among those specified in Article 41?
      —Which type of measures should be first resorted to? Economic? Means of communication? Diplomatic relations?
      —Among economic measures should an arms embargo and/or a halt to oil purchases be the first type of measures resorted to?

3. Arms embargo
—Is this the most obvious first step?
—Is this the most effective first step?
—How is its scope defined (problem of dual use)?
—Can adequate enforcement mechanism be devised, given the variety of channels used to supply arms?
4. Halt to oil purchases
—Can adequate enforcement mechanism be devised given the variety of channels and methods used to sell oil including the particular problem of time swaps?
5. Are there other sanctions which might be practicable and effective?
B. Acceptance of cease-fire in name but de facto rejection or noncompliance.
—How should Council define and determine responsibility for noncompliance?
—Once determined see II. A. above.
C. How should compliance of non-UN members be effected? By making specific provisions in the resolution or by other means?
—How and when should sanctions be terminated? By a time limit as well as a requirement of compliance with the cease-fire?
—Is there a problem of countersanctions?
D. Should there be agreement on all or some of the above measures including enforcement mechanisms for specific sanctions (e.g., arms embargo, halt to oil purchases) before (a) adopting a cease-fire resolution, (b) resorting to any measures to induce compliance?

April 1987: Early Working Draft of Resolution

Acting under Articles 25, 39, and 40,

Determining in accordance with Article 39 that the conflict between Iran and Iraq constitutes a breach of the peace,

1. Reaffirms Security Council Resolution 582 of 24 February 1986;

2. Demands that Iran and Iraq observe an immediate cease-fire, a cessation of all hostilities, and withdrawal of all forces to the internationally recognized boundaries without delay;

3. Urges that a comprehensive exchange of prisoners of war be completed within a short period after the cessation of hostilities in cooperation with the International Committee of the Red Cross;

4. Calls upon Iran and Iraq to cooperate with mediation efforts coordinated through the Secretary-General with a view to achieving a comprehensive, just, and honorable settlement acceptable to both sides, of all outstanding issues, on the basis of the principles contained in the Charter of the United Nations;

5. Calls upon all other States to exercise the utmost restraint and to refrain from any act which may lead to further escalation and widening of the conflict, and thus to facilitate the implementation of the present resolution;

6. Requests the Secretary-General to examine, in consultation with the governments of Iran and Iraq, the question of entrusting an impartial body with inquiring into the responsibility for the initiation of the conflict and to report to the Council as soon as possible;

7. Recognizes the magnitude of the damages inflicted during this conflict and therefore the need for reconstruction efforts, with appropriate international assistance, once the conflict is ended;

8. Further requests the Secretary-General to examine, in consultation with the parties and other concerned governments in the region, measures to be taken to enhance security in the region;

9. Requests the Secretary-General to keep the Council informed of the situation;

10. Decides to remain seized of the matter and to meet again in the event of the continuation of hostilities to consider the adoption of such further measures as may be necessary to ensure compliance with this decision.

14 June 1987: Elements Paper Used by Spokesman for the Five

As you are aware, the Five Permanent Members have been exploring together various ideas that could constitute the basis of action by this Council to end by peaceful means the conflict between Iran and Iraq. We now have been able to agree on elements of a comprehensive approach that we would like to share with you.

I have been authorized to speak today on behalf of the delegations of China, France, the Union of Soviet Socialist Republics, the United Kingdom, and the United States. We would like to inform members of the Council of the elements we believe should be included in a resolution of the Security Council on the conflict between Iran and Iraq.

Since our last briefing to the Council on the subject, we have continued in our joint efforts. As some of the elements we had been considering would request the Secretary-General to take certain action, we have already informed him of our work. We have now all been authorized by our governments to proceed with consultations within the Security Council with a view to obtaining agreement on action by the Council to end the conflict between Iran and Iraq.

We have in mind a draft resolution which would in essence expressly reaffirm and proceed from resolution 582, determine that the conflict constitutes a breach of the peace, and state the Council is acting under Articles 39 and 40 of the Charter.

It is our intention to include the following elements in the operative part of the draft:

(A) A demand that, as a first step towards negotiations, Iran and Iraq observe an immediate cease-fire, discontinue all military actions, and withdraw all forces to the internationally recognized boundaries without delay.

(B) A call for comprehensive exchange of prisoners of war within a short period after the cease-fire.

(C) A call upon Iran and Iraq to cooperate with the mediation efforts of the Secretary-General to achieve a comprehensive, just, honorable settlement, acceptable to both sides, in accordance with the principles contained in the Charter.

(D) A call on other states to exercise the utmost restraint and to refrain from any act which could lead to further escalation and widening of the conflict.

(E) A request for the Secretary-General to explore, in consultation with Iran and Iraq, the question of entrusting an impartial body with inquiring into responsibility for the conflict and to report to the Council as soon as possible.

(F) A recognition of the magnitude of the damage inflicted during the conflict and the need for reconstruction efforts, with appropriate international assistance, once the conflict is ended.

(G) A request for the Secretary-General to examine, in consultation with Iran, Iraq, and other states in the region, measures to enhance the security and stability of the region.

(H) A request to the Secretary-General to keep the Council informed on the implementation of the resolution.

We would like to highlight several points.

—First, our work builds on resolution 582.

—Second, it emphasizes those elements of 582 that aim specifically at bringing this conflict to a peaceful solution.

—Third, the demand for a cease-fire and withdrawal of forces would be binding.

—Fourth, while all of these elements have previously been suggested as possible measures to help bring an end to this war, some have not been included in previous resolutions by the Council. For example, these new elements include: a request to the Secretary-General to explore in consultation with Iran and Iraq the question of entrusting an impartial body with inquiring into responsibility for the conflict; a request for the Secretary-General to examine, in consultation with Iran, Iraq, and other states in the region, measures to enhance the security and stability of the region; and, a recognition of the magnitude of the damage inflicted during the conflict and the need for reconstruction efforts, with appropriate international assistance, once the conflict is ended.

We hope that a resolution drafted along these lines would initiate a process to end a disastrous conflict that has lasted for too long. We hope that, based on today's detailed description of our approach, you will be able to inform us of your views. After receiving your views, we intend to present a proposal in the form of a draft resolution.

July 1987: Iranian Draft for a Resolution

Deploring the initiation of the conflict and deeply concerned that the conflict continues unabated with heavy loss of human life and material destruction,

Equally concerned that further escalation and widening of the conflict may take place,

Determined to find a solution to the conflict which will bring an end to all military actions between Iran and Iraq,

Recalling the obligation of all member states to settle their disputes by peaceful means in such a manner that international peace and security and justice are not endangered,

Reaffirming the obligation of all states to comply with terms and provisions of international law related to armed conflicts,

1. Calls upon Iran and Iraq to cooperate with the Secretary-General in mediation efforts to achieve a comprehensive, just and honourable settlement, acceptable to both sides, of all outstanding issues, in accordance with the principles contained in the Charter of the United Nations;

2. Calls upon all other states to exercise neutrality and utmost restraint and to refrain from any act which may lead to further escalation and widening of the conflict and thus to facilitate the implementation of the present resolution;

3. Demands an immediate halt to all attacks against merchant ships and oil tankers by Iran and Iraq to avoid further escalation of the conflict and its spread to other countries in and outside the region;

4. Calls for an end to the use of chemical weapons, attacks on civilian targets and threats against civil aviation;

5. Invites the two sides to repatriate groups of POW's in accordance with the provisions of the Third Geneva Convention of 1949 and in cooperation with the ICRC;

6. Requests the Secretary-General to explore, in consultation with Iran and Iraq, the question of entrusting an impartial body with determining the party responsible for the conflict and to report to the Security Council as soon as possible;

7. Requests also that the Secretary-General assign a team of experts to evaluate, with the assistance and cooperation of the two sides, the damages inflicted to the parties during the conflict;

8. Further requests the Secretary-General to examine, in consultation with the states in the region, measures to enhance the security and stability of the region;

9. Invites the Secretary-General to keep the Council informed on the implementation of this resolution;

10. Decides to meet again as necessary to consider further steps to ensure progress in efforts to reach a settlement.

20 July 1987: Text of Resolution 598 (1987) with Amendments Proposed by Nonpermanent Members Italicized

The Security Council,

Reaffirming its resolution 582 (1986),

Deeply concerned that, despite its calls for a cease-fire, the conflict *between Iran and Iraq* continues unabated, with further heavy loss of human life and material destruction,

Deploring the initiation and continuation of the conflict,

Deploring also the bombing of purely civilian population centres, attacks on neutral shipping or civilian aircraft, the violation of international humanitarian law and other laws of armed conflict, and, in particular, the use of chemical weapons contrary to obligations under the 1925 Geneva Protocol,

Deeply concerned that further escalation and widening of the conflict may take place,

Determined to bring to an end all military actions between Iran and Iraq,

Convinced that a comprehensive, just, honourable and durable settlement should be achieved between Iran and Iraq,

Recalling the provisions of the Charter of the United Nations, and in particular the obligation of all Member States to settle their international disputes by peaceful means in such a manner that international peace and security and justice are not endangered,

Determining that there exists a breach of the peace as regards the conflict between Iran and Iraq,

Acting under Articles 39 and 40 of the Charter of the United Nations,

1. Demands that, as a first step towards *a negotiated settlement,* Iran and Iraq observe an immediate cease-fire, discontinue all military actions *on land, at sea and in the air,* and withdraw all forces to the internationally recognized boundaries without delay;

2. *Requests the Secretary-General to dispatch a team of United Nations Observers to verify, confirm and supervise the cease-fire and withdrawal and further requests the Secretary-General to make the necessary arrangements in consultation with the Parties and to submit a report thereon to the Security Council;*

3. Urges that prisoners of war be released and repatriated without delay after the cessation of active hostilities *in accordance with the Third Geneva Convention of 12 August 1949;*

4. Calls upon Iran and Iraq to cooperate with the Secretary-General *in implementing this resolution and* in mediation efforts to achieve a comprehensive, just and honourable settlement, acceptable to both sides, of all outstanding issues, in accordance with the principles contained in the Charter of the United Nations;

5. Calls upon all other States to exercise the utmost restraint and to refrain from any act which may lead to further escalation and widening of the conflict, and thus to facilitate the implementation of the present resolution;

6. Requests the Secretary-General to explore, in consultation with Iran and Iraq, the question of entrusting an impartial body with inquiring into responsibility for the conflict and to report to the *Security* Council as soon as possible;

7. Recognizes the magnitude of the damage inflicted during the conflict and the need for reconstruction efforts, with appropriate international assistance, once the conflict is ended *and, in this regard, requests the Secretary-General to assign a team of experts to study the question of reconstruction and to report to the Security Council;*

8. Further requests the Secretary-General to examine, in consultation with Iran and Iraq and with other States of the region, measures to enhance the security and stability of the region;

9. Requests the Secretary-General to keep the *Security* Council informed on the implementation of this resolution;

10. Decides to meet again as necessary to consider further steps to ensure compliance with this resolution.

January 1988: Nonpaper on Arms Embargo

Arms Embargo Resolution: revised elements paper

[1. Decision under Article 41 of the Charter to impose an arms embargo against the noncomplying party in order to ensure compliance with Resolution 598.]
or
[1. Determination that the position taken by Iran toward Resolution 598 warrants resorting to measures provided for in Article 41 of the Charter.]

2. Resolution to draw on precedent of Resolution 418, with particular attention to operative paragraphs 2, 4, 5, 6, and 7.

3. The embargo to cover:
(a) [All types of weapons] [Weapons and military equipment] including missiles, guns and ammunition, all types of combat vehicles including tanks, armoured personnel carriers, naval vessels and military aircraft, helicopters and hovercraft, and spare parts for such [weapons and vehicles] [weapons, vehicles and military equipment].
(b) Military training and provision of technology and equipment to manufacture or maintain banned goods;
(c) Cooperation on manufacture and development of nuclear weapons.

4. A committee to monitor compliance. All states to cooperate fully with the committee.

5. A time limit for the resolution, unless renewed.

6. A call for continued efforts to seek a political settlement to the conflict within the framework of Resolution 598.

7. Secretary-General to report periodically to the Security Council.

February 1988: Nonpaper on Proposal for a Naval Presence

The United Nations Naval Force in the Gulf: revised elements

1. Task: ensuring the safety of commercial navigation in international waters and passage to ports of Gulf States.

2. Composition: naval vessels comprising the UNNF are to be provided by interested States.

3. Number: the number of vessels should be reasonably sufficient to carry out the task outlined in para 1.

4. Types: vessels suitable for escorting ships, and other operations which may be necessary to carry out the task, including minesweeping.

5. Financing: costs are covered by the States providing the vessels and also through deductions from users of sea routes (States, shipping and insurance companies).

6. The UNNF is granted the right to self-defense.

7. The Security Council will decide the questions of establishing the Force, its composition, tasks, functioning, and command, as well as financial aspects.

March 1988: Draft Enforcement Resolution

The Security Council,

Reaffirming its resolution 598 (1987) demanding an immediate cease-fire in the conflict between Iran and Iraq, the discontinuance of all military actions on land, at sea and in the air, and the withdrawal of all forces to the internationally recognised boundaries without delay,

Deeply concerned that, despite this demand and the efforts of the Secretary-General to secure the implementation of resolution 598, the conflict between Iran and Iraq continues with further heavy loss of human life and material destruction,

Determined to bring the conflict between Iran and Iraq to an end,

Convinced of the need for continued efforts to achieve a comprehensive, just, honourable, and durable settlement between Iran and Iraq within the framework of resolution 598 (1987),

Expressing its appreciation to the Secretary-General for his continuing efforts to secure the implementation of resolution 598 (1987) [and its support for his decision to appoint a Special Representative to assist him in conducting urgent consultations on this matter],

Mindful of its responsibilities under the Charter for the maintenance of international peace and security,

Acting under Article 41 of the Charter of the United Nations,

1. Determines that Iran has failed to comply with resolution 598 (1987);

[2. Urges the Secretary-General to renew on an urgent basis consultations with a view to securing full compliance with resolution 598 (1987); and requests that the Secretary-General report to the Council the results of these consultations no later than 30 March 1988;]

2. Decides that [effective 1 April 1988, unless the Security Council determines otherwise,] all States shall cease forthwith, and notwithstanding any contracts entered into or licences granted before the date of the present resolution, the provision to Iran of:

(a) All types of weapons and other military equipment, including missiles, guns, ammunition, and combat vehicles, including tanks, armoured personnel carriers, naval vessels, and military aircraft, helicopters, and hovercraft ("banned goods");
(b) Spare parts for banned goods;
(c) Military training connected with the continuation of the conflict or with banned goods;
(d) All types of equipment and supplies and grants of licensing arrangements, for the manufacture or maintenance of banned goods;

3. Further decides that [effective 1 April 1988,] all States shall refrain from any cooperation with Iran in the manufacture and development of nuclear weapons;

4. Calls upon all States, including States nonmembers of the United Nations, to act strictly in accordance with the provisions of this resolution;

5. Decides to establish, in accordance with rule 28 of the provisional rules of procedure of the Security Council, a Committee of the Security Council consisting of all the members of the Council, to undertake the following tasks and to report on its work to the Council with its observations and recommendations:
(a) To examine the reports on the progress of the implementation of this resolution, which will be submitted by the Secretary-General;
(b) To seek from all States further information regarding the action taken by them concerning the effective implementation of the provisions laid down in this resolution;

6. Calls upon all States to cooperate fully with the committee in the fulfillment of its task, including supplying such information as may be sought by the Committee in pursuance of this resolution;

7. Requests the Secretary-General to provide all necessary assistance to the Committee and to make the necessary arrangements in the Secretariat for that purpose;

8. Requests the Secretary-General to report to the Council on the progress of the implementation of this resolution, the first report to be submitted within three months;

9. Decides that the measures taken in this resolution shall continue in effect for an initial period of two years unless the Council decides otherwise;

10. Decides to keep this item on its agenda for further action as appropriate in the light of developments.

Annual Joint Statements of Permanent Members, 1987–1990

The following communiqués were issued by the foreign ministers of the permanent members of the UN Security Council after annual meetings with the secretary-general.

Joint Statement of Permanent Members,
25 September 1987

On September 25, 1987, the Ministers of Foreign Affairs of the five Permanent Members of the Security Council had a meeting with the Secretary-General of the United Nations, H.E. Mr. Javier Pérez de Cuéllar. Taking part in the meeting were the State Counselor, Minister of Foreign Affairs of the People's Republic of China, H.E. Mr. Wu Xuequian; the Minister of Foreign Affairs of France, H.E. Mr. Jean-Bernard Raimond; the Minister of Foreign Affairs of the Union of Soviet Socialist Republics, H.E. Mr. Eduard A. Shevardnadze; the Secretary of State for Foreign and Commonwealth Affairs of the United Kingdom of Great Britain and Northern Ireland, the Rt. Hon. Sir Geoffrey Howe; and the Secretary of State of the United States of America, H.E. Mr. George Shultz.

The goal of the Permanent Members and of the Security Council as a whole is to bring an end to the Iran-Iraq conflict.

The Permanent Members regard implementation of resolution 598 as the sole basis for a comprehensive, just, honourable and durable settlement of the conflict.

The Permanent Members commend the Secretary-General for his efforts thus far and give full support to his efforts to implement the resolution.

The Permanent Members stated their determination to continue to work with each other within the Security Council. They will, therefore, continue to work on the ways and means to secure full and rapid implementation of resolution 598 and, in this context, on further steps to ensure compliance with that resolution.

Joint Statement of Permanent Members,
28 September 1988

On 28 September 1988, the Ministers of Foreign Affairs of the five Permanent Members of the Security Council had a meeting with the Secretary-General of the United Nations, H.E. Mr. Javier Pérez de Cuéllar. Taking part in the meeting were the Minister of Foreign Affairs of the People's Republic of China, H.E. Mr. Qian Qichen; the State Minister, Minister of Foreign Affairs of France, H.E. Mr. Roland Dumas; the Minister of Foreign Affairs of the Union of Soviet Socialist Republics, H.E. Mr. Eduard A. Shevardnadze; the Secretary of State for Foreign and Commonwealth Affairs of the United Kingdom of Great Britain and Northern Ireland, the

Rt. Hon. Sir Geoffrey Howe; and the Secretary of State of the United States of America, H.E. Mr. George Shultz.

The Ministers and the Secretary-General exchanged views on a wide range of major international issues. They placed particular emphasis on efforts to resolve current regional conflicts in accordance with the principles of the Charter of the United Nations. They noted with satisfaction the marked improvement in international relations at the global level and the general trend towards dialogue and peaceful settlement of disputes which had developed since their previous meeting with the Secretary-General on 25 September 1987. They welcomed the active involvement of the United Nations in this process. They also stressed their continuing confidence in the United Nations, which they believed had an increasingly significant role to play in the achievement of international peace and security. The Ministers expressed their determination to continue to work together to enhance these positive developments.

The Ministers welcomed the cease-fire between Iran and Iraq which came into effect on 20 August 1988. They also welcomed the start of direct talks between the Parties under the auspices of the Secretary-General in order to secure full implementation of Security Council Resolution 598 (1987).

The Secretary-General briefed the Ministers on his current efforts to consolidate the cease-fire in all its aspects and to bring about a settlement in accordance with the resolution. The Ministers reiterated their complete support for the Secretary-General's endeavors and their determination to work in cooperation with him to ensure that the resolution be fully implemented as an integral whole. They also expressed the conviction that the two Parties now had before them the opportunity to reach a comprehensive, just, honourable and durable peace. They urged the need for substantive and continuous talks and, in this respect, they welcomed the decision to continue the talks on 1 October. They called on both sides to display restraint, flexibility and readiness to search for mutually acceptable solutions.

The Ministers further reaffirmed their strong commitment to the sovereignty, independence and territorial integrity of Lebanon.

The Ministers thanked the Secretary-General for his invitation to the meeting, which they considered most useful. In view of the primary responsibility of the Security Council under the Charter for the maintenance of international peace and security, they expressed their determination to continue to work together for the prevention and settlement of international conflicts.

Joint Statement of Permanent Members, 29 September 1989

On 29 September 1989, the Ministers of Foreign Affairs of the five Permanent Members of the Security Council were guests at a luncheon given by the Secretary-General of the United Nations, H.E. Javier Pérez de Cuéllar. Taking part were the Minister of Foreign Affairs of the People's Republic of China, H.E. Mr. Qian Qichen; the Minister of State, Minister of Foreign Affairs of France, H.E. Mr. Roland Dumas; the Minister of Foreign Affairs of the Union of Soviet Socialist Republics, H.E. Mr. Eduard A. Shevardnadze; the Secretary of State for Foreign and Commonwealth Affairs of the United Kingdom of Great Britain and Northern Ireland, H.E. Mr. John Major; and the Secretary of State for the United States of America, H.E. Mr. James A. Baker, III.

The Ministers and the Secretary-General exchanged views on a wide range of major international issues and also reviewed developments over those issues since their previous meeting with the Secretary-General on 28 September 1988. They agreed that at the present time of positive change in the international political climate from confrontation to relaxation and interaction among states, the United Nations has an important role to play.

The Ministers placed particular emphasis on the efforts to resolve the current regional conflicts in accordance with the principles of the Charter of the United Nations. They noted with satisfaction the trend toward dialogue and peaceful settlement of disputes which had developed in recent years. They welcomed the active involvement of the United Nations in this process.

The Ministers expressed their firm commitment to the cause of independence of Namibia through the holding of free and fair elections under the auspices of the United Nations. They expressed their strong support for the Secretary-General in his efforts to ensure that Security Council Resolution 435 (1978) is fully implemented. They urged all Parties concerned scrupulously to abide by their obligations under the settlement plan.

Having reviewed developments in the Middle East, the Ministers reaffirmed their support for an active peace process in which all relevant Parties would participate, leading to a comprehensive, just and lasting peace in the region. They reiterated their full support for the efforts of the Arab League Tripartite Committee to put an end to the trials of the Lebanese people through the implementation of a plan for the settlement of the Lebanese crisis in all its aspects by guaranteeing the full sovereignty, independence, territorial integrity, and national unity of Lebanon. In this regard, they expressed the strong hope that the resumed inter-Lebanese dialogue would develop constructively.

The Ministers expressed their support for the Secretary-General's efforts to secure the full implementation by Iran and Iraq of Security Council Resolution 598 (1987) as an integral whole and urged both governments to cooperate with the Secretary-General in that regard.

They reaffirmed their support for the peace process in Central America on the basis of the Esquipulas agreement and subsequent agreements by the Central American states and for the efforts of the Secretary-General in this connection.

The Ministers expressed their concern at the current situation in Afghanistan and supported the efforts of the Secretary-General to encourage and facilitate the early realization of a comprehensive political settlement. They called on the Parties concerned to implement faithfully the Geneva agreement and last year's General Assembly resolution.

The Ministers reviewed the situation in Cambodia in the light of the outcome of the Paris conference. They advocated a comprehensive political settlement, which would ensure the independent, sovereign, and neutral status of Cambodia and a continuation of the negotiating process initiated toward this end.

The Ministers exchanged views on international cooperation against terrorism. They condemned all acts of terrorism in whatever form and demanded the immediate safe release of all hostages. The Ministers called for strengthened international cooperation aimed at combating illicit international drug trafficking.

The Ministers commended the peacekeeping operations of the United Nations, which in their view illustrate the vital role of the organization in preventing and resolving regional conflicts. They underlined the importance of the effective functioning of these operations.

In view of the primary responsibility of the Security Council for the maintenance of international peace and security under the Charter, the Ministers expressed their satisfaction at the improved working relations within the Council and with the Secretary-General. They expressed their determination to continue to work together and in cooperation with the Secretary-General for the prevention and resolution of international conflicts.

The Ministers expressed their deep appreciation to the Secretary-General for his contribution to the cause of international peace and cooperation. They thanked him for the invitation to the meeting, which they considered a most useful occasion for an exchange of views.

Joint Statement of Permanent Members, 28 September 1990

On 28 September 1990, the Ministers for Foreign Affairs of the five Permanent Members of the Security Council were the guests at a luncheon given by the Secretary-General of the United Nations, H.E. Mr. Javier Pérez de Cuéllar. Taking part were the Minister of Foreign Affairs of the People's Republic of China, H.E. Mr. Qian Qichen; the Minister of State, Minister of Foreign Affairs of France, H.E. Mr. Roland Dumas; the Minister of Foreign Affairs of the Union of Soviet Socialist Republics, H.E. Mr. Eduard A. Shevardnadze; the Secretary of State for Foreign and Commonwealth Affairs of the United Kingdom of Great Britain and Northern Ireland, H.E. Mr. Douglas Hurd; and the Secretary of State of the United States of America, H.E. Mr. James A. Baker III.

The Ministers welcomed the considerable success achieved by the United Nations over the past year, in particular in Namibia, and the progress made towards settlement of conflicts in Central America, Western Sahara and Afghanistan. They agreed that the United Nations faced important new opportunities and challenges. They stressed the crucial contribution which the United Nations could make in this new era of intensified cooperation and interaction among States.

They paid particular attention to the most serious crisis the international community is facing now, caused by Iraq's invasion of Kuwait.

The Ministers affirmed that this aggressive action must not be tolerated. They condemned the continuing occupation of the State of Kuwait and the increasing persecution of its citizens.

They welcomed, in this regard, the firm and decisive role played by the United Nations and the good offices of the Secretary-General. They reaffirmed their support for the relevant Resolutions adopted by the Security Council since the Iraqi invasion of Kuwait and re-emphasized their commitment to seek together, in full compliance with them, a peaceful solution of the crisis.

They demanded that Iraq comply with the will of the international community and withdraw unconditionally and without delay from Kuwait, thus restoring Kuwait's full sovereignty under the authority of its legitimate Government, free all hostages held in Iraq and Kuwait, allow all foreign nationals wishing to leave Iraq or Kuwait to do so and respect the immunity of diplomatic personnel and the inviolability of diplomatic premises in Kuwait.

They called upon all States to apply strictly the relevant resolutions of the Security Council.

The Ministers expressed their deep concern at the aggravation of tensions in the Near East. They reaffirmed their determination to support an active negotiating process in which all relevant Parties would participate, leading to a comprehensive, just and lasting peace. They agreed that such negotiations should be based on Resolutions 242 (1967) and 338 (1973) of the Security Council and should take into account the right to security for all States in the region, including Israel, and the legitimate rights of the Palestinian people.

The Ministers also reaffirmed their strong commitment to the sovereignty, independence, unity, and territorial integrity of Lebanon and renewed their support for the Taif agreement as the basis for the resolution of the Lebanese crisis.

Finally, the Ministers welcomed the agreement by the Cambodian parties to form the Supreme National Council as well as their acceptance in its entirety of the framework for a comprehensive settlement of the Cambodia conflict worked out by the five Permanent Members and the endorsement of that framework by the Security Council. They called on all Cambodians to intensify their efforts to achieve national reconciliation and reiterated, as stated in the framework document, that should Prince Norodom Sihanouk be elected by the Supreme National Council as its President, the five would welcome that decision.

They expressed the view that the Paris International Conference on Cambodia should be reconvened at the earliest possible date to elaborate and adopt a comprehensive political settlement, which will include an important role for the United Nations.

The Ministers stressed the importance of a further development of the ability of the Security Council to respond quickly to challenges to international peace and security. They reaffirmed their determination to continue to work together and with the other members of the Security Council as well as in co-operation with the Secretary-General for the prevention and resolution of international conflicts.

They noted the importance of the meeting of the Security Council at the level of Foreign Ministers on 25 September 1990 and expressed their readiness to participate in such meetings should the need arise.

They expressed once again their deep appreciation to the Secretary-General for his untiring efforts with regard to the cause of international peace and security. They thanked him for the invitation to the meeting, which they viewed as a very useful and positive one, and agreed to continue their consultations.

(S/21835, 2 October 1990)

Table of Kuwait Resolutions, August–November 1990

Resolution 660 (2 August): Condemned Iraq's invasion of Kuwait and demanded unconditional withdrawal.

Resolution 661 (6 August): Imposed comprehensive sanctions against Iraq and set up a committee to monitor compliance.

Resolution 662 (9 August): Declared Iraq's purported annexation of Kuwait to be null and void.

Resolution 664 (18 August): Condemned Iraq for holding foreign nationals hostage and demanded their release.

Resolution 665 (25 August): Called upon states with maritime forces in the area to use such measures as may be necessary to ensure strict implementation of the sanctions.

Resolution 666 (13 September): Established guidelines for humanitarian food and medicine shipments to Iraq and Kuwait.

Resolution 667 (16 September): Condemned Iraqi violation of diplomatic premises.

Resolution 669 (24 September): Entrusted the committee established under 661 with examining requests for assistance from third states injured by compliance with the sanctions.

Resolution 670 (25 September): Tightened embargo on air traffic to Iraq.

Resolution 674 (29 October): Held Iraq responsible for Kuwait's financial losses, pressed Iraq to permit departure of third country nationals, and sought evidence of human rights abuses.

Resolution 677 (28 November): Condemned Iraqi attempts to alter the demographic composition of Kuwait's population.

Resolution 678 (29 November): Authorized states cooperating with Kuwait to use all necessary means to secure implementation of Resolution 660 and subsequent relevant resolutions and to restore international peace and security in the area.

Note on Endnotes

Much of the information in chapters 1 and 7–15 is based on the author's personal involvement, contemporaneous notes, conversations with other diplomats, and reference to unpublished negotiating texts, several of which are included in the Documentary Annex. Wherever possible, public sources have been used and have been identified in the notes. The Documentary Annex also contains the annual joint statements of the foreign ministers of the permanent members for 1987–1990 and a chronology of resolutions passed regarding the Iraq-Kuwait crisis in 1990.

UN documents in these notes are referred to by the standard marking system—UNSCOR (Security Council Official Records, available for the period up to the mid-1980s), UNGAOR (General Assembly Official Records, available for the period up to the mid-1980s), S (Security Council documents or provisional verbatim records), and A (General Assembly documents or provisional verbatim records).

NOTES

1. A Structure for Diplomacy

1. S/PV.2943, 25 September 1990, p. 7.
2. Ibid., p. 8.
3. Ibid., p. 18.
4. Ibid., p. 22.
5. Ibid., pp. 31–32.
6. Ibid., p. 63.
7. Ibid., pp. 74–75.
8. Ernest B. Haas, "Regime Decay: Conflict Management and International Organizations, 1945–81," *International Organization* 37, no. 2 (Spring 1983): 189–256.
9. *New York Post*, 4 September 1990, p. 19.
10. David J. Scheffer, "The United Nations in the Gulf Crisis and Options for U.S. Policy," no. 1, October 1990, United Nations Association of the USA, New York, p. 9.
11. Davidson Nicol, ed., *Paths to Peace: The UN Security Council and Its Presidency* (New York: Pergamon, 1981), p. 86.

2. Setting Out

1. UNSCOR, 1st meeting, 17 January 1946, p. 9.
2. UNSCOR, First Year, First Series, Supplement no. 1, p. 17.
3. Ibid., p. 73.
4. Ibid., p. 76.
5. Ibid., p. 25.
6. *Foreign Relations of the United States (FRUS)*, 1946, vol. 7, *The Near East and Africa* (Washington: Government Printing Office, 1969), pp. 289–568 in general for Iran.
7. UNSCOR, First Year, 3rd meeting, 28 January 1946, pp. 31–43.

8. Ibid., 4th meeting, 29 January 1946, p. 53.

9. George Kennan, *Memoirs: 1925–50*, vol. 1 (Boston: Little Brown, 1967), p. 556.

10. *FRUS*, p. 337.

11. Ibid., p. 341.

12. Hugh Thomas, *Armed Truce: The Beginnings of the Cold War, 1945–46* (New York: Atheneum, 1987), p. 508.

13. *FRUS*, p. 357.

14. UNSCOR, First Year, First Series, Supplement no. 2, p. 44.

15. Trygve Lie, *In the Cause of Peace: Seven Years with the United Nations* (New York: Macmillan, 1954), p. 75.

16. UNSCOR, First Year, First Series, Supplement no. 2, p. 44.

17. James F. Byrnes, *All in One Lifetime* (New York: Harper, 1958), p. 352.

18. Aryeh Y. Yodfat, *The Soviet Union and Revolutionary Iran* (London: Croom Helm, 1983), p. 18.

19. UNSCOR, First Year, First Series, Supplement no. 2, p. 46.

20. Ibid., p. 122.

21. Ibid., p. 54 (S/68).

22. Ibid., p. 305.

23. UNGAOR, 32nd session, Supplement no. 2 (A/32/2), p. 64.

24. *FRUS*, p. 442.

25. Ibid., p. 532.

26. *New York Times*, 20 June 1961, 1:4.

27. Helen Chapin Metz, *Iraq: A Country Study* (Washington: United States Government, 1990), p. 50.

28. *New York Times*, 26 June 1961, 1:4.

29. Husain M. Albaharna, *The Arabian Gulf States: Their Legal and Political Status and Their International Problems* (Beirut: Librairie du Liban, 1975), p. 250 et seq.

30. UNSCOR, Supplement for July, August, and September 1961 (S/4844).

31. Ibid., S/4847.

32. Ibid.

33. Ibid., S/4848.

34. *New York Times*, 4 July 1961, 1:4.

35. UNSCOR, 957th meeting, 2 July 1961, p. 11.

36. UNSCOR, Supplement for July, August, and September 1961, p. 5 (S/4855).

37. Ibid., p. 6 (S/4856).

38. *New York Times*, 21 July 1961, 5:5.

39. UNSCOR, Supplement for July, August, and September 1961, S/4966.

40. *New York Times*, 3 June 1961, 1:4.

41. Judith Miller and Laurie Mylroie, *Saddam Hussein and the Crisis in the Gulf* (New York: Times Books, 1990), p. 82.

42. Albaharna, *The Arabian Gulf States*, p. 251.

43. *New York Times*, 14 March 1963, 16:8.

44. Albaharna, *The Arabian Gulf States*, p. 252.

45. *United Nations Treaty Series* (UNTS), vol. 485 (1964), p. 321.

46. Albaharna, *The Arabian Gulf States*, p. 330.

47. Ibid.

48. *Guardian*, 9 October 1971.

49. UNSCOR, Supplement for April, May, and June 1969 (S/9185 and S/9190); also Murray Gordon, *Conflict in the Persian Gulf* (New York: Facts on File, 1981), p. 33.

50. UNSCOR, Supplement for April, May, and June 1969 (S/9200).

51. S. H. Amin, "The Iran-Iraq Conflict: Legal Implications," *International and Comparative Law Quarterly* 31 (January 1982): 175.

52. Abdullah Omran Tarryam, *The Establishment of the United Arab Emirates 1950–85* (London: Croom Helm, 1987), p. 31.

53. UNSCOR, Supplement for January, February, and March 1970 (S/9726).

54. UNSCOR, Supplement for April, May, and June 1970, p. 169 (S/9772).

55. Davidson Nicol, ed., *Paths to Peace: The UN Security Council and Its Presidency*, p. 82.

56. *New York Times*, 13 August 1970, 2:5.

57. Tarryam, *The Establishment of the United Arab Emirates 1950–85*, p. 188.

58. UNSCOR, Supplement for October, November, and December 1971, p. 79 (S/10409).

59. UNSCOR, 1609th meeting, 8 December 1971.

60. UNSCOR, 1610th meeting, 9 December 1971, p. 20.

61. Kaiyan Homi Kaikobad, *The Shatt al-Arab Boundary Question: A Legal Reappraisal* (Oxford: Clarendon Press, 1988), pp. 7–8.

62. Ibid., p. 51.

63. Ibid., p. 53.

64. Majid Khadduri, *The Gulf War: The Origins and Implications of the Iraq-Iran Conflict* (New York: Oxford University Press, 1988), p. 40.

65. UNSCOR, Supplement for January, February, and March 1974, p. 96 (S/11216).

66. Robert D. Tomasek, "The Resolution of Major Controversies between Iran and Iraq," *World Affairs* 139, no. 3 (Winter 1976–77): 219 et seq.

67. UNSCOR, 1764th meeting, 28 February 1974, p. 1.

68. Ibid., p. 2.

69. UNSCOR, Supplement for April, May, and June 1974, pp. 125–29 (S/11291).

70. UNSCOR, 1770th meeting, 28 May 1974, p. 4.

71. J. M. Abdulghani, *Iran and Iraq: The Years of Crisis* (London: Croom Helm, 1984), p. 157. From *Christian Science Monitor*, 7 May 1975.

3. Over the Edge to War

1. UNSCOR, Supplement for October, November, and December 1979, p. 61 (S/13615).

2. Ibid. (S/13616).

3. Cyrus Vance, *Hard Choices: Critical Years in American Foreign Policy* (New York: Simon and Schuster, 1983), p. 377.

4. UNSCOR, Supplement for October, November, December 1979, pp. 68–69 (S/13626).

5. Gary Sick, *All Fall Down: America's Tragic Encounter with Iran* (New York: Penguin, 1986), p. 226.

6. Ibid.

7. Kurt Waldheim, *In the Eye of the Storm: A Memoir* (Bethesda: Adler and Adler, 1986), p. 2.

8. UNSCOR, Supplement for October, November, December 1979, p. 83 (S/13646).

9. UNSCOR, 2172nd meeting, 27 November 1979, p. 2.

10. Sick, *All Fall Down*, p. 226.

11. Ibid., p. 235.

12. UNSCOR, 2175th meeting, 1 December 1979, p. 2.

13. Warren Christopher et al., *American Hostages in Iran: The Conduct of a Crisis* (New Haven: Yale University Press, 1985), p. 98.

14. Sick, *All Fall Down*, p. 242.

15. UNSCOR, Supplement for October, November, December 1979, pp. 139–40 (S/13704).

16. Ibid., p. 140 (S/13705).

17. Sick, *All Fall Down*, p. 247.
18. In Christopher et al., *American Hostages in Iran*, p. 101.
19. UNSCOR, 2182nd meeting, 29 December 1979, p. 2.
20. Brian Urquhart, *A Life in Peace and War* (New York: Harper and Row, 1987), p. 323.
21. Vance, *Hard Choices*, p. 399.
22. *New York Times*, 31 December 1979, 1.
23. Ibid., 12 December 1979, 1:4.
24. Waldheim, *In the Eye of the Storm*, p. 5.
25. Ibid., p. 8.
26. Ibid., p. 7.
27. UNSCOR, Supplement for January, February, March 1980, pp. 4–6 (S/13730).
28. Zbigniew Brzezinski, *Power and Principle: Memoirs of the National Security Adviser, 1977–81* (New York: Farrar Straus Giroux, 1983), p. 485.
29. UNSCOR, 2186th meeting, 5 January 1980, p. 6.
30. UNSCOR, Supplement for January, February, March 1980, p. 4 (S/13729).
31. Ibid., p. 10 (S/13735).
32. UNSCOR, 2192nd meeting, 13 January 1980, p. 4.
33. Ibid., p. 5.
34. Ibid., p. 15.
35. Christopher et al., *American Hostages in Iran*, p. 8.
36. Ibid., p. 11.
37. Cameron R. Hume, "Pérez de Cuéllar and the Iran-Iraq War," *Negotiation Journal* (April 1992): 173–84.
38. Howard Raiffa, *The Art and Science of Negotiation* (Cambridge: Harvard/Belknap, 1982), p. 22.
39. Ibid., pp. 108–109.
40. Ibid., p. 23.
41. Arthur W. Rovine, *The First Fifty Years: The Secretary-General in World Politics 1920–70* (Leyden: Sithoff, 1970), p. 204.
42. UNGAOR, Introduction to the Report of the Secretary-General on the Work of the Organization, 1961, A/4800, Add. 1, p. 1.
43. UNGAOR, 1972, Supplement 1A, A/27/01/Add. 1.
44. Tareq Y. Ismael, *Iran and Iraq: Roots of Conflict* (Syracuse: Syracuse University Press, 1982), p. 24.
45. Saddoun Hammadi, *A Conversation with Dr. Saddoun Hammadi: Iraq's Foreign Policy* (Washington: American Enterprise Institute, 1981), p. 6.
46. *New York Times*, 18 September 1980, 8:1.
47. Article 70 of the Vienna Convention on the Law of Treaties.
48. Kaiyan Homi Kaikobad, *The Shatt al-Arab Boundary Question: A Legal Appraisal*, p. 99.
49. UNSCOR, Supplement for July, August, September 1980, pp. 113–14 (S/14191).
50. Ibid., p. 118 (S/14196).
51. Yearbook of the United Nations 1980, vol. 31, p. 313.
52. *New York Times*, 16 September 1981, 8:1.
53. Steven B. Kashkett, "Iraq and the Pursuit of Nonalignment," *Orbis* 26, no. 2 (Summer 1982): 492.
54. *New York Times*, 16 September 1981, 9:1.
55. Ibid., 26 September 1980, 8:1.
56. UNSCOR, 2247th meeting, 26 September 1980, p. 3.
57. *New York Times*, 27 September 1980, 4:1.
58. Urquhart, *A Life in Peace and War*, p. 324.
59. *New York Times*, 28 September 1980, 18:1.

60. Ibid., 29 September 1980, 1:6.
61. Gary Sick, "Moral Choice and the Iran-Iraq Conflict," *Ethics and International Affairs* 3 (1989): 122.
62. UNSCOR, 2248th meeting, 28 September 1980, p. 11.
63. *New York Times*, 2 October 1980, 1:5.
64. UNSCOR, Supplement for October, November, December 1980, p. 3 (S/14206).
65. UNSCOR, 2250th meeting, 15 October 1980, p. 6.
66. UNSCOR, 2251st meeting, 17 October 1980, pp. 4–5.
67. Waldheim, *In the Eye of the Storm*, p. 165.
68. *Yearbook of the United Nations 1980*, vol. 34, p. 317.

4. Five Years of War

1. *Yearbook of the United Nations 1980*, vol. 34, p. 317.
2. *New York Times*, 13 November 1980, 14:4.
3. Jan Eliasson, "Sweden and International Mediation," Stockholm, Ministry of Foreign Affairs, 1989, p. 13.
4. *New York Times*, 21 November 1980, 14:3.
5. Ibid.
6. Ibid., 25 November 1980, 8:5.
7. Ibid., 30 December 1980, 9:5.
8. Remy George, "Zwischen Arabisher Weidergeburt und Islamischer Revolution: mit Olof Palme in Irak und Iran," *Vereinte Nationen* 1 (1987): 13.
9. *New York Times*, 17 January 1981, 2:5.
10. Ibid., 18 January 1981, 14:6.
11. George, "Zwischen Arabisher Weidergeburt und Islamischer Revolution," p. 13.
12. *New York Times*, 19 January 1981, 7:5.
13. Ibid., 24 January 1981, 3:3.
14. Ahmed Sékou Touré, *Du Conflit Irano-Irakien* (Conakry, R.P.R.G.: Imprimerie Nationale "Patrice Lumumba," 1981), p. 10.
15. Ibid., p. 26.
16. Aage Eknes, "From Scandal to Success: The United Nations and the Iran-Iraq War 1980–1988" (Oslo: Norwegian Institute of International Affairs, 1989), p. 14.
17. *New York Times*, 2 March 1982, 4:3.
18. Gary Sick, "Moral Choice and the Iran-Iraq Conflict," p. 126.
19. Gary Sick, "Trial by Error: Reflections on the Iran-Iraq War," *Middle East Journal* 43 (Spring 1989): 236–37.
20. Anthony H. Cordesman, *The Iran-Iraq War and Western Security 1984–87* (London: Jane's, 1987), p. 50.
21. UNGAOR, A/38/PV. 12, 1 October 1983, p. 66.
22. UNSCOR, Supplement for April, May, June 1983.
23. Ibid., S/15834.
24. *Times* (London), 11 October 1984, p. 6e.
25. *The Economist*, 21 July 1984, p. 14.
26. *New York Times*, 27 March 1985, 8:4.
27. Ibid., 1 April 1985, 9:1.
28. Ibid., 10 April 1985, 11:1.
29. Ibid., 16 April 1985, 11:5.
30. UNGAOR, Introduction to the Report of the Secretary-General on the Work of the Organization, 1982, A/37/1, p. 1.

31. Ibid.
32. Ibid., p. 2.
33. *New York Times*, 25 April 1983, 2:3.
34. UNGAOR, 5 October 1983, A/38/PV.19, p. 307.
35. In Adam Roberts (with Benedict Kingsbury), ed., *United Nations, Divided World: The UN's Role in International Relations* (Oxford: Clarendon Press, 1988), pp. 50–51.
36. *New York Times*, 9 September 1985, 12:4.
37. *The Economist*, 19 October 1985, p. 48.

5. The Permanent Members

1. See John C. Campbell, "The Gulf Region in the Global Setting," in Hossein Amirsadeghi, ed., *The Security of the Persian Gulf* (New York: St. Martin's Press, 1981), pp. 1–25.
2. Shahram Chubin, *The Role of Outside Powers in the Persian Gulf*, vol. 4 (London: International Institute for Strategic Studies, 1981), p. 112.
3. Ibid., p. 131.
4. John George Stoessinger, *The United Nations and the Superpowers: China, Russia, and America* (New York: Random House, 1973), p. 217.
5. Evan Luard, *The United Nations: How It Works and What It Does* (New York: St. Martin's Press, 1979), p. 27.
6. Gary Sick, "An American Perspective," in Paul Jabber et al., *Great Power Interests in the Persian Gulf* (New York: Council on Foreign Relations, 1989), p. 32.
7. *Times* (London), 24 September 1980, p. 1c.
8. Ibid., 1 October 1980, p. 7a.
9. Ibid.
10. UNSCOR, PV. 2288, 19 June 1981, p. 14.
11. Ibid., p. 16.
12. *Times* (London), 14 July 1982, p. 1c.
13. Ibid., 12 October 1982, p. 8g.
14. Frederick W. Axelgard, *A New Iraq?: The Gulf War and Implications for U.S. Policy* (New York: Praeger, 1988), p. 65.
15. *Times* (London), 20 December 1983, p. 1g.
16. Nizar Hamdoon, "The United States, Iraq, and the Gulf War," *American-Arab Affairs* (Fall 1985): 95.
17. *New York Times*, 27 November 1984, 1:5.
18. James A. Bill, *The Eagle and the Lion: The Tragedy of American-Iranian Relations* (New Haven: Yale University Press, 1988), p. 306.
19. Eric Hooglund, "The Policy of the Reagan Administration toward Iran," in Nikki R. Keddie and Mark J. Gasiorowski, eds., *Neither East nor West: Iran, the Soviet Union, and the United States* (New Haven: Yale University Press, 1990), p. 190.
20. Anthony H. Cordesman, *The Gulf and the West: Strategic Relations and Military Realities* (Boulder: Westview, 1988), p. 270.
21. Chubin, *The Role of Outside Powers in the Persian Gulf*, vol. 4, p. 80.
22. Ibid., p. 76.
23. Arye H. Yodfat, *The Soviet Union and Revolutionary Iran*, pp. 145–46.
24. Dennis Ross, "Soviet Views toward the Gulf War," *Orbis* 28 (Fall 1984): 437–47.
25. *Times* (London), 3 October 1980, p. 8f.
26. Yodfat, *The Soviet Union and Revolutionary Iran*, p. 93 (from *Pravda* of 9 October 1980).
27. *Times* (London), 6 October 1980, p. 1g.

28. *New York Times*, 11 December 1980, 12:3.
29. *Times* (London), 10 March 1982, p. 32c.
30. Yodfat, *The Soviet Union and Revolutionary Iran*, p. 134.
31. *Facts on File*, 5 November 1982, p. 826.
32. *Times* (London), 5 May 1983, p. 1a.
33. Robert O. Freedman, "Gorbachev, Iran, and the Iran-Iraq War," in Keddie and Gasiorowski, eds., *Neither East nor West*, p. 118.
34. *Times* (London), 5 February 1986, p. 7a.
35. *Washington Post*, 26 August 1986, p. A 1.
36. Alvin Z. Rubinstein, "Perspectives on the Iran-Iraq War," *Orbis* 29 (Fall 1985): 606.
37. Dominique Moisie, "A European Perspective," in Jabber et al., *Great Power Interests in the Persian Gulf*, p. 61.
38. *New York Times*, 2 February 1981, 6:3.
39. Ibid., 8 February 1981, pt. IV, 4:1.
40. Ibid., 6 August 1981, 3:4.
41. Ibid., 5 February 1983, 4:6.
42. *Times* (London), 6 September 1983, p. 10b.
43. *New York Times*, 16 September 1983, 3:1.
44. Aage Eknes, "From Scandal to Success: The United Nations and the Iran-Iraq War 1980–1988," p. 18.
45. *New York Times*, 10 October 1983, 3:4.
46. *Times* (London), 11 November 1983, p. 6g.
47. *New York Times*, 25 February 1986, 9:5.
48. Ibid., 6 March 1986, 15:1.
49. Ibid., 20 April 1986, 14:1.
50. Chubin, *The Role of Outside Powers in the Persian Gulf*, vol. 4, p. 65.
51. U.S. Arms Control and Disarmament Agency (ACDA), *World Military Expenditures and Arms Transfers, 1988*, pp. 113–14.
52. *Facts on File*, 31 October 1980, p. 821.
53. Charles Kupchan, *The Persian Gulf and the West: The Dilemma of Security* (Boston: Allen and Unwin, 1987), p. 160.
54. Anthony Parsons, "A British Perception of the Gulf," in B. R. Pridham, ed., *The Arab Gulf and the West* (London: Croom Helm, 1985), p. 39.
55. *Facts on File*, 21 November 1980, p. 879.
56. *Times* (London), 5 November 1980, p. 8f.
57. Valerie Yorke, *The Gulf in the 1980s* (London: The Royal Institute of International Affairs, 1980), p. 72.
58. *Times* (London), 4 January 1984, p. 8b.
59. *Facts on File*, 31 December 1985, p. 972; *Times* (London), 1 October 1985, p. 11a.
60. ACDA, *World Military Expenditures and Arms Transfers, 1988*, p. 22.
61. Anthony H. Cordesman, *The Iran-Iraq War and Western Security 1984–87: Strategic Implications and Policy Options* (London: Jane's, 1987), pp. 28, 30.
62. Anthony Parsons, "Iran and Western Europe," *Middle East Journal* 43 (Spring 1989): 220.
63. *Times* (London), 16 May 1986, p. 6h.
64. Valerie Yorke (with Louis Turner), *European Interests and Gulf Oil* (Brookfield, VT: Gower, 1986), p. 19.
65. Cordesman, *The Gulf and the West*, p. 290.
66. Ibid., p. 292.
67. Yorke, *European Interests and Gulf Oil*, p. 6.
68. Ibid., p. 8.
69. *Facts on File*, 8 September 1978, p. 675.

70. *Times* (London), 31 August 1978, p. 4e.
71. *Facts on File*, 17 October 1980, p. 774.
72. *Washington Post*, 31 August 1986, p. A 14.
73. ACDA, *World Military Expenditures and Arms Transfers, 1988*, p. 22.
74. Ibid., pp. 111, 113.
75. *Christian Science Monitor*, 14 September 1987, p. 9:1.
76. Ibid., 5 June 1987, p. 1:3.
77. Cordesman, *The Gulf and the West*, p. 56.

6. Signs of Change

1. Rouhollah K. Ramazani, *Revolutionary Iran* (Baltimore: Johns Hopkins University Press, 1986), p. 261.
2. Ibid., p. 259.
3. Ibid., p. 3.
4. Erik R. Peterson, *The Gulf Cooperation Council: Search for Unity in a Dynamic Region* (Boulder: Westview, 1988), pp. 239–45.
5. Ibid., p. 287.
6. Ibid., p. 288.
7. Ibid., p. 203.
8. Ibid., p. 291.
9. Ibid., p. 122.
10. Anthony H. Cordesman, *The Gulf and the West: Strategic Relations and Military Realities*, p. 398.
11. Peterson, *The Gulf Cooperation Council*, p. 294.
12. UNSCOR, Supplement for April, May, June 1984, letter dated 21 May 1984 (S/16574).
13. See, for example, Cordesman, *The Gulf and the West*: one table on page 319 shows that in 1984 Iraq made 36 such attacks and Iran 18 (adapted from *The Economist*); another table on page 398 shows that in 1984 Iraq made 16 attacks on targets in the tanker war and Iran 53 (adapted from the *Washington Post*).
14. Peterson, *The Gulf Cooperation Council*, p. 296.
15. Ibid., p. 298.
16. Herbert Honsowitz, "Markt und Makler der Interessen: Sicherheitsrat und Generalsekretar: Versuche zur Beilegung des Golfkreigs," *Vereinte Nationen* (January 1987): 10.
17. Ibid.
18. *New York Times*, 11 October 1986, 2:3.
19. Ibid., 12 December 1981, 6:4.
20. *The International Who's Who* (London: Europa, 1989), p. 1216.
21. *Times* (London), 12 December 1981, p. 4b.
22. *New York Times*, 12 December 1981, 6:4.
23. *Times* (London), 12 December 1981, p. 4b.
24. *New York Times*, 12 December 1981, 6:4.
25. Ibid.
26. *Times* (London), 26 December 1981, p. 5c.
27. UNGAOR, 36th session, 98th meeting, 15 December 1981, p. 1760.
28. UNGAOR, 1982, A/37/1, p. 2.
29. UNGAOR, 1983, A/38/1, p. 2.
30. UNGAOR, 1986, A/41/1, p. 2.
31. UNGAOR, 1982, A/37/1, p. 3.
32. UNGAOR, 1985, A/40/1, p. 3(f).
33. UNGAOR, 1986, A/41/1, p. 2.

34. UNGAOR, 1982, A/37/1, p. 3.

35. UNGAOR, 1983, A/38/1, p. 2.

36. Ibid.

37. Diego Cordovez, "Strengthening United Nations Diplomacy for Peace: The Role of the Secretary-General," in Davidson Nicol, ed., *The United Nations Security Council: Towards Greater Effectiveness* (New York: UNITAR, 1982).

38. UNGAOR, 1982, A/37/1, p. 3.

39. UNGAOR, 1986, A/41/1, p. 7.

40. Javier Pérez de Cuéllar, "The Role of the Secretary-General," in Adam Roberts (with Benedict Kingsbury), ed., *United Nations, Divided World: The UN's Role in International Relations*, p. 68.

41. Ibid., p. 69.

42. *Times* (London), 11 October 1986, p. 6f.

43. Ibid., 26 July 1986, p. 5d.

44. Ibid., 11 September 1986, p. 12a.

45. *New York Times*, 11 October 1986, 2:3.

46. UNGAOR, 13 October 1986, A/41/PV. 33, pp. 8–10.

47. *New York Times*, 22 February 1985, 3:1.

48. *Washington Post*, 31 August 1986, p. A 14.

49. S/PV.2663, 18 February 1986, p. 12.

50. Anthony H. Cordesman, *The Iran-Iraq War and Western Security 1984–87: Strategic Implications and Policy Options*, p. 48.

51. Ibid., p. 52.

52. Ibid., p. 49.

53. Frederick W. Axelgard, *A New Iraq?: The Gulf War and Implications for U.S. Policy*, p. 89.

54. United States Department of State, Special Report no. 166, *U.S. Policy in the Persian Gulf*, July 1987, p. 3.

55. UNSCOR, 3 October 1986, S/PV.2709, p. 7.

56. UNSCOR, 8 October 1986, S/PV.2713, p. 44.

57. *New York Times*, 2 October 1986, 7:3.

58. Rouhollah K. Ramazani, "Iran's Foreign Policy: Contending Orientations," *Middle East Journal* 43, no. 2 (Spring 1989): 213.

59. James A. Bill, "The U.S. Overture to Iran, 1985–1986," in Nikki R. Keddie and Mark J. Gasiorowski, eds., *Neither East nor West: Iran, the Soviet Union, and the United States*, p. 172.

60. *The Tower Commission Report* (New York: Bantam Books/Time Books, 1987), p. 41.

61. Ibid., p. 46.

62. Murray Waas and Craig Unger, "In the Loop: Bush's Secret Mission," *The New Yorker*, 2 November 1992, p. 80.

63. Ibid., p. 50.

64. Cordesman, *The Iran-Iraq War and Western Security 1984–87*, p. 30.

65. James A. Bill, *The Eagle and the Lion: The Tragedy of American-Iranian Relations*, p. 313.

66. James Schlesinger, "Reykjavik and Revolutions: A Turn of the Tide?" *Foreign Affairs* 65, no. 3 (1987): 440.

67. *New York Times*, 21 November 1986, 6:1.

68. Staff Report to the Committee on Foreign Relations, *War in the Persian Gulf: The U.S. Takes Sides*, United States Senate, October 1987, p. 28.

69. Ibid., p. 39.

70. Ibid., p. 48.

71. Secretary of Defense Caspar W. Weinberger, *A Report to the Congress on Security Arrangements in the Persian Gulf*, 15 June 1987, p. 14.

72. Cordesman, *The Iran-Iraq War and Western Security 1984–87*, p. 124.
73. Ibid., p. 128.
74. *Washington Post*, 16 January 1987, p. 27 (or *Christian Science Monitor*, 20 January 1987, p. 1).
75. *New York Times*, 20 January 1987, 8:1 & 5.
76. Ibid., 4 February 1987, 6:1.
77. Ibid., 12 January 1987, 1:6.

7. Pérez de Cuéllar's Move

1. Press Release SG/SM/3956, 13 January 1987, pp. 6–7.
2. Ibid., p. 7.
3. Howard Raiffa, *The Art and Science of Negotiation*, pp. 108–109.
4. But for a different version that U.S. official sources could not confirm see George L. Sherry, *The United Nations Reborn: Conflict Control in the Post-Cold War Era* (New York: Council on Foreign Relations, 1990), p. 12.
5. Raiffa, *The Art and Science of Negotiation*, p. 23.
6. Shahram Chubin, *The Role of Outside Powers in the Persian Gulf*, vol. 4, p. 142.
7. Fred C. Iklé, *How Nations Negotiate* (New York: Harper and Row, 1965), p. 135.
8. Ibid., p. 90.
9. *Who's Who 1990* (London: Black, 1990), p. 1805.
10. Ibid., p. 1811.
11. *International Who's Who 1988–89* (London: Europa, 1990), p. 933.
12. *Qui Est Qui en France: 1988–89* (Paris: Editions Jacques Lafitte, 1988), p. 895.
13. Ibid., p. 260.
14. *International Who's Who: 1989–90* (London: Europa, 1990), p. 126.
15. *Forbes*, 20 April 1987, vol. 139, no. 8, p. 17.
16. *Current Biography Yearbook 1988* (New York: Wilson, 1988), p. 595.
17. "March 1987: Nonpaper Used to Brainstorm," reproduced in the Documentary Annex.
18. "April 1987: Early Working Draft of Resolution," in Documentary Annex.
19. United States Department of State, *U.S. Policy in the Persian Gulf*, Special Report no. 166, July 1987, p. 8.
20. Ibid.
21. Secretary of Defense Caspar W. Weinberger, "A Report to the Congress on Security Arrangements in the Persian Gulf," 15 June 1987, p. 10.
22. Department of State, *U.S. Policy in the Persian Gulf*, p. 11.
23. *New York Times*, 26 March 1987, 26:1.
24. Joseph W. Twinam, "U.S. Interests in the Arabian Gulf," *American-Arab Affairs* 21 (Summer 1987): 14.
25. Robert O. Freedman, "Gorbachev, Iran, and the Iran-Iraq War," in Nikki R. Keddie and Mark J. Gasiorowski, eds., *Neither East nor West*, p. 122.
26. *Times* (London), 27 April 1987, p. 7d.
27. Carol R. Saivetz, *The Soviet Union and the Gulf in the 1980's* (Boulder: Westview, 1989), p. 91.
28. *Washington Post*, 8 May 1987, p. 17b.
29. *New York Times*, 8 May 1987, 15:5.
30. *Times* (London), 12 May 1987, p. 6g.
31. "April 1987: Nonpaper Used to Brainstorm," in Documentary Annex.
32. Fred C. Iklé, *How Nations Negotiate*, p. 87.

8. A Meeting of the Minds

1. *Washington Post*, 9 May 1987, p. 1a.
2. *New York Times*, 19 May 1987, 9:5.
3. Ibid., 27 May 1987, 14:3, and 28 May 1987, 13:1.
4. Ibid., 30 May 1987, 7:1.
5. Ibid., 7 June 1987, 1:5.
6. Robert O. Freedman, "Gorbachev, Iran, and the Iran-Iraq War," in Nikki R. Keddie and Mark J. Gasiorowski, eds., *Neither East nor West*, p. 125.
7. *New York Times*, 3 July 1987, 6:5.
8. Anthony H. Cordesman, *The Gulf and the West: Strategic Relations and Military Realities*, p. 331.
9. *New York Times*, 4 June 1987, 8:4.
10. Department of State, "U.S. Policy in the Persian Gulf," p. 12.
11. Secretary of Defense Caspar W. Weinberger, "A Report to the Congress on Security Arrangements in the Persian Gulf," p. 25.
12. "14 June 1987: Elements Paper Used by Spokesman for the Five," in Documentary Annex.
13. *New York Times*, 17 July 1990, 8:6.
14. Ibid., 19 July 1987, 1:4.
15. Ibid., 22 July 1987, 10:1.
16. Ibid., 3 July 1987, 6:5.
17. Ibid., 4 July 1987, 1:6.
18. Freedman, "Gorbachev, Iran, and the Iran-Iraq War," in Keddie and Gasiorowski, eds., *Neither East nor West*, p. 127.
19. "July 1987: Iranian Draft for a Resolution," in Documentary Annex.
20. George Joffe (with Keith McLachlan), *Iran and Iraq: The Next Five Years* (London: Economist Intelligence Unit, 1987), p. 15.
21. "20 July 1987: Text of Resolution 598 (1987) with Amendments Proposed by Nonpermanent Members Italicized," in Documentary Annex.
22. S/PV.2750, 20 July 1987, p. 22.
23. George P. Shultz, *Turmoil and Triumph: My Years as Secretary of State* (New York: Scribner's, 1993), p. 932.
24. S/PV.2750, 20 July 1987, p. 62.
25. Ibid., pp. 64–65.
26. Ibid., p. 72.

9. Making It Work

1. *New York Times*, 21 July 1987, 10:5.
2. S/19045, 14 August 1987, Letter dated 23 July 1987 from the deputy prime minister and minister for foreign affairs of Iraq addressed to the secretary-general, p. 3.
3. *New York Times*, 24 July 1987, 2:3.
4. Ibid., 28 July 1987, 6:3.
5. Ibid., 5 August 1987, 1:2.
6. Ibid., 1 August 1987, 4:1.
7. S/19031, 11 August 1987, p. 2.
8. Ibid.
9. *New York Times*, 1 September 1987, 1:6.
10. Ibid., 31 August 1987, 1:5.

11. Ibid., 12 September 1987, 1:3.
12. Ibid., 13 September 1987, 3:4.
13. Ibid., 14 September 1987, 3:1.
14. Ibid., 15 September 1987, 3:4.
15. Department of State Noon Briefing, 18 September 1987.
16. *New York Times*, 19 September 1987, 3:3.
17. Ibid., 20 September 1987, 1:5.
18. A/42/PV.6, 24 September 1987, p. 37.
19. Ibid., p. 40.
20. Ibid., p. 42.
21. Ibid., p. 43.
22. Ibid., p. 48.
23. A/42/PV.13, 29 September 1987, p. 24.
24. Ibid., p. 36.
25. Ibid., p. 46.
26. *New York Times*, 25 September 1987, 1:6.
27. Ibid., 1 October 1987, 1:6.
28. The communiqué of this meeting is reproduced in the Documentary Annex as "Joint Statement of the Permanent Members, 25 September 1987."
29. 15 October 1987, paper approved during Security Council informal consultations.
30. *New York Times*, 17 October 1987, 1:1.
31. Ibid., 18 October 1987, 22:2.
32. *New York Times*, 20 October 1987, 11:1.
33. Ibid., 23 October 1987, 1:1.
34. Ibid., 28 October, 3:1.
35. Ibid., 4 November 1987, 3:1.
36. Ibid., 25 October 1987, 8:5.
37. Ibid., 1 November 1987, 27:1.
38. 21 October 1987, statement by UN press spokesman.
39. *New York Times*, 2 November 1987, 6:1; Anthony H. Cordesman, *The Gulf and the West: Strategic Relations and Military Realities*, p. 413.
40. *New York Times*, 8 November 1987, 5:1.
41. Ibid., 17 November 1987, 3:1.
42. Ibid., 28 November 1987, 1:1.
43. Ibid., 2 December 1987, 1:2.
44. Ibid., 13 December 1987, 14:1.
45. A/42/779–S/19274, 18 November 1987, p. 4.
46. *New York Times*, 3 November 1987, 3:4.
47. Ibid., 8 November 1987, 17:1.
48. Ibid., 26 November 1987, 7:1.
49. Ibid., 28 November 1987, 3:2.
50. Robert O. Freedman, "Gorbachev, Iran, and the Iran-Iraq War," in Nikki R. Keddie and Mark J. Gasiorowski, eds., *Neither East nor West*, p. 131.
51. *Department of State Bulletin*, vol. 88, no. 2131, February 1988, p. 15.
52. Ibid., p. 17.

10. Peacekeeping or Sanctions

1. Statement by Under Secretary for Political Affairs Michael H. Armacost, before the Senate Foreign Relations Committee, 16 June 1987, in United States Department of State, Special Report no. 166, *U.S. Policy in the Persian Gulf*, p. 11.

2. Secretary of Defense Caspar W. Weinberger, "A Report to the Congress on Security Arrangements in the Persian Gulf," 15 June 1987, p. 3.

3. Department of State, *U.S. Policy in the Persian Gulf*, pp. 11–12.

4. Anthony H. Cordesman, *The Gulf and the West: Strategic Relations and Military Realities*, p. 375.

5. Ibid., p. 385.

6. Ibid., p. 407.

7. Ibid., p. 332.

8. Ibid., p. 337.

9. Ibid., p. 347.

10. Department of State, *U.S. Policy in the Persian Gulf*, p. 5.

11. *New York Times*, 8 July 1987, 24.

12. A/42/574–S/19143, 18 September 1987, p. 2 et seq.

13. S/19143, 18 September 1987, p. 6.

14. Ibid., p. 7.

15. Ibid., p. 10.

16. A/42/PV.9, 25 September 1987, p. 13.

17. Ibid., p. 19.

18. Secretary of State Shultz, remarks to the press, 17 December 1987, London.

19. *New York Times*, 26 February 1989, 17:1.

20. Letter dated 19 January 1988 from Iranian foreign minister.

21. Letter dated 19 January 1988 from Iranian foreign minister.

22. "January 1988: Nonpaper on Arms Embargo," in Documentary Annex.

23. S/19448, 23 January 1988.

24. Letter dated 1 February 1988 from Alternate Permanent Representative of Iraq.

25. *New York Times*, 16 January 1988, 1:1.

26. Cordesman, *The Gulf and the West*, p. 426.

27. See "February 1988: Nonpaper on Proposal for a Naval Presence," in Documentary Annex.

28. *New York Times*, 7 February 1988, 14:1.

29. Letter dated 28 February 1988 from Iranian foreign minister.

30. *New York Times*, 6 March 1988, 1:5.

31. "March 1988: Draft Enforcement Resolution," in Documentary Annex.

11. Diplomacy Yields to War

1. Anthony H. Cordesman, *The Gulf and the West: Strategic Relations and Military Realities*, p. 429.

2. *New York Times*, 7 March 1988, 3:4.

3. Maziar Behrooz, "Trends in the Foreign Policy of the Islamic Republic," in Nikki R. Keddie and Mark J. Gasiorowski, eds., *Neither East nor West*, p. 27.

4. *New York Times*, 8 March 1988, 6:6.

5. S/19626, 16 March 1988.

6. *New York Times*, 9 April 1988, 8:4.

7. Ibid.

8. S/19637, 17 March 1988.

9. S/19639, 17 March 1988.

10. S/19650, 18 March 1988.

11. S/19664, 21 March 1988, p. 2.

12. Ibid.

13. S/19665, 21 March 1988.

14. S/19682, 25 March 1988.

15. Ibid., pp. 1–2.
16. S/19823, 25 April 1988, pp. 12–13.
17. Ibid., p. 13.
18. Ibid., p. 16.
19. Ibid., p. 6.
20. Ibid., p. 1.
21. Ibid., p. 3.
22. Judith Miller and Laurie Mylroie, *Saddam Hussein and the Crisis in the Gulf* (New York: Times Books, 1990), pp. 162, 175.
23. S/PV.2812, p. 2.
24. *New York Times*, 9 March 1988, 9:1.
25. Ibid., 10 March 1988, 11:1.
26. Ibid., 13 March 1988, 11:1.
27. Ibid., 1 April 1988, 6:4.
28. Ibid., 2 April 1988, 6:1.
29. Ibid., 23 April 1988, 7:1.
30. Ibid., 24 April 1988, pt. IV, 25:1.
31. Cordesman, *The Gulf and the West*, p. 437.
32. *New York Times*, 19 April 1988, 11:4.
33. Ibid., 23 April 1988, 1:3.
34. Ibid., 30 April 1988, 3:1.
35. Ibid., 19 April 1988, 11:1.
36. Ibid., 1 July 1988, 2:3.
37. Ibid., 5 June 1988, 6:1.
38. Ibid., 3 June 1988, 3:4.
39. Ibid., 6 July 1988, 1:1; ibid., 8 July 1988, 6:3.
40. Ibid., 6 July 1988, 10:5.
41. Ibid., 4 May 1988, 8:4.
42. Ibid., 6 May 1988, 6:3.
43. Ibid., 16 June 1988, 14:1.
44. Ibid., 24 June 1988, 3:4.
45. Ibid., 4 July 1988, 4:5.
46. Ibid.
47. Ibid., 25 May 1988, 12:1.
48. Conversation with the author, July 1990.
49. Richard Morgan Wilbur, "The Iran-Iraq War: An Analysis of the Cease-fire," *The Fletcher Forum of World Affairs* 14, no. 1 (Winter 1990): 124.
50. William I. Zartman, ed., *The Negotiation Process: Theories and Applications* (Beverly Hills: Sage, 1978), p. 73.
51. Wilbur, "The Iran-Iraq War," p. 125.

12. From Tragedy to Cease-Fire

1. *New York Times*, 4 July 1988, 6:5.
2. Ibid., 4:5.
3. Ibid., 8 July 1988, 6:1.
4. Ibid., 6 July 1988, 10:1.
5. Ibid., 4 July 1988, 4:5.
6. Ibid., 6 July 1988, 10:3.
7. Ibid., 5 July 1988, 9:1–2.
8. Ibid., 9:1.
9. Ibid., 6 July 1988, 23:6.
10. S/19981, 5 July 1988.

11. *New York Times,* 6 July 1988, 10:4.
12. Ibid., 4 July 1988, 5:2.
13. Ivor Richard, "The Council President as Politician," in Davidson Nicol, ed., *Paths to Peace: The UN Security Council and Its Presidency,* p. 253.
14. *New York Times,* 11 July 1988, 11:1.
15. Ibid., 12 July 1988, 1:6.
16. Ibid., 14 July 1988, 23:1.
17. Ibid., 13 July 1988, 7:1.
18. Ibid.
19. S/PV.2818, 14 July 1988, pp. 28–30.
20. Ibid., pp. 34–35.
21. Ibid., p. 46.
22. Ibid., p. 47.
23. Ibid., p. 51.
24. Ibid., pp. 59–60.
25. S/PV.2819, 15 July 1988, pp. 19–20.
26. Ibid., pp. 29–30.
27. *New York Times,* 15 July 1988, 8:4.
28. Ibid., 18 July 1988, 1:3.
29. Ibid., 8:2.
30. Ibid., 19 July 1988, 9:5.
31. Ibid., 1:3.
32. Ibid., 21 July 1988, 1:1.
33. Ibid., 20 July 1988, 6:3.
34. Efraim Karsh, "Military Lessons of the Iran-Iraq War," *Orbis* 33 (Spring 1989): 214.
35. S/PV.2821, 20 July 1988, p. 7.
36. Ibid., p. 8,
37. Ibid., p. 14.
38. *New York Times,* 20 July 1990, 1:1.
39. Ibid., 21 July 1988, 8:4; 22 July 1988, 1:2.
40. Ibid., 21 July 1988, 8:1.
41. Ibid., 22 July 1988, 6:4.
42. Ibid.
43. Ibid.
44. Ibid., 23 July 1988, 5:5.
45. Ibid., 27 July 1988, 10:6.
46. Ibid., 10:2.
47. Ibid., 28 July 1988, 8:1.
48. Ibid., 30 July 1988, 4:3.
49. Ibid., 31 July 1988, 6:1.
50. Ibid., 2 August 1988, 1:1.
51. Ibid., 3 August 1988, 1:4.
52. Ibid., 6 August 1988, 3:3.
53. Aage Eknes, "From Scandal to Success: The United Nations and the Iran-Iraq War 1980–1988," p. 31.
54. *New York Times,* 7 August 1988, 1:6.
55. Ibid., 8 August 1988, 1:6.
56. S/20095, 8 August 1988.
57. S/20093, 7 August 1988, pp. 1–2.
58. *New York Times,* 26 August 1988, 8:1.
59. Ibid., 27 August 1988, 3:5.
60. Anthony H. Cordesman, *The Iran-Iraq War and Western Security 1984–87: Strategic Implications and Policy Options,* p. 155.

61. *New York Times,* 29 August 1988, 9:1.
62. Ibid., 9:2.
63. Ibid., 30 August 1988, 8:1.
64. Ibid., 1 September 1988, 14:1.
65. BIO/2354, 2 September 1988, UN Department of Public Information.
66. *New York Times,* 27 September 1988, 17:5.
67. "Joint Statement of Permanent Members, 28 September 1988," in Documentary Annex.
68. Ibid., 1 October 1988, 6:1.
69. Ibid., 4 October 1988, 8:1.
70. Ibid., 28 November 1988, 14:3.
71. S/20442, 2 February 1989, p. 10.

13. The Permanent Members Working Together

1. "Joint Statement of Permanent Members, 28 September 1988," in Documentary Annex.
2. "Joint Statement of Permanent Members, 29 September 1989," in Documentary Annex.
3. Press Release, United States Mission to the United Nations, March 1989.
4. *Philadelphia Inquirer,* 2 September 1990.
5. *New York Times,* 10 November 1990, 7:4.
6. BIO/2467, United Nations, 28 May 1990.
7. BIO/2469, United Nations, 12 June 1990.
8. BIO/2501, United Nations, 11 September 1990.
9. See Chester A. Crocker, *High Noon in Southern Africa: Making Peace in a Rough Neighborhood* (New York: Norton, 1992), and Charles W. Freeman, Jr., "The Angola/Namibia Accords," *Foreign Affairs* 68, no. 3 (Summer 1989): 126–41.
10. *New York Times,* 20 December 1988, 3:4.
11. Ibid., 28 December 1988, 5:1.
12. S/20412, 23 January 1989, p. 16.
13. *New York Times,* 1 January 1989, 9:1.
14. Ibid., 25 January 1989, 11:1.
15. S/20412, 23 January 1989, p. 18.
16. *New York Times,* 12 February 1989, 8:1.
17. Speech by Secretary of State Baker, delivered to the American Committee on U.S.-Soviet Relations, 19 October 1990, Washington.
18. Jean-Pierre Lafosse, "The Paris Conference on Cambodia (August 1989) and Its Aftermath," CFIA, Harvard University, Cambridge, Massachusetts, May 1990, p. 10.
19. Ibid., p. 14.
20. Ibid., p. 15.
21. S/21087, 18 January 1990, pp. 2–3.
22. S/21149, 15 February 1990, p. 3.
23. S/21196, 16 March 1990, p. 6.
24. S/21318, 29 May 1990, p. 3.
25. S/21404, 23 July 1990, p. 2.
26. S/21985, 6 December 1990, p. 3.
27. S/20862, 22 September 1989, p. 10.
28. FBIS-NES-89-223, 21 November 1989, pp. 21–22.
29. *New York Times,* 15 December 1989, 7:1.
30. S/21070, 8 January 1990, pp. 2–3.
31. *New York Times,* 7 January 1990, 8:1.

32. S/21200, 22 March 1990, p. 10.
33. *New York Times*, 13 May 1990, 16:1.
34. United Nations DPI Daily Press Briefing, 3 July 1990.
35. *New York Times*, 4 July 1990, 1:4.
36. United Nations DPI Daily Press Briefing, 4 July 1990.
37. S/21528, 15 August 1990, pp. 9–10.

14. Opening the New Era

1. *New York Times*, 3 August 1990, 10:1.
2. S/PV.2932, 2 August 1990, p. 18.
3. S/PV.2934, 9 August 1990, pp. 19–20.
4. S/PV.2932, 2 August 1990, p. 6.
5. Ibid., p. 7.
6. Ibid., pp. 11–12.
7. Ibid., pp. 13–15.
8. Ibid., pp. 19–21.
9. See "Table of Kuwait Resolutions, August-November 1990," in the Documentary Annex.
10. S/21472, 9 August 1990.
11. *New York Times*, 6 August 1990, 6:1.
12. S/PV.2933, 6 August 1990, p. 12.
13. Ibid., p. 18.
14. Ibid., pp. 27–28.
15. Ibid., p. 31.
16. *New York Times*, 7 August 1990, 9:4.
17. S/PV.2934, 9 August 1990, pp. 9–10.
18. Ibid., p. 12.
19. Ibid., p. 18.
20. Ibid., p. 32.
21. *Washington Post*, 10 August 1990, p. A 1.
22. Ibid., p. A 30.
23. S/21556, 17 August 1990, p. 4.
24. S/21528, 15 August 1990, p. 6.
25. S/21621, 24 August 1990, p. 2.
26. S/21494, 12 August 1990, p. 2.
27. Ibid.
28. Ibid., p. 3.
29. Ibid.
30. S/21499, 13 August 1990, p. 2.
31. Reuters, 16 August 1990.
32. Ibid.
33. S/PV.2937, 18 August 1990, p. 31.
34. Ibid., p. 52.
35. S/21651, 27 August 1990, p. 5.
36. *New York Times*, 11 August 1990, 7:2.
37. Ibid., 13 August 1990, 11:1.
38. Ibid., 30 August 1990, 1:4.
39. *Washington Post*, 14 August 1990, p. A 1.
40. *Financial Times*, 15 August 1990, p. 3.
41. *New York Times*, 30 August 1990, 1:4.
42. *Financial Times*, 15 August 1990, p. 3.
43. *Washington Post*, 14 August 1990, p. A 1.

44. *Financial Times*, 15 August 1990, p. 1.
45. *New York Times*, 30 August 1990, 15:2.
46. Ibid., 20 August 1990, 7:1.
47. *Washington Post*, 21 August 1990, p. A 7.
48. Ibid., 22 August 1990, p. A 29.
49. *New York Times*, 30 August 1990, 15:2.
50. Ibid., 22 August 1990, 12:3.
51. *Financial Times*, 23 August 1990, p. 3.
52. *New Yorker*, 8 October 1990, p. 104.
53. *Washington Post*, 23 August 1990, p. A 1.
54. *Financial Times*, 24 August 1990, p. 3.
55. *New York Times*, 30 August 1990, 15; *Washington Post*, 24 August 1990, A 29.
56. *New York Times*, 30 August 1990, 15.
57. Reuters, 24 August 1990, 0544.
58. *New Yorker*, 8 October 1990, p. 104; *New York Times*, 30 August 1990, 15.
59. S/PV.2938, 25 August 1990, pp. 7–25.
60. Ibid., pp. 26–31.
61. Ibid., p. 48.
62. Ibid., p. 54.
63. S/21650, 27 August 1990, p. 3.
64. *Wall Street Journal*, 30 August 1990, p. A 4:5.
65. *New York Times*, 5 September 1990, 17:1.
66. Ibid., 7 September 1990, 9:1.
67. Ibid., 10 September 1990, 7:1.
68. Ibid., 8:1.
69. Ibid., 11 September 1990, 18:4.
70. Ibid., 19 September 1990, 11:1.
71. S/PV.2939, 13 September 1990, p. 41.
72. S/21790, 19 September 1990.
73. *Financial Times*, 17 September 1990, p. 2.

15. Into the Future

1. *Washington Post*, 27 August 1990, p. A 14:4.
2. Richard Murphy, 18 September 1990, USIA telephone press conference.
3. *New York Times*, 24 September 1990, 13.
4. *New Yorker*, 8 October 1990, pp. 103–104.
5. A/45/PV.6, 28 September 1990, p. 63.
6. A/45/PV.5, 28 September 1990, p. 42.
7. A/45/PV.8, 1 October 1990, p. 33.
8. Ibid., p. 37.
9. *New York Times*, 7 October 1990, pt. IV, 19:5.
10. *New York Post*, 25 September 1990, p. 21.
11. A/45/PV.14, 5 October 1990, p. 67.
12. A/45/PV.16, 11 October 1990, p. 72.
13. A/45/585, 5 October 1990, p. 2.
14. S/21919, 31 October 1990, p. 5.
15. S/PV.2946, 8 October 1990, p. 7.
16. Ibid., p. 33. See also "Joint Statement of Permanent Members, 28 September 1990," in Documentary Annex.
17. *New York Times*, 12 October 1990, 12:1.
18. Ibid., 13 October 1990, 5:5.
19. *Washington Post*, 14 October 1990, p. A 27.

20. *New York Times,* 16 October 1990, 1:3.
21. *Washington Post,* 16 October 1990, p. A 1.
22. *International Herald Tribune,* 16 October 1990.
23. A/45/236, 6 November 1990.
24. *International Herald Tribune,* 10 November 1990, p. 4.
25. *Christian Science Monitor,* 15 October 1990, p. 18.
26. S/21986, 7 December 1990.
27. Transcript, Bush News Conference, 8 November 1990.
28. Ibid.
29. *The Wall Street Journal,* 5 November 1990, p. A 24.
30. *New York Times,* 4 November 1990, 16:5.
31. Ibid., 7 November 1990, 19:4.
32. *Financial Times,* 8 November 1990, p. 1.
33. *Washington Post,* 8 November 1990, p. A 1.
34. Ibid., 7 November 1990, p. A 7.
35. *New York Times,* 8 November 1990, 14:3.
36. Ibid., 2 December 1990, 1:5.
37. Ibid., 19:3.
38. Press transcript, Baker-Shevardnadze briefing, 8 November 1990.
39. Reuter, 9 November 1990.
40. *New York Times,* 2 December 1990, 19:6.
41. Ibid., 19:5.
42. Ibid., 18 November 1990, 14:5.
43. Ibid., 19 November 1990, 1:6.
44. Ibid.
45. Ibid., 2 December 1990, 19:6.
46. Ibid., 20 November 1990, 15:1.
47. Ibid., 21 November 1990, 10:3.
48. Ibid., 22 November 1990, 20:1.
49. Ibid., 2 December 1990, 19:6.
50. Ibid., 24 November 1990, 4:1.
51. Ibid., 28 November 1990, 8:3.
52. S/PV.2963, 29 November 1990, p. 6.
53. Ibid., p. 22.
54. Ibid., p. 27.
55. Ibid., p. 40.
56. Ibid., p. 58.
57. Ibid., p. 62.
58. Ibid., p. 68.
59. Ibid., p. 81.
60. Ibid., p. 92.
61. Ibid., pp. 104–105.
62. *Le Monde,* 15 May 1991, p. 2.
63. *Washington Post,* 2 November 1990, p. A 16.
64. *New York Times,* 21 December 1990, 17:1.
65. Bruce Russet and James S. Sutterlin, "The U.N. in a New World Order," *Foreign Affairs* 70, no. 2 (Spring 1991): 69–83.
66. *Financial Times,* 17 September 1990, p. 2; *Washington Post,* 9 November 1990, p. A 27.

Bibliography

Books

Abdulghani, J. M. *Iraq and Iran: The Years of Crisis.* London: Croom Helm, 1984.

Al-Ebraheem, Hassan Ali. *Kuwait and the Gulf: Small States and the International System.* London: Croom Helm, 1984.

Allsebrook, Mary. *Prototypes of Peacemaking: The First Forty Years of the United Nations.* Essex, UK: Longman, 1986.

Amirsadeghi, Hossein, ed. *The Security of the Persian Gulf.* New York, St. Martin's Press, 1981.

Axelgard, Frederick W. *Iraq in Transition: A Political, Economic, and Strategic Perspective.* Boulder: Westview, 1986.

———. *A New Iraq?: The Gulf War and Implications for U.S. Policy.* New York, Praeger, 1988.

Bailey, Sydney D. *The Procedure of the UN Security Council.* Oxford, Clarendon Press, 1975.

Balta, Paul. *Iran-Iraq: Une Guerre de 5000 Ans.* Paris: Anthropos, 1987.

Bendahmane, Diane B., and John W. McDonald, Jr., eds. *International Negotiation: Art and Science.* Washington: Department of State, 1984.

Berridge, G. R., and A. Jennings, eds. *Diplomacy at the UN.* New York: St. Martin's Press, 1985.

Bill, James A. *The Eagle and the Lion: The Tragedy of American-Iranian Relations.* New Haven: Yale University Press, 1988.

Binnendijk, Hans, ed. *National Negotiating Styles.* Washington: Department of State, 1987.

Boyd, Andrew. *Fifteen Men on a Powderkeg: A History of the UN Security Council.* New York: Steen and Day, 1971.

Brzezinski, Zbigniew. *Power and Principle: Memoirs of the National Security Adviser, 1977–81.* New York: Farrar Straus Giroux, 1983.

Byrnes, James F. *All in One Lifetime.* New York: Harper, 1958.

Carter, Jimmy. *Keeping Faith: Memoirs of a President.* New York: Bantam, 1982.

Christopher, Warren, et al. *American Hostages in Iran: The Conduct of a Crisis.* New Haven: Yale University Press, 1985.

Chubin, Shahram. *The Role of Outside Powers in the Persian Gulf.* Vol. 4. London: International Institute for Strategic Studies, 1981.

———. *Soviet Policy toward Iran and the Gulf.* London: International Institute for Strategic Studies, 1980 (#204).

Chubin, Shahram (with Charles Tripp). *Iran and Iraq at War.* London: Tauris, 1988.

Cordesman, Anthony H. *The Gulf and the West: Strategic Relations and Military Realities.* Boulder: Westview, 1988.

———. *The Iran-Iraq War and Western Security 1984–87: Strategic Implications and Policy Options.* London: Jane's, 1987.

Crocker, Chester A. *High Noon in South Africa: Making Peace in a Rough Neighborhood.* New York: Norton, 1992.

Curzon, George Nathaniel. *Persia and the Persian Question.* New York: Barnes and Noble, 1966.

Davidow, Jeffrey. *A Peace in Southern Africa: The Lancaster House Conference on Rhodesia.* Boulder: Westview, 1979.

Franck, Thomas M. *Nation against Nation: What Happened to the UN Dream and What the U.S. Can Do about It.* New York: Oxford University Press, 1985.

Gardner, J. Anthony. *The Iraq-Iran War: A Bibliography.* London: Mansell, 1988.

Ghani, Cyrus. *Iran and the West: A Critical Bibliography.* New York: K. Paul International, 1987.

Goodrich, Leland M. (with Anne P. Simons). *The United Nations and the Maintenance of International Peace and Security.* Washington: Brookings Institution, 1955.

Gordon, Murray. *Conflict in the Persian Gulf.* New York: Facts on File, 1981.

Gromyko, Andrei. *Memories.* London: Hutchinson, 1984.

Halliday, Fred. *Threat from the East?: Soviet Policy from Afghanistan and Iran to the Horn of Africa.* New York: Penguin, 1982.

Hammadi, Saddoun. *A Conversation with Dr. Saddoun Hammadi: Iraq's Foreign Policy.* Washington: American Enterprise Institute for Public Policy Research, 1982.

Heller, Mark. *The Iran-Iraq War: Implications for Third Parties.* Cambridge: CFIA Harvard, 1984.

Helms, Christine Moss. *Iraq: Eastern Flank of the Arab World.* Washington: Brookings Institution, 1984.

Hiro, Dilip. *The Longest War: The Iran-Iraq Military Conflict.* New York: Routledge, 1990.

Hunter, Shireen T. *The Gulf Cooperation Council: Problems and Prospects.* Washington: CSIS, 1984.

———. *Iran and the World: Continuity in a Revolutionary Decade.* Bloomington: Indiana University Press, 1990.

Hussein, Saddam. *Saddam Hussein on Current Events in Iraq.* London: Longman, 1977.

Iklé, Fred C. *How Nations Negotiate.* New York: Harper and Row, 1965; reprint ed., Washington: Institute for the Study of Diplomacy, Georgetown University, 1979.

The Iraqi-Iranian Conflict: Documentary Dossier. Baghdad: Ministry of Foreign Affairs of the Republic of Iraq, 1981.

The Iraqi-Iranian Dispute: Facts v. Allegations. Baghdad: Ministry of Foreign Affairs of the Republic of Iraq, 1981.

Ismael, Tareq Y. *Iran and Iraq: Roots of Conflict.* Syracuse: Syracuse University Press, 1982.

Izzi, Khalid. *The Shatt al Arab Dispute: A Legal Study.* London: Third World Centre for Research and Publication, 1981.

Jabber, Paul, et al. *Great Power Interests in the Persian Gulf.* New York: Council on Foreign Relations, 1989.

Joffe, George (with Keith McLachlan). *Iran and Iraq: The Next Five Years.* London: Economist Intelligence Unit, 1987.

Kaikobad, Kaiyan Homi. *The Shatt al-Arab Boundary Question: A Legal Appraisal.* Oxford: Clarendon Press, 1988.

Karsh, Efraim. *The Iran-Iraq War: A Military Analysis.* London: International Institute for Strategic Studies, 1987.

Keddie, Nikki R., and Mark J. Gasiorowski, eds. *Neither East nor West: Iran, the Soviet Union, and the United States.* New Haven: Yale University Press, 1990.

Kennan, George. *Memoirs: 1925–50.* Boston: Little Brown, 1967.

Khadduri, Majid. *The Gulf War: The Origins and Implications of the Iraq-Iran Conflict.* New York: Oxford University Press, 1988.

Khan, Riaz M. *Untying the Afghan Knot: Negotiating Soviet Withdrawal.* An Institute for the Study of Diplomacy Book. Durham, NC: Duke University Press, 1991.

King, Ralph. *The Iran-Iraq War: The Political Implications.* London: Institute for Strategic Studies, 1987.

Kupchan, Charles. *The Persian Gulf and the West: The Dilemma of Security.* Boston: Allen and Unwin, 1987.

Lall, Arthur S. *Multilateral Negotiation and Mediation: Instruments and Methods,* 1985.

Lewis, Bernard. *The Political Language of Islam.* Chicago: University of Chicago Press, 1988.

Lie, Trygve. *In the Cause of Peace: Seven Years with the United Nations.* New York: Macmillan, 1954.

Limbert, John. *Iran at War with History.* Boulder: Westview, 1987.

Luard, Evan. *The United Nations: How It Works and What It Does.* New York: St. Martin's Press, 1979.

McLachlan, K. S. *The Gulf War: A Survey of Political Issues and Economic Consequences* (with George Joffe). London: Economist Intelligence Unit, 1984.

Marr, Phebe. *The Modern History of Iraq.* Boulder: Westview, 1985.

Maull, Hanns, and Otto Pick, eds. *The Gulf War: Regional and International Dimensions.* New York: St. Martin's Press, 1990.

Miller, E. Willard. *The Third World, Iran, Iran and Iraq War, Iran Arms-Contra Affair, Iraq: A Bibliography* (with Ruby M. Miller). Monteville, IL: Vance Bibliographies, 1989.

Miller, Judith, and Laurie Mylroie. *Saddam Hussein and the Crisis in the Gulf.* New York: Times Books, 1990.

Mitchell, C. R., and K. Webb, eds. *New Approaches to International Mediation.* New York: Greenwood, 1988.

Naff, Thomas, ed. *Gulf Security and the Iran-Iraq War.* Washington: National Defense University Press, 1985.

Nicol, Davidson, ed. *Paths to Peace: The UN Security Council and Its Presidency.* New York: Pergamon, 1981.

———. *The United Nations Security Council: Towards Greater Effectiveness.* New York: UNITAR, 1982.

O'Ballance, Edgar. *The Gulf War.* London: Brassey's Defense, 1988.

Parsons, Anthony. *Pride and the Fall: Iran 1974–79.* London: Capew, 1984.

Peterson, Erik R. *The Gulf Cooperation Council: Search for Unity in a Dynamic Region.* Boulder: Westview, 1988.

Pridham, B. R., ed. *The Arab Gulf and the West.* London: Croom Helm, 1985.

Raiffa, Howard. *The Art and Science of Negotiation.* Cambridge: Harvard/Belknap, 1982.

Ramazani, Rouhollah K. *The Gulf Cooperation Council, Record and Analysis.* Charlottesville: University Press of Virginia, 1988.

———. *Revolutionary Iran.* Baltimore: Johns Hopkins University Press, 1986.

———, ed. *Iran's Revolution: The Search for Consensus.* Bloomington: Indiana University Press, 1990.

Renwick, Robin. *Economic Sanctions.* Cambridge, MA: CFIA, 1981.

Roberts, Adam (with Benedict Kingsbury), ed. *United Nations, Divided World: The UN's Role in International Relations.* Oxford: Clarendon Press, 1988.

Rovine, Arthur. *The First Fifty Years: The Secretary-General in World Politics, 1920–70.* Leyden: Sithoff, 1970.

Saivetz, Carol R. *The Soviet Union and the Gulf in the 1980's.* Boulder: Westview, 1989.

Schwebel, Stephen M. *The Secretary-General of the United Nations: His Political Powers and Practice.* Cambridge: Harvard University Press, 1952.

Shelling, Thomas. *Arms and Influence.* Cambridge: Harvard University Press, 1988.

———. *The Strategy of Conflict.* Cambridge: Harvard University Press, 1960.

Sherry, George L. *The United Nations Reborn: Conflict Control in the Post–Cold War Era.* New York: Council on Foreign Relations, 1990.

Shultz, George P. *Turmoil and Triumph: My Years as Secretary of State.* New York: Scribner's, 1993.
Sick, Gary. *All Fall Down: America's Tragic Encounter with Iran.* New York: Penguin, 1986.
Sindelar, H. Richard III (with J. E. Peterson), ed. *Crosscurrents in the Gulf: Arab, Regional and Global Interests.* For the Middle East Institute. New York: Routledge, 1988.
Sirriyeh, Hussein. *U.S. Policy in the Gulf, 1968–77: Aftermath of the British Withdrawal.* London: Ithaca Press, 1984.
Souresrafil, Behrouz. *The Iran-Iraq War.* United States, Guinan Co., 1989.
Stoessinger, John George. *The United Nations and the Superpowers: China, Russia, and America.* New York: Random House, 1973.
Tahir-Kheli, Shirin, and Shaheen Ayubi. *The Iran-Iraq War: New Weapons, Old Conflicts.* New York: Praeger, 1983.
Tarryam, Abdullah Omran. *The Establishment of the United Arab Emirates 1950–85.* London: Croom Helm, 1987.
Thomas, Hugh. *Armed Truce: The Beginnings of the Cold War, 1945–46.* New York: Atheneum, 1987.
Touré, Ahmed Sékou. *Du Conflit Irano-Irakien.* Conakry, R.P.R.G.: Imprimerie Nationale "Patrice Lumumba," 1981.
Trager, Oliver, ed. *The Iran-Contra Arms Scandal: A Foreign Policy Disaster.* New York: Facts on File, 1988.
UNITAR. *The United Nations and the Maintenance of International Peace and Security.* The Netherlands: Nijhoff, 1987.
U.S. Congress. *Report of Congressional Committees Investigating the Iran-Contra Affair.* USGPO, 1987.
U.S. Department of State. Special Report no. 166. *U.S. Policy in the Persian Gulf.* July 1987.
U.S. Senate. *Chemical Weapons Use in Kurdistan: Iraq's Final Offensive. A Staff Report to the Committee on Foreign Relations.* 1988.
U.S. Senate. *Persian Gulf: Report to the Majority Leader, United States Senate,* from Senator John Glenn and Senator John Warner on their trip to the Persian Gulf. 22 May to 4 June 1987.
U.S. Senate. Committee on Foreign Relations. *U.S. Policy in the Persian Gulf: Hearings before the Committee on Foreign Relations.* 1988.
United States. *President's Special Review Board, The Tower Commission Report.* New York: Bantam Books//Time Books, 1987.
Urquhart, Brian. *Decolonization and World Peace.* Austin: University of Texas Press, 1989.
———. *A Life in Peace and War.* New York: Harper and Row, 1987.
Vance, Cyrus. *Hard Choices: Critical Years in American Foreign Policy.* New York: Simon and Schuster, 1983.
Waldheim, Kurt. *In the Eye of the Storm: A Memoir.* Bethesda: Adler and Adler, 1986.
Yodfat, Arye H. *The Soviet Union and Revolutionary Iran.* London: Croom Helm, 1983.
Yorke, Valerie (with Louis Turner). *European Interests and Gulf Oil.* Brookfield, VT: Gower, 1986.
———. *The Gulf in the 1980s.* London: The Royal Institute of International Affairs, 1980.
Zartman, I. William, ed. *The 50% Solution.* New Haven: Yale University Press, 1987.
———. *The Negotiation Process: Theories and Applications.* Beverly Hills, CA: Sage, 1978.

Articles and Periodicals

Ahriri, Mohammed E. "Iran and the Superpowers in the Gulf." *SAIS Review* 7 (Winter-Spring 1987): 921–49.

Amin, S. H. "The Iran-Iraq Conflict: Legal Implications." *International and Comparative Law Quarterly* 31 (January 1982): 167–88.

Anderson, H. "A Showdown with Tehran." *Newsweek,* 27 July 1987, 110:28–30.

Anthony, John Duke. "The Gulf Cooperation Council." *Orbis* 28 (Fall 1984): 447–50.

Arend, Anthony Clark. "The Obligation to Pursue Peaceful Settlement of International Disputes during Hostilities." *Virginian Journal of International Law* 24, 1 (Fall 1983): 97–123.

Axelgard, Frederick W. "U.S./Iraqi Relations: A Status Report." *American-Arab Affairs,* no. 30 (Summer 1985): 1–9.

Chubin, Shahram. "The Soviet Union and Iran." *Foreign Affairs* 61, no. 4 (1983): 921–49.

———. "The Super-powers, Regional Conflicts, and World Order." In *The Changing Strategic Landscape,* Adelphi paper 237 (1989), p. 84 et seq.

Cordesman, Anthony H. "The Gulf Crisis and Strategic Interests: A Military Analysis." *American-Arab Affairs* (Summer 1984): 8–15.

Eknes, Aage. "From Scandal to Success: The United Nations and the Iran-Iraq War 1980–88." Oslo: Norwegian Institute of International Affairs, 1989.

Eliasson, Jan. "Sweden and International Mediation." Stockholm: Ministry for Foreign Affairs, 1989.

"Enter, the Gang of Five." *The Nation,* 20 February 1989, 248:217.

Franck, T. M. "Soviet Initiatives: U.S. Responses: New Opportunities for Reviving the United Nations System." *American Journal of International Law* 83 (July 1989): 599–604.

Freeman, Charles W., Jr. "The Angola/Namibia Accords." *Foreign Affairs* 68, no. 3 (Summer 1989): 126–41.

Ghareeb, Edmund. "The Forgotten War." *American-Arab Affairs* 5 (Summer 1983): 59–75.

Haas, Ernst B. "Regime Decay: Conflict Management and International Organizations, 1945–81." *International Organization* 37, no. 2 (Spring 1983): 189–256.

Hamdoon, Nizar (with Thomas Stauffer). "The United States, Iraq, and the Gulf War." *American-Arab Affairs* 95 (Fall 1985): 95–116.

Hellman, Gunther. "Der Kreig um Kuwait: Katalysator einer 'neuen Weltordnung' oder Vorbite neuer Konflikte." *Aus Politik und Zeitgeschichte,* B 7–8/91 (8 February 1991): 12–26.

Howar, L. "Iran: Peace Feelers." *Newsweek,* 8 February 1988, 111:7.

Hume, Cameron R. "Negotiations before Peacekeeping." Occasional Paper on Peacekeeping No. 5, International Peace Academy. New York, 1991.

———. "Pérez de Cuéllar and the Iran-Iraq War." *Negotiation Journal* (April 1992): 173–84.

Hunter, Shireen T. "After the Ayatollah." *Foreign Policy* (Spring 1987): 77–97.

Janson, Godfrey. "The Gulf War: The Contest Continues." *Third World Quarterly* 6, no. 4 (October 1984): 950–63.

Karsh, E. "Geopolitical Determinism: The Origins of the Iran-Iraq War." *Middle East Journal* 44, no. 2 (Spring 1990): 256–68.

———. "Military Lessons of the Iran-Iraq War." *Orbis* 33 (Spring 1989): 209–23.

Kashkett, Steven B. "Iraq and the Pursuit of Nonalignment." *Orbis* 26, no. 2 (Summer 1982): 477–94.

Khalilzad, Zalmay. "Islamic Iran: Soviet Dilemma." *Problems of Communism* 33 (January–February 1984): 1–20.

Kono, Tom. "The Cease-Fire and After: Entering a New Phase in the Gulf Conflict." Unpublished, Columbia University, 1990.

Krauthammer, C. "Let It Sink." *New Republic,* 24 August 1987, 197:18–23.

Lauterpacht, Eli. "River Boundaries: Legal Aspects of the Shatt-al-Arab Frontier," *International and Comparative Law Quarterly* 9, no. 2 (April 1960): 208–36.

Lorenz, Joseph P. "Ending the Iran-Iraq War; The Prenegotiation Phase." Washington: The Center for the Study of Foreign Affairs, Foreign Service Institute, 1984.

Luard, Evan. "The Superpowers and Regional Conflicts." *Foreign Affairs* (Summer 1986): 1006–25.

McLaurin, R. D. "Soviet Policy in the Persian Gulf." In *Conflict and Cooperation in the Persian Gulf,* Mohammed Mughisuddin, ed. New York: Praeger, 1977, pp. 116–39.

Maull, Hanns W. "Containment, Competition and Cooperation: Superpower Strategies in the Persian Gulf." *SAIS Review* 8 (Summer/Fall 1986): 103–19.

MERIP Reports. "The Strange War in the Gulf," 14, 6/7 (July/September 1984): 3–50.

Murphy, Richard. "Developments in the Persian Gulf," 12/15/87. *Department of State Bulletin* 88:74–76.

Mylroie, Laurie. "After the Guns Fell Silent: Iraq in the Middle East." *Middle East Journal* 43 (Winter 1989): 51–67.

———. "The Baghdad Alternative." *Orbis* 32 (Summer 1988): 339–54.

———. "The Superpowers and the Iran-Iraq War." *American-Arab Affairs* (Summer 1987): 47–56.

Neuman, Stephanie. "Arms, Aid, and Superpowers." *Foreign Affairs* (Summer 1988): 1044–65.

Newhouse, John. "The Diplomatic Round: Building a Cage." *New Yorker,* 8 October 1990, pp. 102–108.

Olson, William J. "The Gulf War: Peace in our Time?" *Parameters* 16 (Winter 1986): 47–56.

Page, Stephen. "The Soviet Union and the GCC States: A Search for Openings." *American-Arab Affairs* 20 (Spring 1987): 38–56.

Parsons, Anthony. "Iran and Western Europe." *Middle East Journal* 43 (Spring 1989): 218–29.

———. "The Iranian Revolution." *Middle East Review* 20, no. 3 (Spring 1988): 3–8.

Pederson, R. F. "National Representation in the United Nations." *International Organization* (Spring 1961): 256–66.

Peterson, J. E. "The GCC and Regional Security." *American-Arab Affairs* 20 (Spring 1987): 62–90.

Precht, Henry. "Ayatollah Realpolitik." *Foreign Policy* (Spring 1988): 109–28.

Putnam, Robert D. "Diplomacy and Domestic Politics: The Logic of Two-Level Games." *International Organization* 42, no. 3 (Summer 1988): 427–60.

Quandt, William B. "The Gulf War: Policy Options and Regional Implications." *American-Arab Affairs* (Summer 1984): 1–7.

Ramati, Johanan. "Iraq and Arab Security." *Global Affairs* (Winter 1990): 116–27.

Ramazani, R. K. "Iran's Foreign Policy: Contending Orientations." *Middle East Journal* 43, no. 2 (Spring 1989): 202–17.

Renfrew, Nita M. "Who Started the War?" *Foreign Policy* (Spring 1987): 98–108.

Ross, Dennis. "Soviet Views toward the Gulf War." *Orbis* 28 (Fall 1984): 437–47.

Rubinstein, Alvin Z. "Perspectives on the Iran-Iraq War." *Orbis* 29 (Fall 1985): 597–608.

Russett, Bruce, and James S. Sutterlin. "The U.N. in a New World Order." *Foreign Affairs* 70, no. 2 (Spring 1991): 69–83.

Sackal, Amin. "Soviet Policy toward Southwest Asia." *Annals of American Academy of Political and Social Science* 481 (September 1985): 104–16.

Scheffer, David J. "The United Nations in the Gulf Crisis and Options for U.S. Policy." New York: UN Association of the U.S.A., no. 1, October 1990.

Schlesinger, James. "Reykjavik and Revolutions: A Turn of the Tide?" *Foreign Affairs* 65, no. 3 (1987): 426–46.

Segal, David. "The Iran-Iraq War: A Military Analysis." *Foreign Affairs* (Summer 1988): 946–64.

Sibiude, Jean-Luc. "The Iran-Iraq War: Reflections on a Cease-fire." Unpublished CFIA, Harvard University, 1989.

Sick, Gary. "Iran's Quest for Superpower Status." *Foreign Affairs* (Spring 1987): 697–715.

———. "Moral Choice and the Iran-Iraq Conflict." *Ethics and International Affairs* 3 (1989): 117–33.

———. "Trial by Error: Reflections on the Iran-Iraq War." *Middle East Journal* 43 (Spring 1989): 230–45.

Smolansky, O. M. "Soviet Policy in Iran and Afghanistan." *Current History* 80 (October 1981): 321–24.

Sobhani, Sohrab C. "Ending the Iran-Iraq War." In David D. Newsom, ed., *The Diplomatic Record 1989–1990.* Boulder: Westview, 1991.

Sterner, Michael. "The Iran-Iraq War." *Foreign Affairs* 63 (Fall 1984): 128–43.

Tomasek, Robert D. "The Resolution of Major Controversies between Iran and Iraq." *World Affairs* 139, no. 3 (Winter 1976–77): 206–30.

Twinam, Joseph W. "U.S. Interests in the Arabian Gulf." *American-Arab Affairs* 21 (Summer 1987): 1–14.

Viorst, Milton. "Iraq at War." *Foreign Affairs* 65 (Winter 1986–87): 349–65.

Waas, Murray, and Craig Unger. "In the Loop: Bush's Secret Mission." *New Yorker,* 2 November 1992, pp. 64–83.

Wilbur, Richard Morgan. "The Iran-Iraq War: An Analysis of the Cease-fire." *The Fletcher Forum of World Affairs* 14, no. 1 (Winter 1990): 111–27.

Wright, Claudia. "Implications of the Iraq-Iran War." *Foreign Affairs* 59 (1980–81): 275–303.

Index

CAMERON HUME, a United States Foreign Service officer, was assigned in 1994 as Minister-Counselor for Political Affairs at the U.S. Mission to the United Nations. Previously he served as deputy chief of mission at the U.S. Embassy to the Holy See, as senior adviser to the U.S. Mission to the United Nations, and in posts at the U.S. embassies in Beirut, Tunis, and Damascus and the U.S. Consulate General in Palermo.